MANGA CORNER
He's creepy...
BLOOP

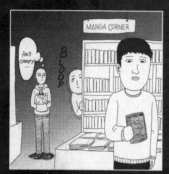

O N E

I saw someone at the bookstore buying *One-Punch Man*. I couldn't help but stare. I'm not some kind of weirdo.

—ONE

Manga creator ONE began *One-Punch Man* as a webcomic, which quickly went viral, garnering over 10 million hits. In addition to *One-Punch Man*, ONE writes and draws the series *Mob Psycho 100* and *Makai no Ossan*.

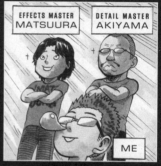

EFFECTS MASTER
MATSUURA
DETAIL MASTER
AKIYAMA
ME

Y U S U K E M U R A T A

(AND THE CURRENT MEMBERS OF VILLAGE STUDIO)

The elite members of the studio continue to aim for new heights and polish their skills every day. If one looks like he's asleep, that's just your imagination.

—Yusuke Murata

A highly decorated and skilled artist best known for his work on *Eyeshield 21*, Yusuke Murata won the 122nd Hop Step Award (1995) for *Partner* and placed second in the 51st Akatsuka Award (1998) for *Samui Hanashi*.

ONE-PUNCH MAN | 04

ONE + YUSUKE MURATA

HEH

★ THE STORIES, CHARACTERS AND INCIDENTS MENTIONED IN THIS PUBLICATION ARE ENTIRELY FICTIONAL.

ONE-PUNCH MAN

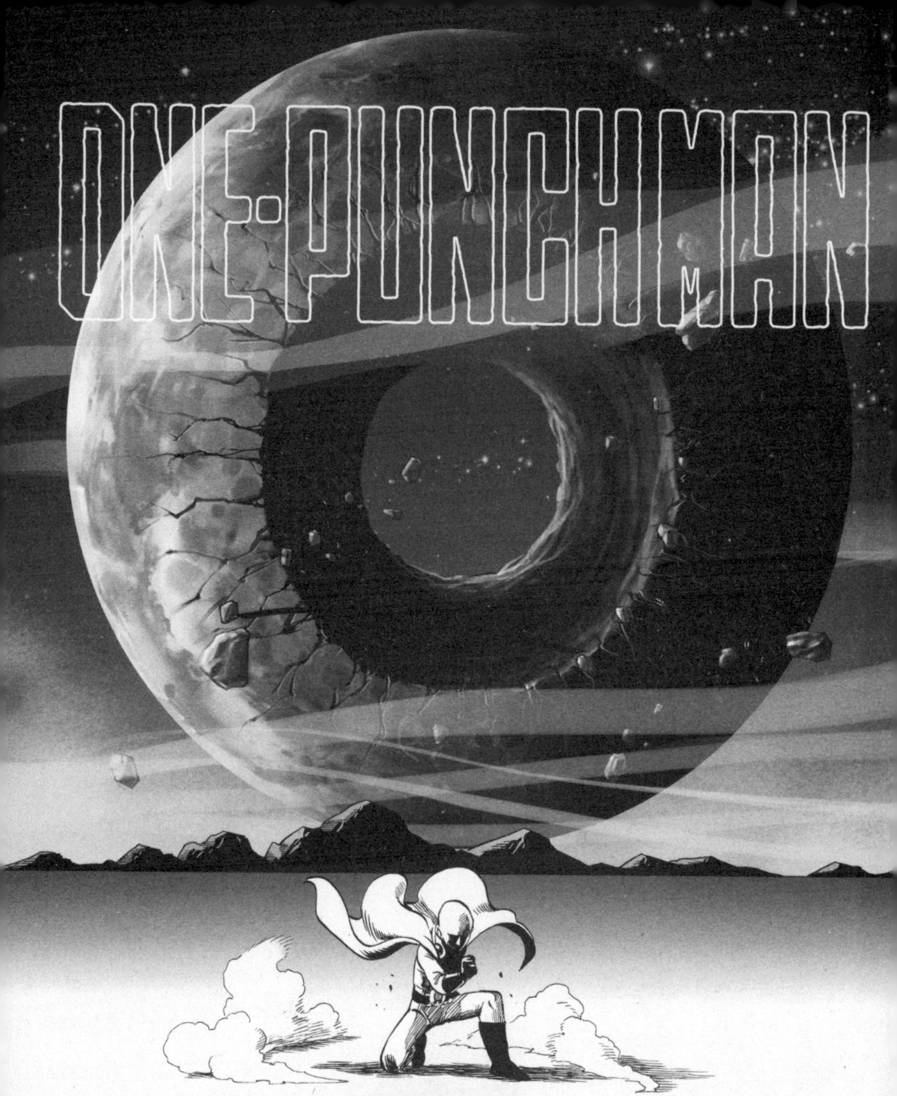

04

STORY BY
ONE

ART BY
YUSUKE MURATA

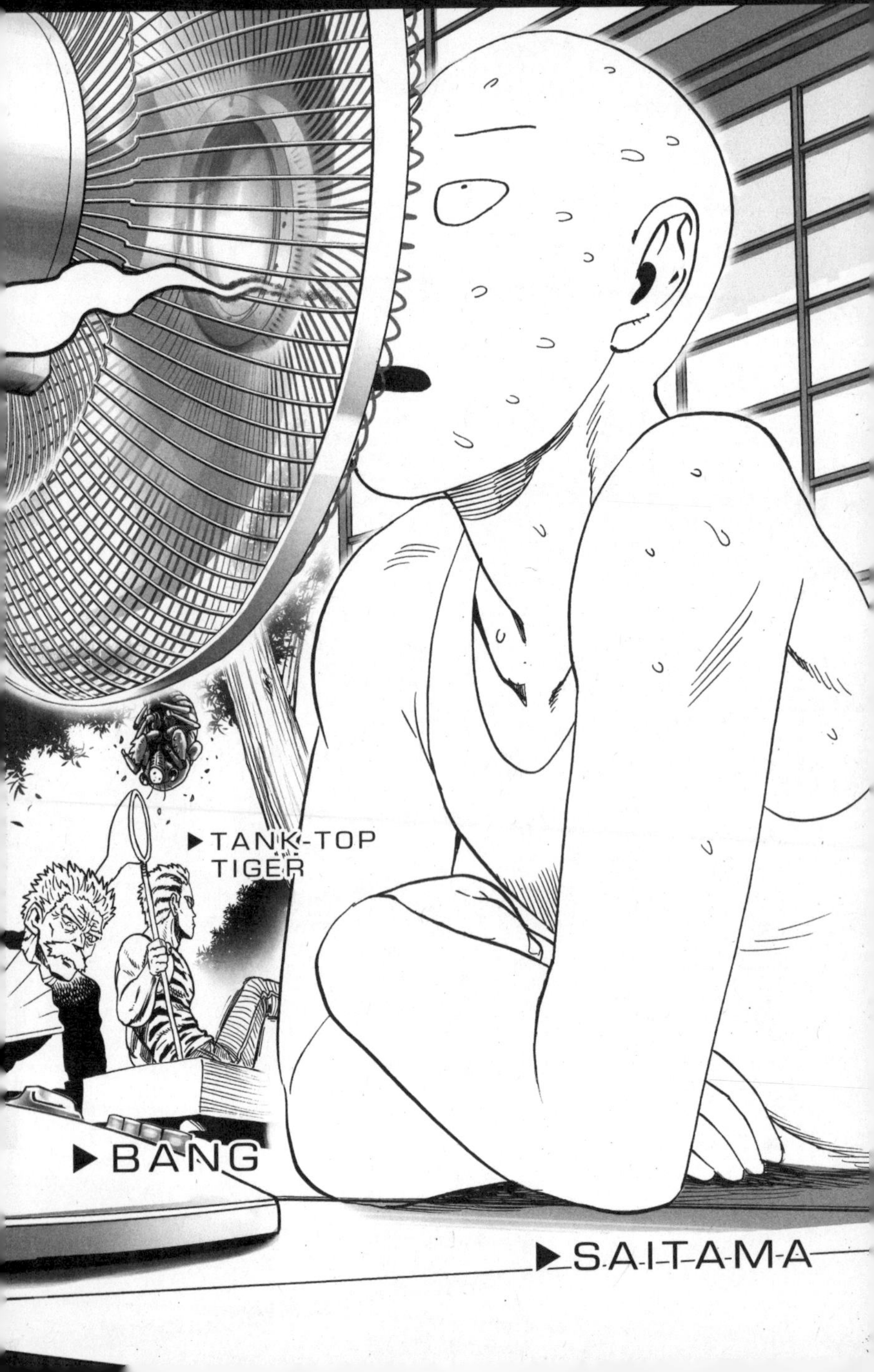
▶TANK-TOP TIGER
▶BANG
▶S-A-I-T-A-M-A

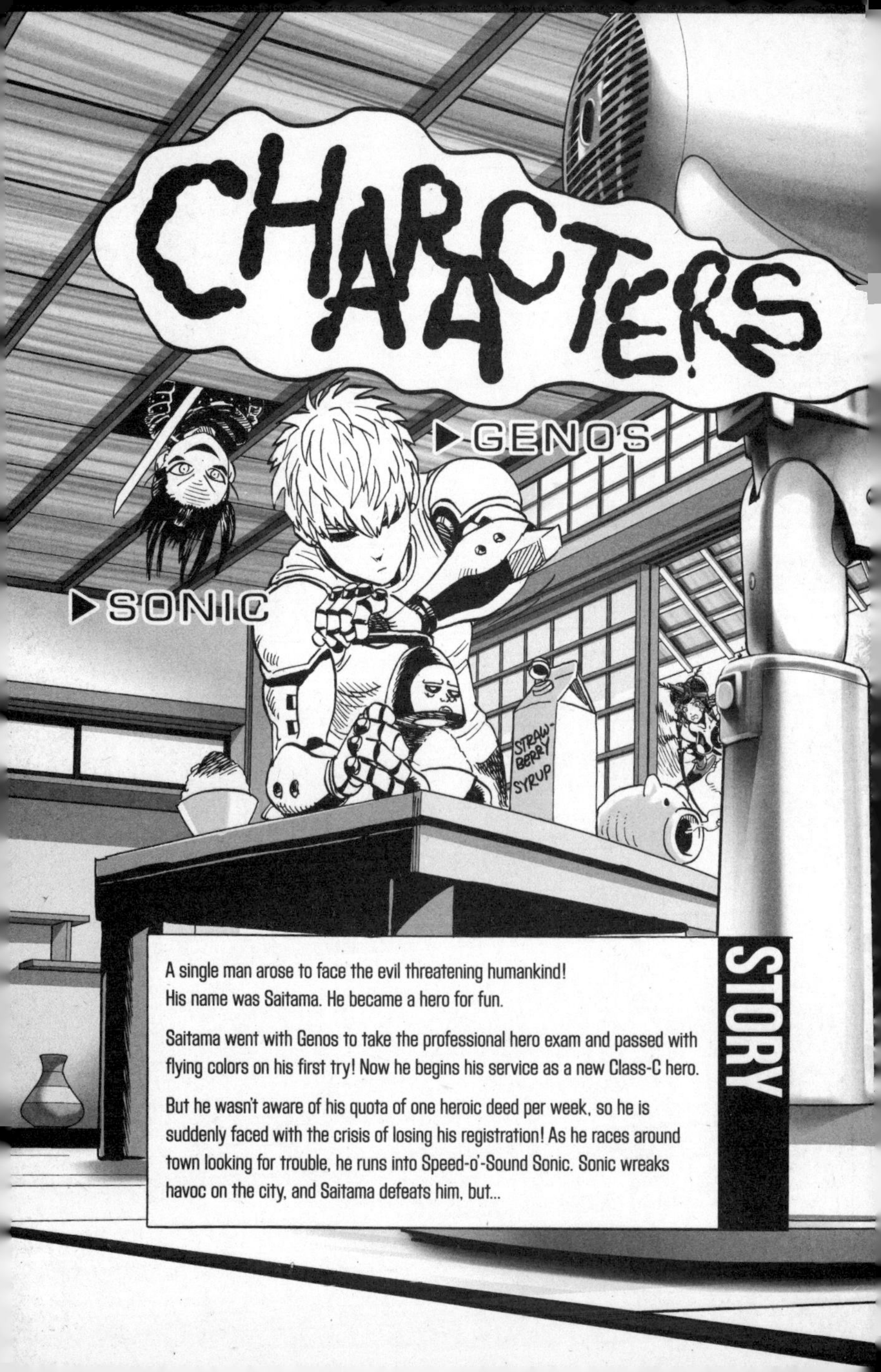
CHARACTERS
▶GENOS
▶SONIC
STRAW-BERRY SYRUP

STORY

A single man arose to face the evil threatening humankind!
His name was Saitama. He became a hero for fun.

Saitama went with Genos to take the professional hero exam and passed with flying colors on his first try! Now he begins his service as a new Class-C hero.

But he wasn't aware of his quota of one heroic deed per week, so he is suddenly faced with the crisis of losing his registration! As he races around town looking for trouble, he runs into Speed-o'-Sound Sonic. Sonic wreaks havoc on the city, and Saitama defeats him, but...

CONTENTS

ONE-PUNCH MAN VOLUME FOUR

ONE-PUNCH MAN
ONE + YUSUKE MURATA

My name is Saitama. I am a hero. My hobby is heroic exploits. I got too strong. And that makes me sad. I can defeat any enemy with one blow. I lost my hair. And I lost all feeling. I want to feel the rush of battle. I would like to meet an incredibly strong enemy. And I would like to defeat it with one blow. That's because I am One-Punch Man.

04

GIANT METEOR

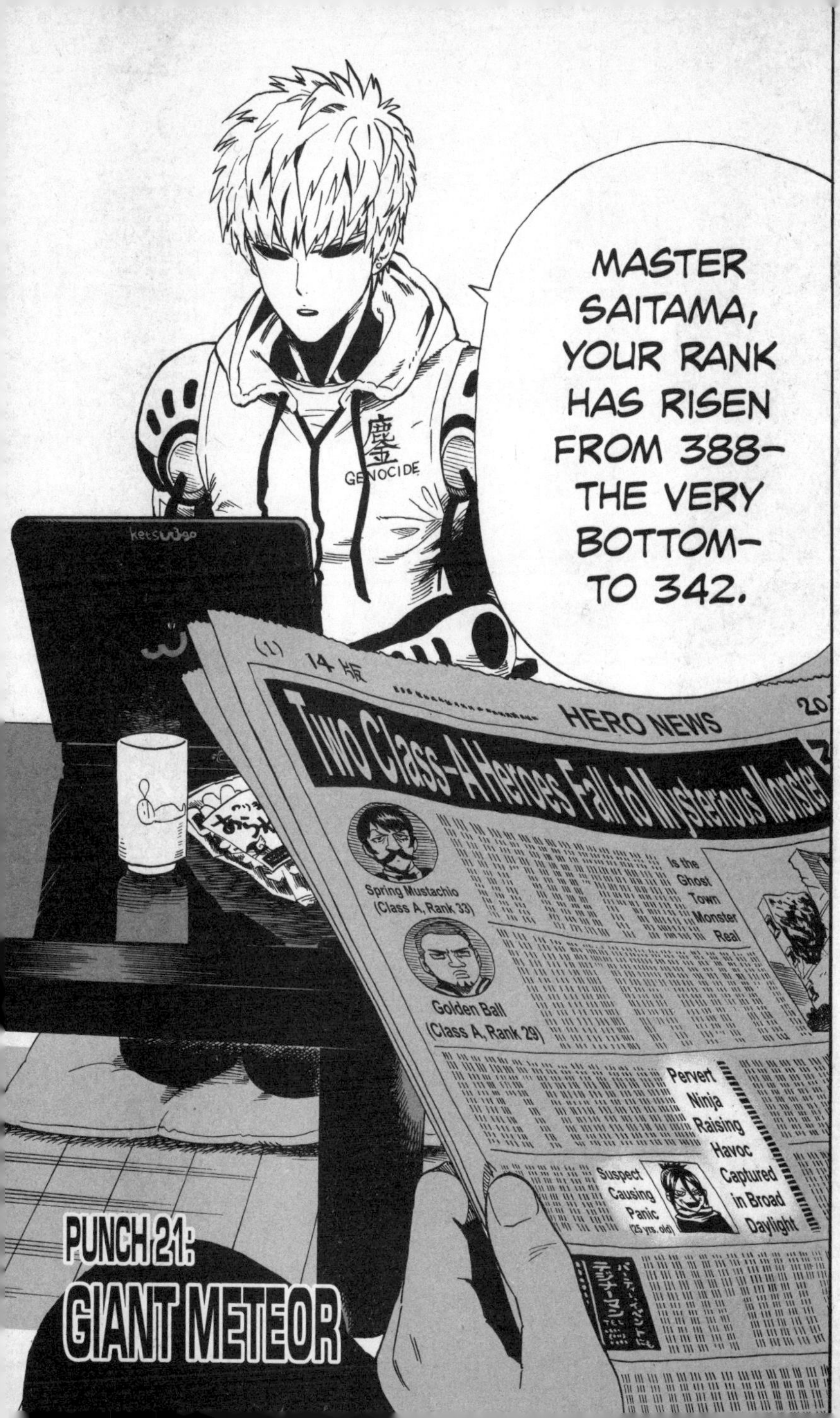
MASTER SAITAMA, YOUR RANK HAS RISEN FROM 388—THE VERY BOTTOM—TO 342.
GENOCIDE
HERO NEWS
Two Class-A Heroes Fall to Mysterious Monster
Spring Mustachio (Class A, Rank 33)
Golden Ball (Class A, Rank 29)
Is the Ghost Town Monster Real
Pervert Ninja Raising Havoc Captured in Broad Daylight
Suspect Causing Panic (25 yrs. old)

PUNCH 21: GIANT METEOR

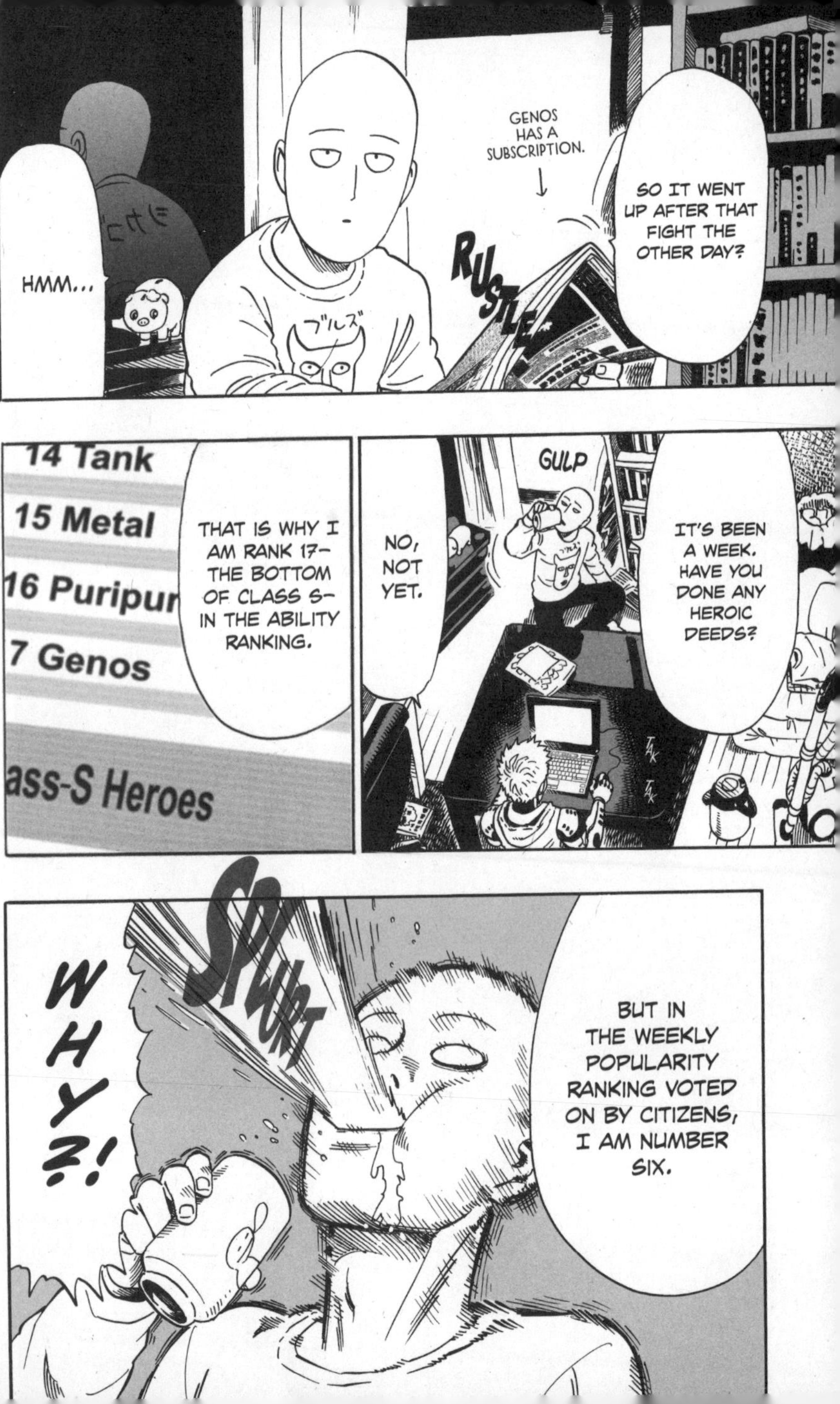
SO IT WENT UP AFTER THAT FIGHT THE OTHER DAY?
GENOS HAS A SUBSCRIPTION.
RUSTLE
HMM...
IT'S BEEN A WEEK. HAVE YOU DONE ANY HEROIC DEEDS?
GULP
NO, NOT YET.
TAK
TAK
THAT IS WHY I AM RANK 17— THE BOTTOM OF CLASS S— IN THE ABILITY RANKING.
14 Tank
15 Metal
16 Puripur
7 Genos
ass-S Heroes
BUT IN THE WEEKLY POPULARITY RANKING VOTED ON BY CITIZENS, I AM NUMBER SIX.
SPLURT
WHY?!

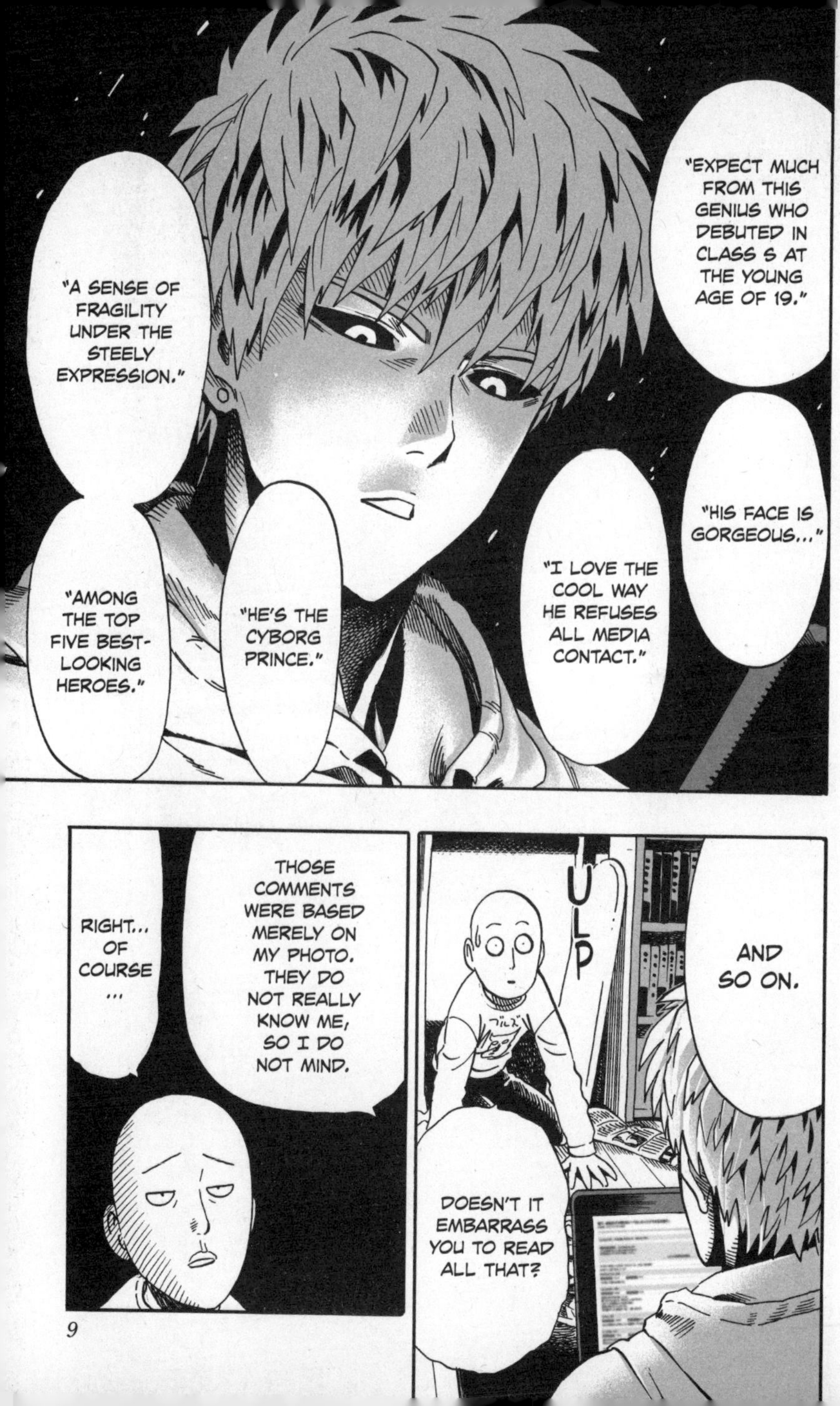
"EXPECT MUCH FROM THIS GENIUS WHO DEBUTED IN CLASS S AT THE YOUNG AGE OF 19."
"HIS FACE IS GORGEOUS..."
"I LOVE THE COOL WAY HE REFUSES ALL MEDIA CONTACT."
"HE'S THE CYBORG PRINCE."
"A SENSE OF FRAGILITY UNDER THE STEELY EXPRESSION."
"AMONG THE TOP FIVE BEST-LOOKING HEROES."
AND SO ON.
ULP
DOESN'T IT EMBARRASS YOU TO READ ALL THAT?
THOSE COMMENTS WERE BASED MERELY ON MY PHOTO. THEY DO NOT REALLY KNOW ME, SO I DO NOT MIND.
RIGHT... OF COURSE ...

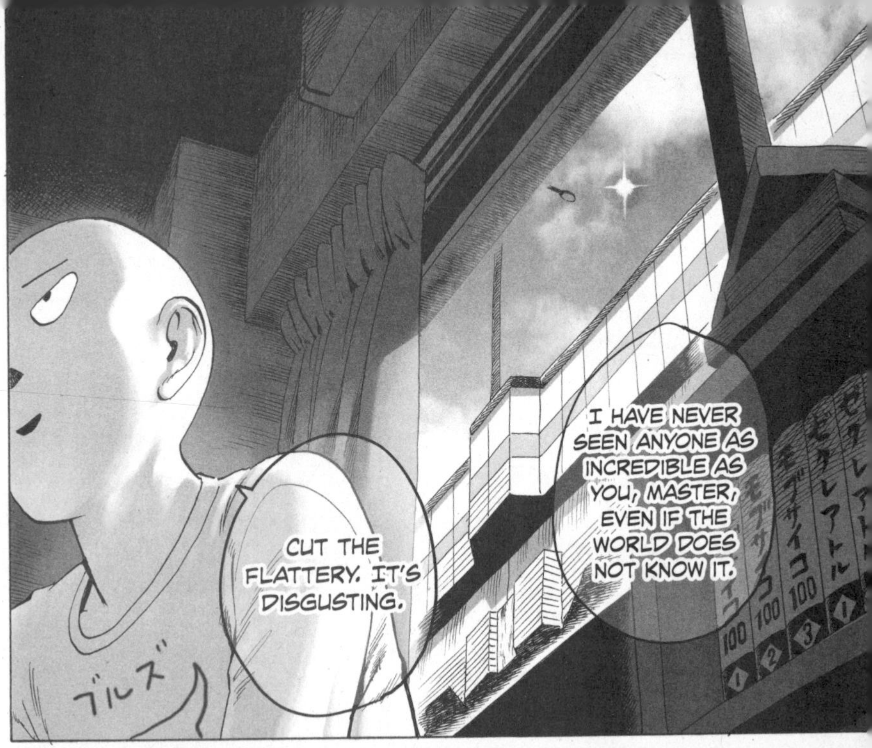
I HAVE NEVER SEEN ANYONE AS INCREDIBLE AS YOU, MASTER, EVEN IF THE WORLD DOES NOT KNOW IT.
CUT THE FLATTERY. IT'S DISGUSTING.
ブルズ

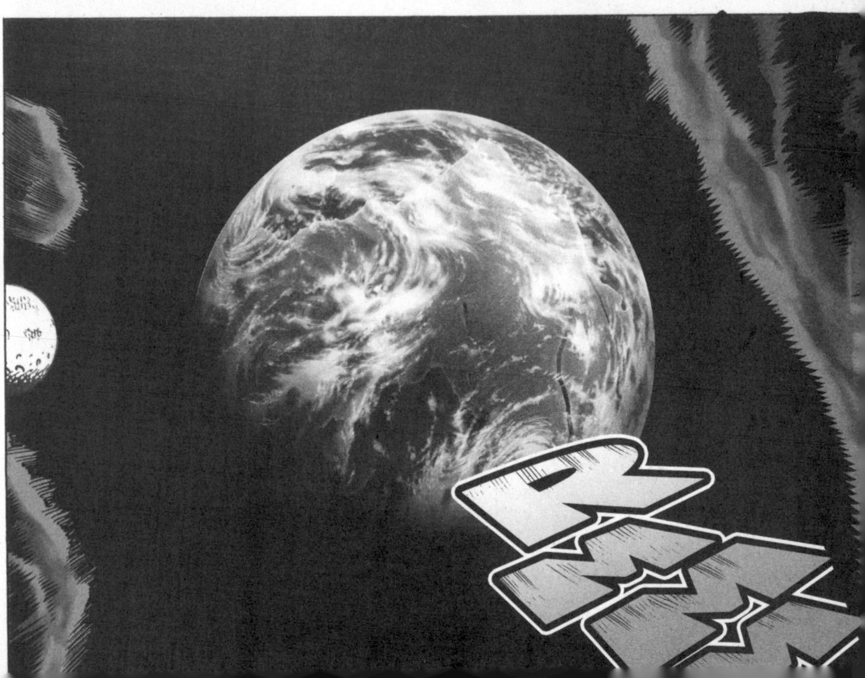

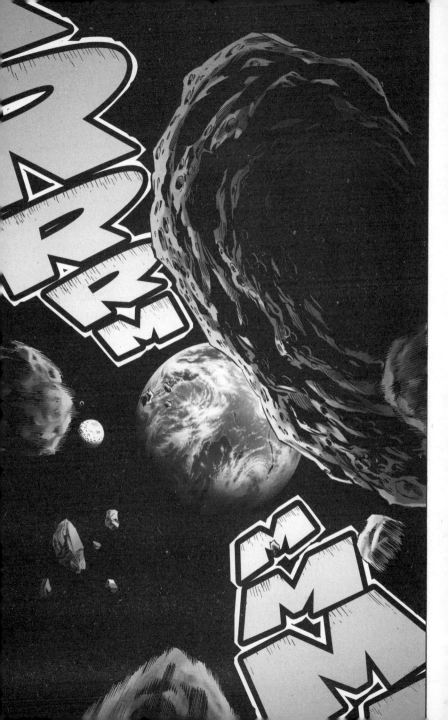

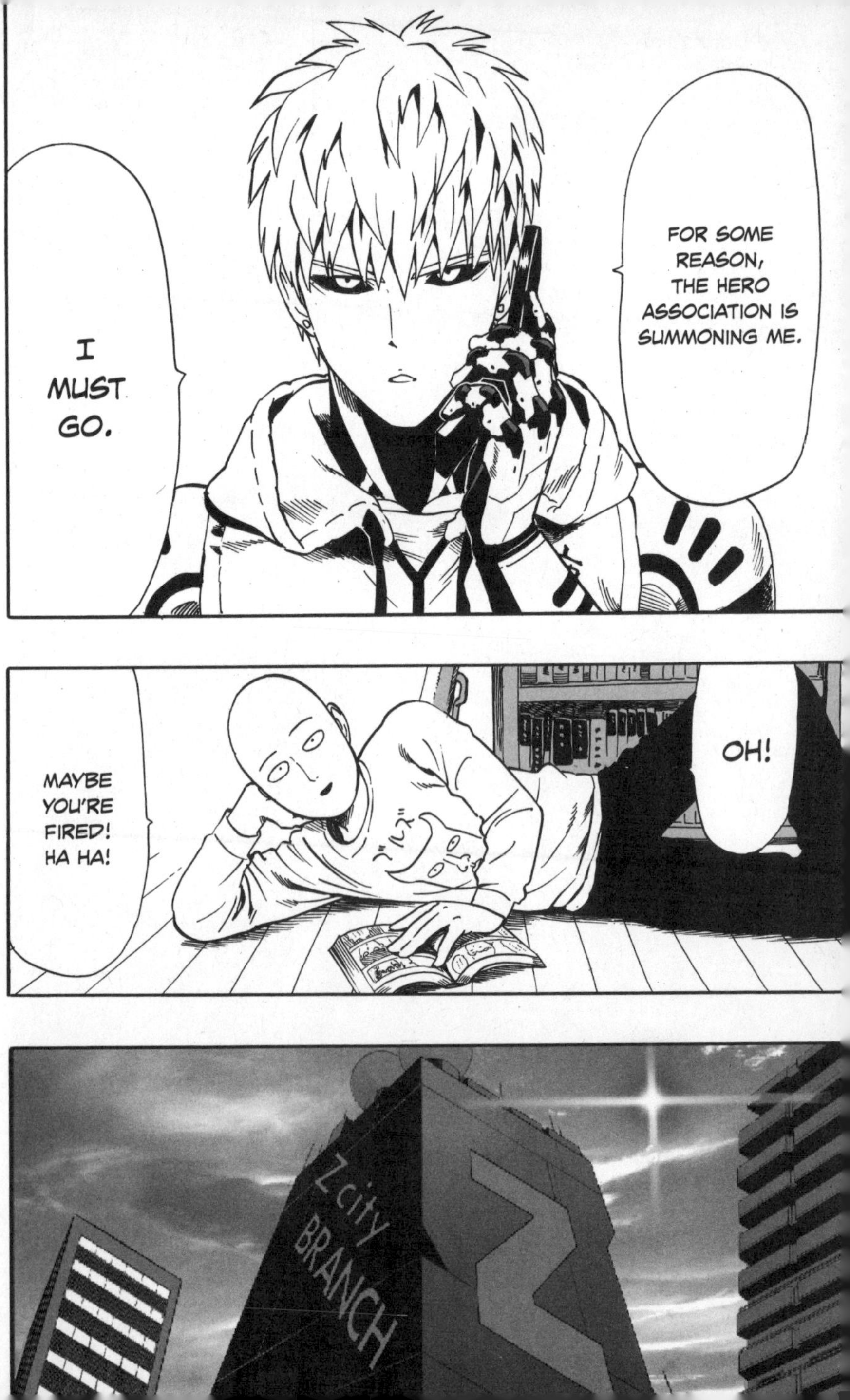
FOR SOME REASON, THE HERO ASSOCIATION IS SUMMONING ME.
I MUST GO.
OH!
MAYBE YOU'RE FIRED! HA HA!
Z city BRANCH

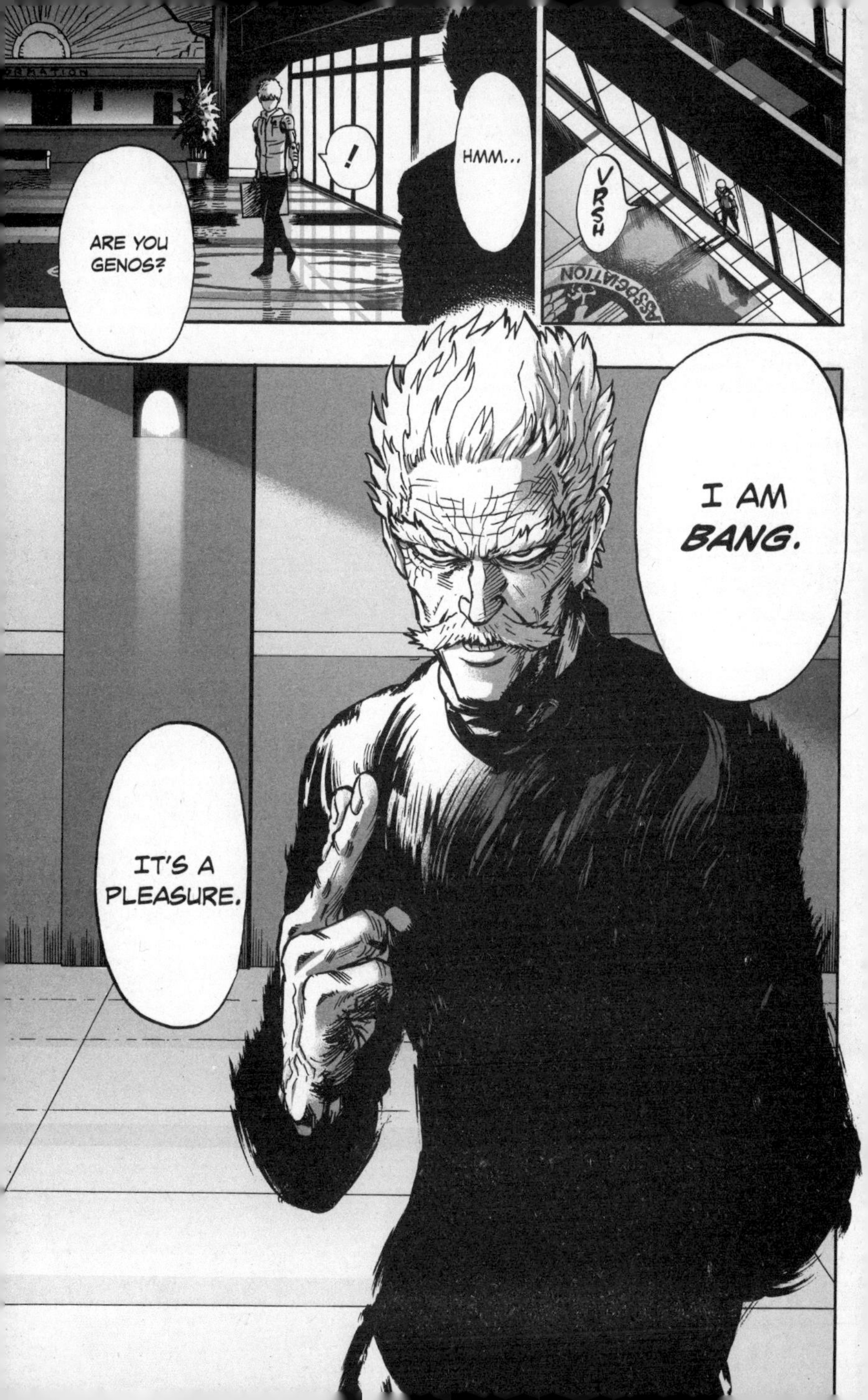
VRSH
HMM...
!
ARE YOU GENOS?
I AM BANG.
IT'S A PLEASURE.

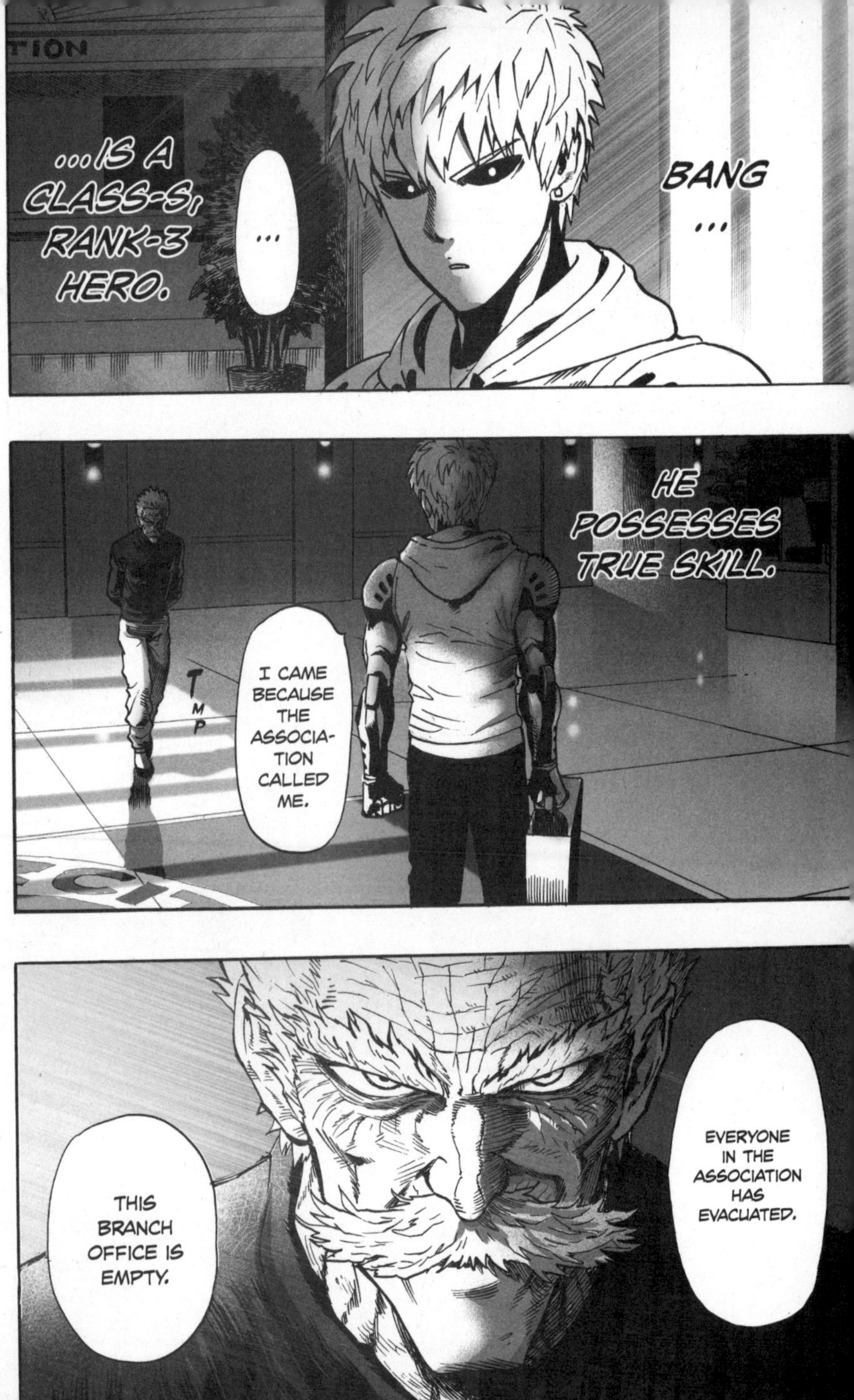
BANG ...
...
...IS A CLASS-S, RANK-3 HERO.
HE POSSESSES TRUE SKILL.
I CAME BECAUSE THE ASSOCIATION CALLED ME.
TMP
EVERYONE IN THE ASSOCIATION HAS EVACUATED.
THIS BRANCH OFFICE IS EMPTY.

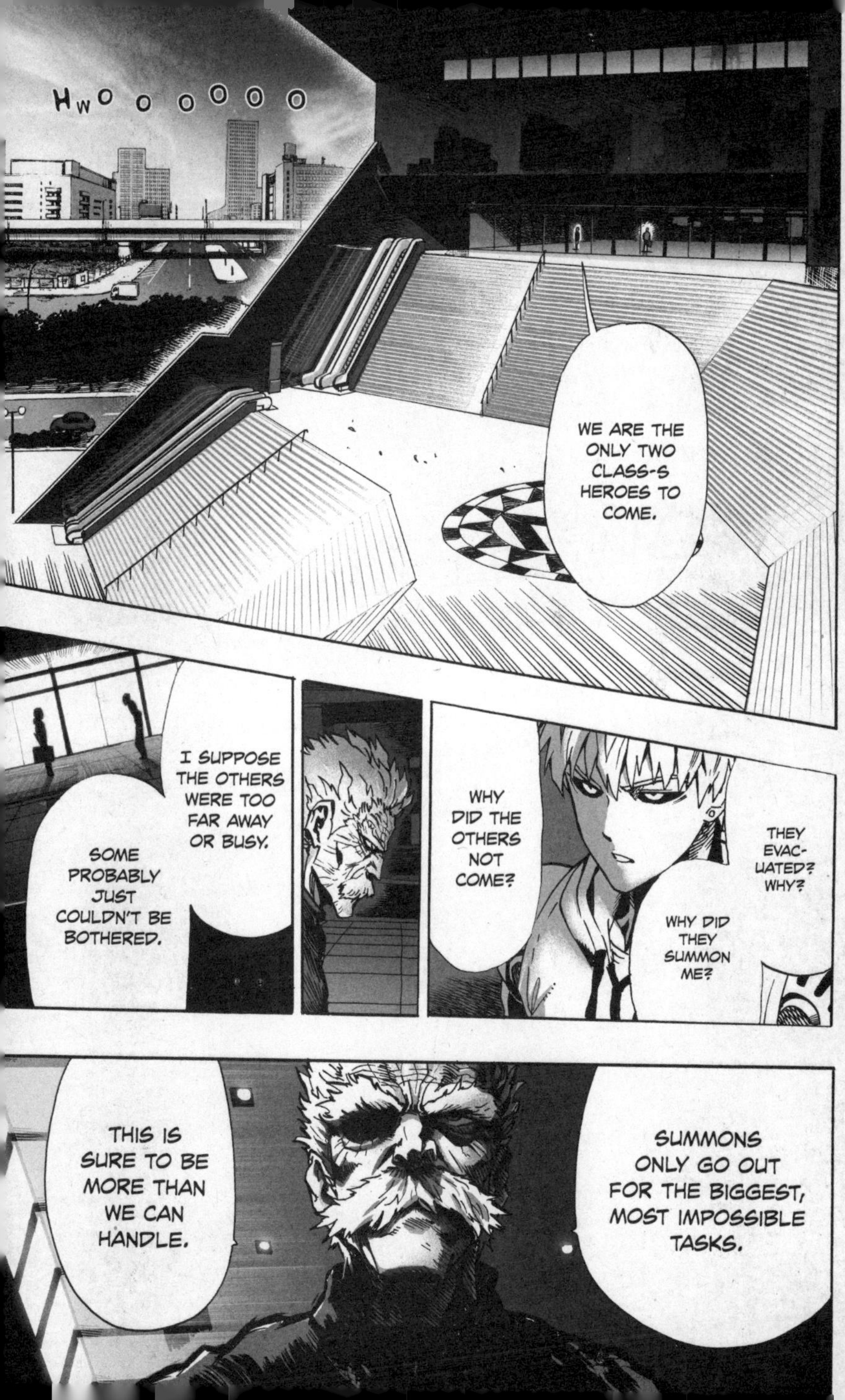
HWOOOOOO
WE ARE THE ONLY TWO CLASS-S HEROES TO COME.
THEY EVACUATED? WHY?
WHY DID THEY SUMMON ME?
WHY DID THE OTHERS NOT COME?
I SUPPOSE THE OTHERS WERE TOO FAR AWAY OR BUSY.
SOME PROBABLY JUST COULDN'T BE BOTHERED.
SUMMONS ONLY GO OUT FOR THE BIGGEST, MOST IMPOSSIBLE TASKS.
THIS IS SURE TO BE MORE THAN WE CAN HANDLE.

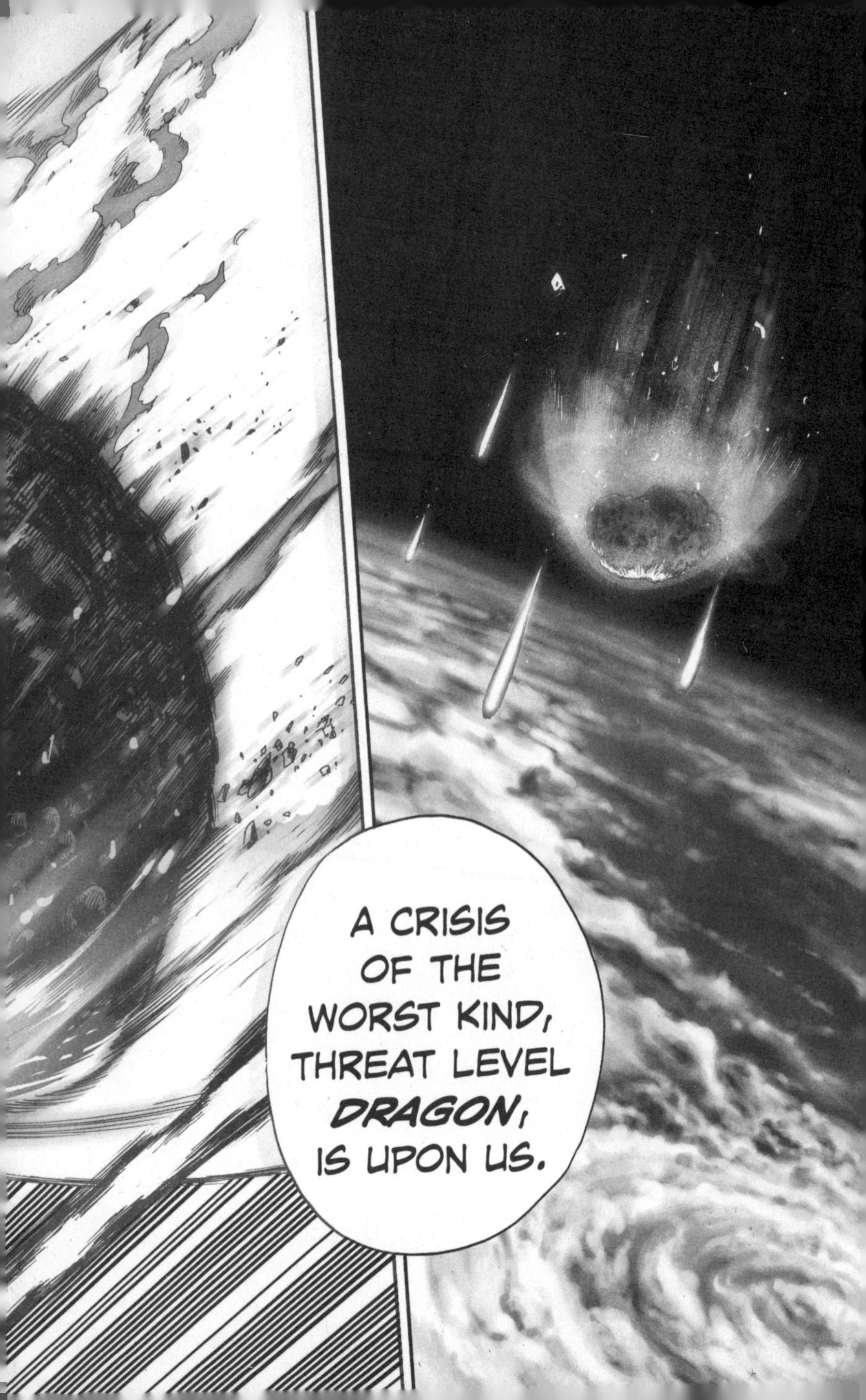
A CRISIS OF THE WORST KIND, THREAT LEVEL DRAGON, IS UPON US.

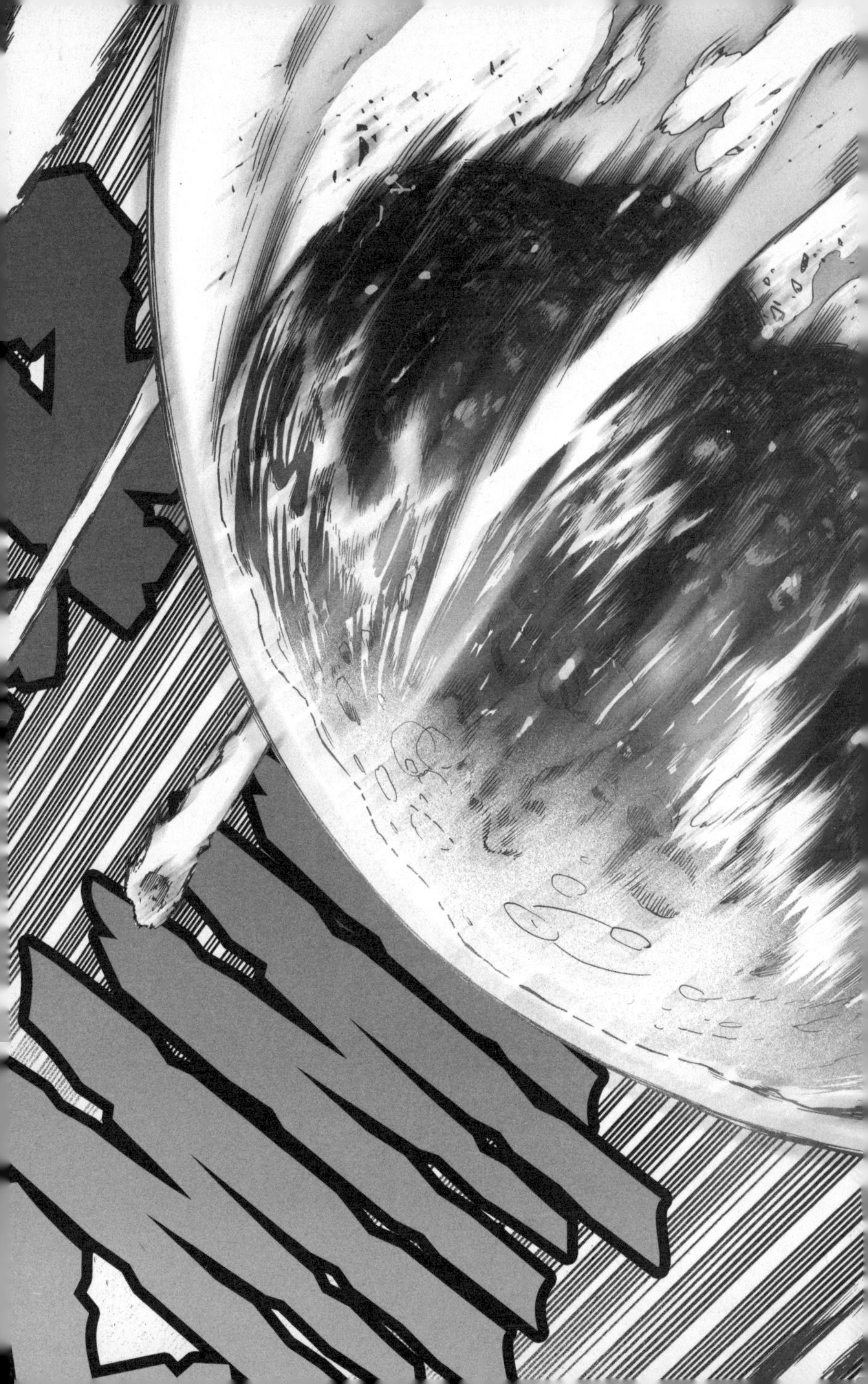

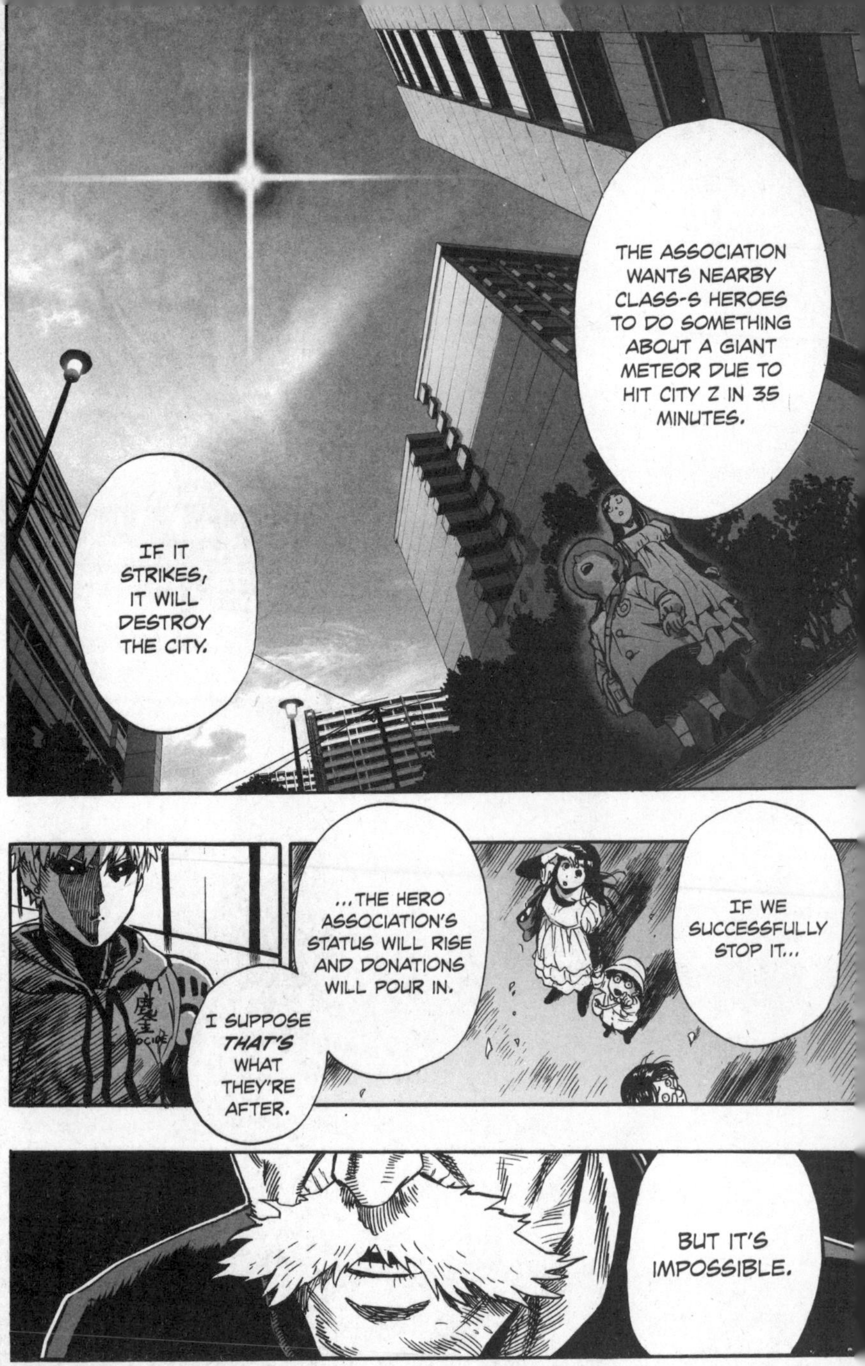
THE ASSOCIATION WANTS NEARBY CLASS-S HEROES TO DO SOMETHING ABOUT A GIANT METEOR DUE TO HIT CITY Z IN 35 MINUTES.
IF IT STRIKES, IT WILL DESTROY THE CITY.
IF WE SUCCESSFULLY STOP IT...
...THE HERO ASSOCIATION'S STATUS WILL RISE AND DONATIONS WILL POUR IN.
I SUPPOSE *THAT'S* WHAT THEY'RE AFTER.
BUT IT'S IMPOSSIBLE.

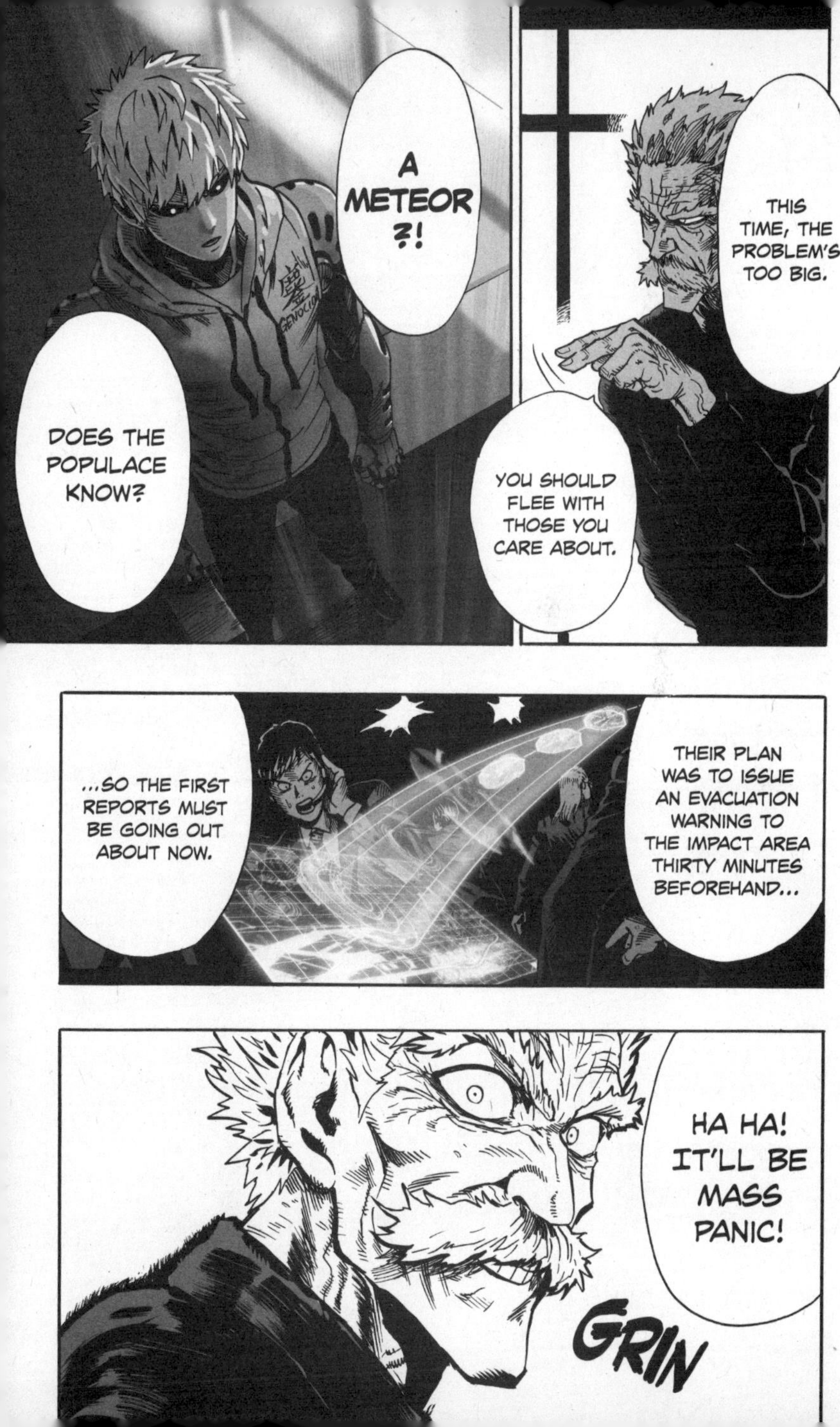
THIS TIME, THE PROBLEM'S TOO BIG.
YOU SHOULD FLEE WITH THOSE YOU CARE ABOUT.
A METEOR?!
DOES THE POPULACE KNOW?
THEIR PLAN WAS TO ISSUE AN EVACUATION WARNING TO THE IMPACT AREA THIRTY MINUTES BEFOREHAND...
...SO THE FIRST REPORTS MUST BE GOING OUT ABOUT NOW.
HA HA! IT'LL BE MASS PANIC!
GRIN

WOOOOO

WOOOOOOOO

...A
WARNING!

...WARNING...

...HAS ISSUED...

THE HERO ASSOCIATION HAS ISSUED...

WOOOOO

WHAT WILL YOU DO, OLD FELLOW?

ADDRESS ME AS MR. BANG.

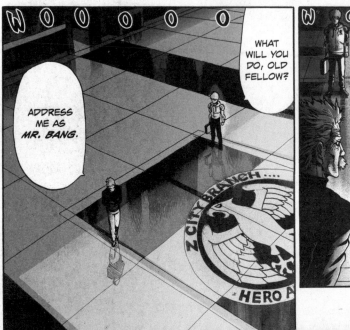

Z CITY BRANCH....

HERO A

WOOOO

AH...

There it is...

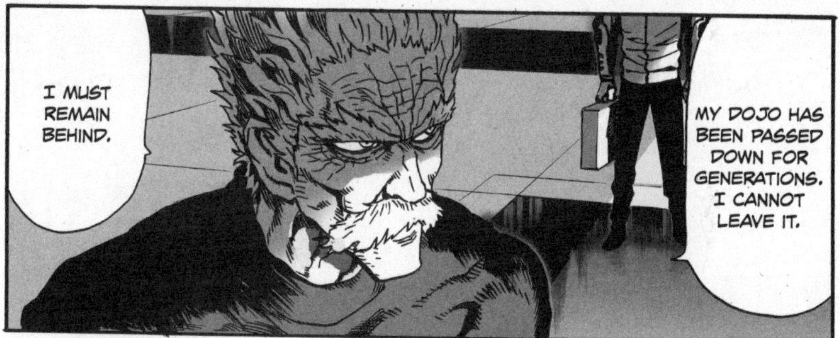
MY DOJO HAS BEEN PASSED DOWN FOR GENERATIONS. I CANNOT LEAVE IT.
I MUST REMAIN BEHIND.

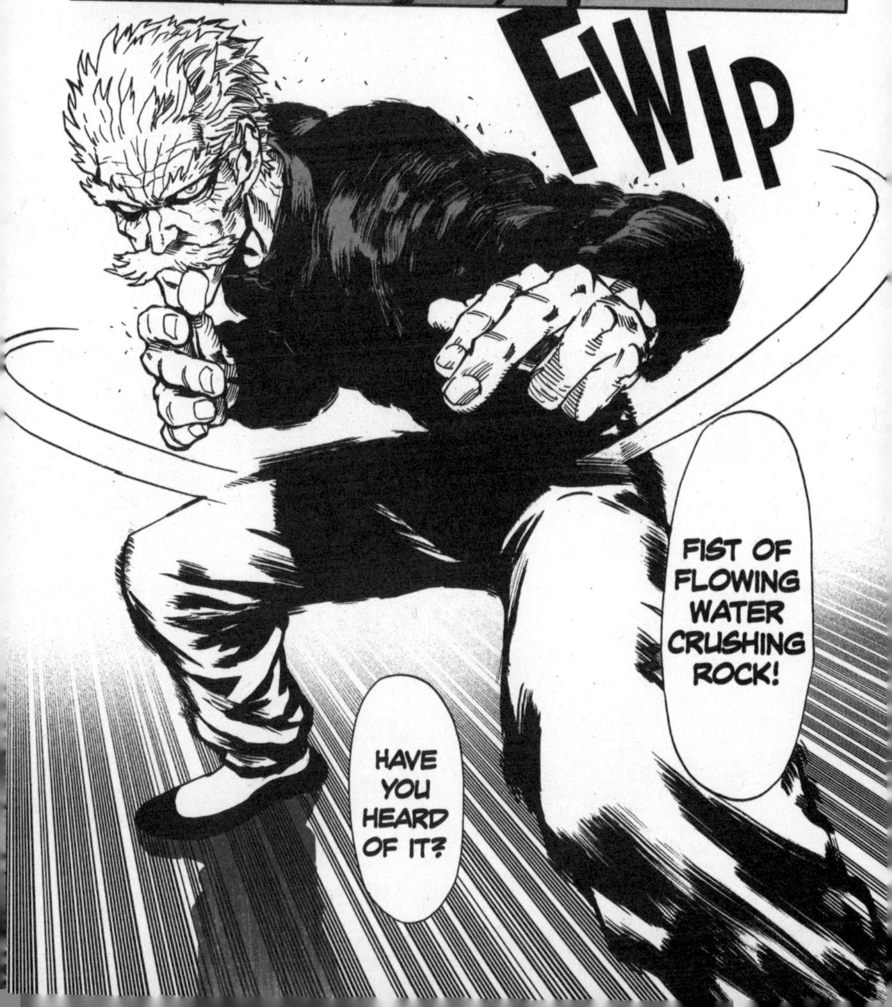
FWIP
FIST OF FLOWING WATER CRUSHING ROCK!
HAVE YOU HEARD OF IT?

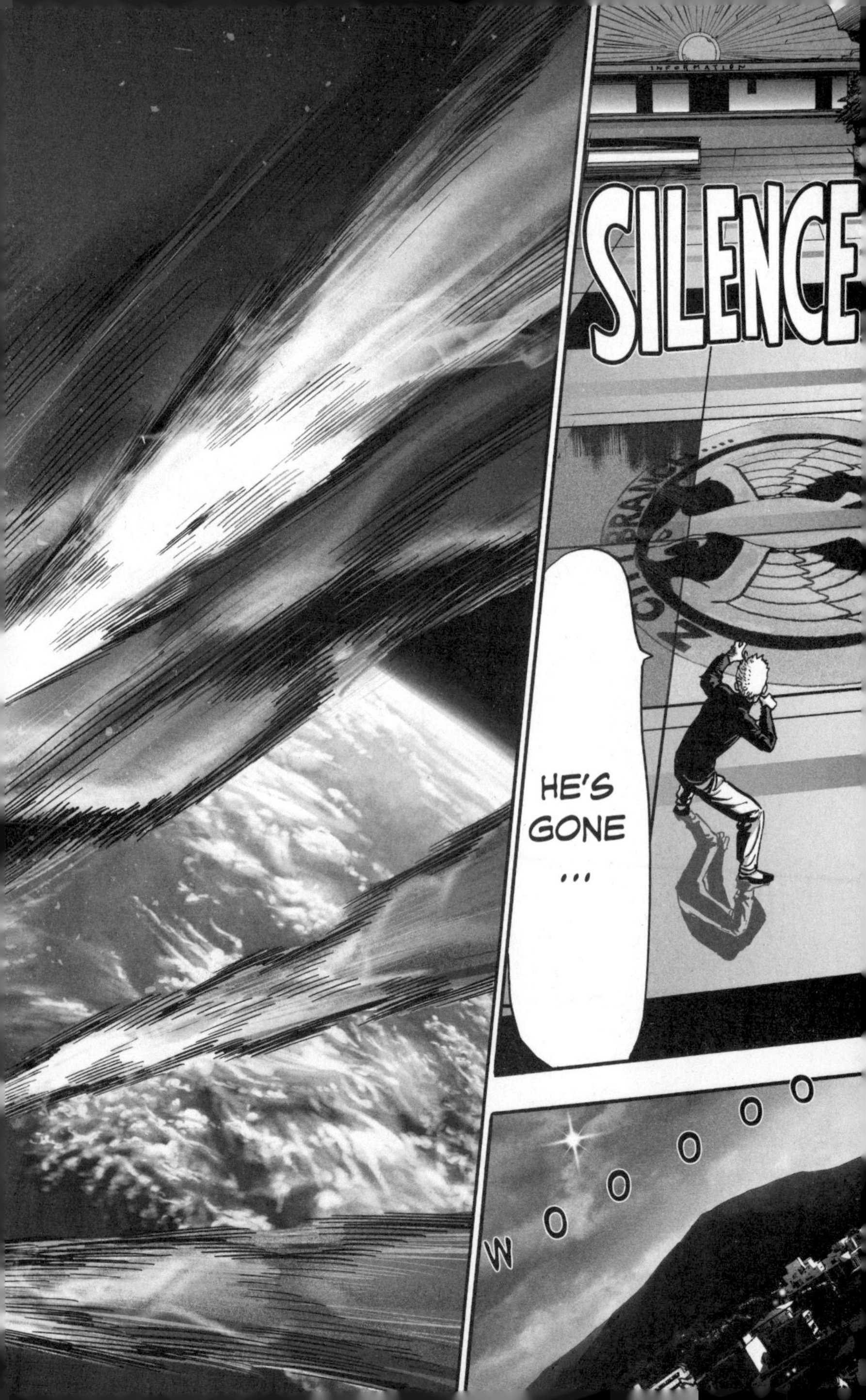
INFORMATION
SILENCE
HE'S GONE ...
WOOOOOO

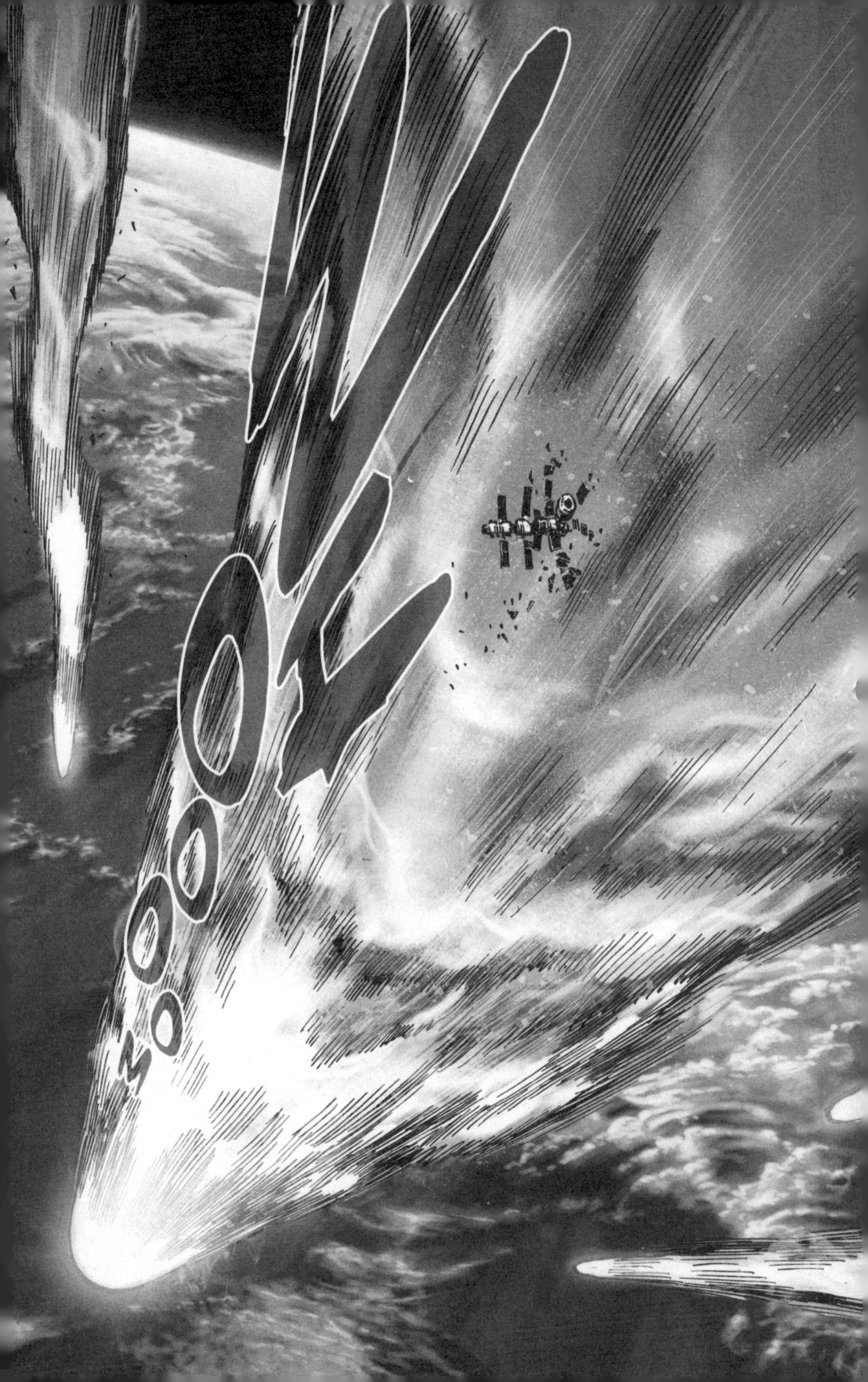

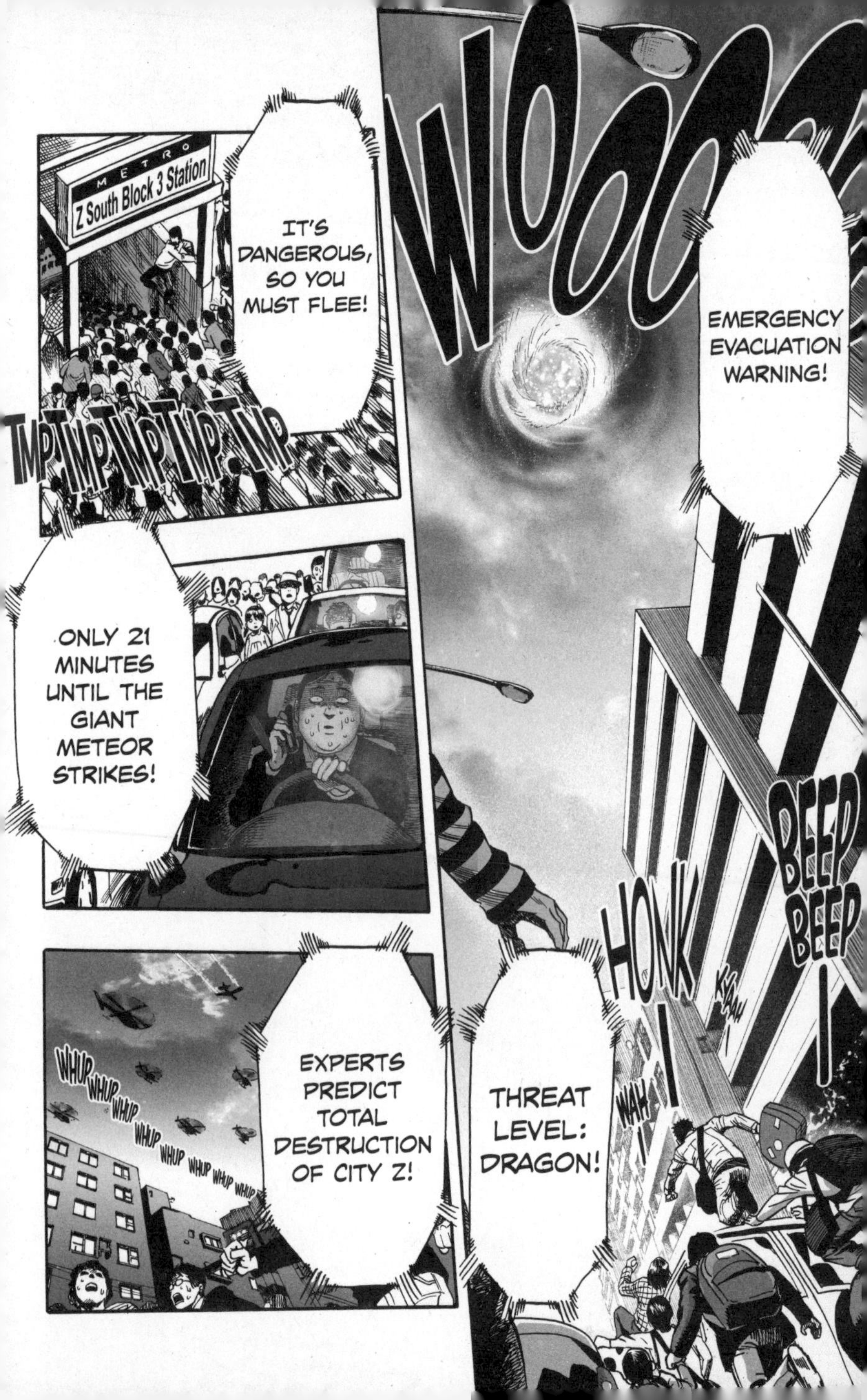
WOOO
EMERGENCY EVACUATION WARNING!
BEEP BEEP
HONK
KYAAH
WAH
THREAT LEVEL: DRAGON!
METRO
Z South Block 3 Station
IT'S DANGEROUS, SO YOU MUST FLEE!
TMP TMP TMP TMP TMP TMP
ONLY 21 MINUTES UNTIL THE GIANT METEOR STRIKES!
EXPERTS PREDICT TOTAL DESTRUCTION OF CITY Z!
WHUP WHUP WHUP WHUP WHUP WHUP WHUP WHUP

...

RUN AS QUICKLY AND AS FAR AS YOU CAN!

I WANTED A GIRLFRIEND BEFORE I DIED...

WOOOOOOO

WE'RE DOOMED...

IPPAN ZIN

IT'S HUGE...

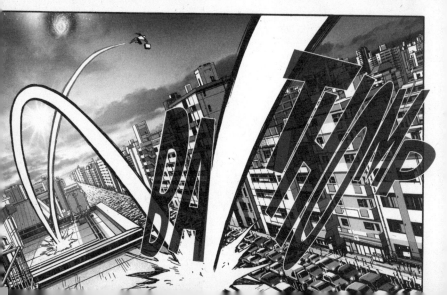

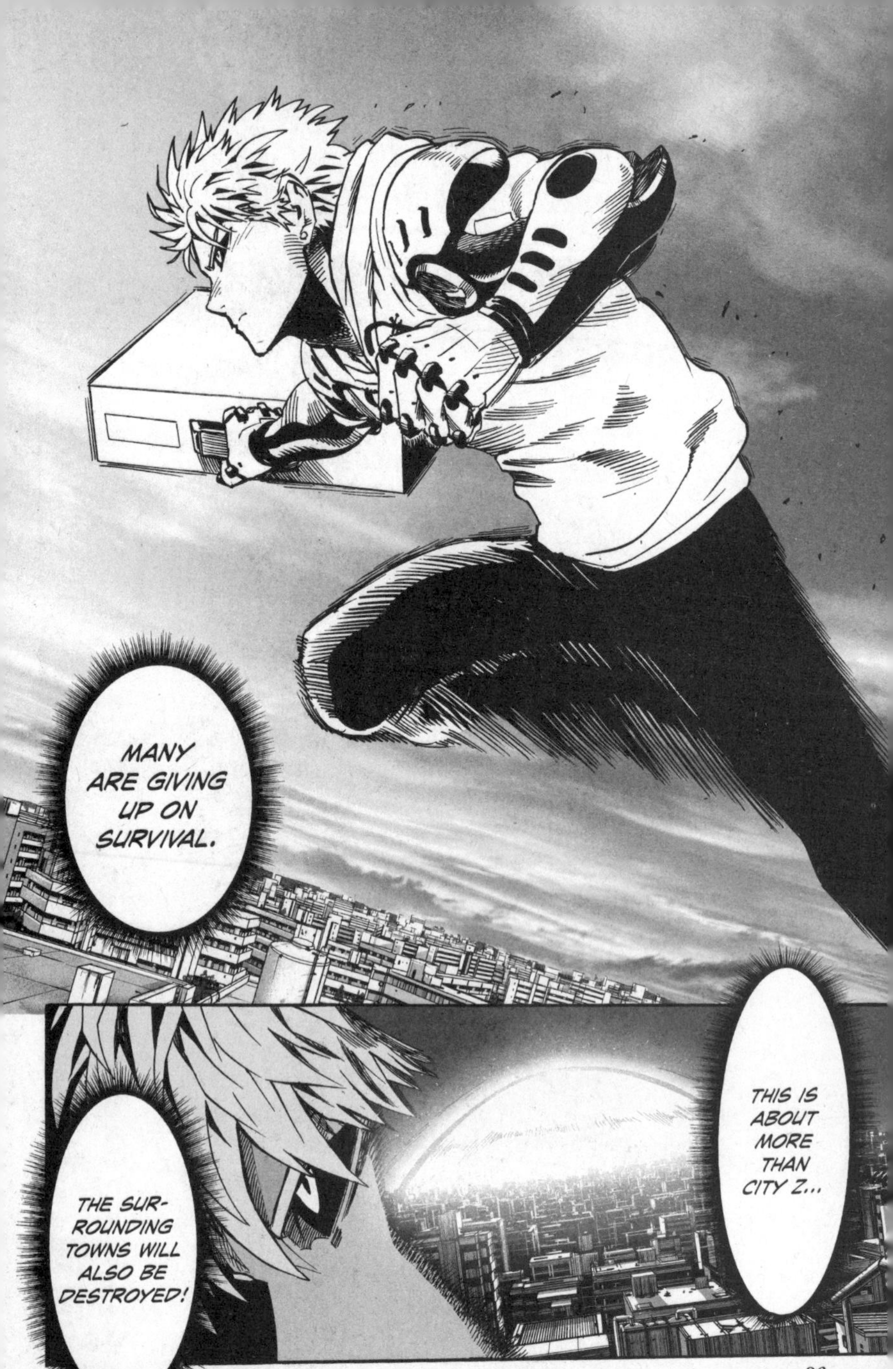
MANY ARE GIVING UP ON SURVIVAL.
THIS IS ABOUT MORE THAN CITY Z...
THE SUR-ROUNDING TOWNS WILL ALSO BE DESTROYED!

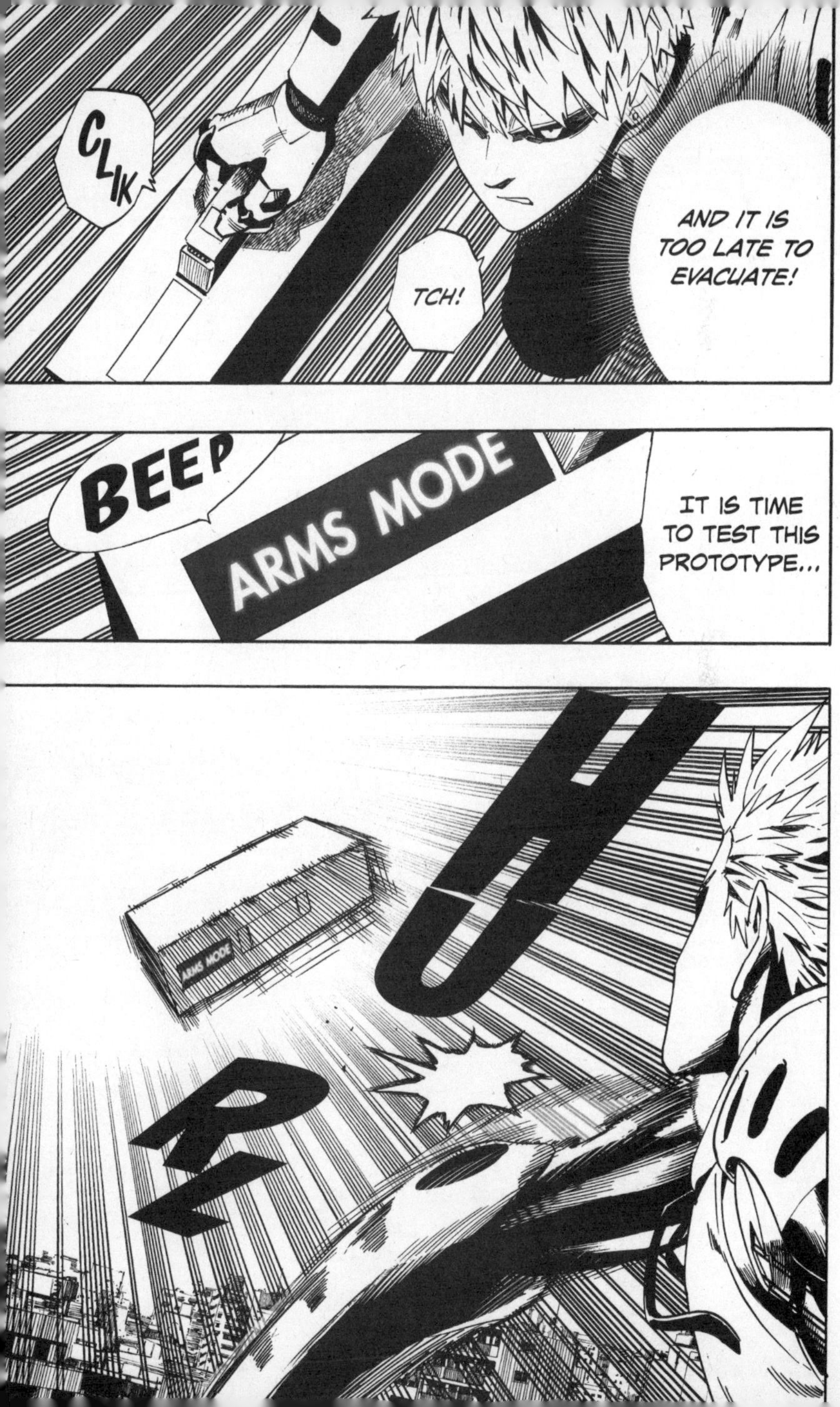
AND IT IS TOO LATE TO EVACUATE!
TCH!
CLIK
IT IS TIME TO TEST THIS PROTOTYPE...
ARMS MODE
BEEP
ARMS MODE

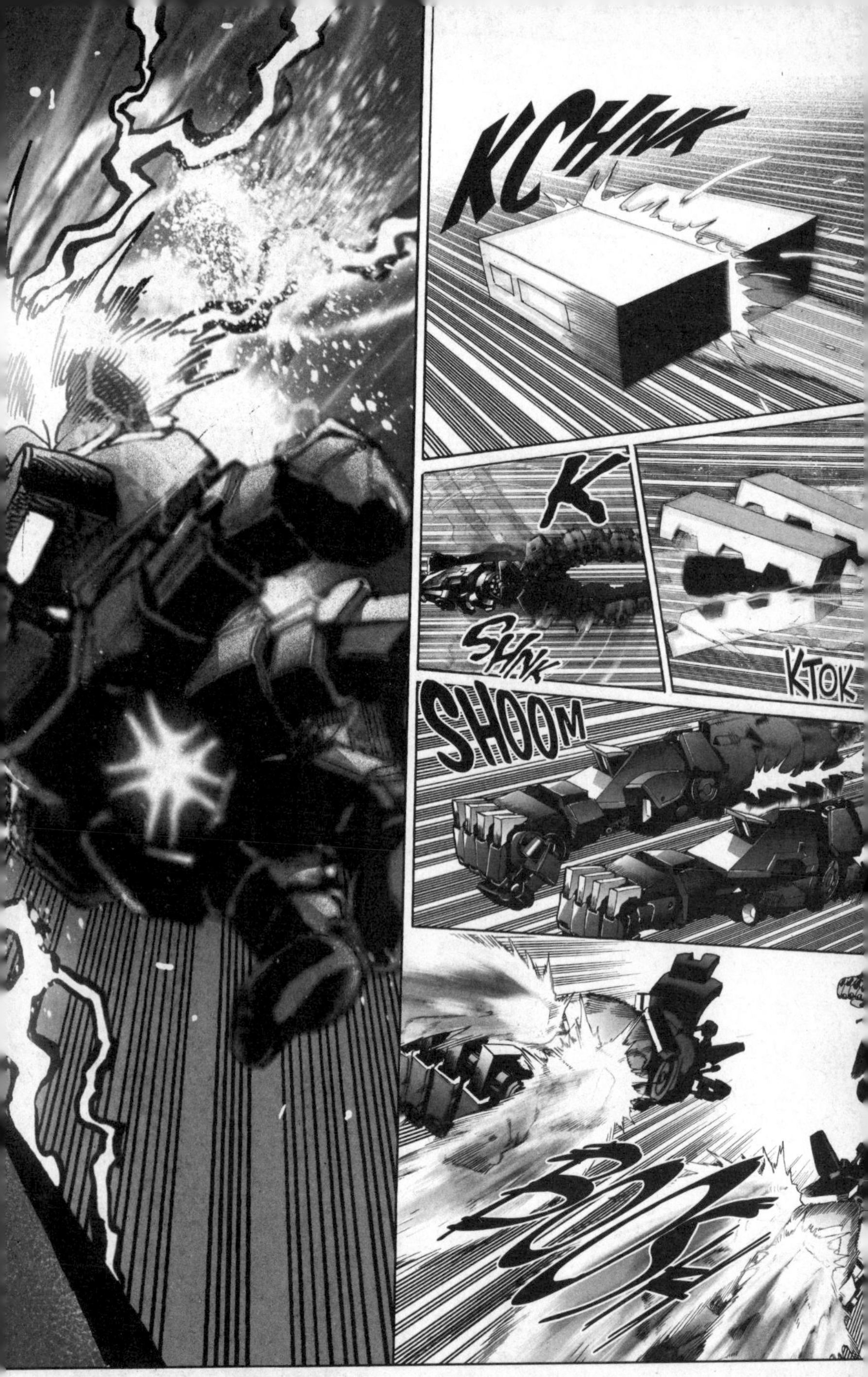
KCHAK
KTOK
K
SHUNK
SHOOM

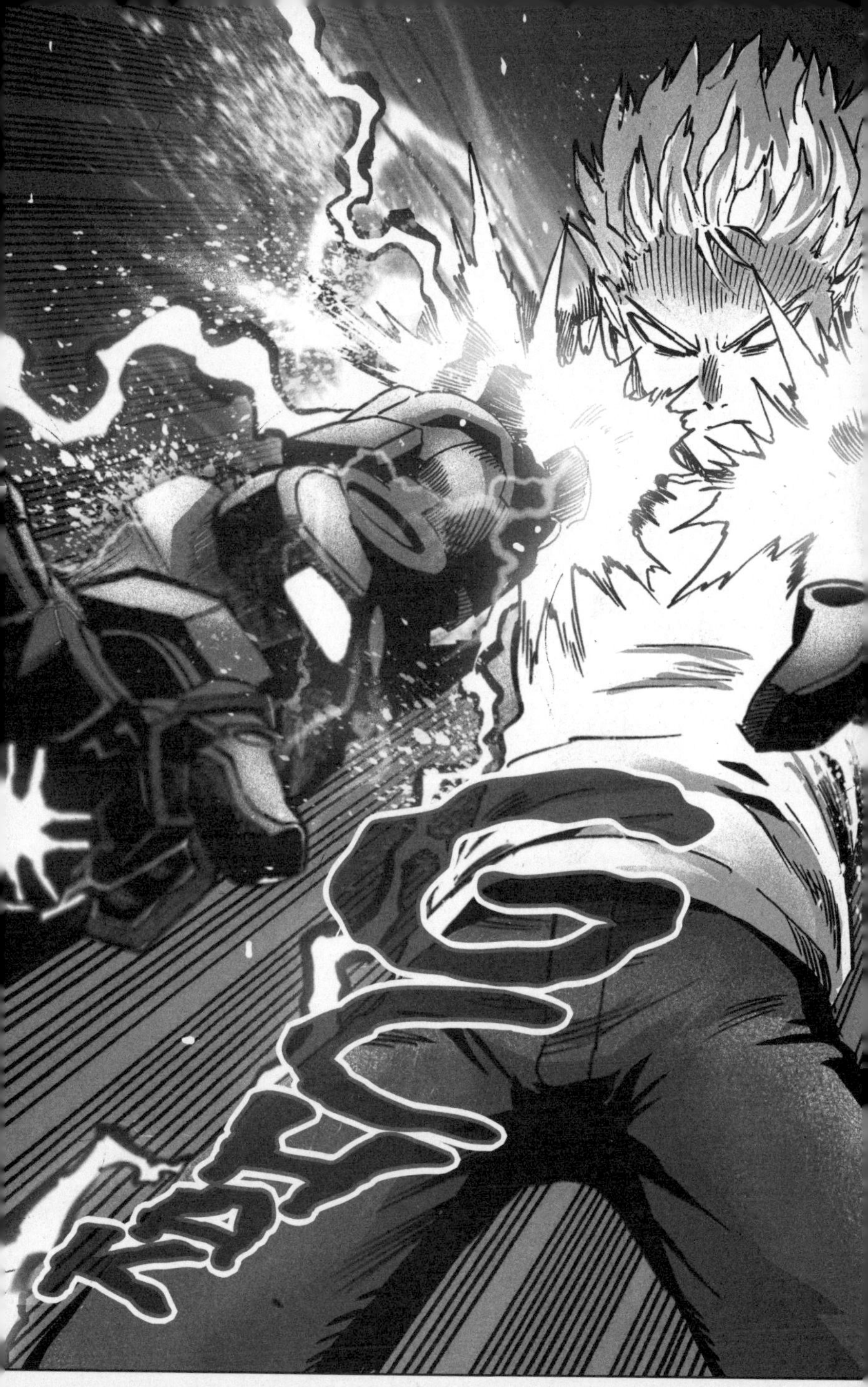

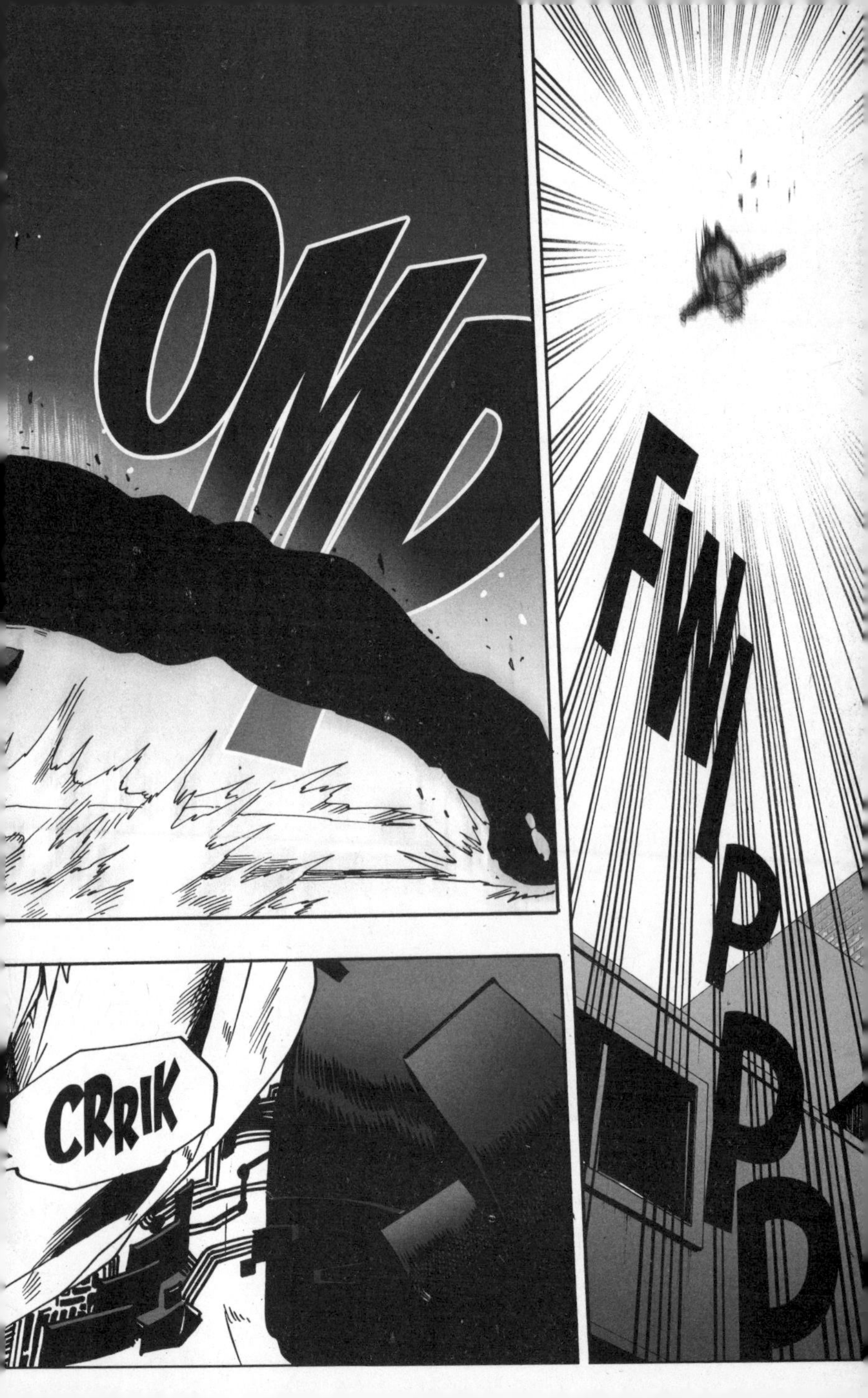
FWIP
OMD
CRRIK

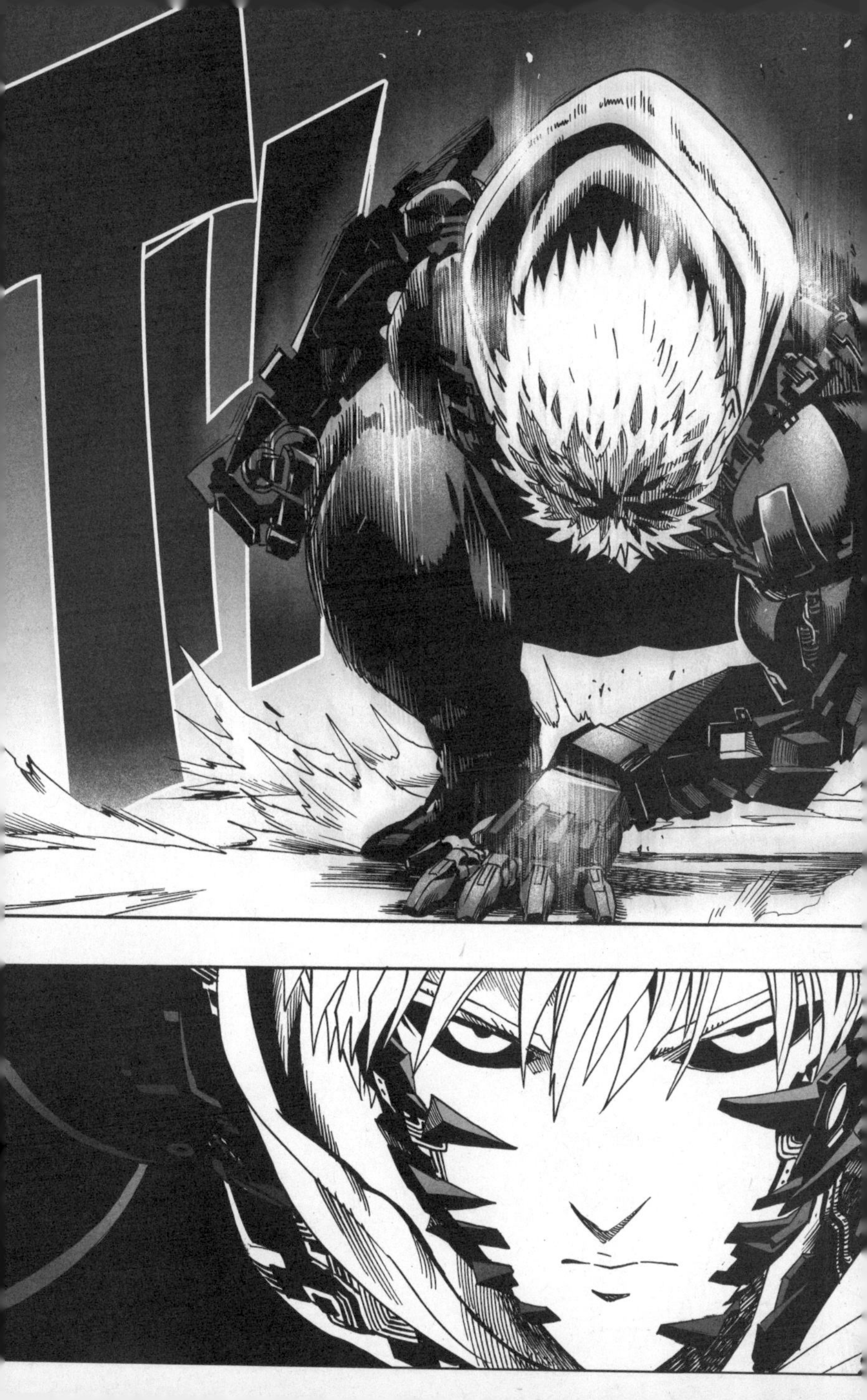

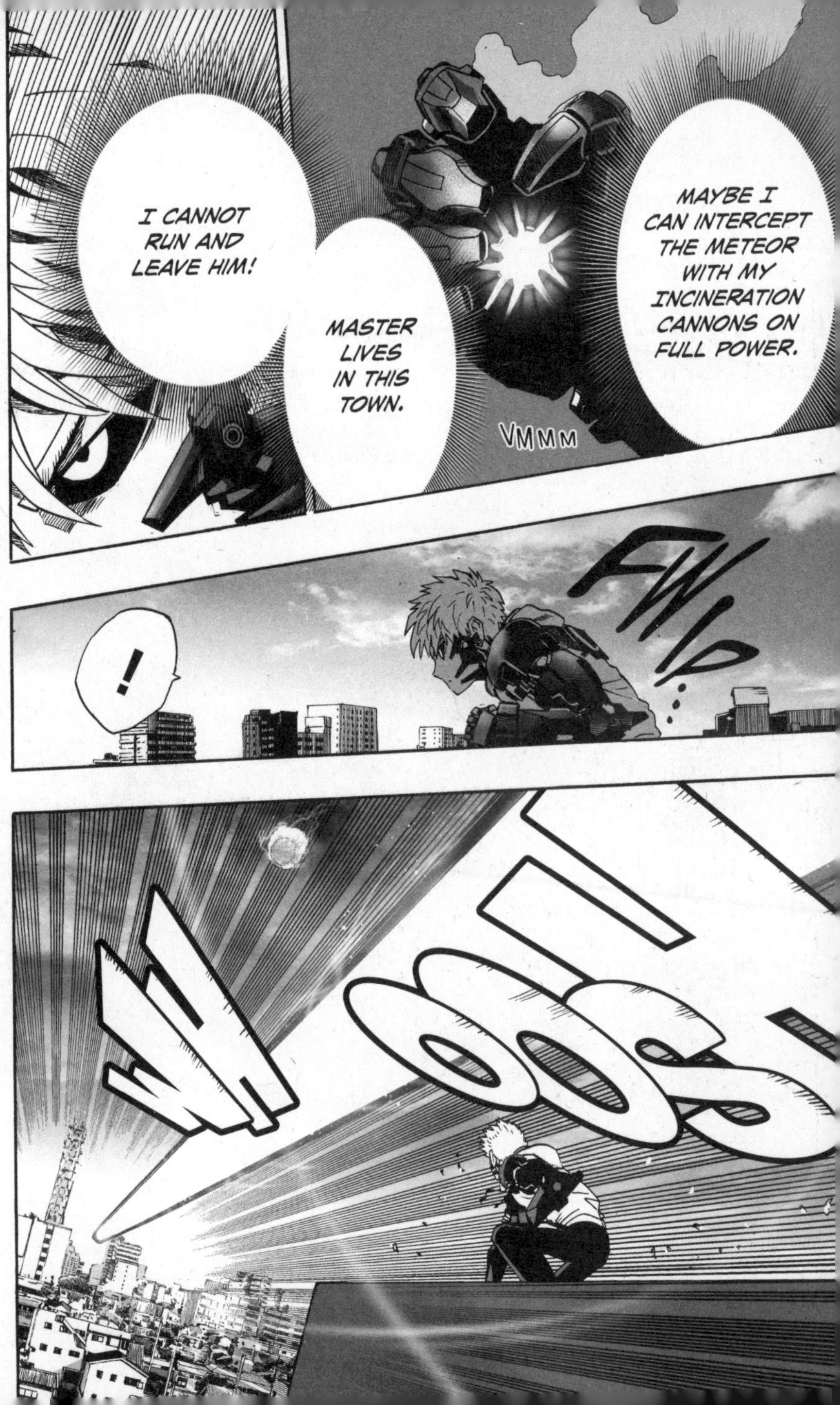
MAYBE I CAN INTERCEPT THE METEOR WITH MY INCINERATION CANNONS ON FULL POWER.
MASTER LIVES IN THIS TOWN.
VMMM
I CANNOT RUN AND LEAVE HIM!
FWIP...
!
WHOOSH

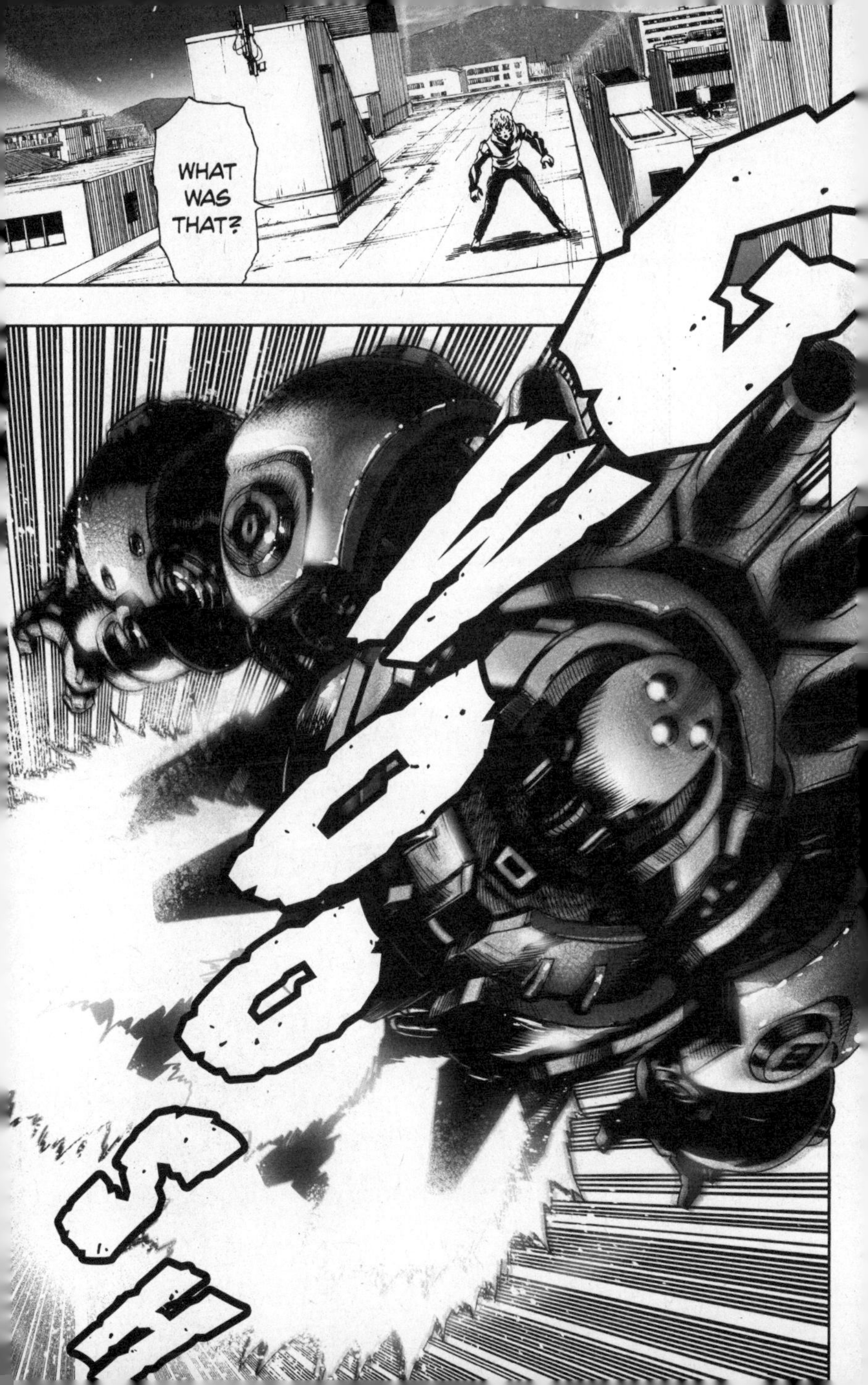
WHAT WAS THAT?

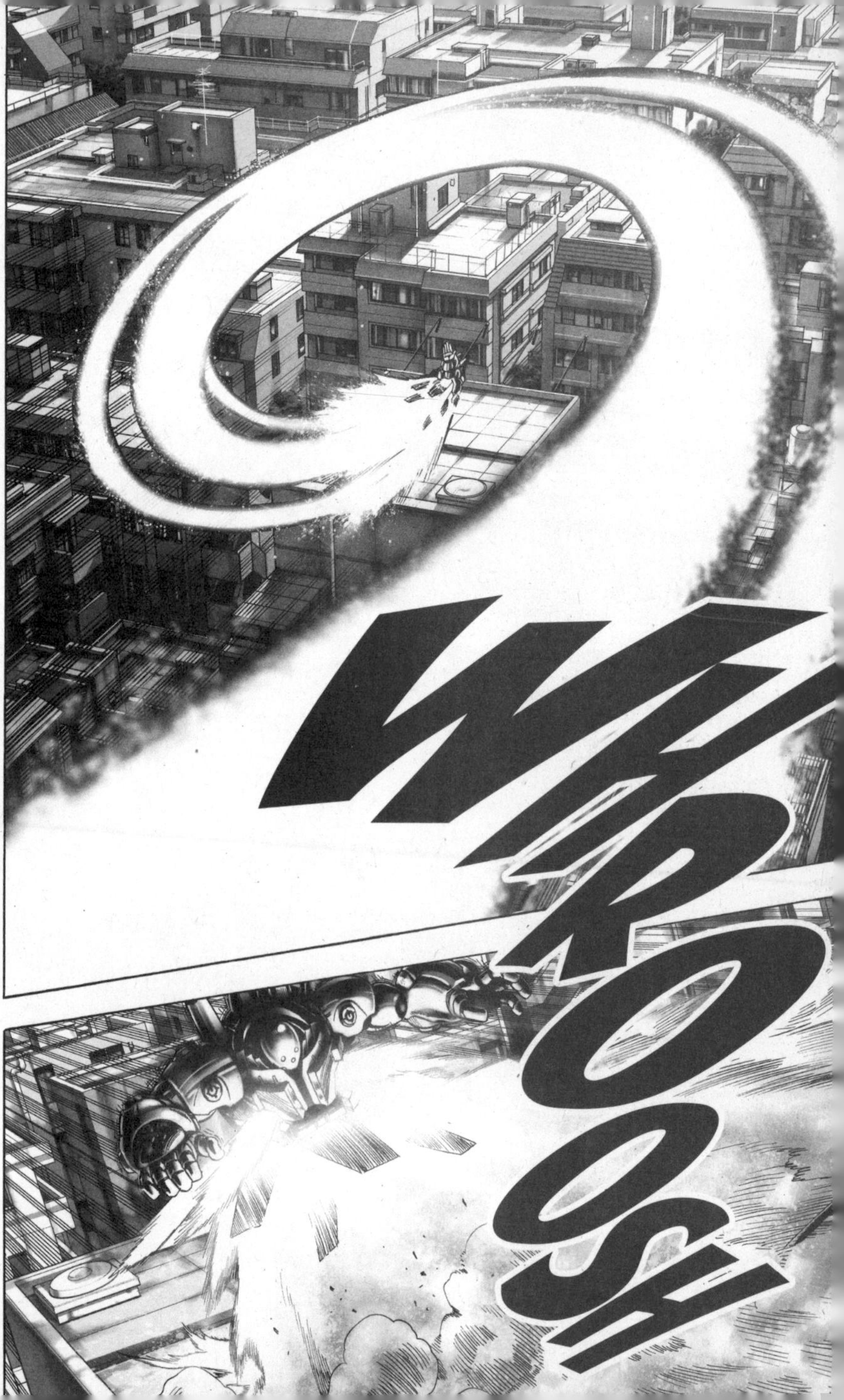
WHOOSH!

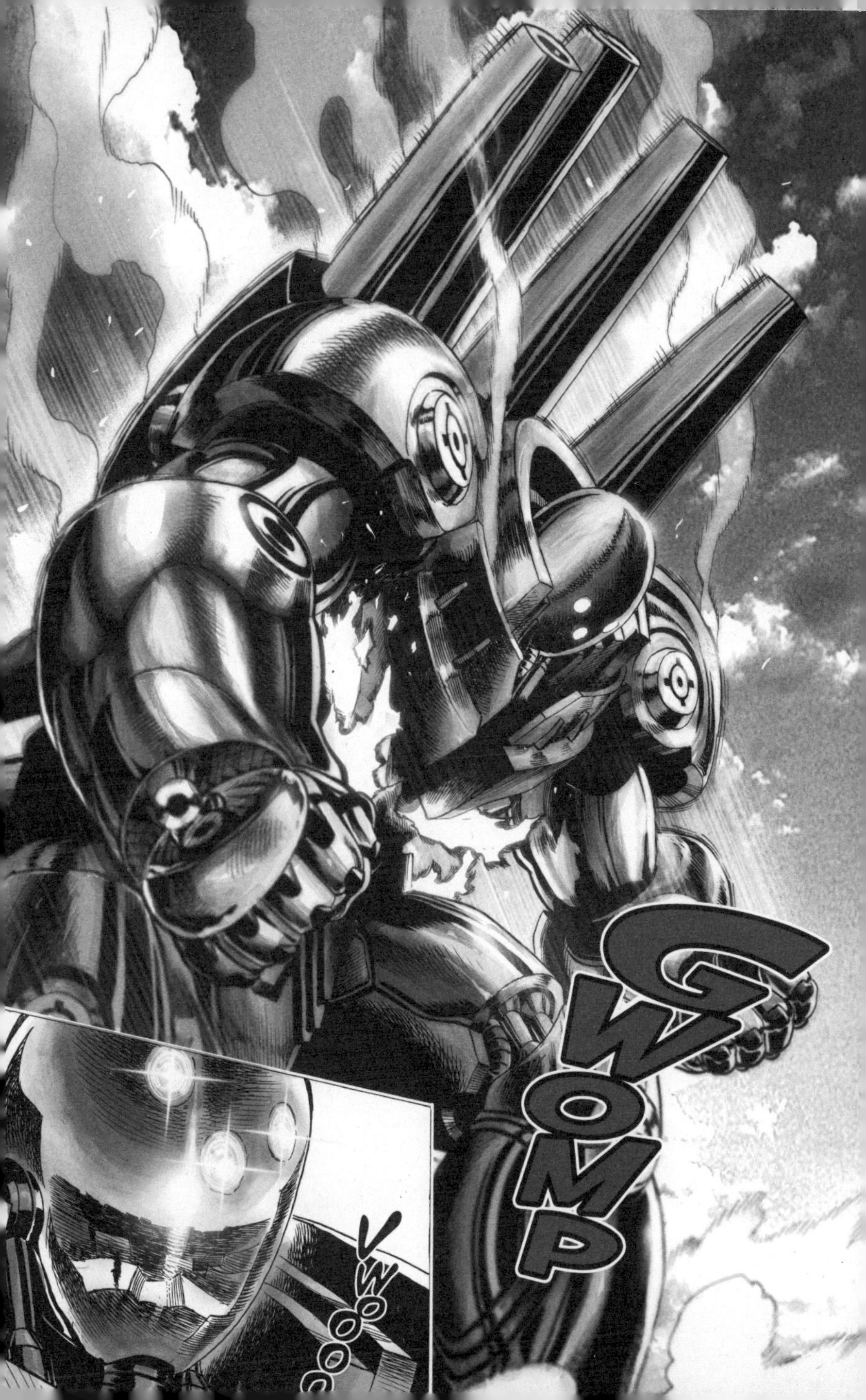
GWOMP
VWOOOO

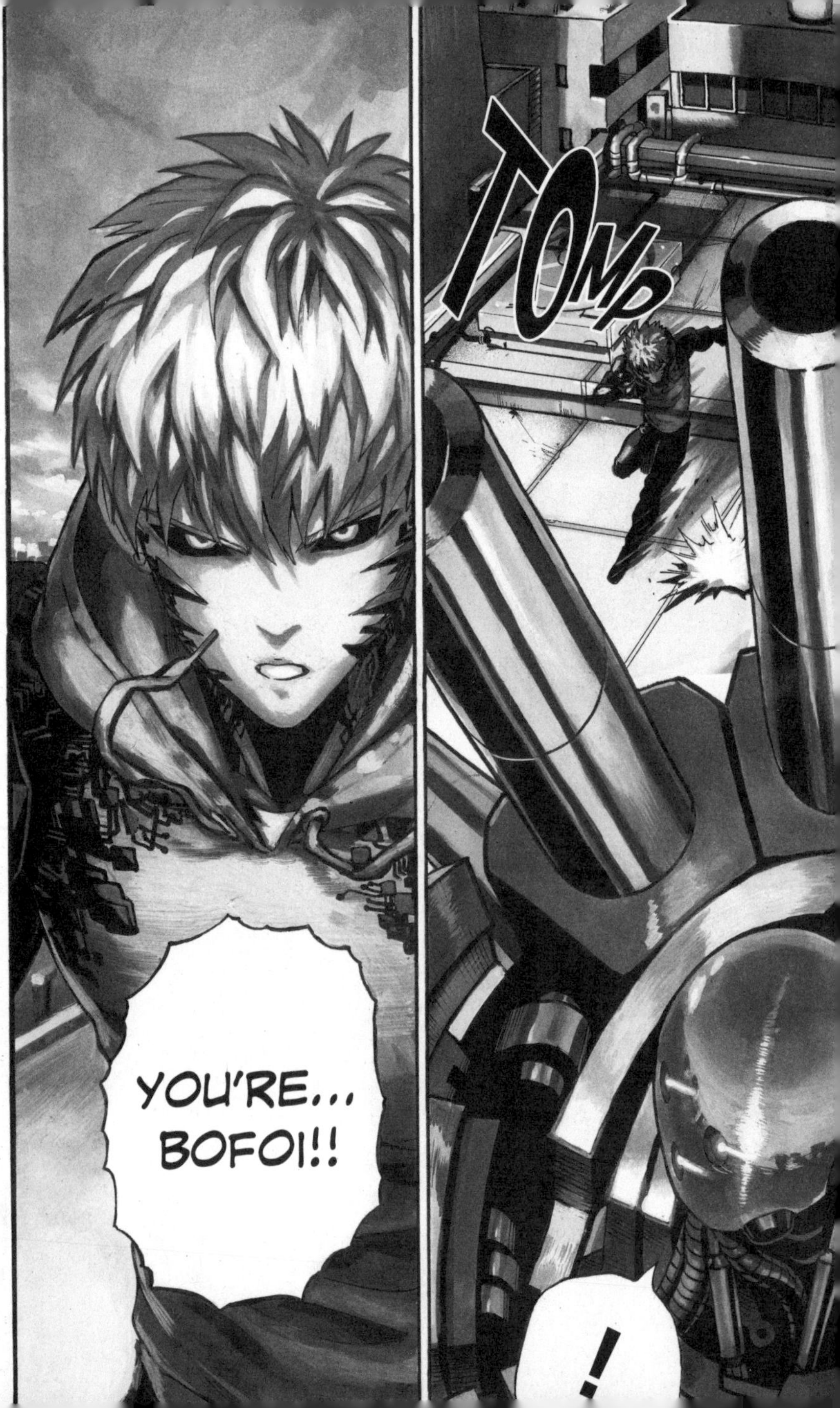
TOMP
!
YOU'RE... BOFOI!!

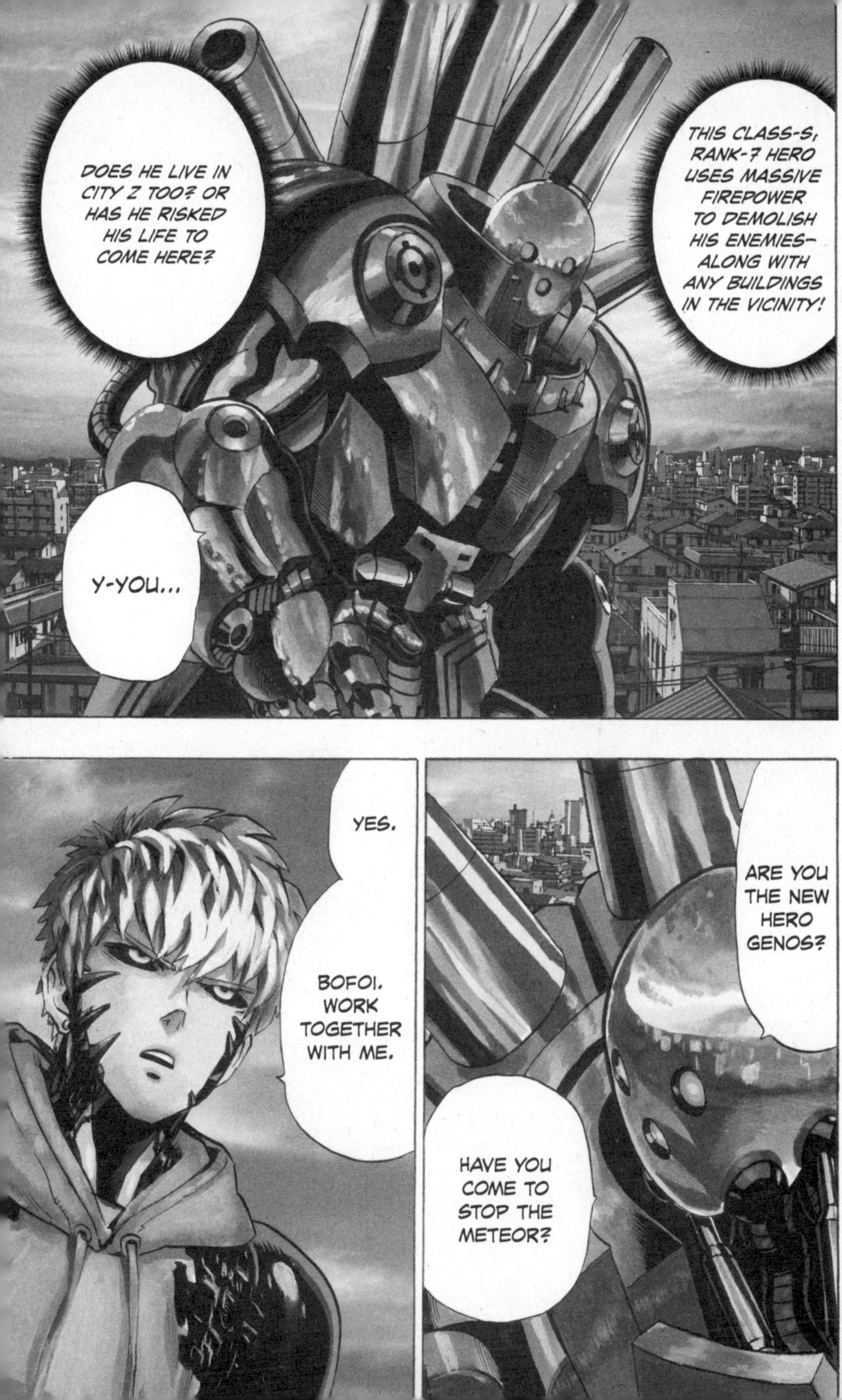
THIS CLASS-S, RANK-7 HERO USES MASSIVE FIREPOWER TO DEMOLISH HIS ENEMIES–ALONG WITH ANY BUILDINGS IN THE VICINITY!
DOES HE LIVE IN CITY Z TOO? OR HAS HE RISKED HIS LIFE TO COME HERE?
Y-YOU...
ARE YOU THE NEW HERO GENOS?
HAVE YOU COME TO STOP THE METEOR?
YES.
BOFOI. WORK TOGETHER WITH ME.

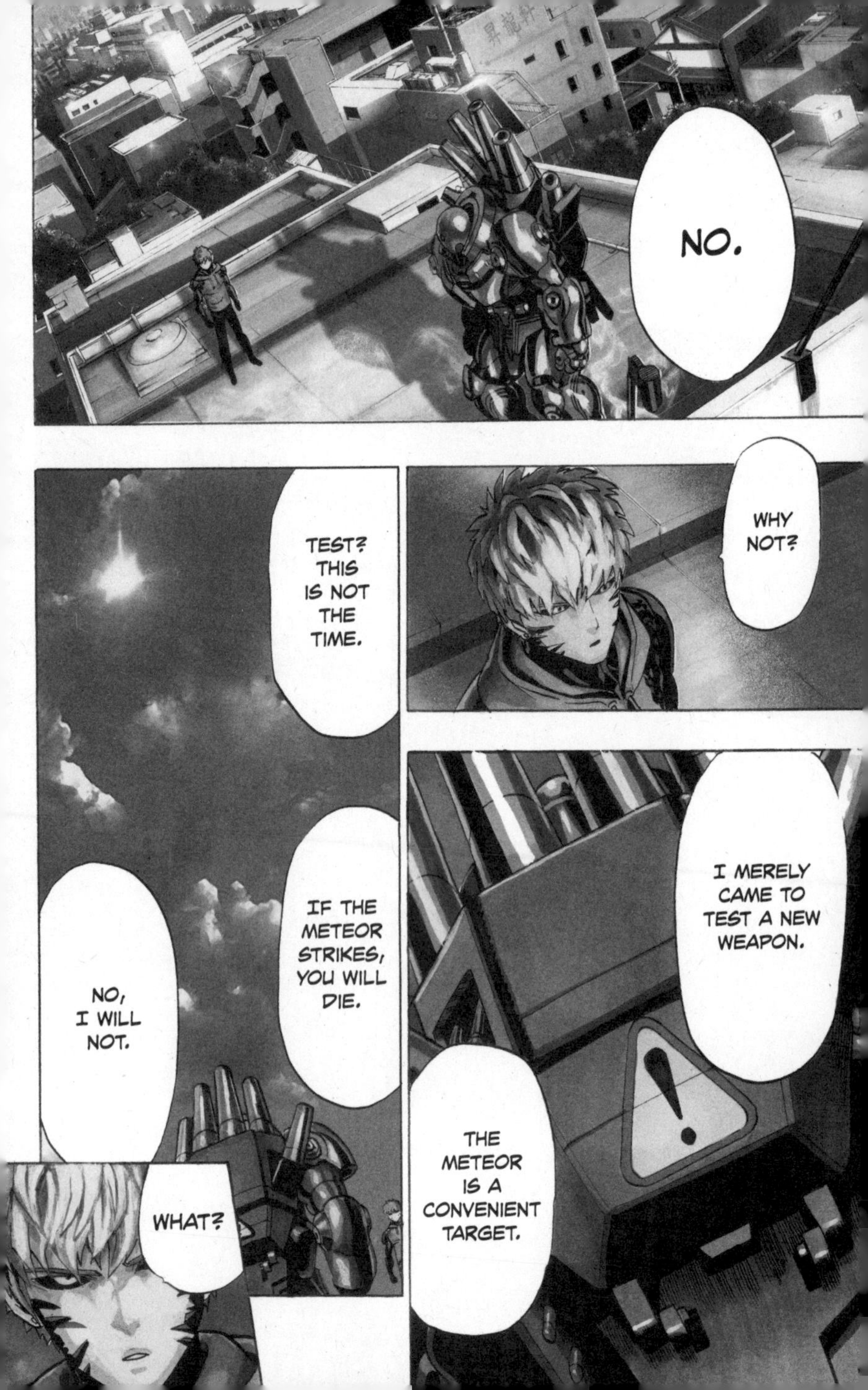
NO.
WHY NOT?
I MERELY CAME TO TEST A NEW WEAPON.
THE METEOR IS A CONVENIENT TARGET.
TEST? THIS IS NOT THE TIME.
IF THE METEOR STRIKES, YOU WILL DIE.
NO, I WILL NOT.
WHAT?

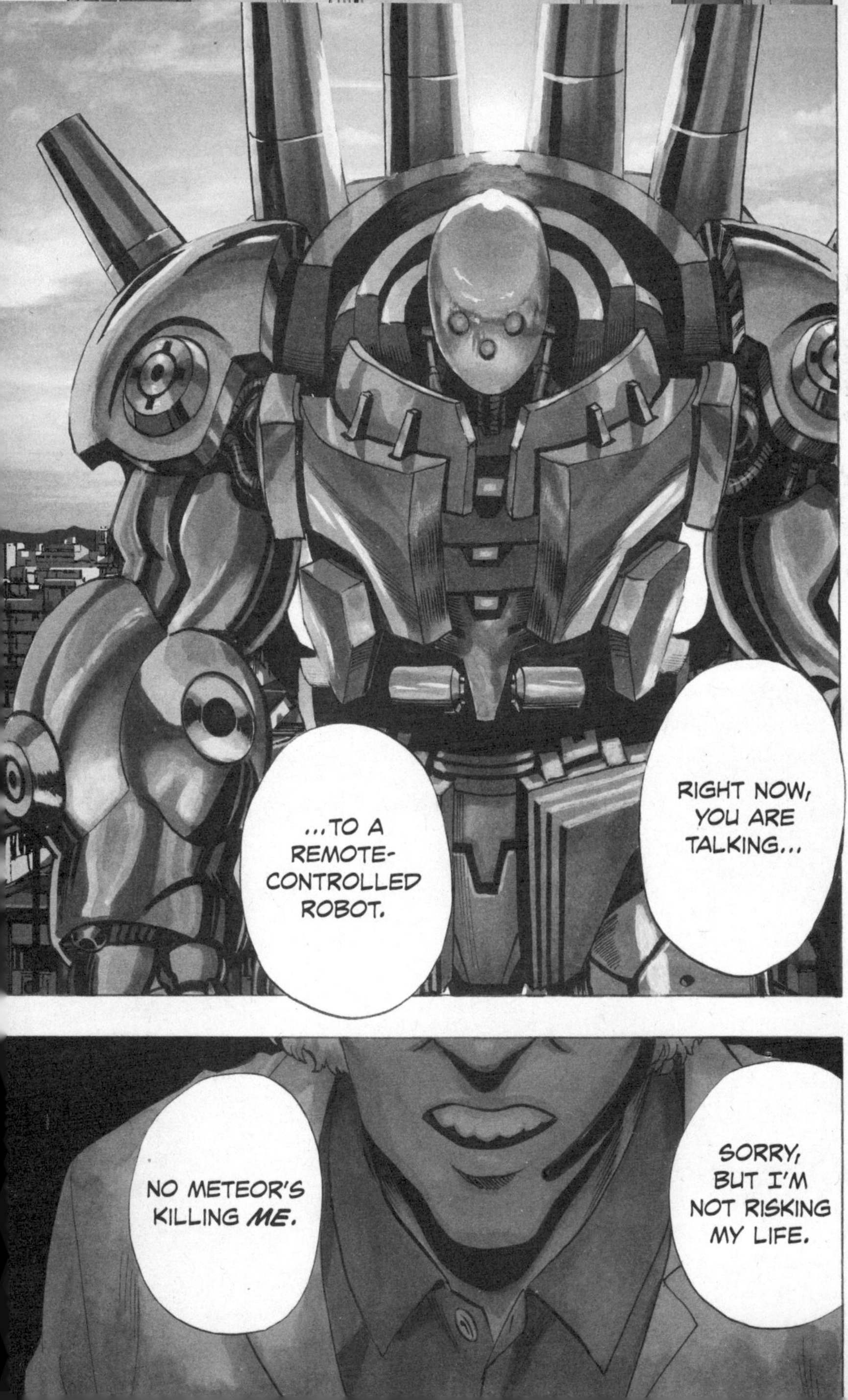
RIGHT NOW, YOU ARE TALKING...
...TO A REMOTE-CONTROLLED ROBOT.
SORRY, BUT I'M NOT RISKING MY LIFE.
NO METEOR'S KILLING *ME*.

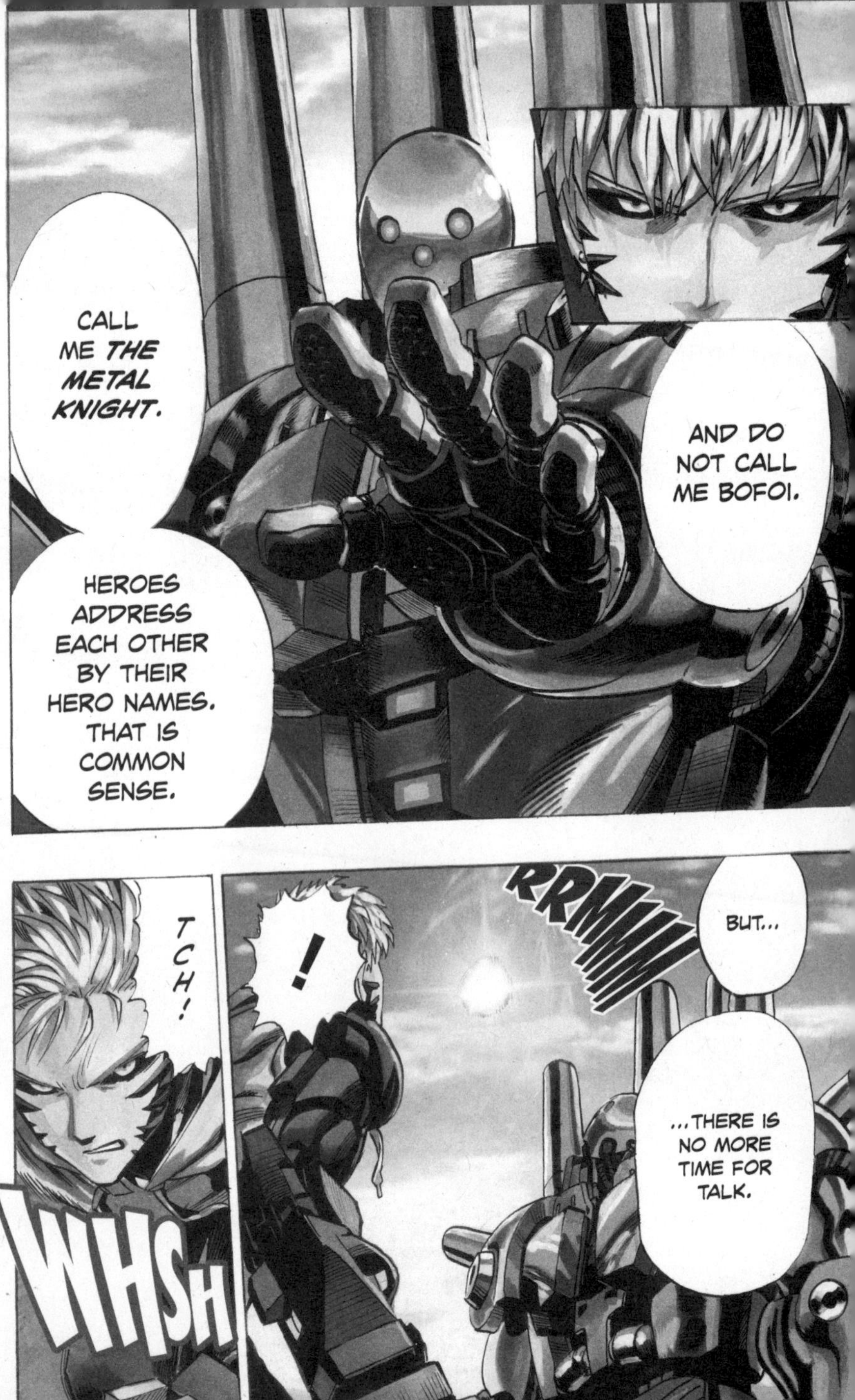
CALL ME *THE METAL KNIGHT*.
AND DO NOT CALL ME BOFOI.
HEROES ADDRESS EACH OTHER BY THEIR HERO NAMES. THAT IS COMMON SENSE.
BUT...
RRMMM
!
...THERE IS NO MORE TIME FOR TALK.
TCH!
WHSH

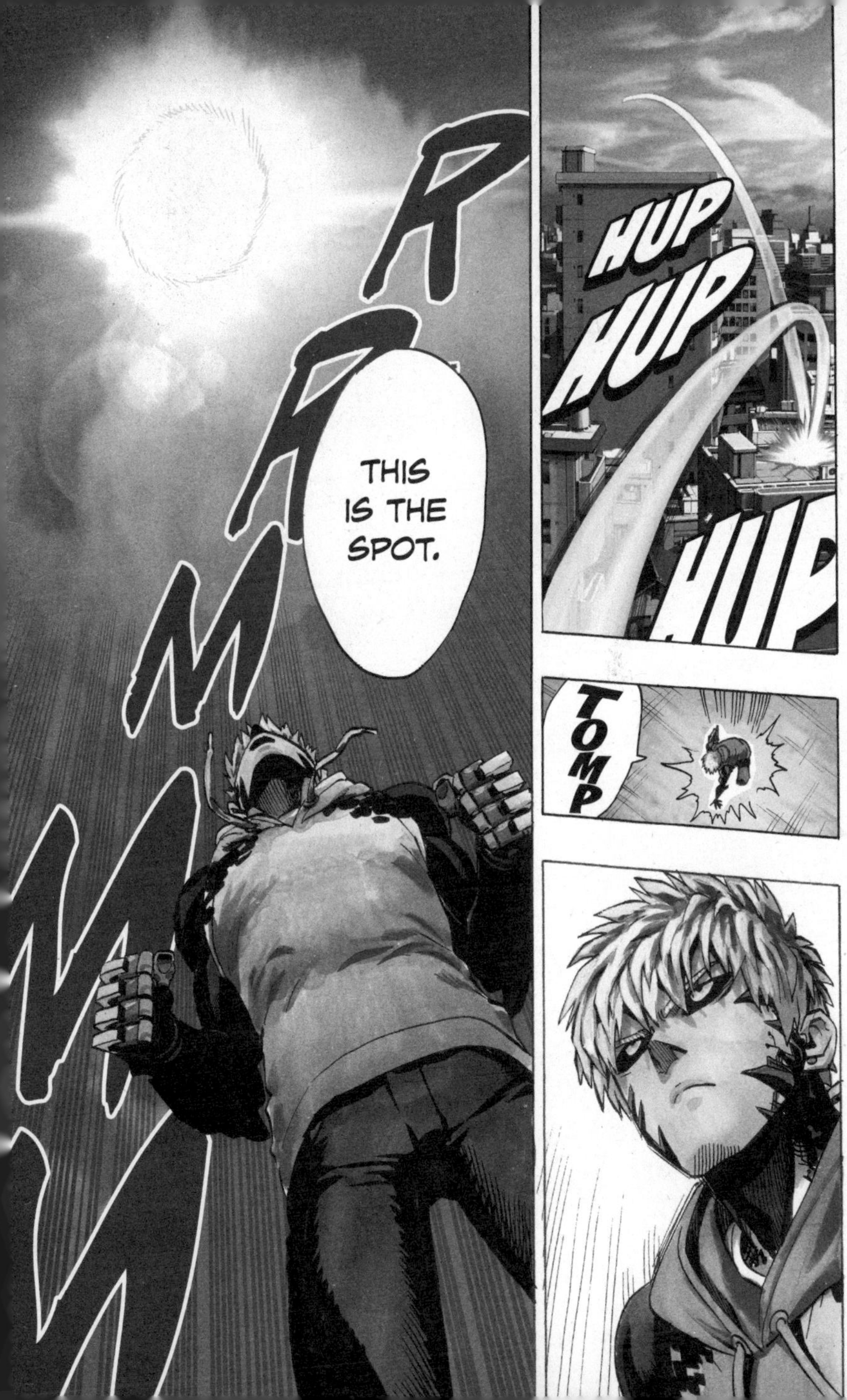
HUP
HUP
HUP
TOMP
THIS IS THE SPOT.

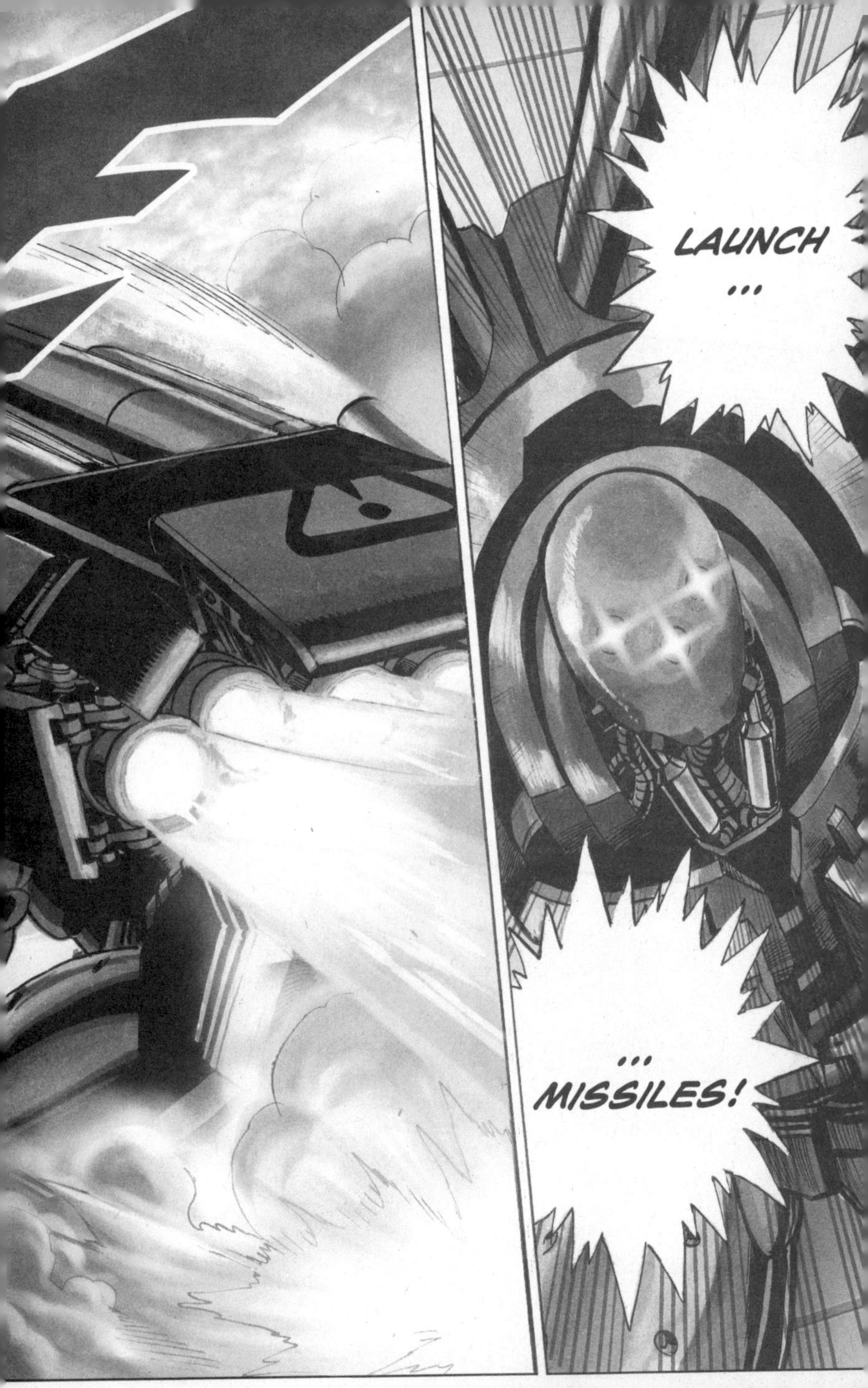
LAUNCH ...
... MISSILES!

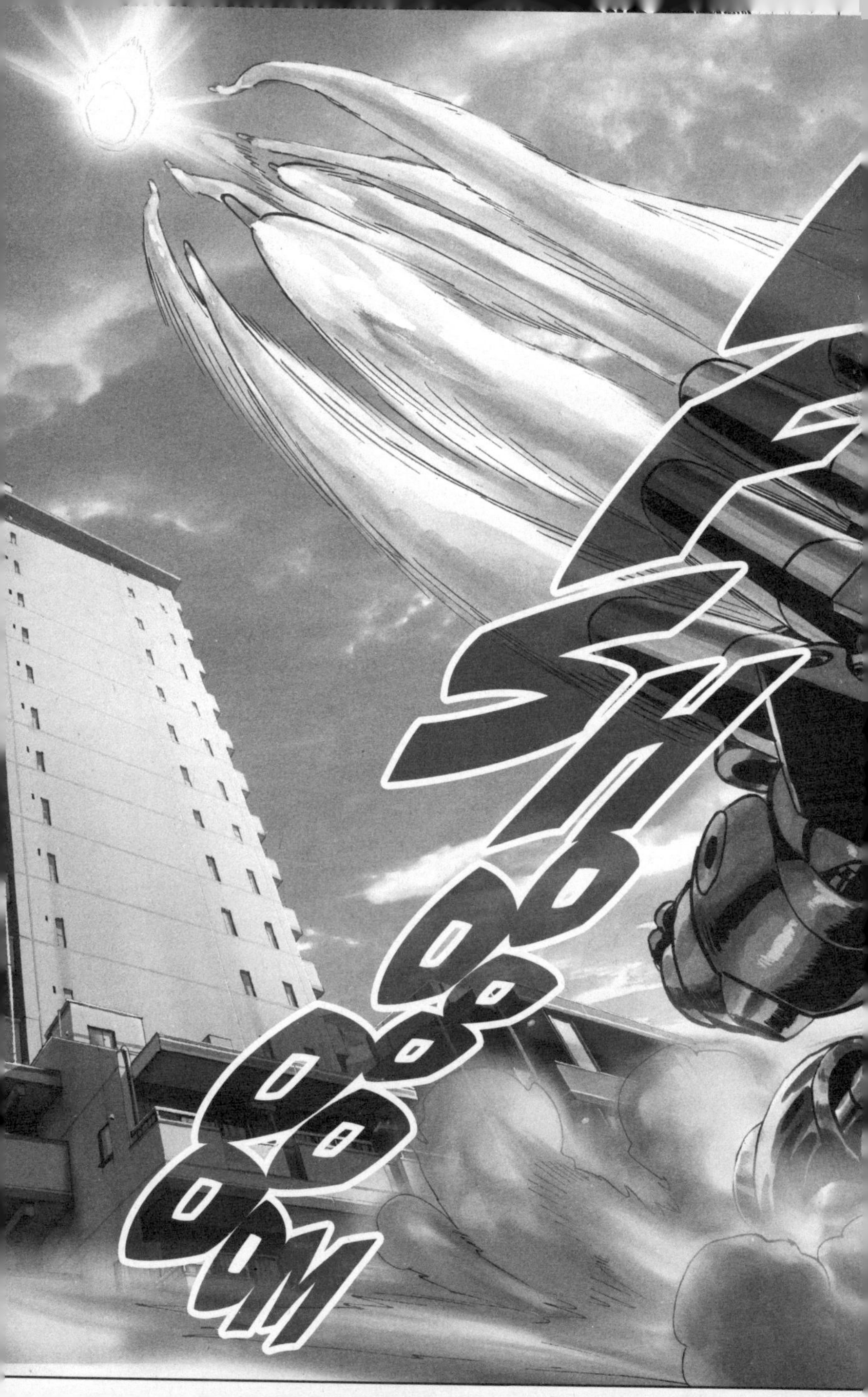

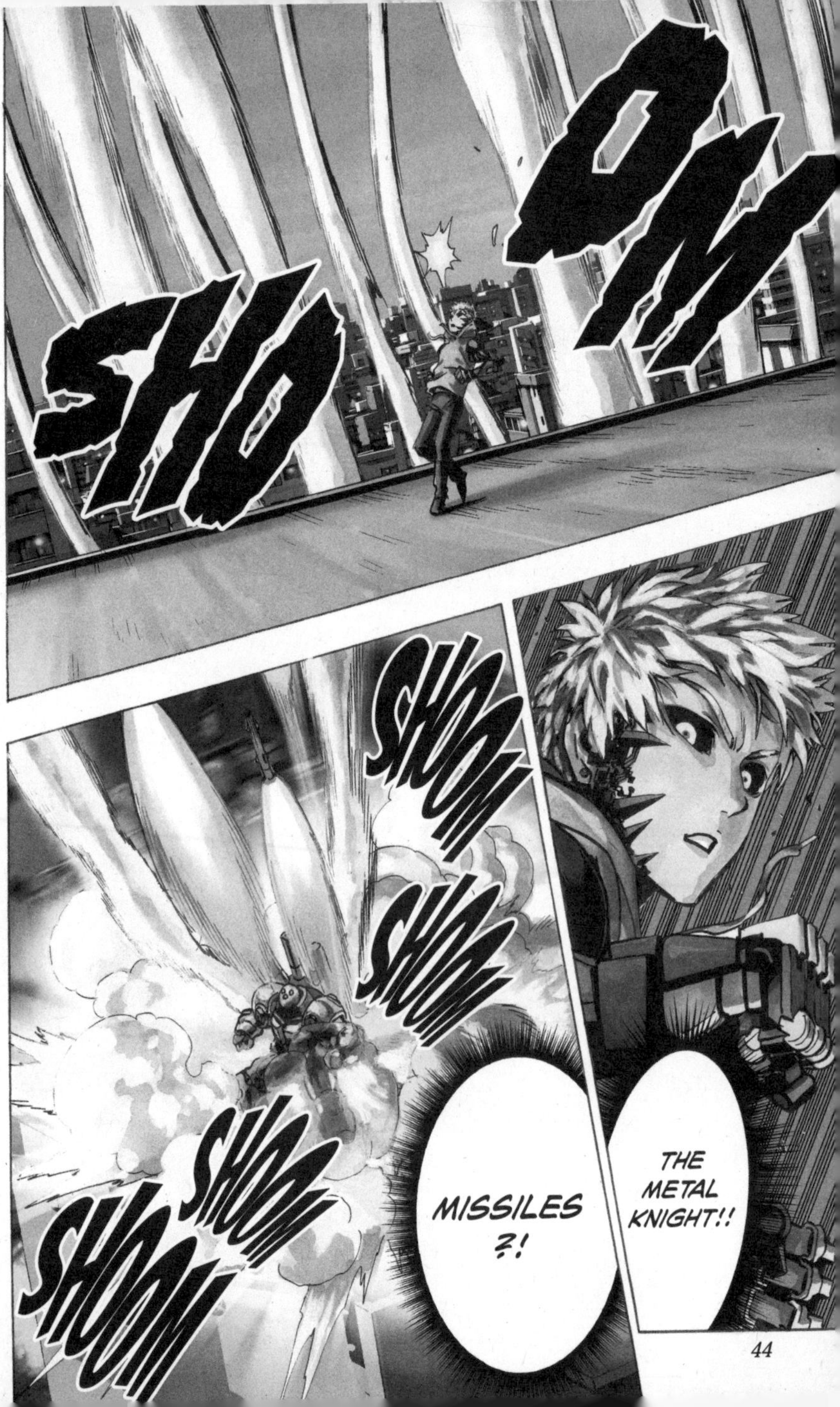
SHOOM
THE METAL KNIGHT!!
SHOOM
SHOOM
SHOOM
SHOOM
MISSILES ?!

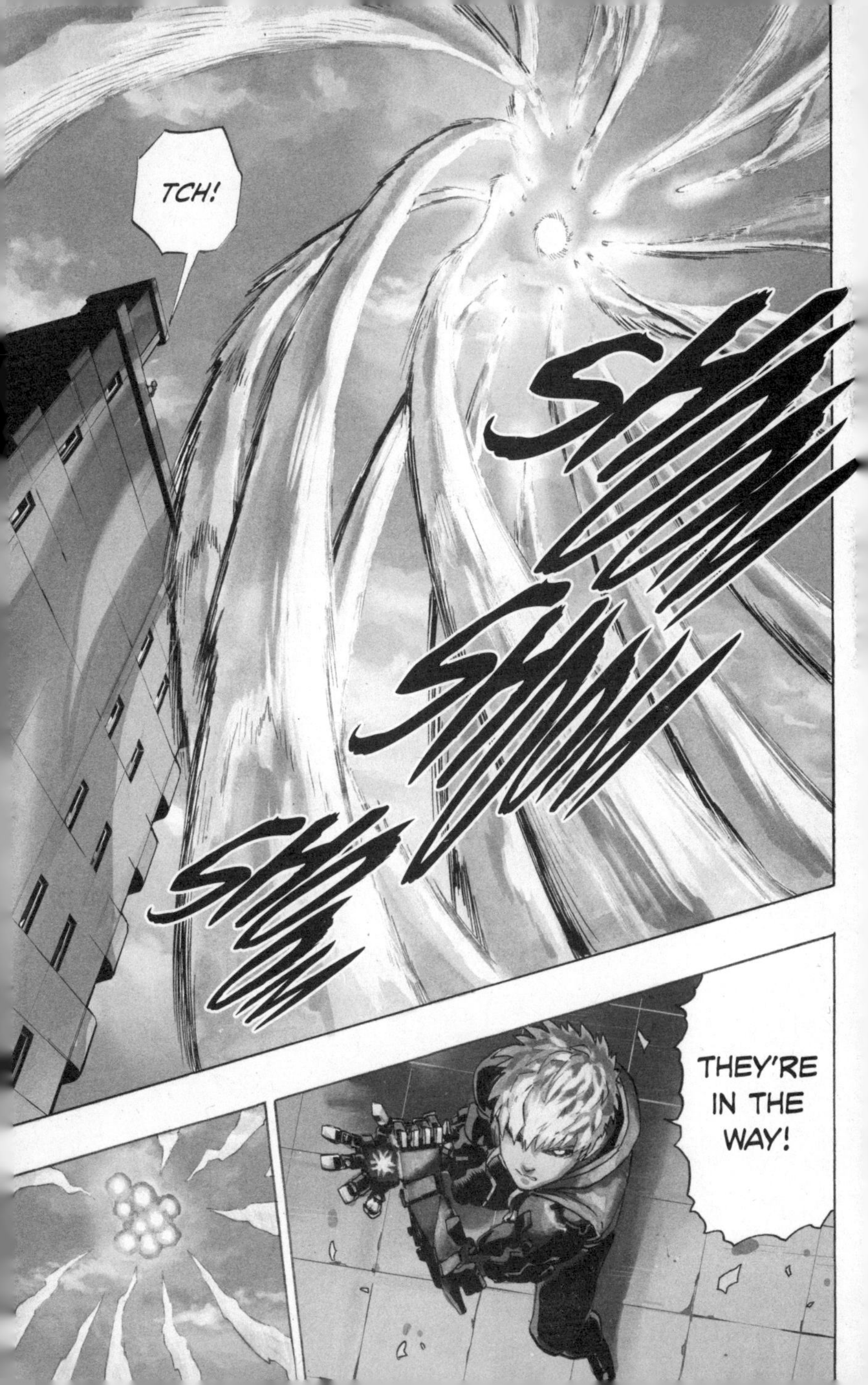
TCH!
THEY'RE IN THE WAY!

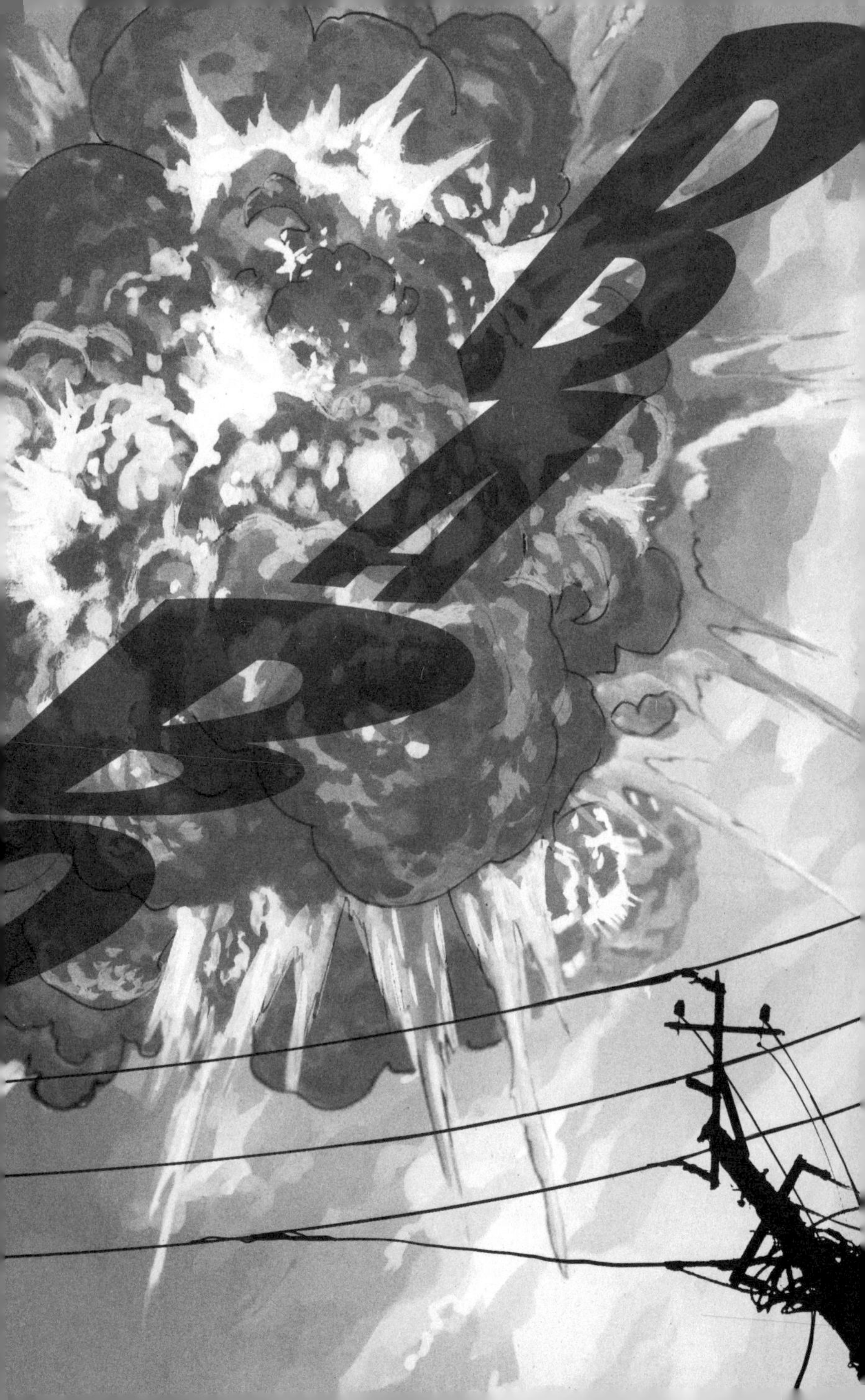

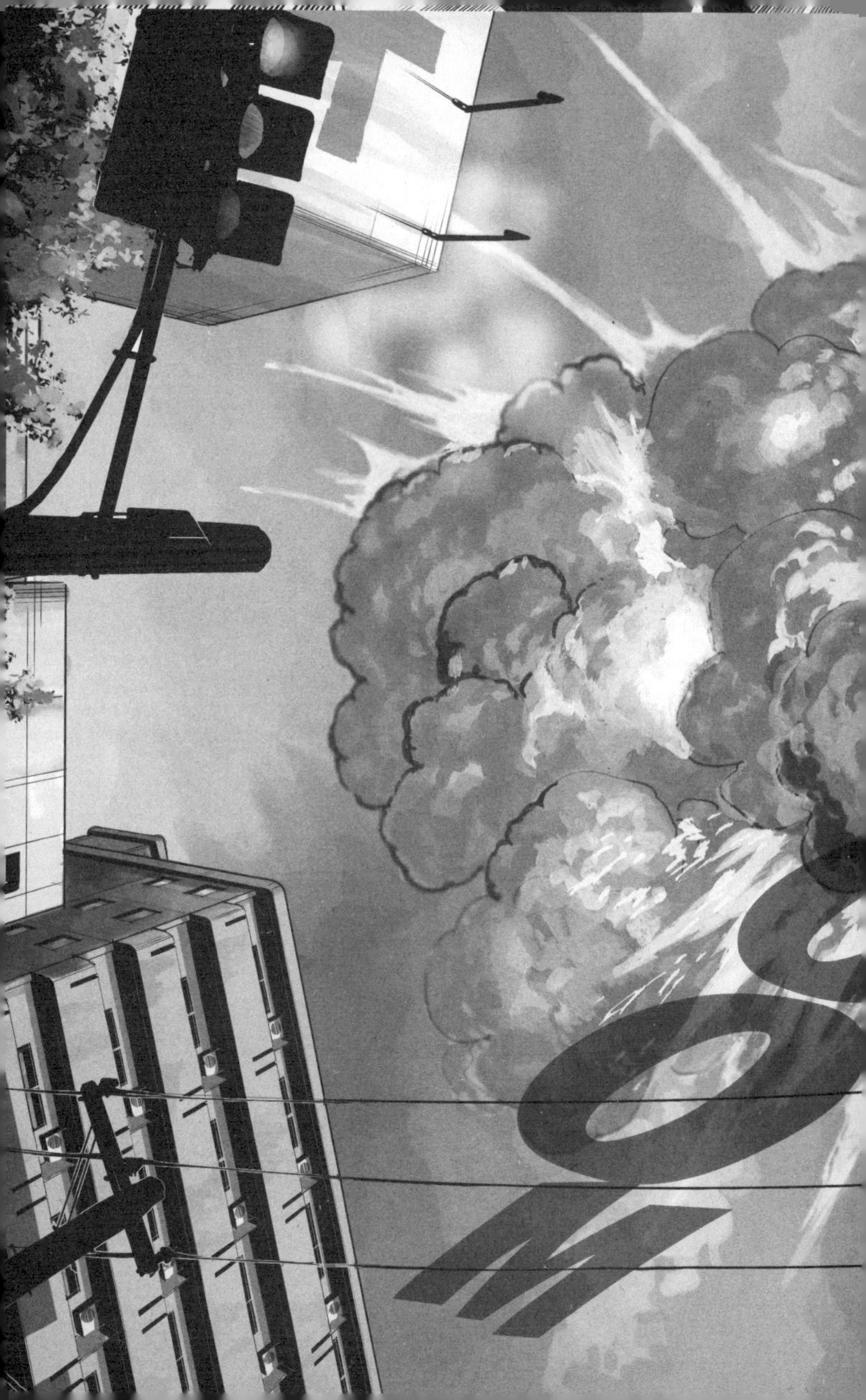

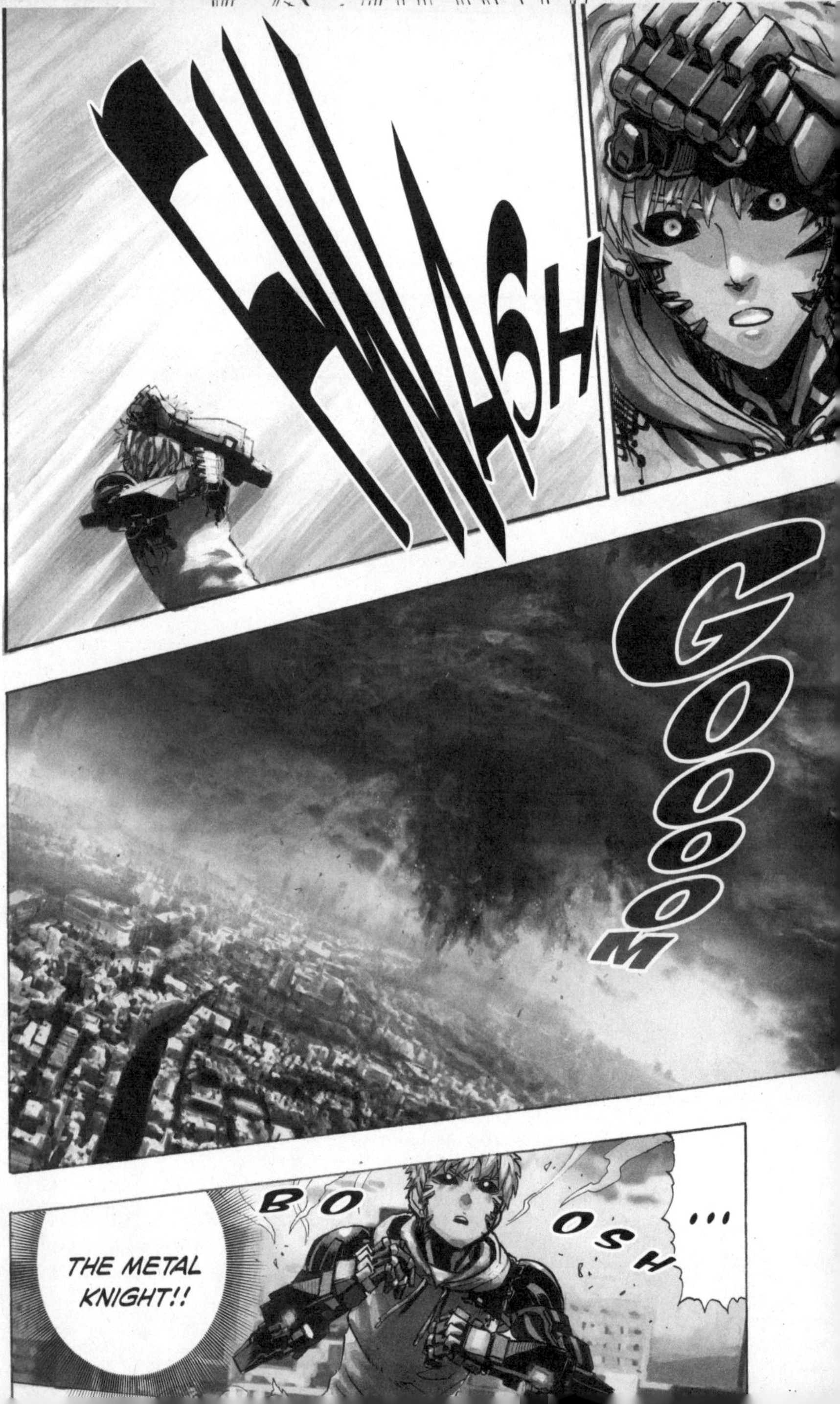
FWASH
GOOOOOM
BOOSH...
THE METAL KNIGHT!!

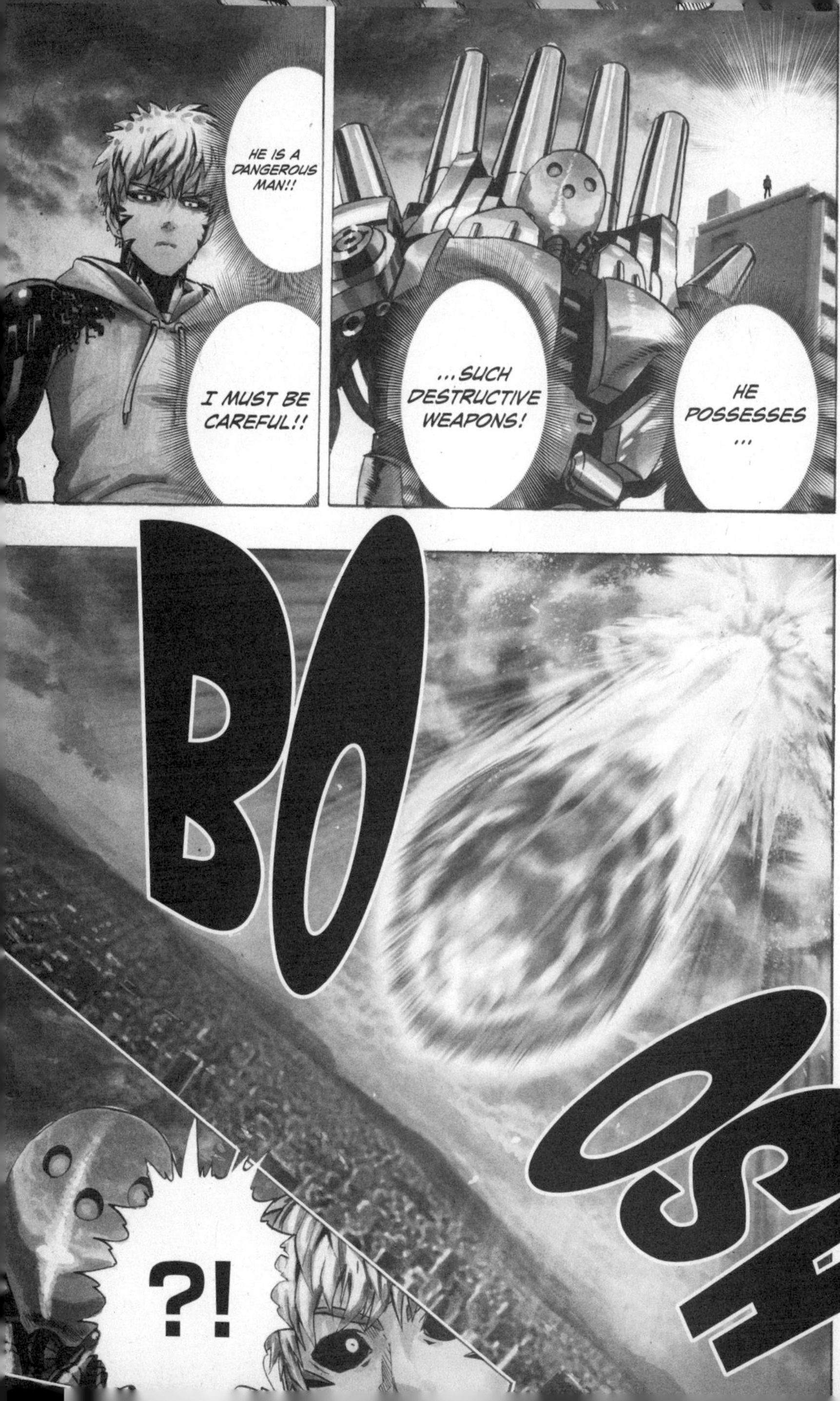
HE POSSESSES ...
...SUCH DESTRUCTIVE WEAPONS!
HE IS A DANGEROUS MAN!!
I MUST BE CAREFUL!!
BOOSH
?!

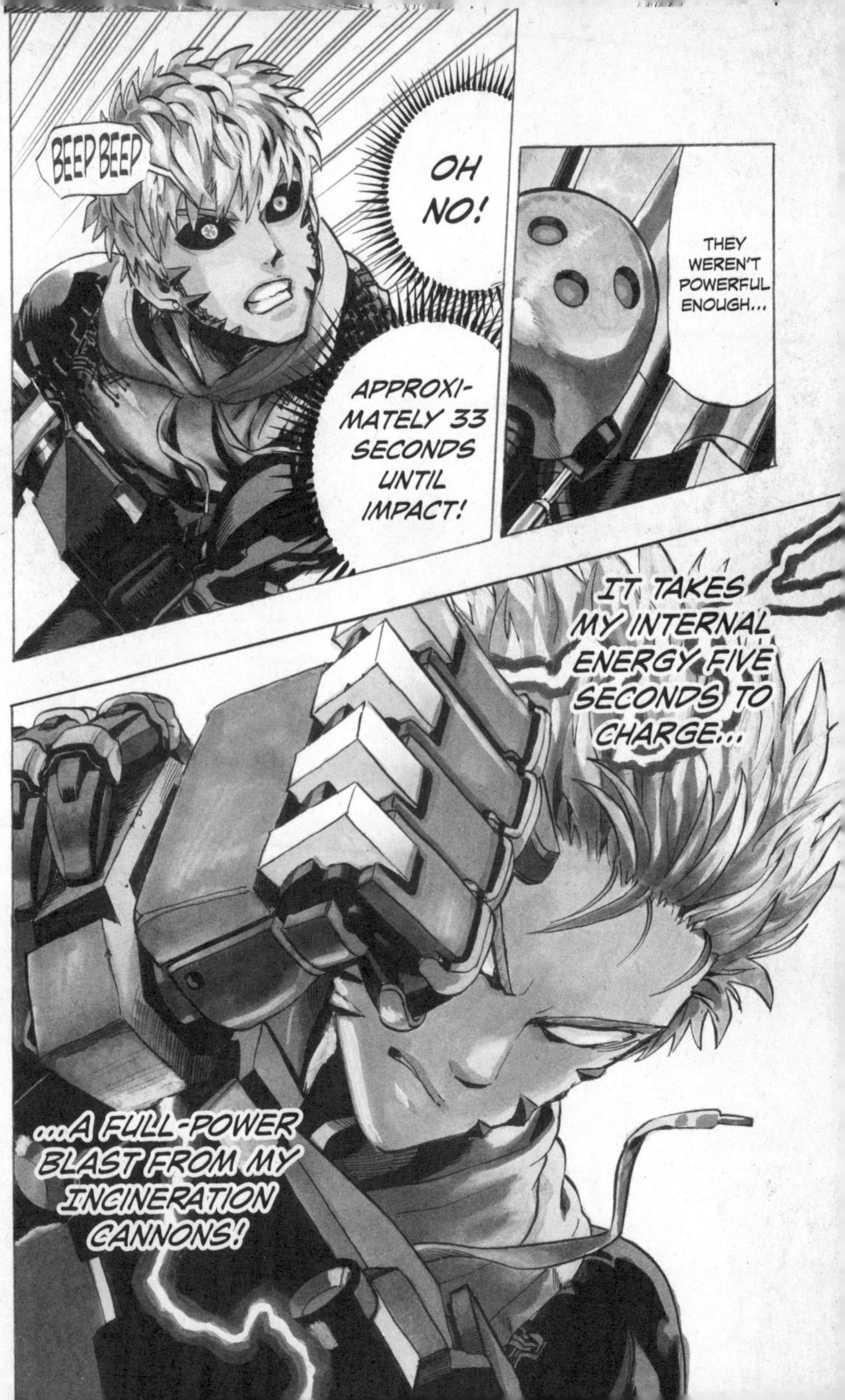
THEY WEREN'T POWERFUL ENOUGH...
OH NO!
BEEP BEEP
APPROXI-MATELY 33 SECONDS UNTIL IMPACT!
IT TAKES MY INTERNAL ENERGY FIVE SECONDS TO CHARGE...
...A FULL-POWER BLAST FROM MY INCINERATION CANNONS!

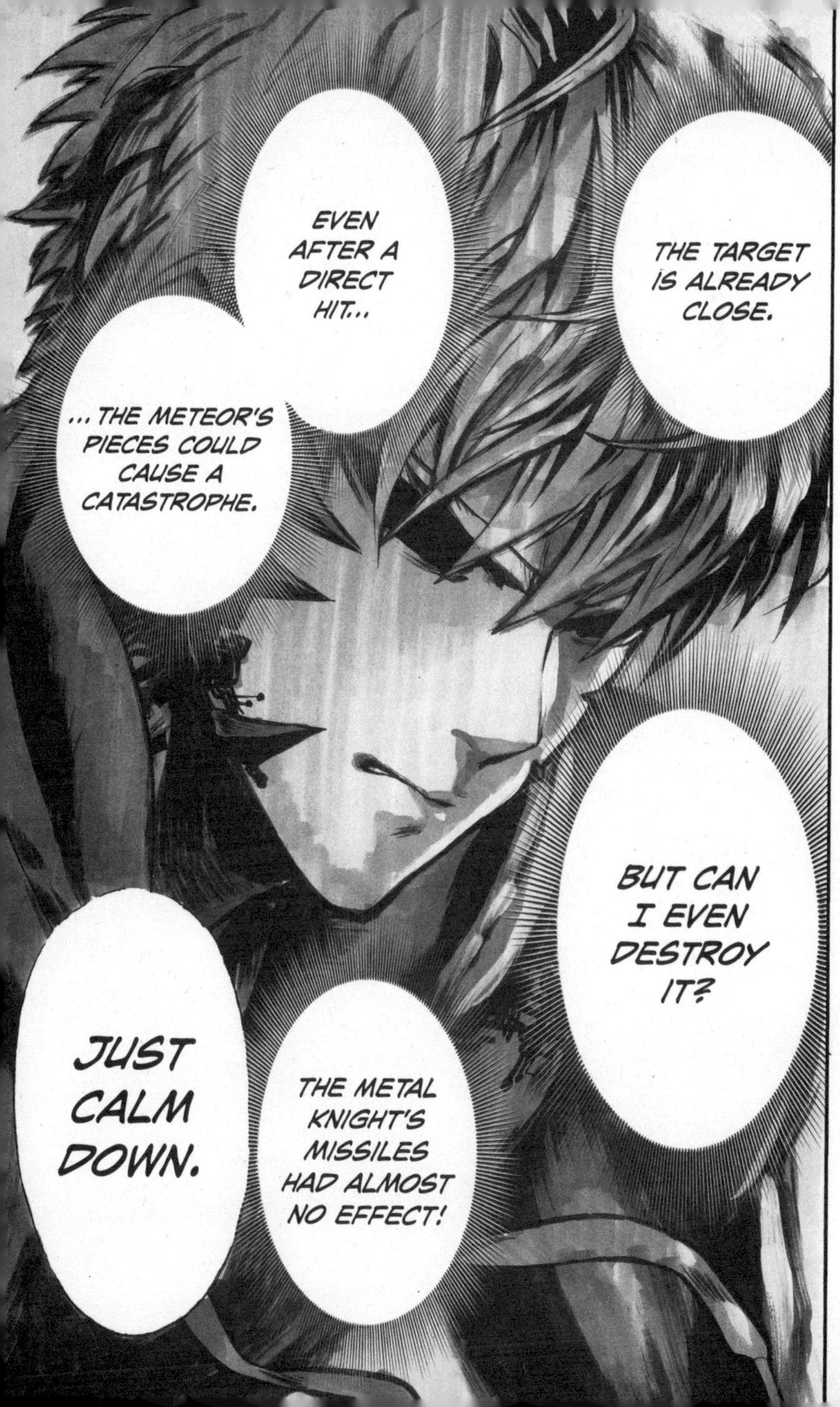
THE TARGET IS ALREADY CLOSE.
EVEN AFTER A DIRECT HIT...
...THE METEOR'S PIECES COULD CAUSE A CATASTROPHE.
BUT CAN I EVEN DESTROY IT?
THE METAL KNIGHT'S MISSILES HAD ALMOST NO EFFECT!
JUST CALM DOWN.

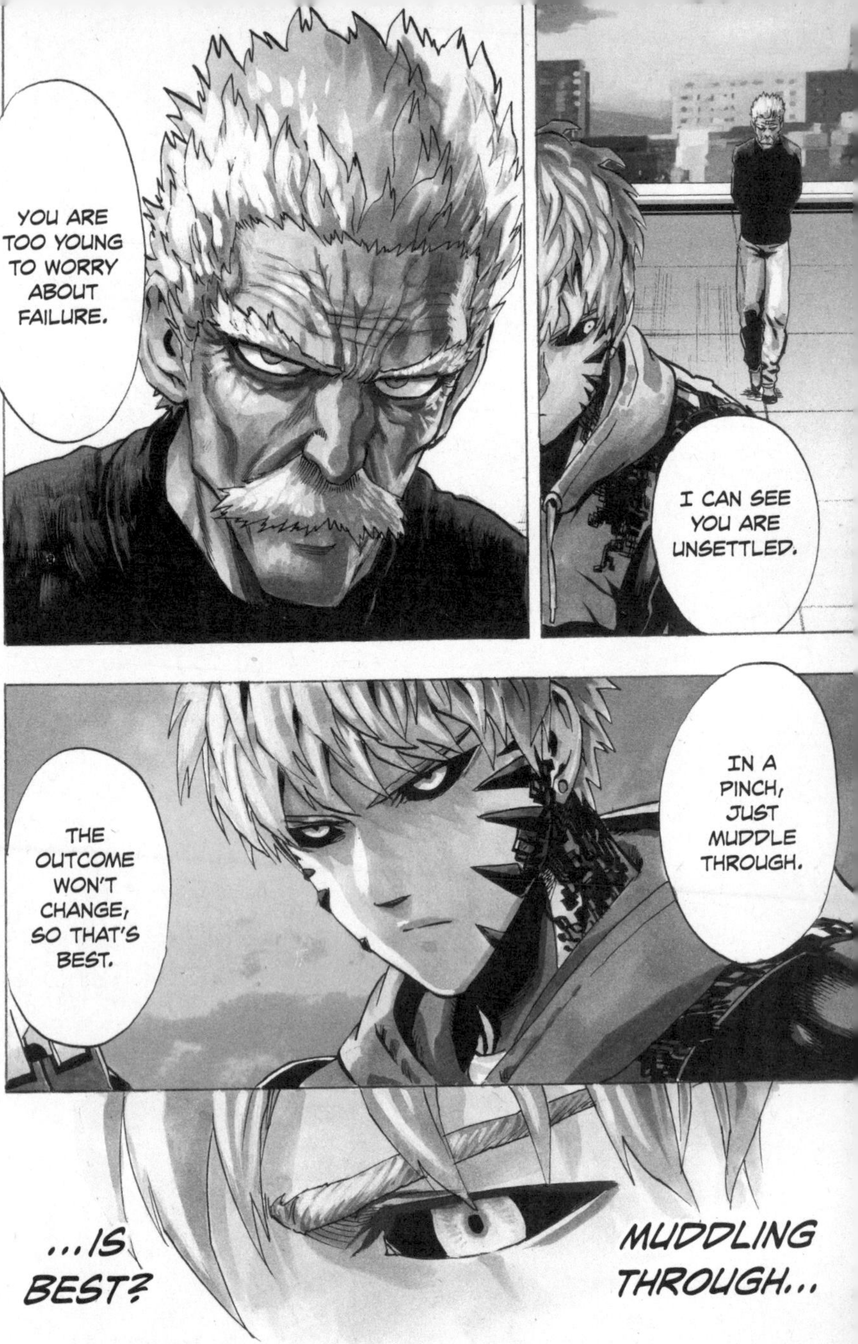
I CAN SEE YOU ARE UNSETTLED.
YOU ARE TOO YOUNG TO WORRY ABOUT FAILURE.
IN A PINCH, JUST MUDDLE THROUGH.
THE OUTCOME WON'T CHANGE, SO THAT'S BEST.
MUDDLING THROUGH...
...IS BEST?

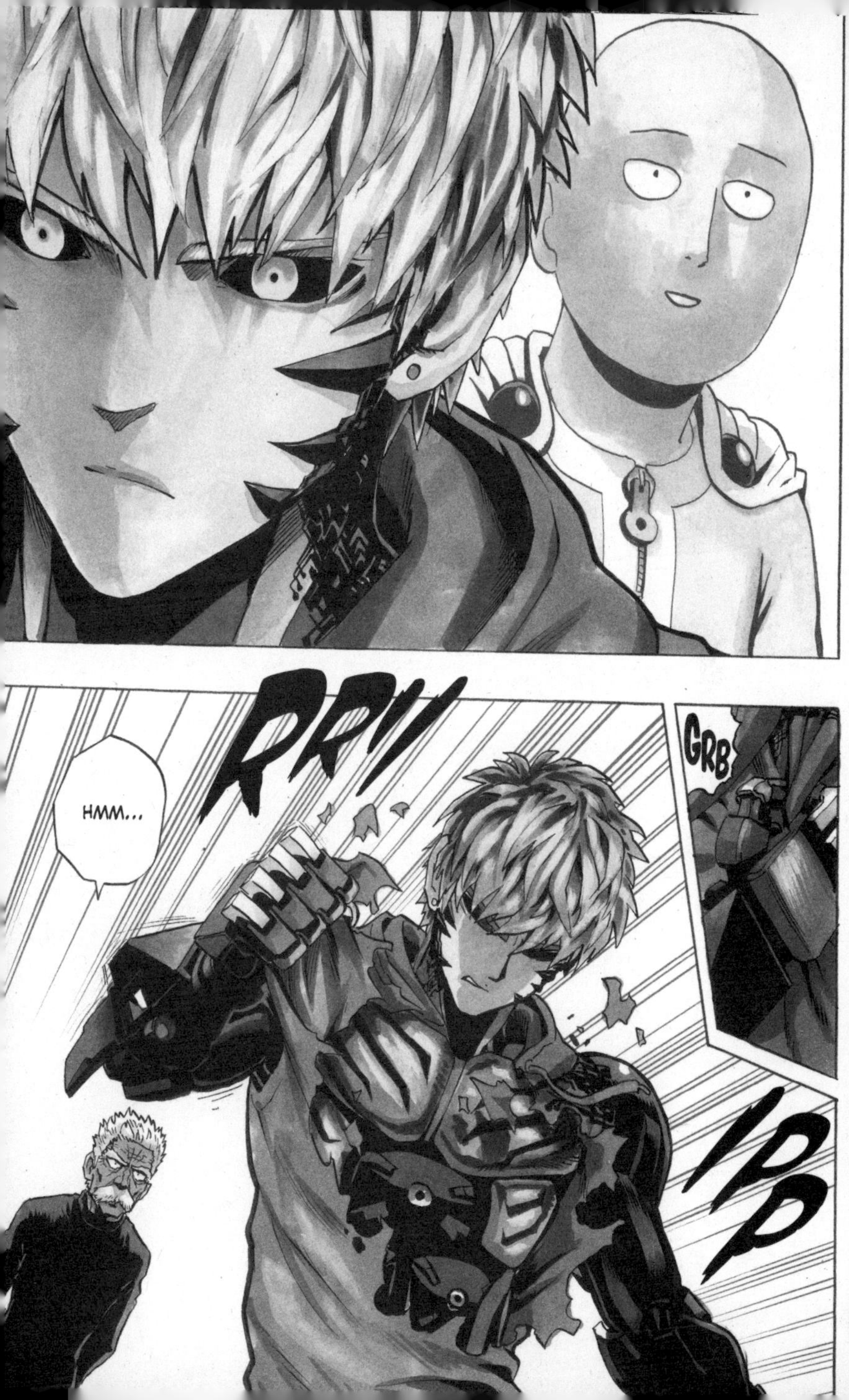
GRB
RRII
HMM...
IPP

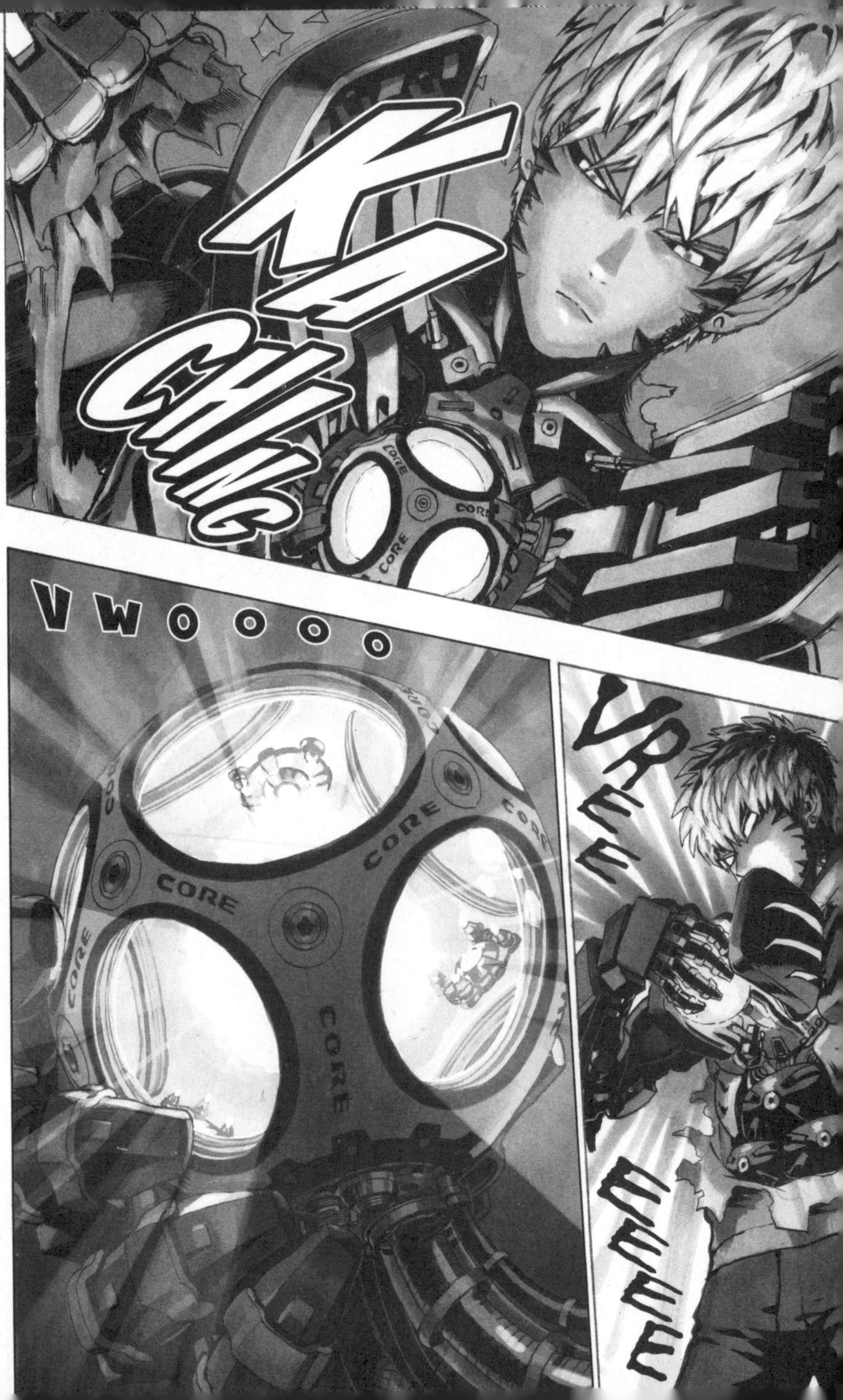
KA CHING
VREE
EEEEE
VWOOOO

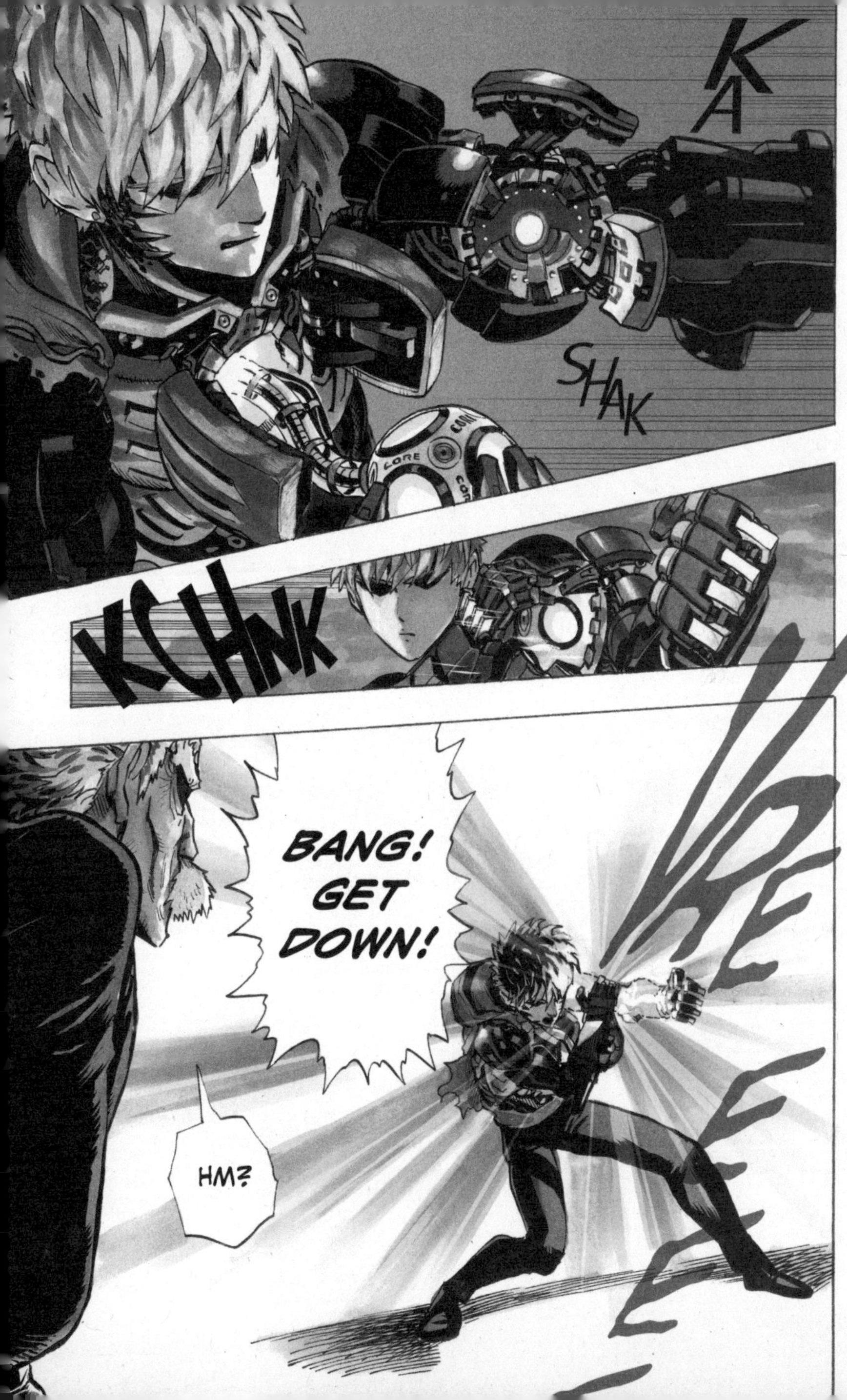
KA
SHAK
KCHNK
BANG! GET DOWN!
HM?

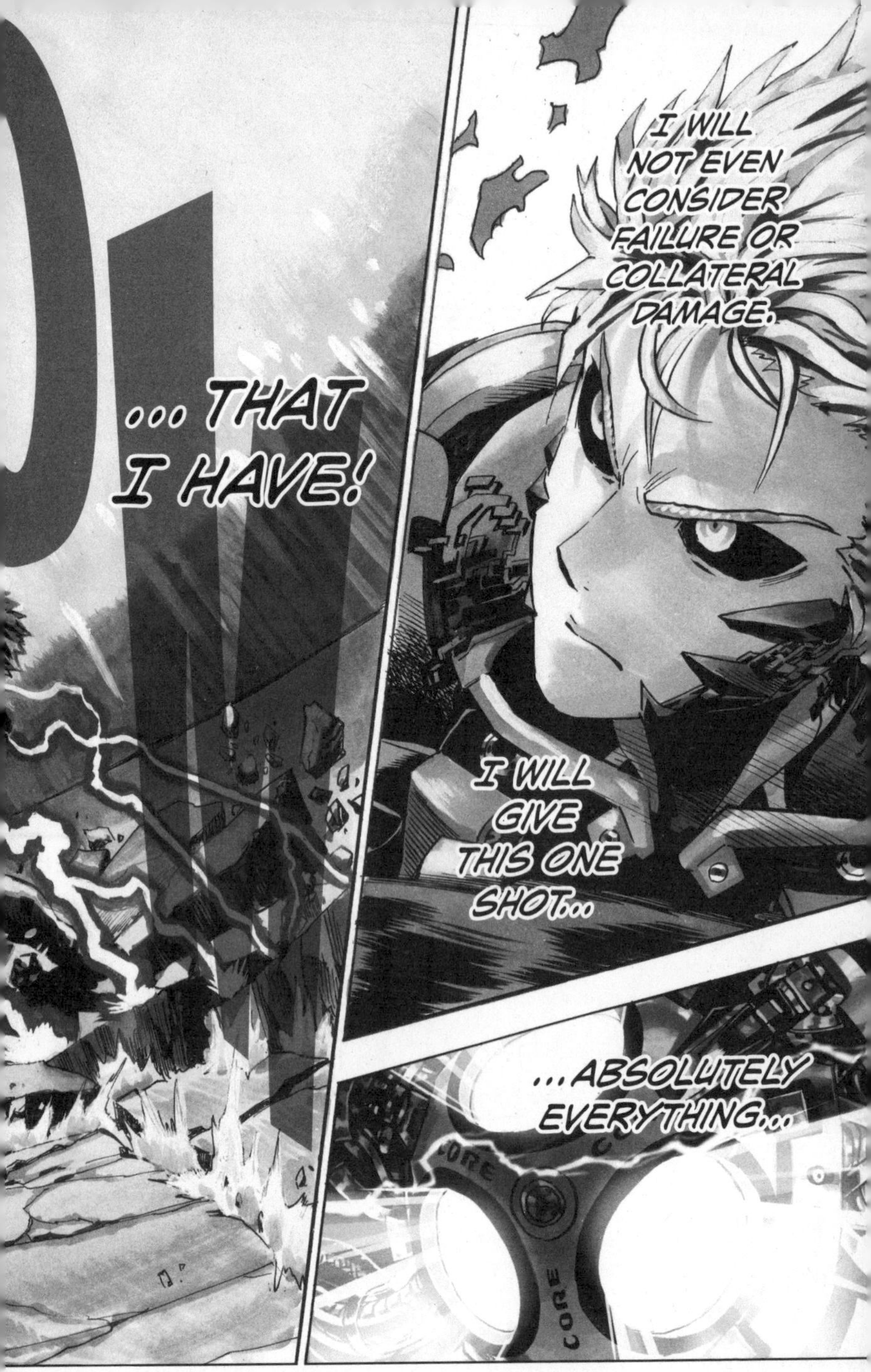
I WILL NOT EVEN CONSIDER FAILURE OR COLLATERAL DAMAGE.
I WILL GIVE THIS ONE SHOT...
...ABSOLUTELY EVERYTHING...
...THAT I HAVE!

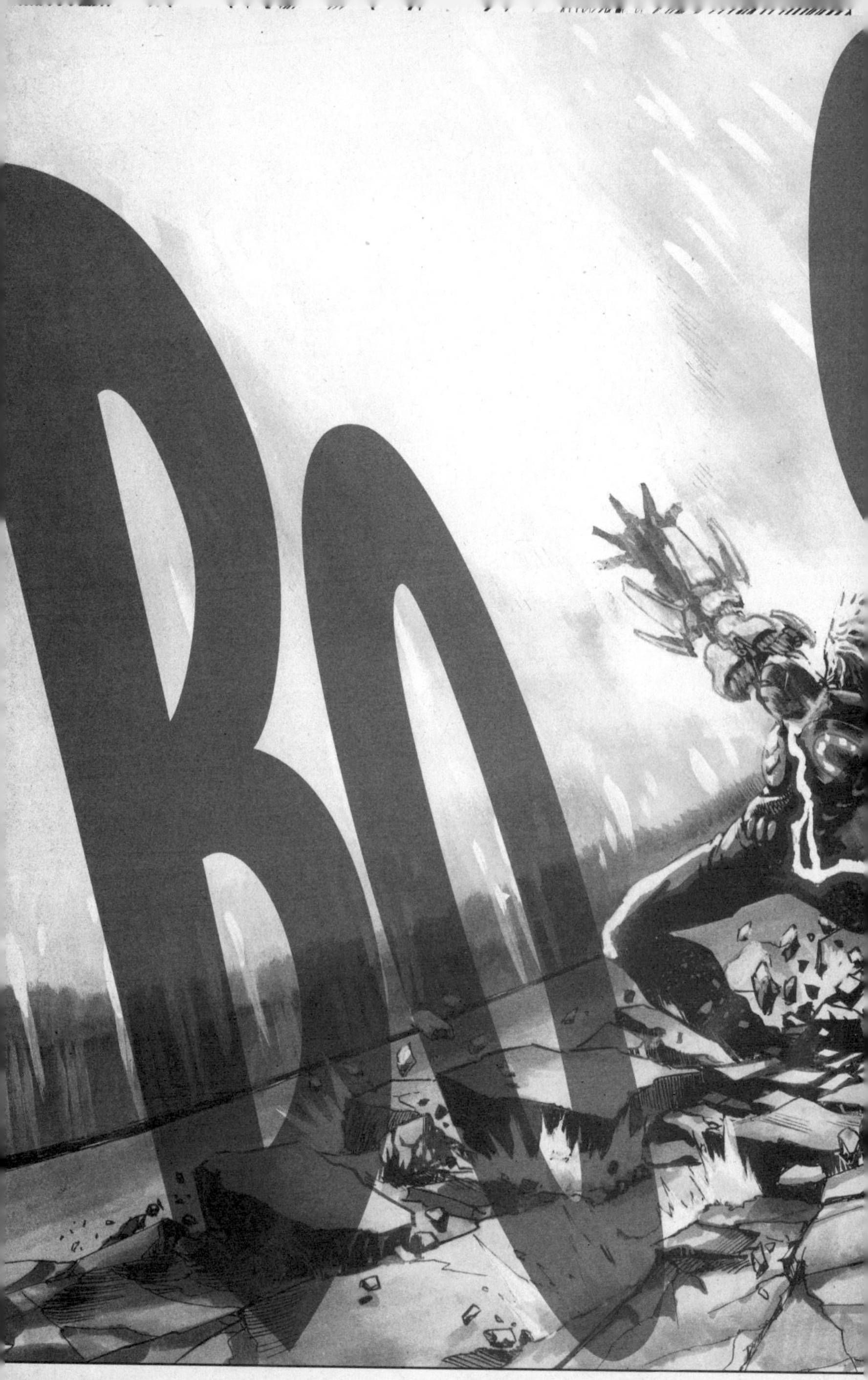
BO

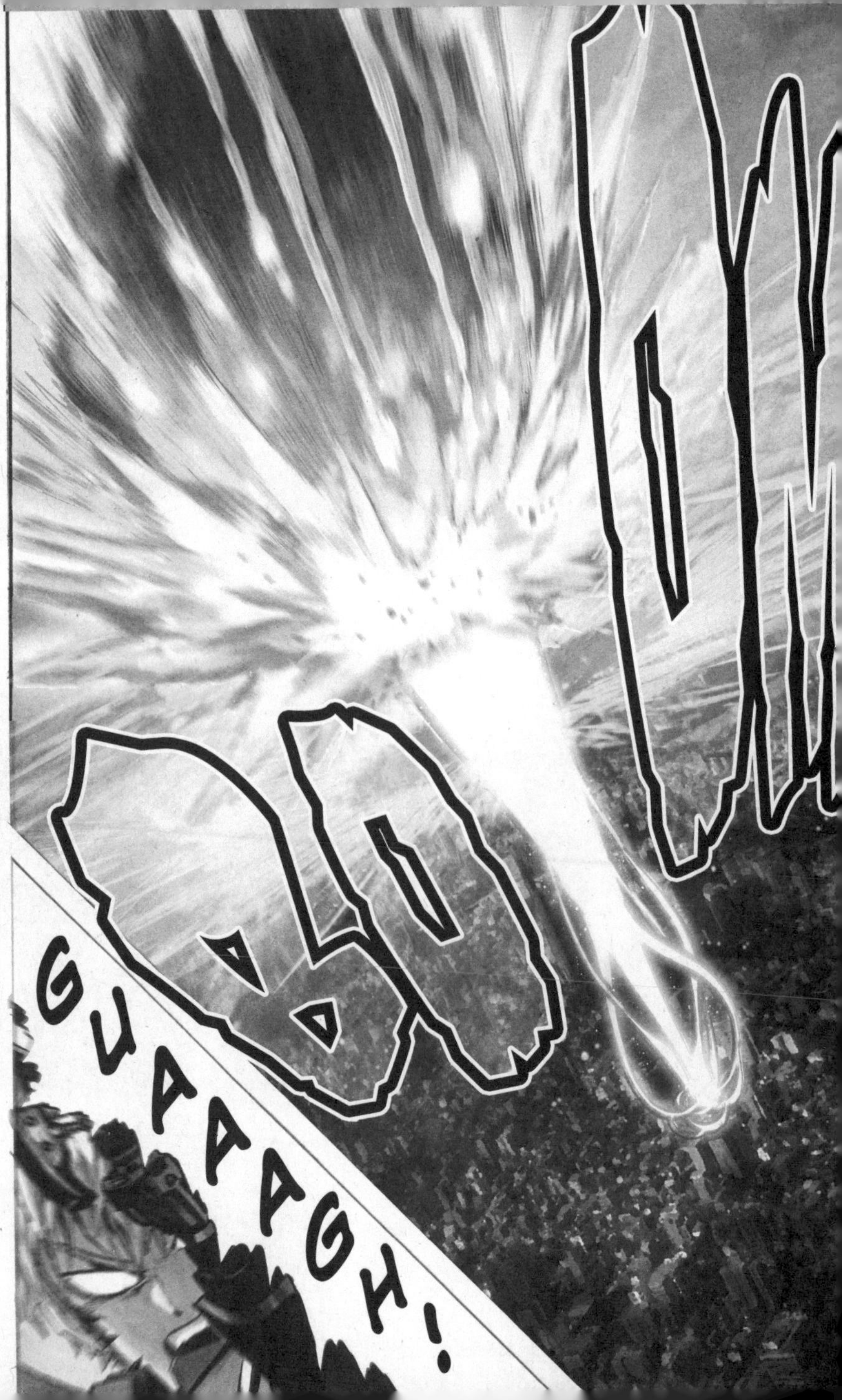
GUAAAGH!

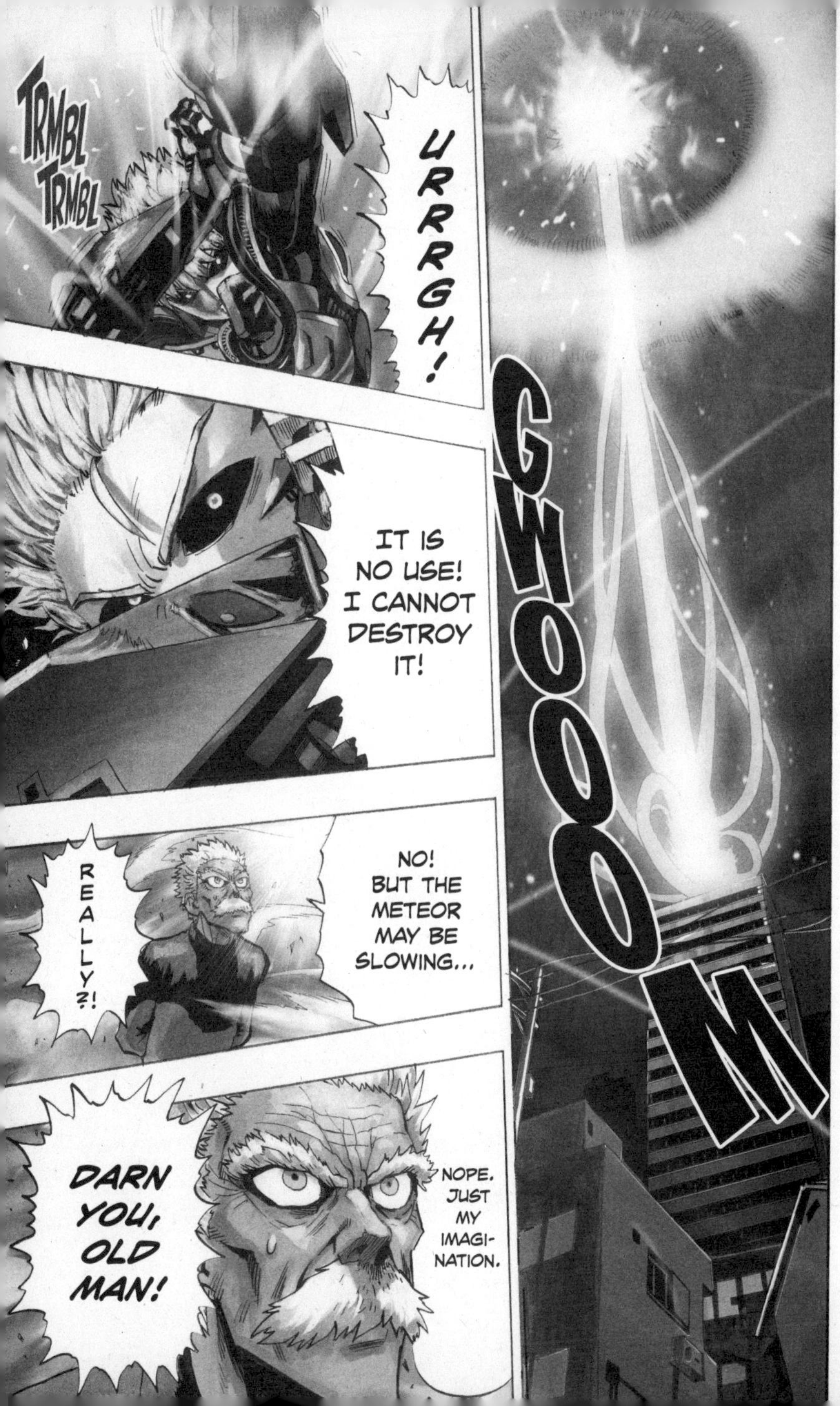
GWOOOOM
URRRGH!
TRMBL TRMBL
IT IS NO USE! I CANNOT DESTROY IT!
NO! BUT THE METEOR MAY BE SLOWING...
REALLY?!
NOPE. JUST MY IMAGINATION.
DARN YOU, OLD MAN!

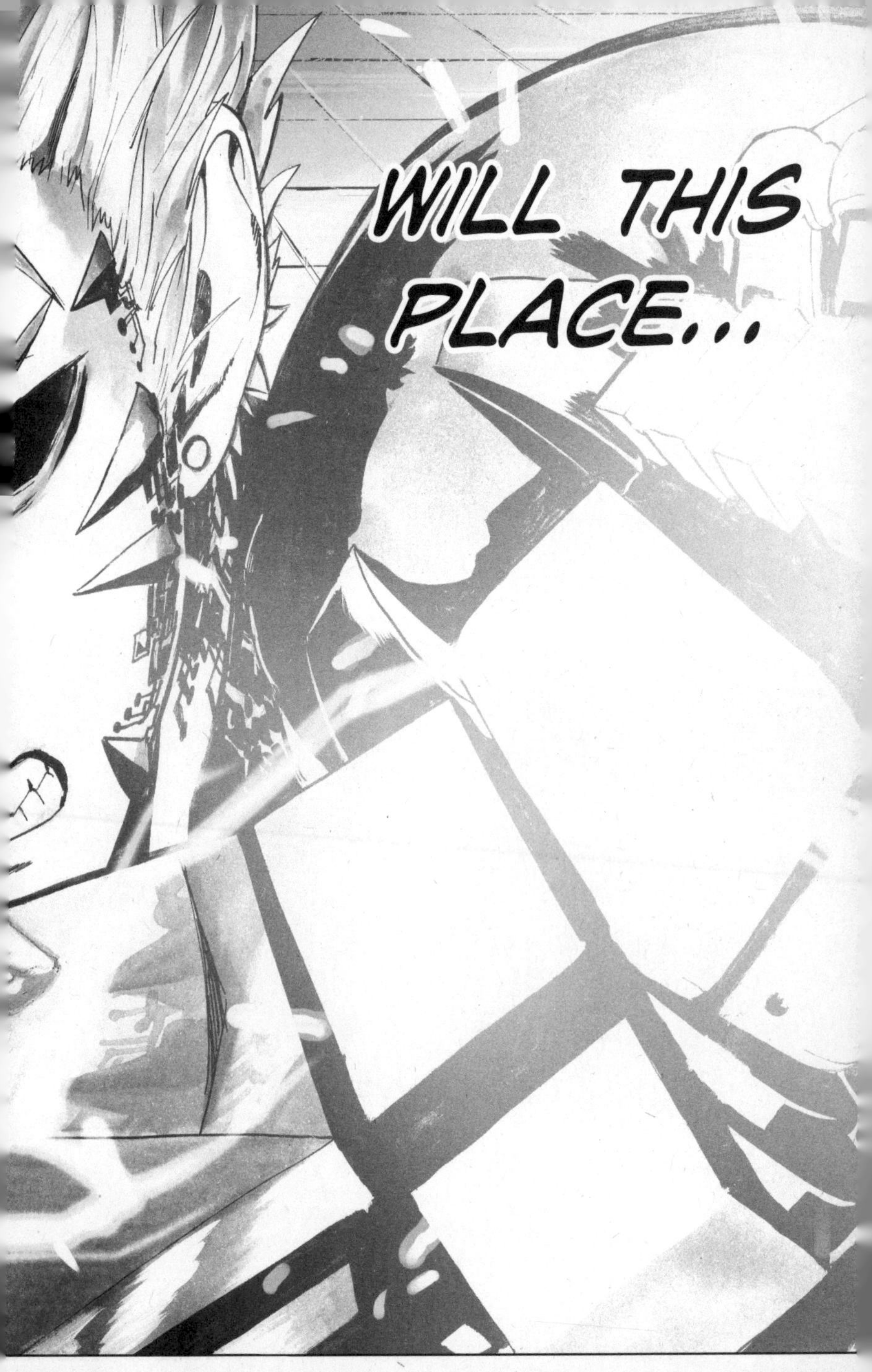
WILL THIS PLACE...

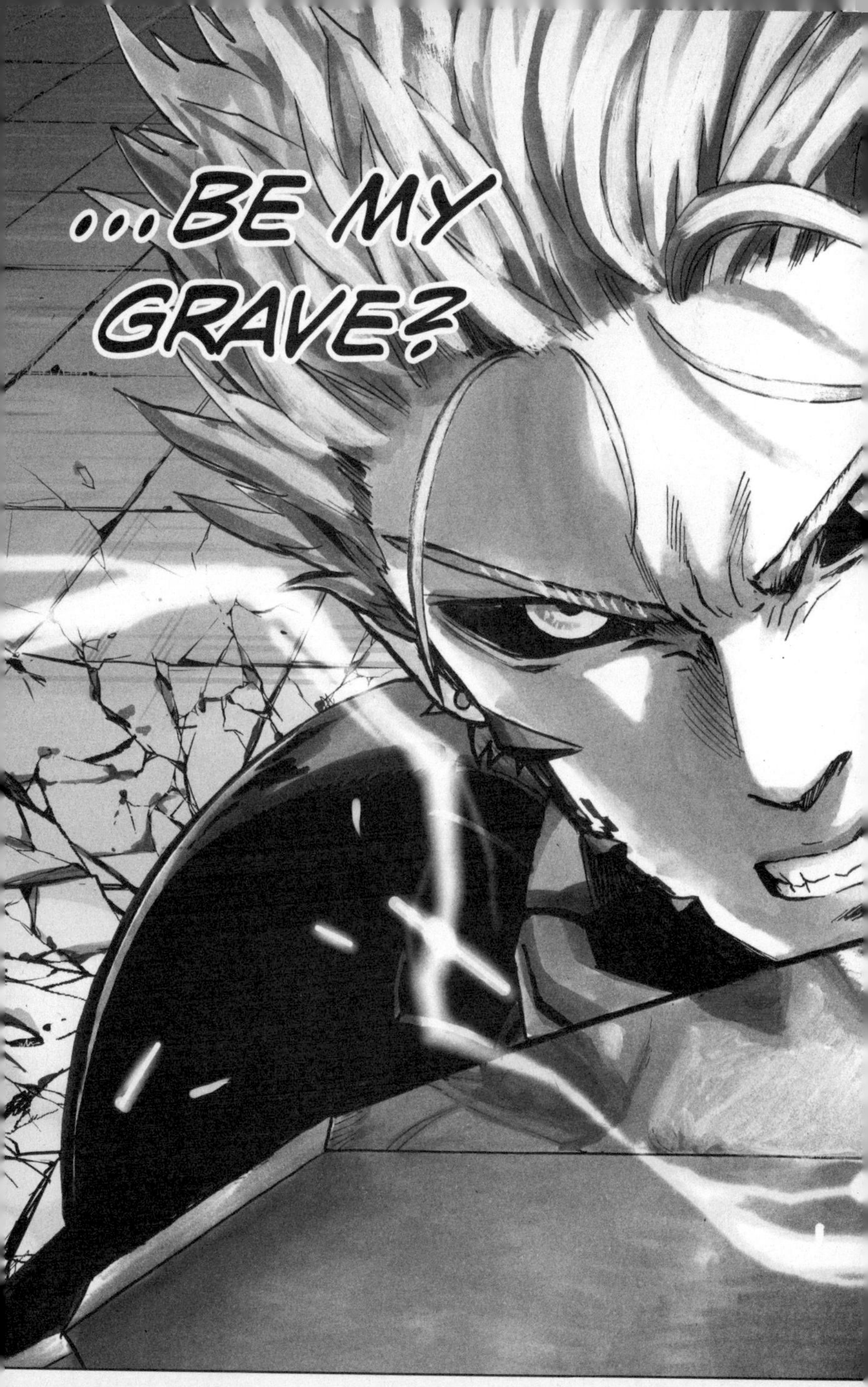
...BE MY GRAVE?

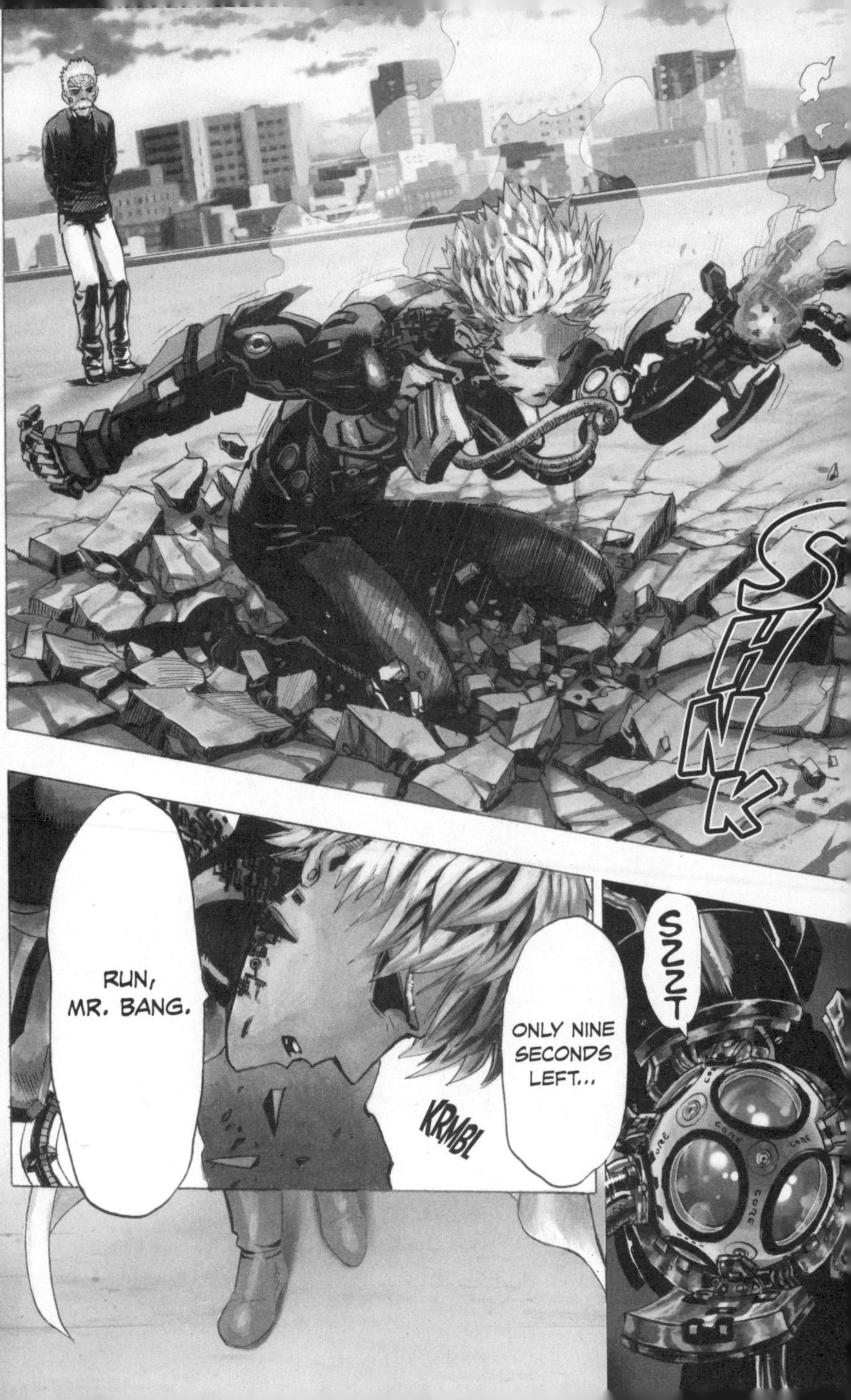
SHINK
SZZT
ONLY NINE SECONDS LEFT...
KRMBL
RUN, MR. BANG.

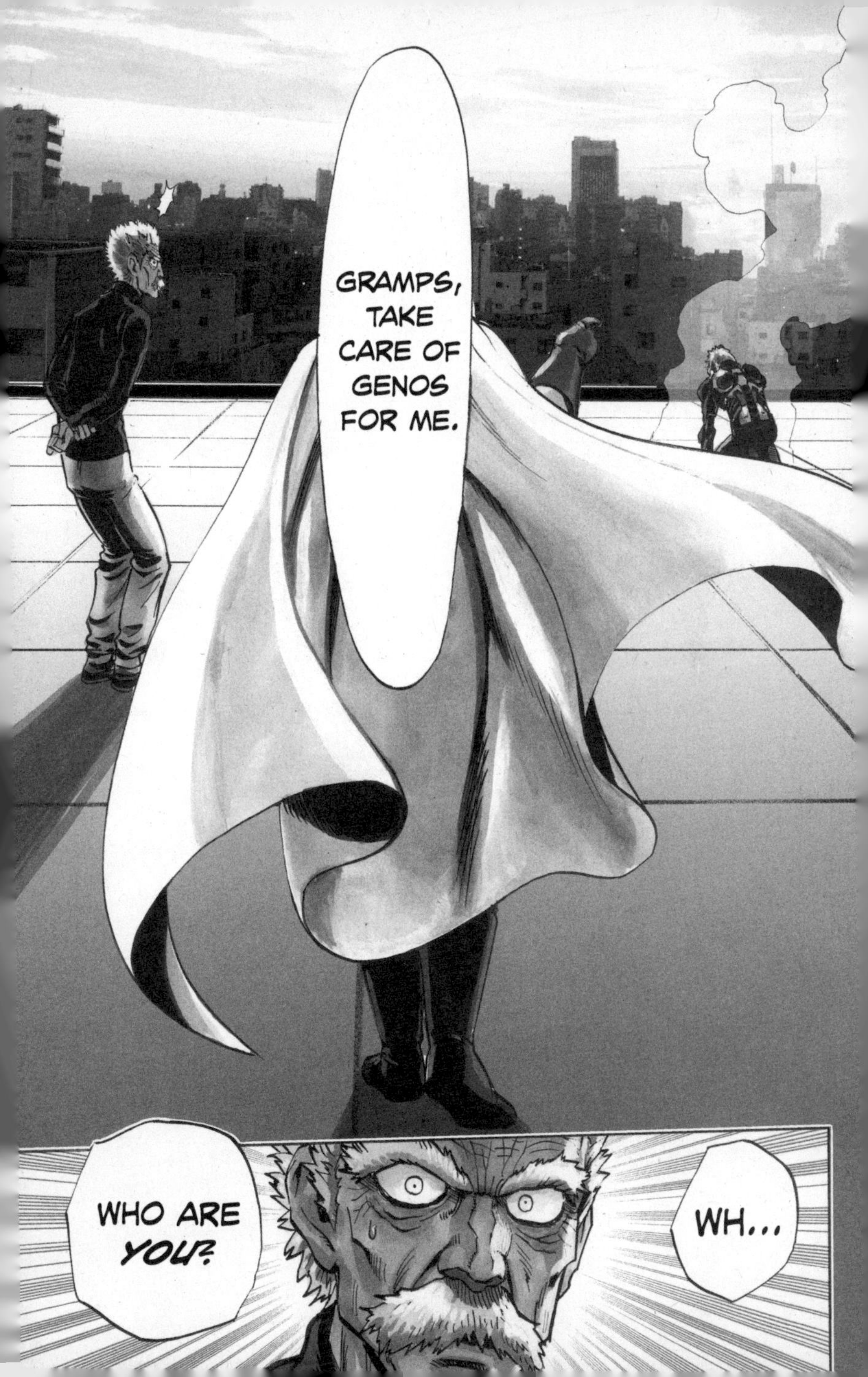
GRAMPS, TAKE CARE OF GENOS FOR ME.
WH...
WHO ARE YOU?

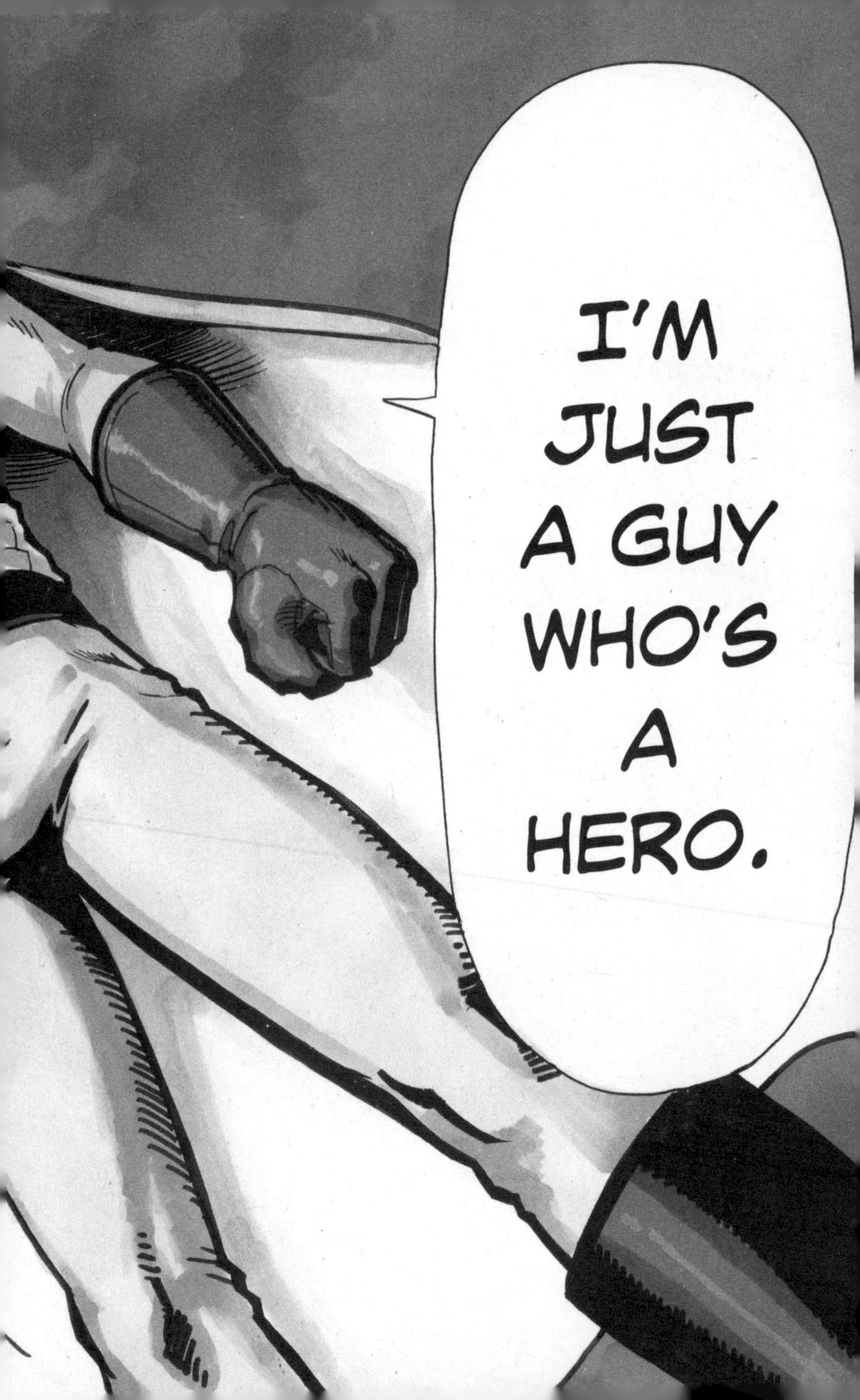
I'M JUST A GUY WHO'S A HERO.

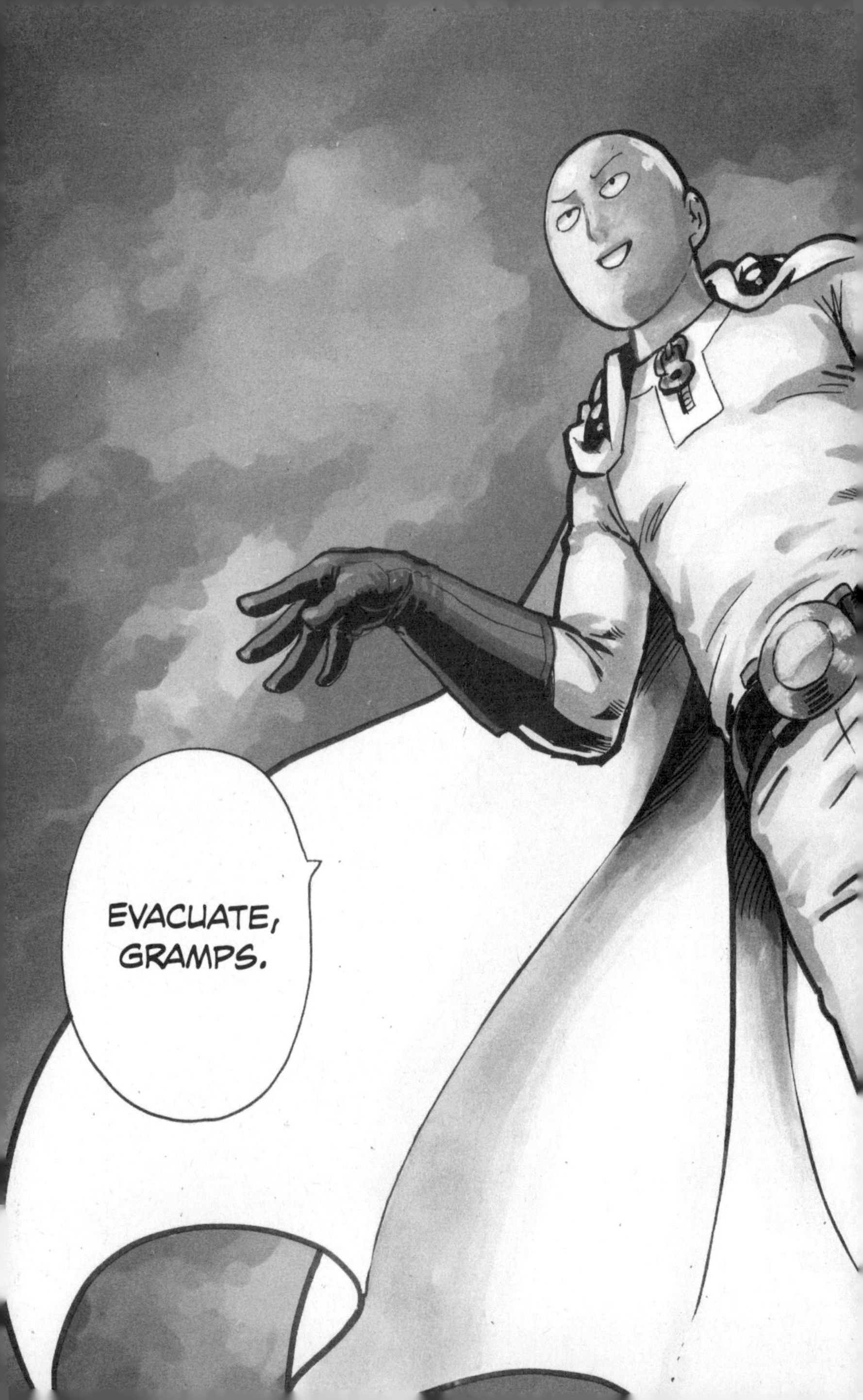
EVACUATE, GRAMPS.

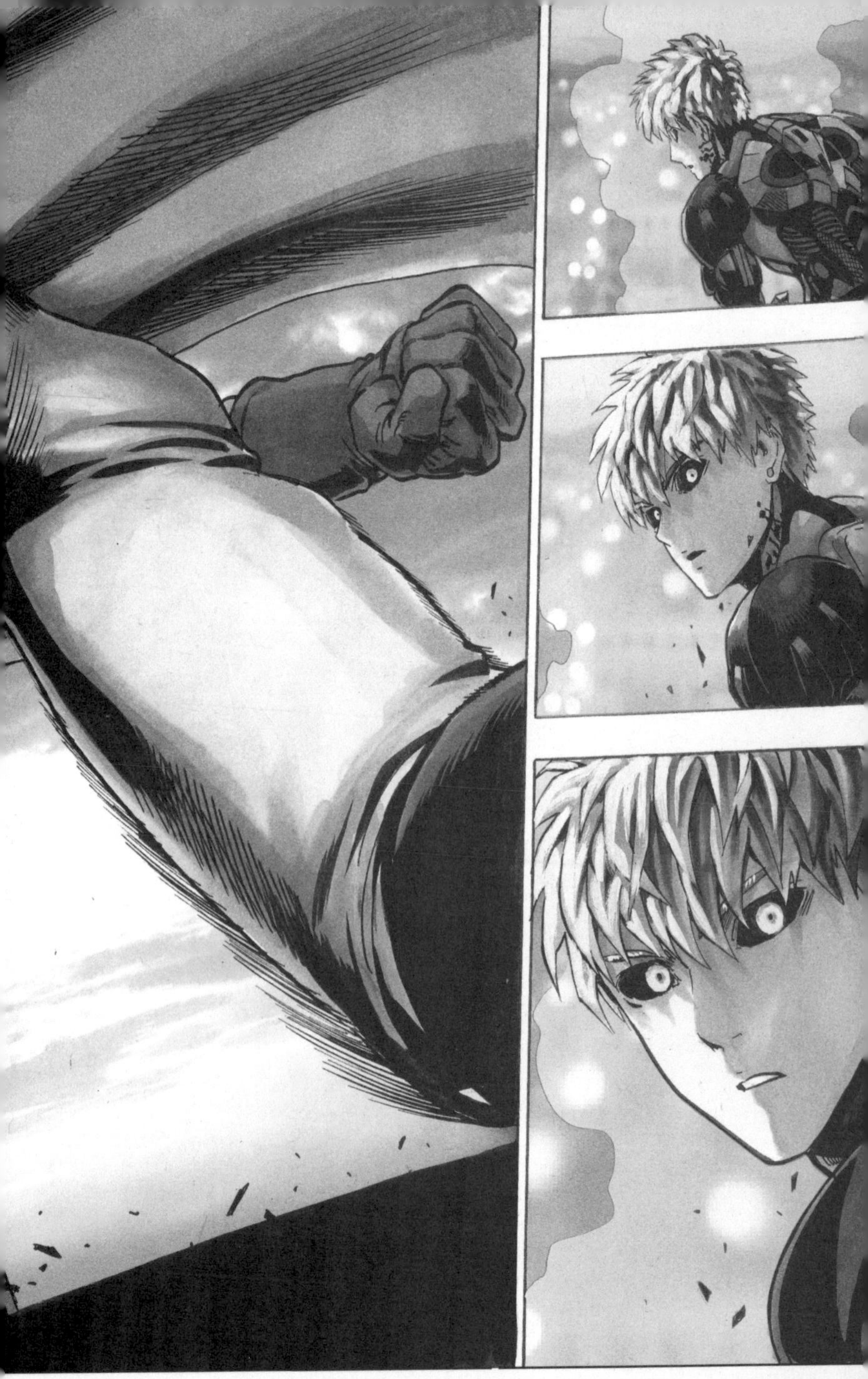

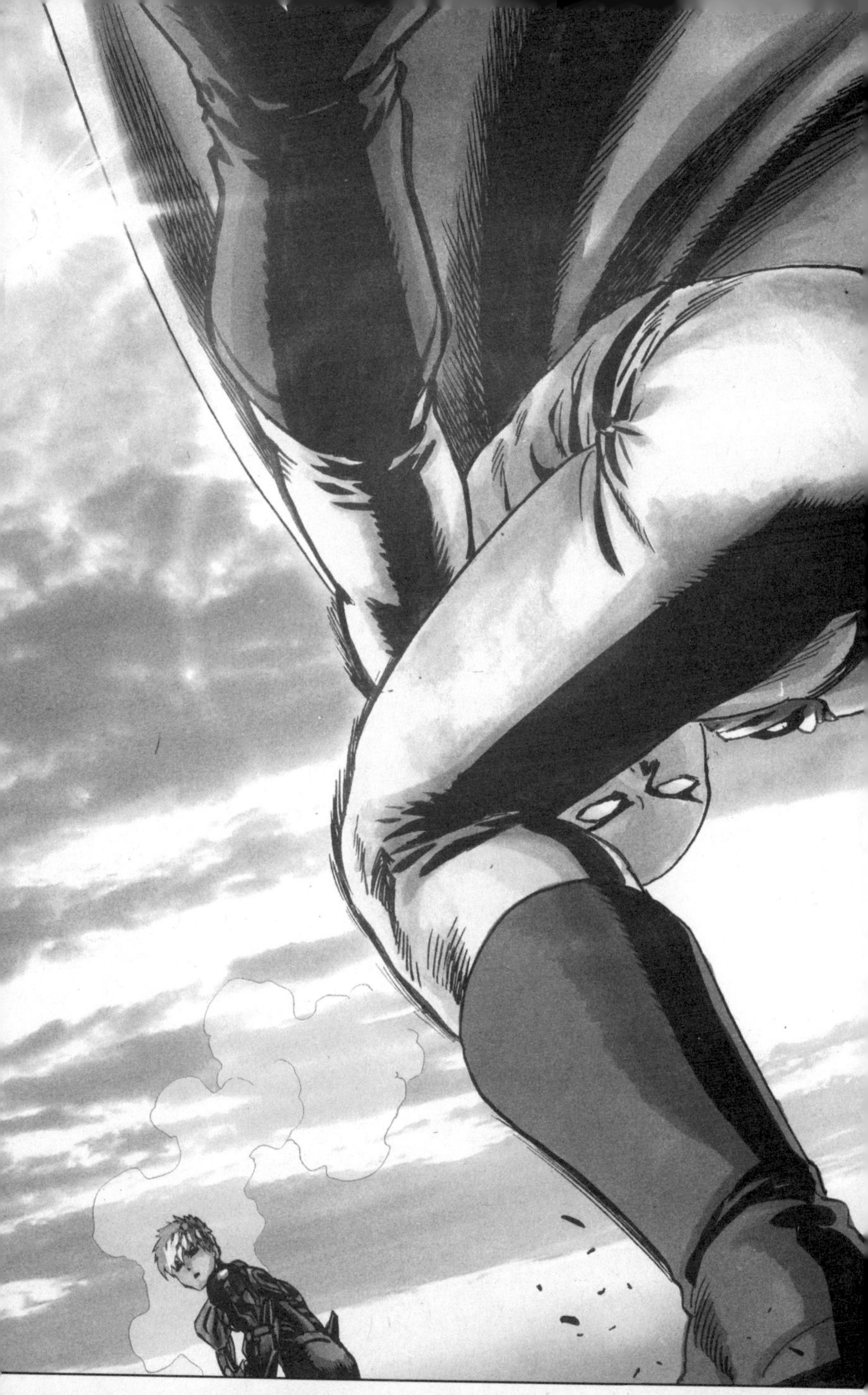

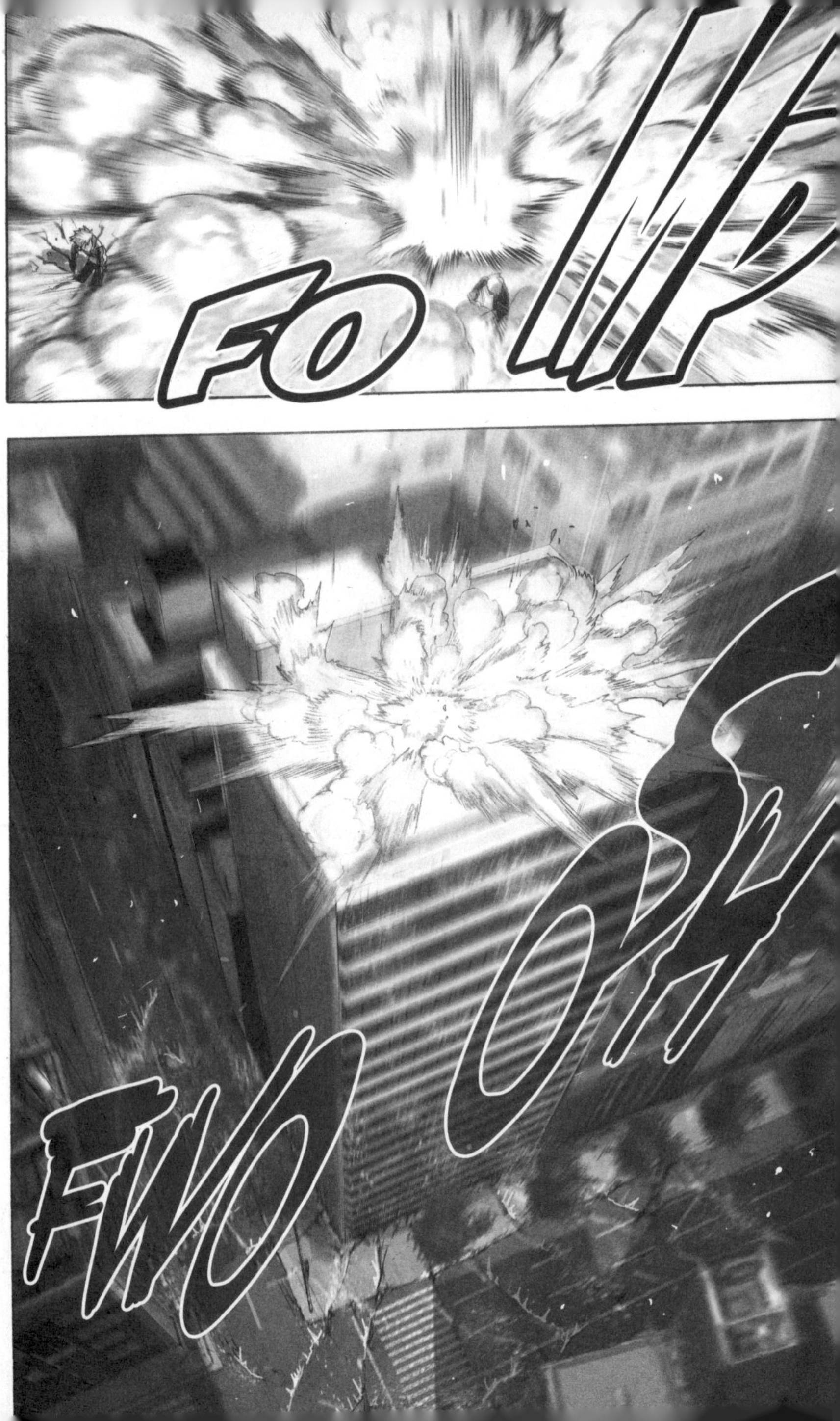
FOUMP
FWOOSH

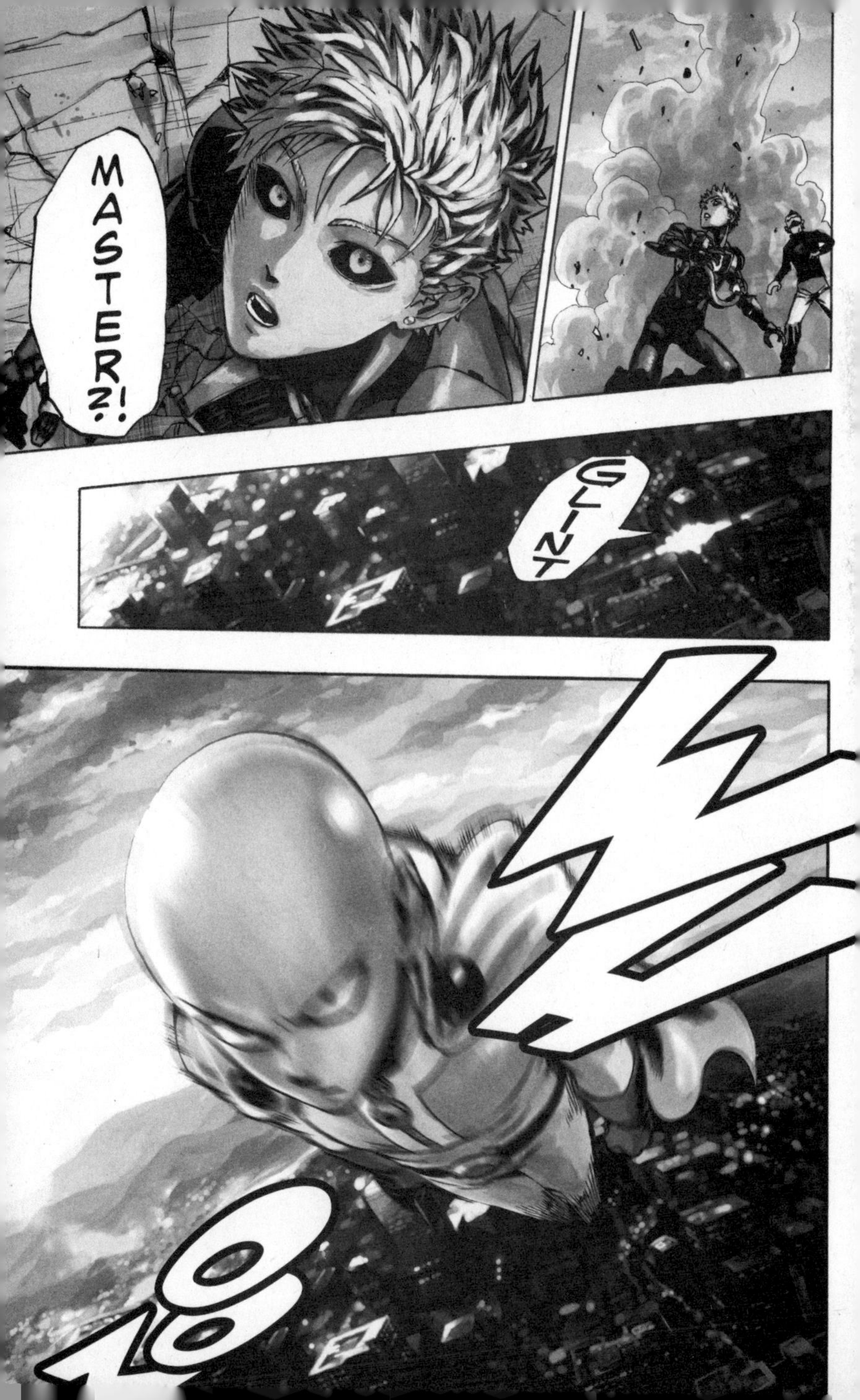
MASTER?!
GLINT

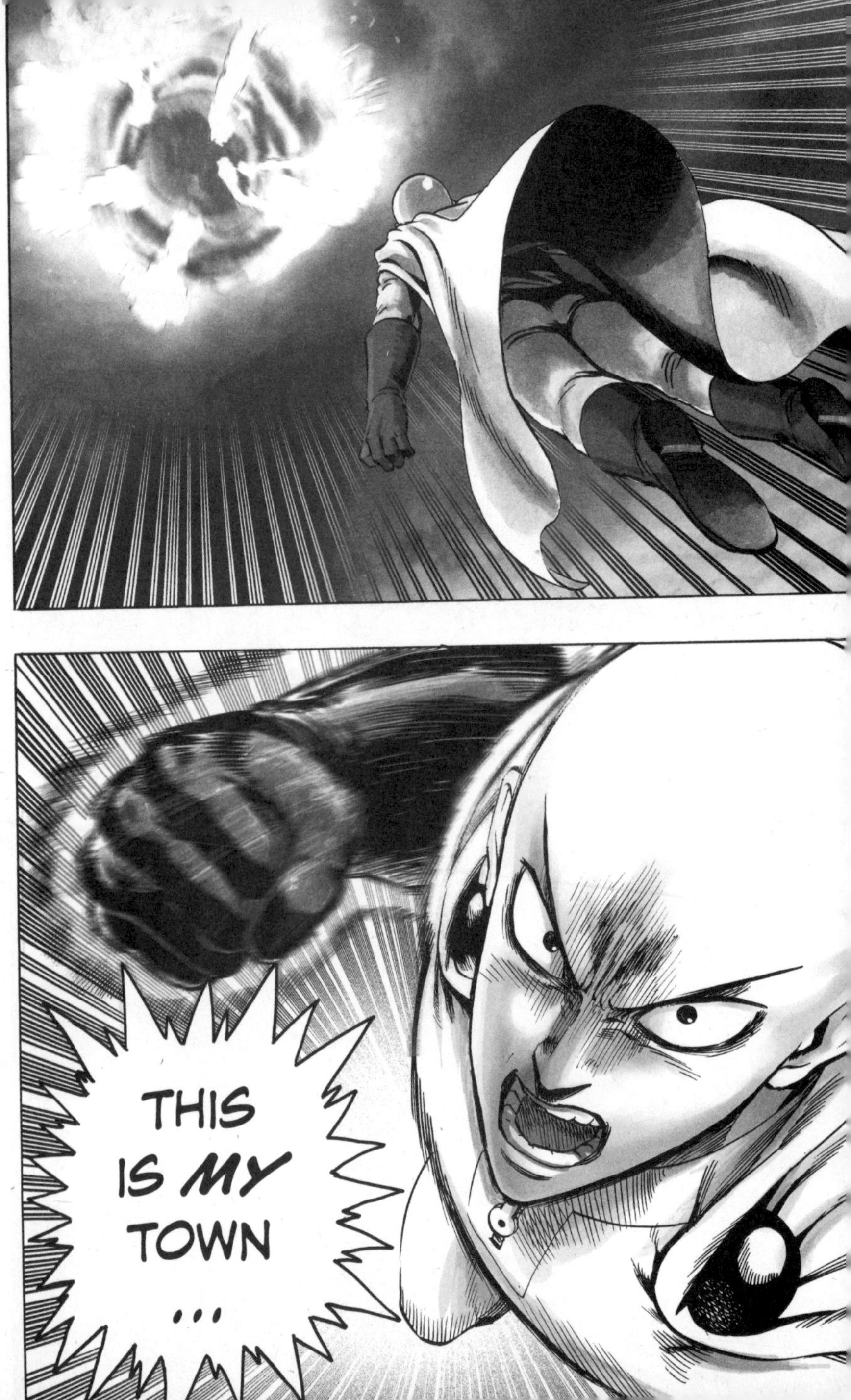
THIS IS *MY* TOWN ...

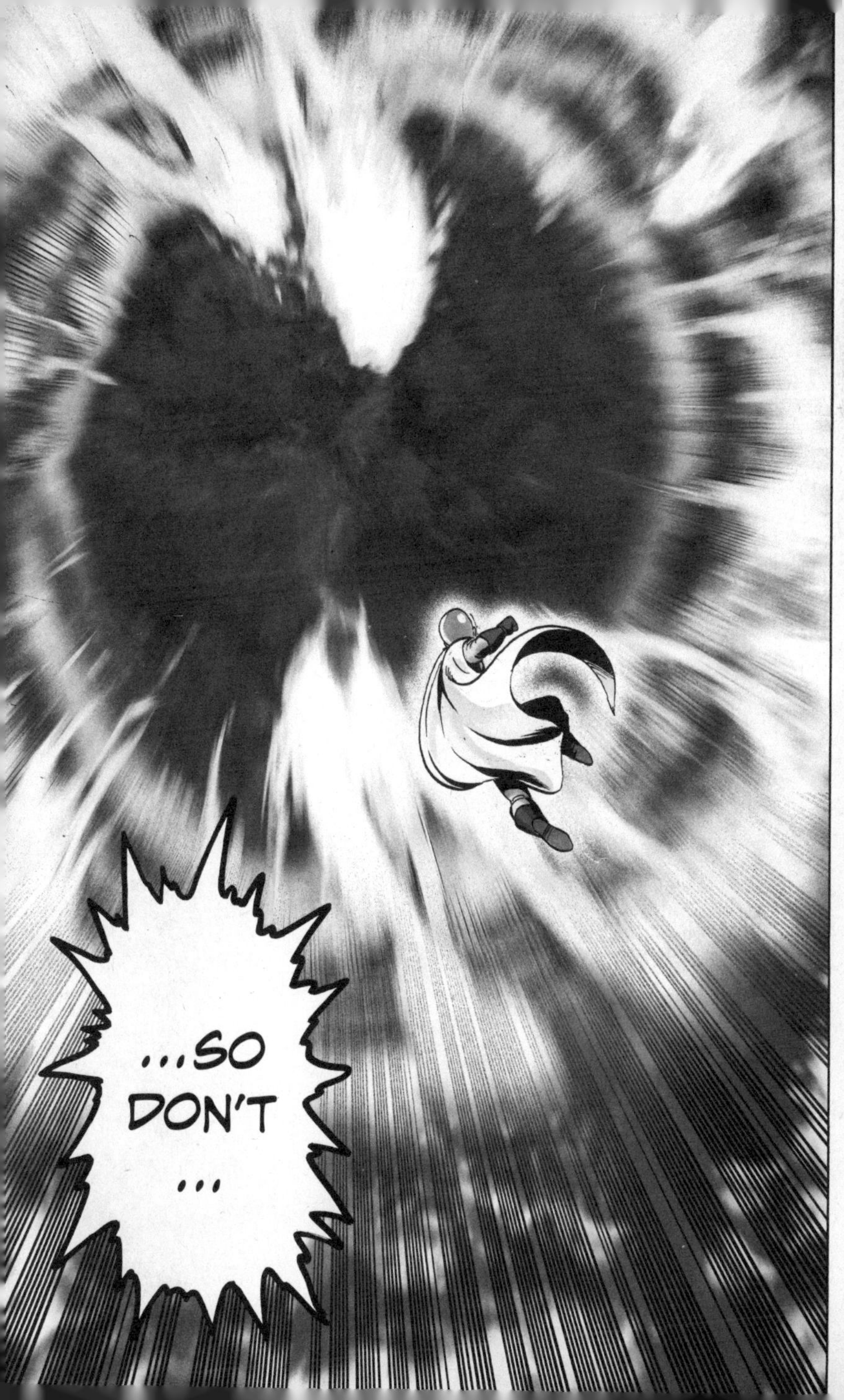
...SO DON'T ...

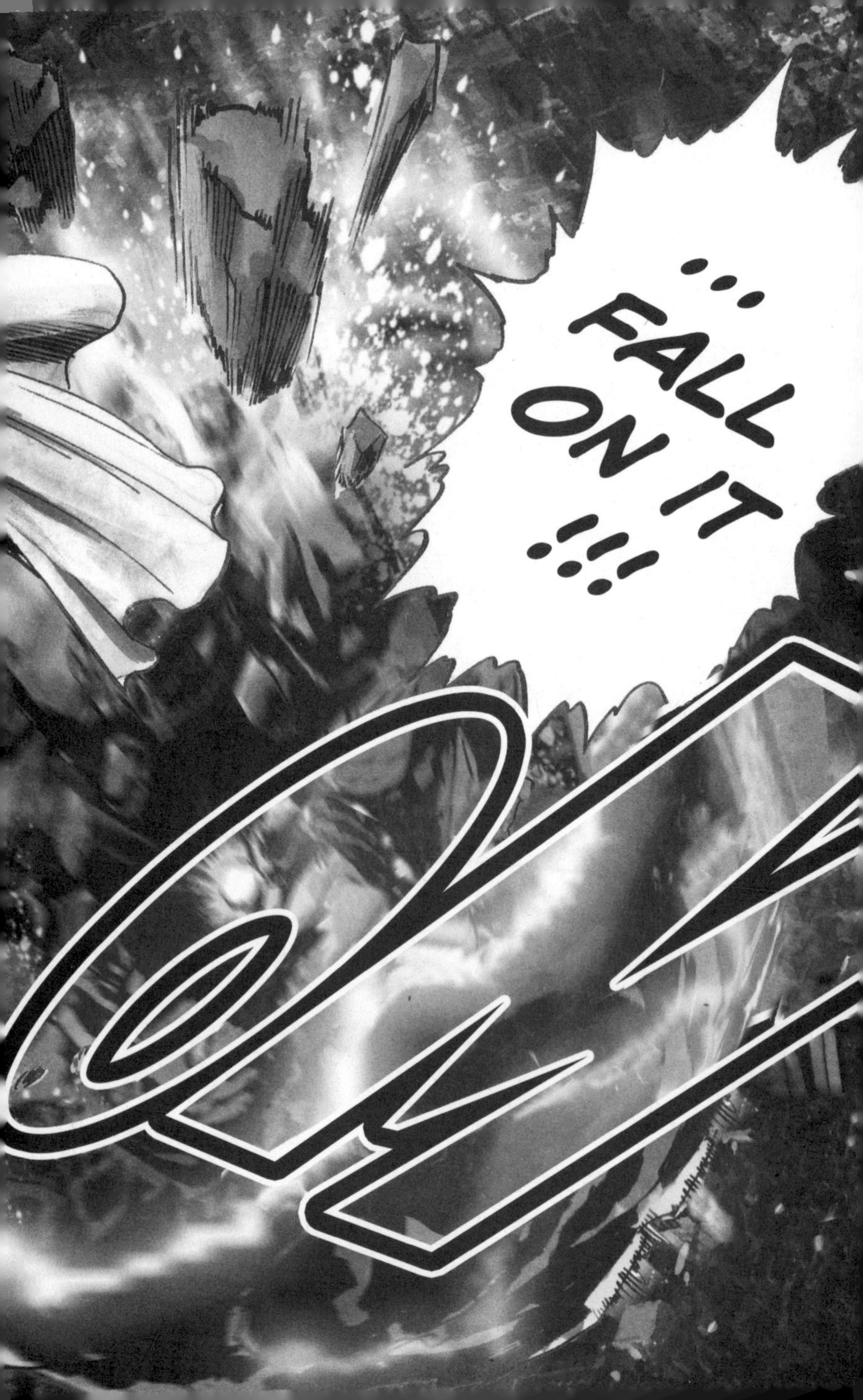
...FALL ON IT...!!

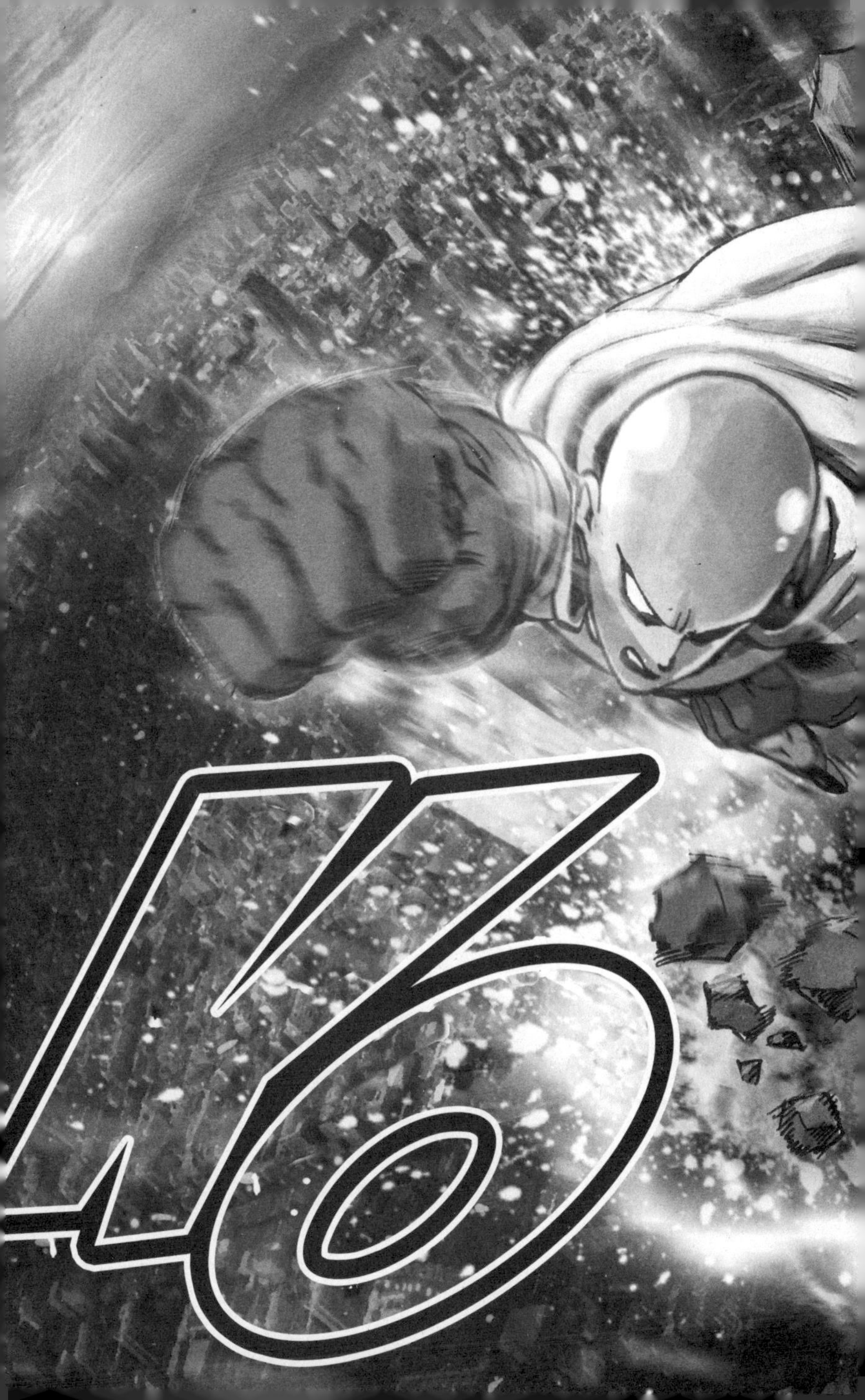
46

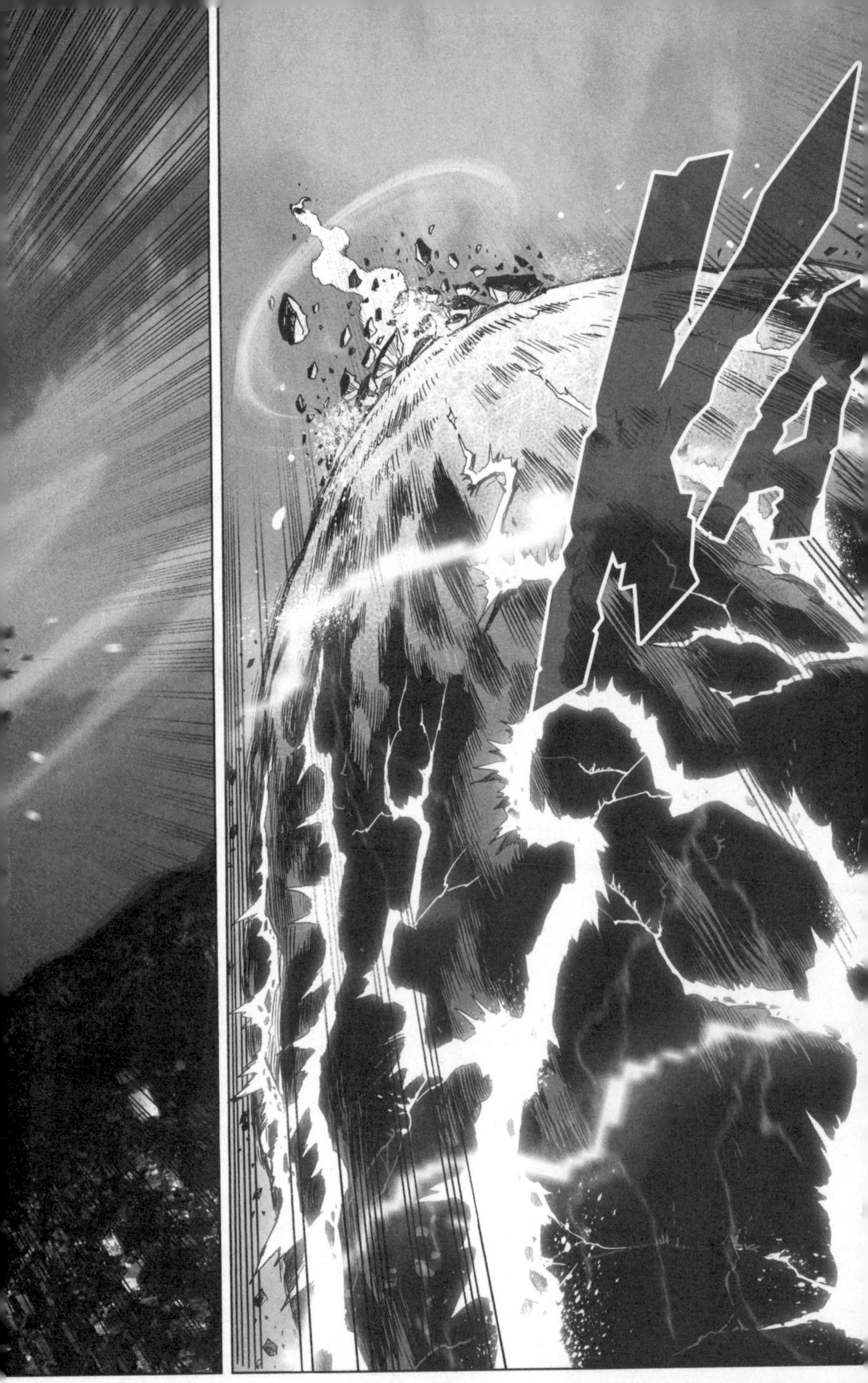

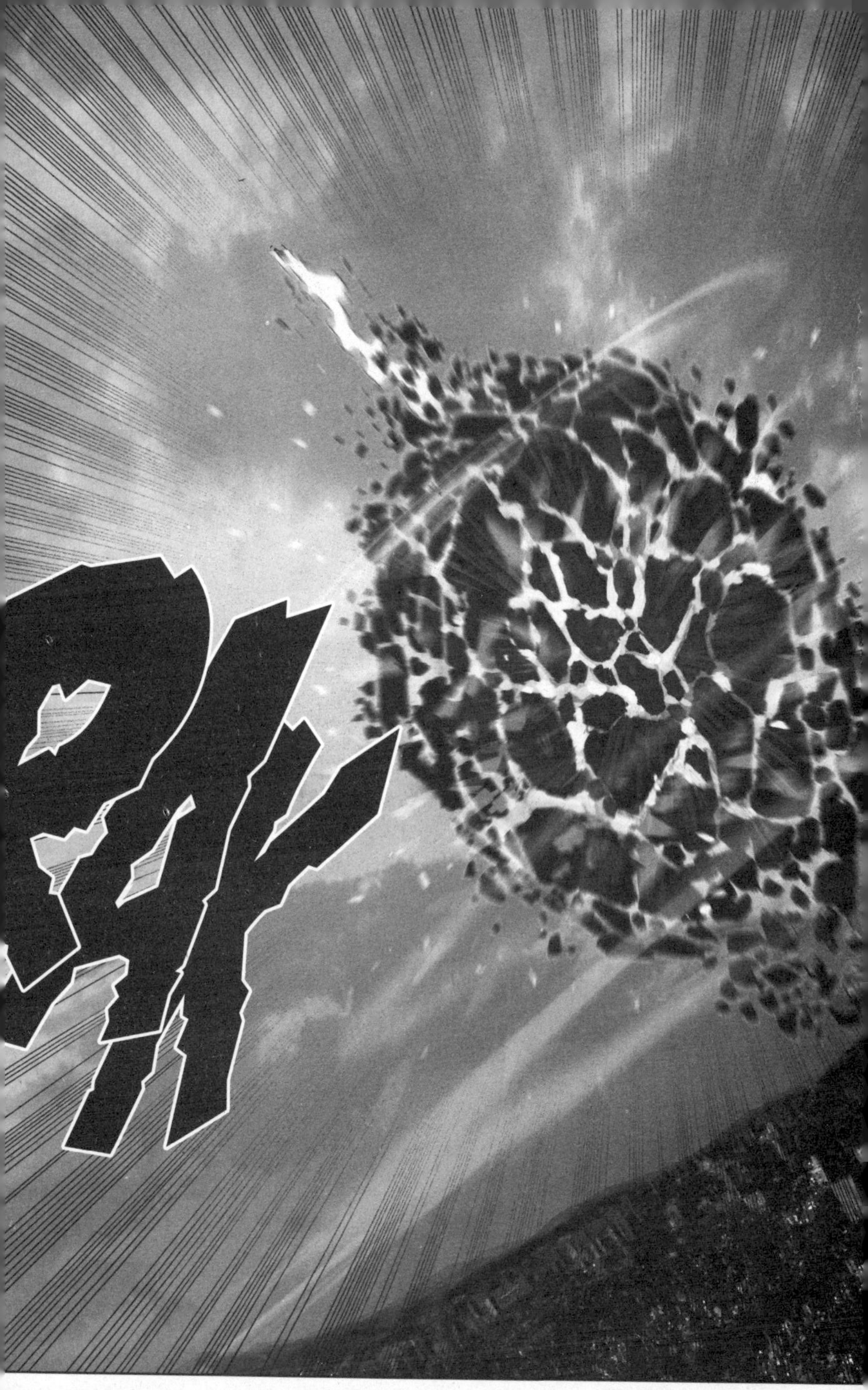

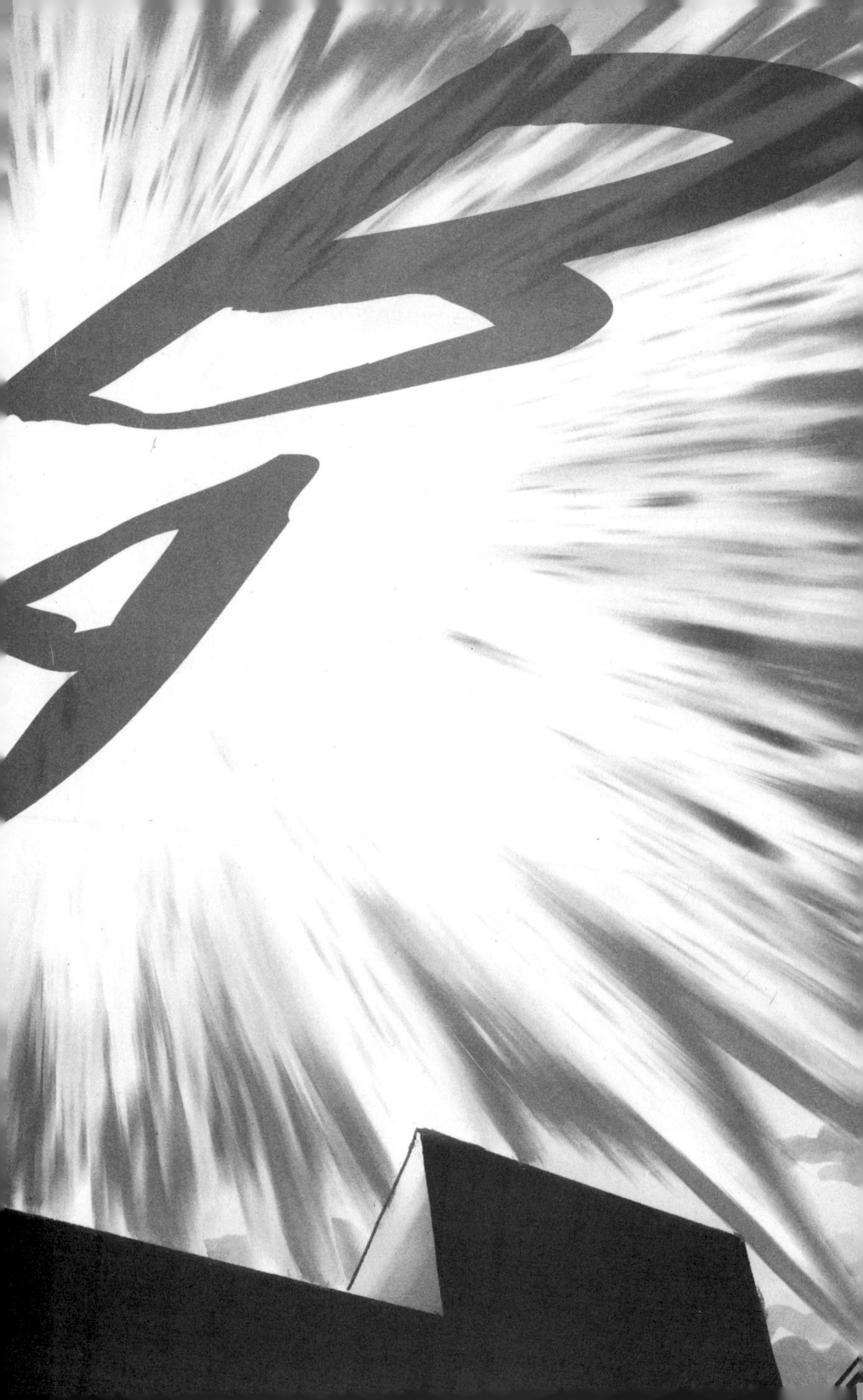

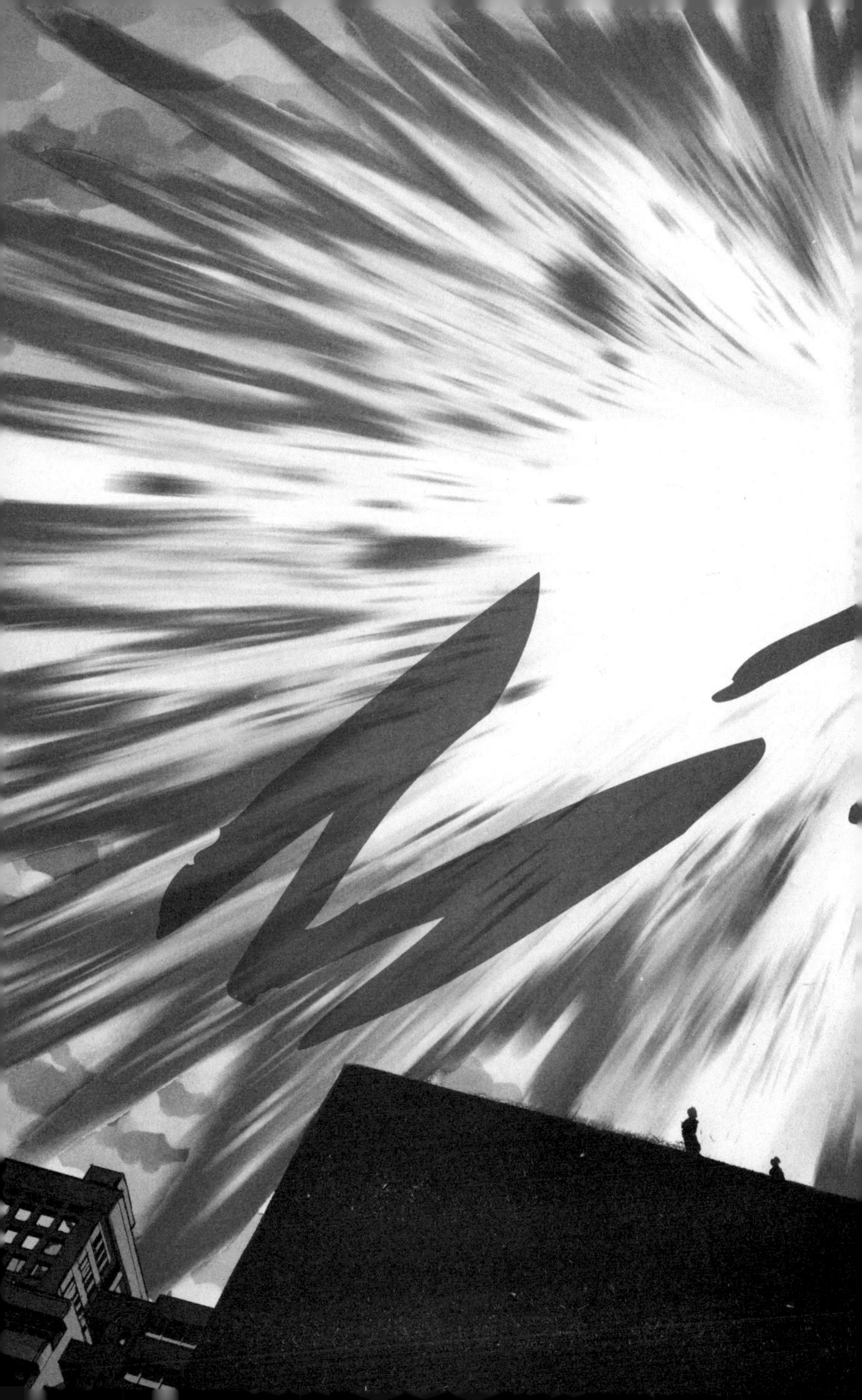

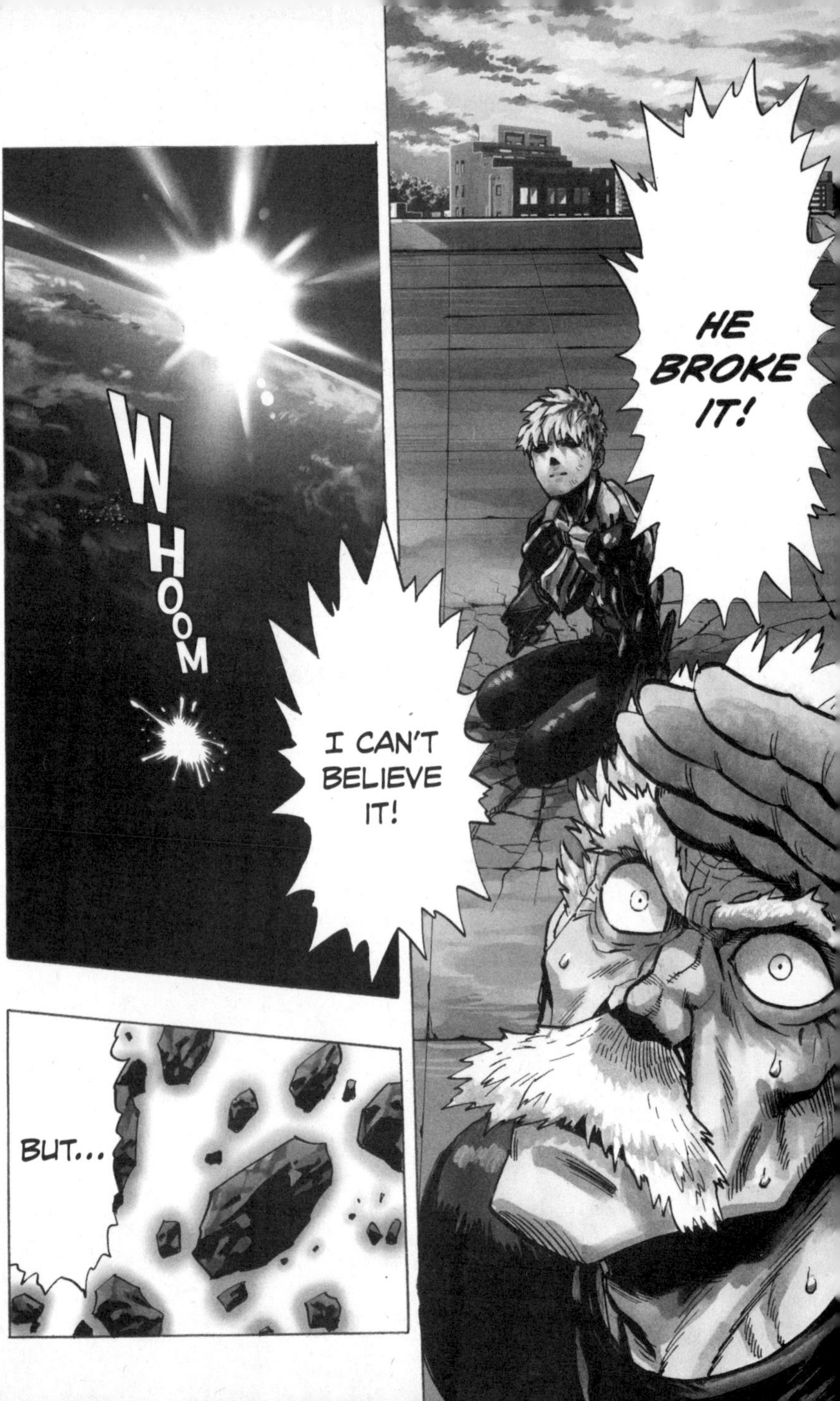
HE BROKE IT!
I CAN'T BELIEVE IT!
WHOOM
BUT...

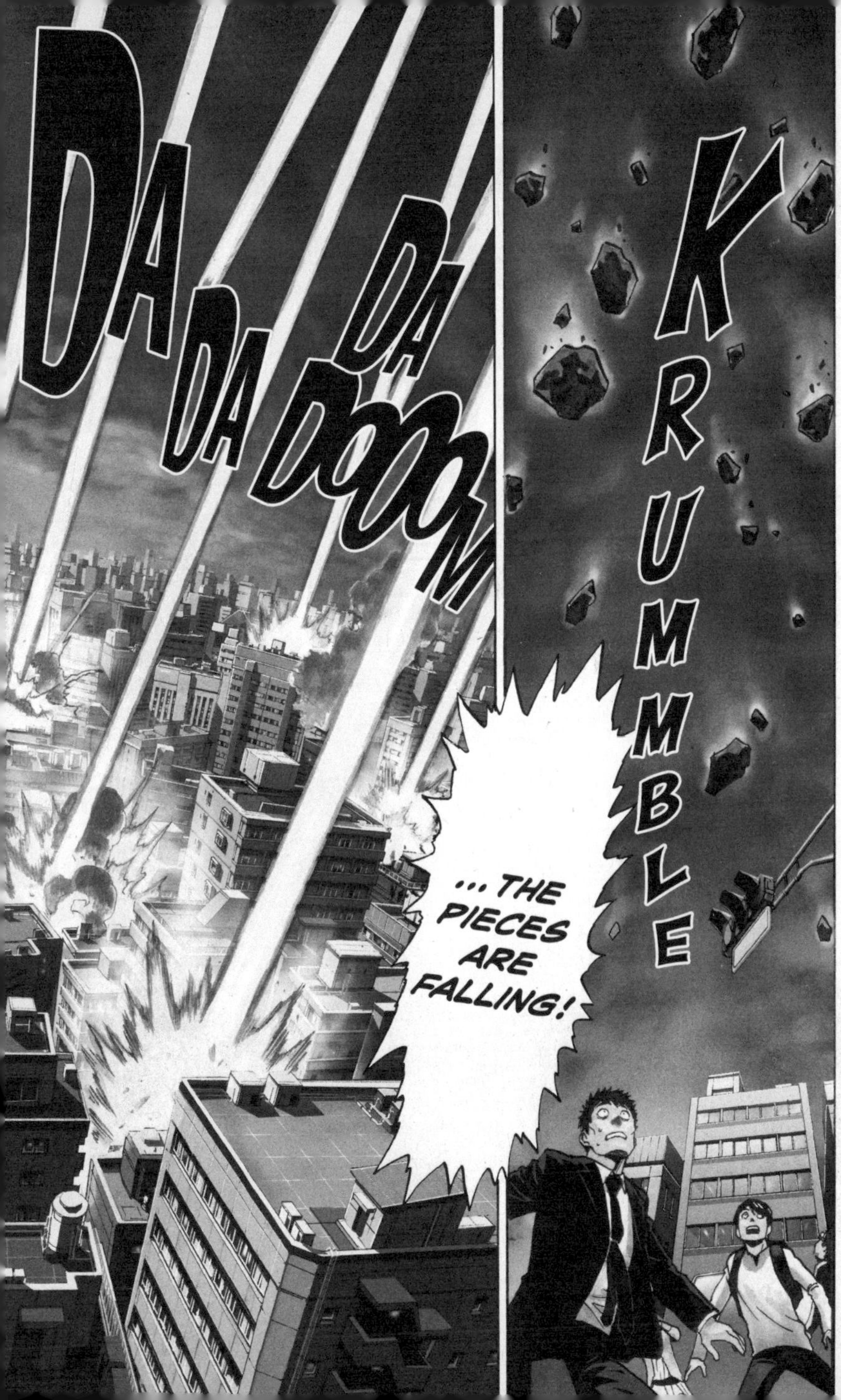
KRUMMBLE
...THE PIECES ARE FALLING!
DA DA DA DA DOOOM

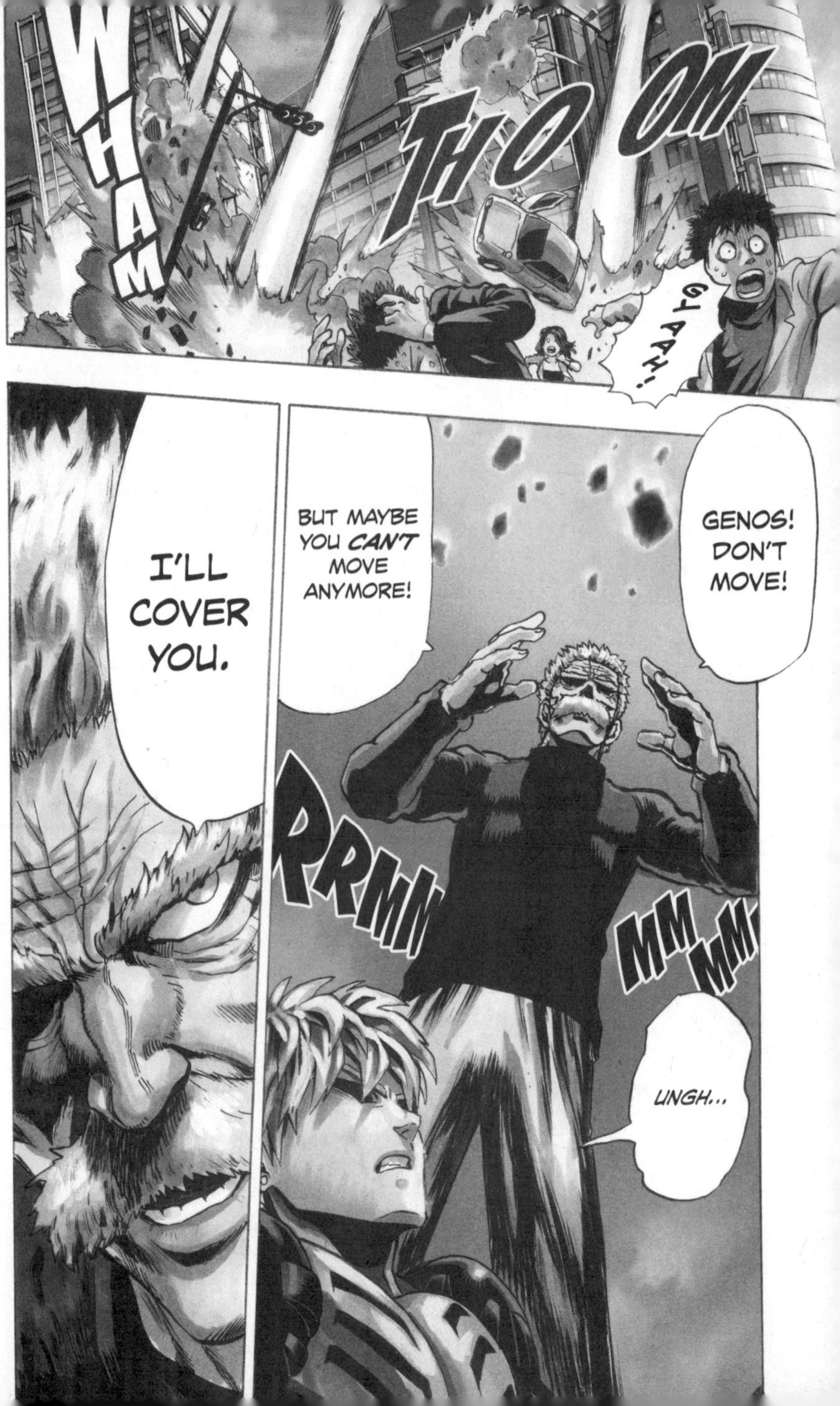
THOOM
GYAAH!
WHAM
GENOS! DON'T MOVE!
BUT MAYBE YOU *CAN'T* MOVE ANYMORE!
RRMMMMMM
UNGH...
I'LL COVER YOU.

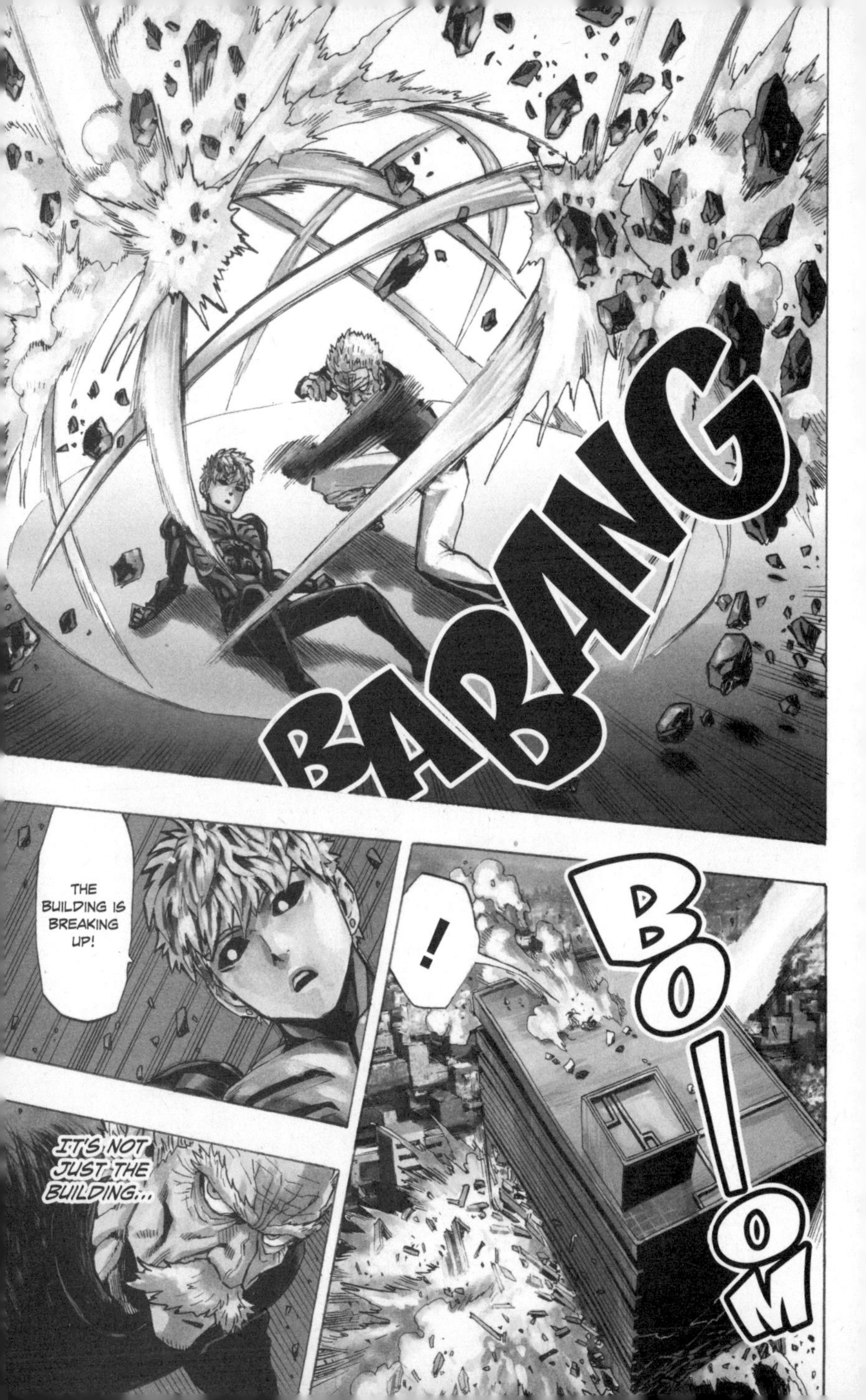
BABANG
!
BOOOM
THE BUILDING IS BREAKING UP!
IT'S NOT JUST THE BUILDING...

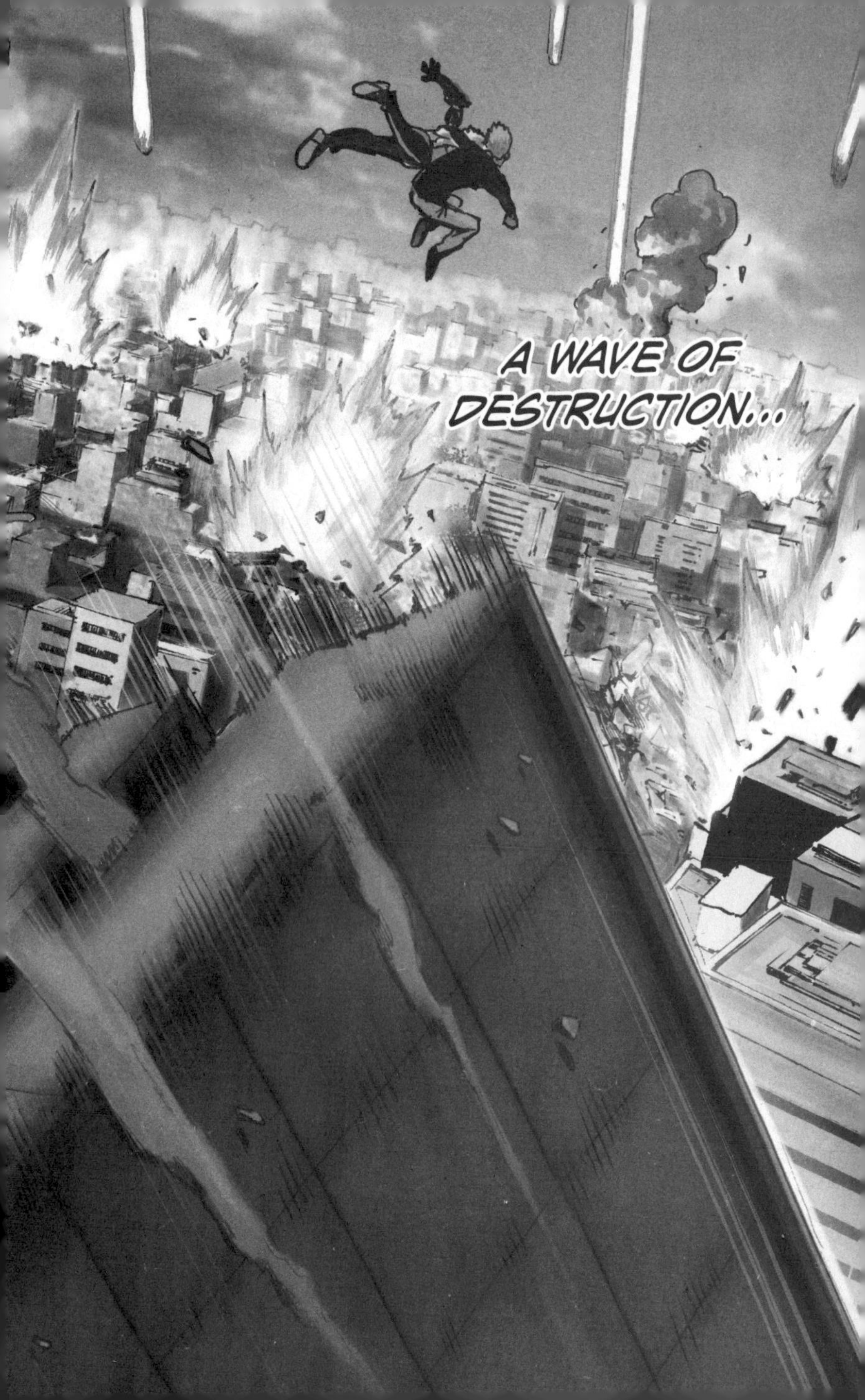
A WAVE OF DESTRUCTION...

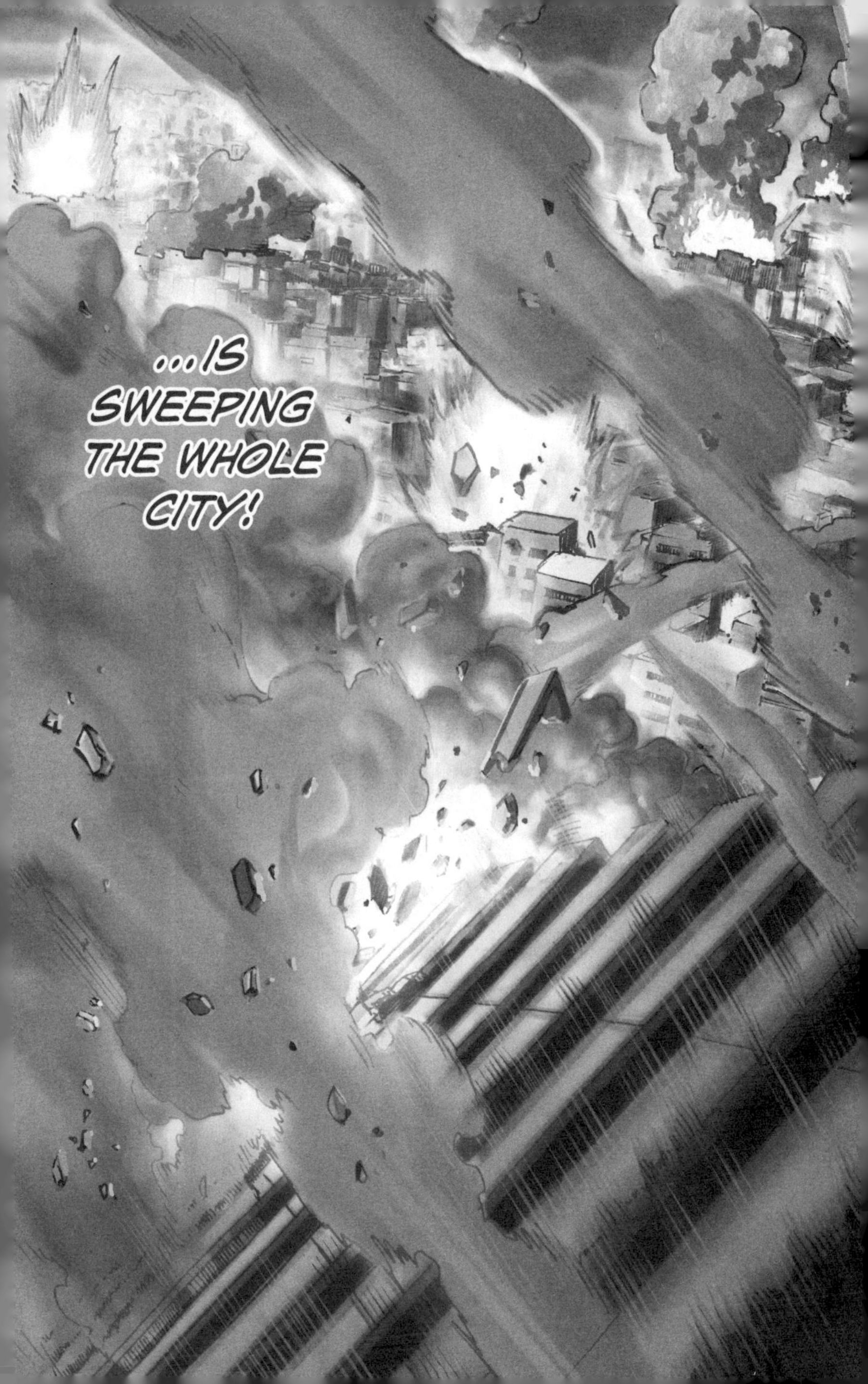
...IS SWEEPING THE WHOLE CITY!

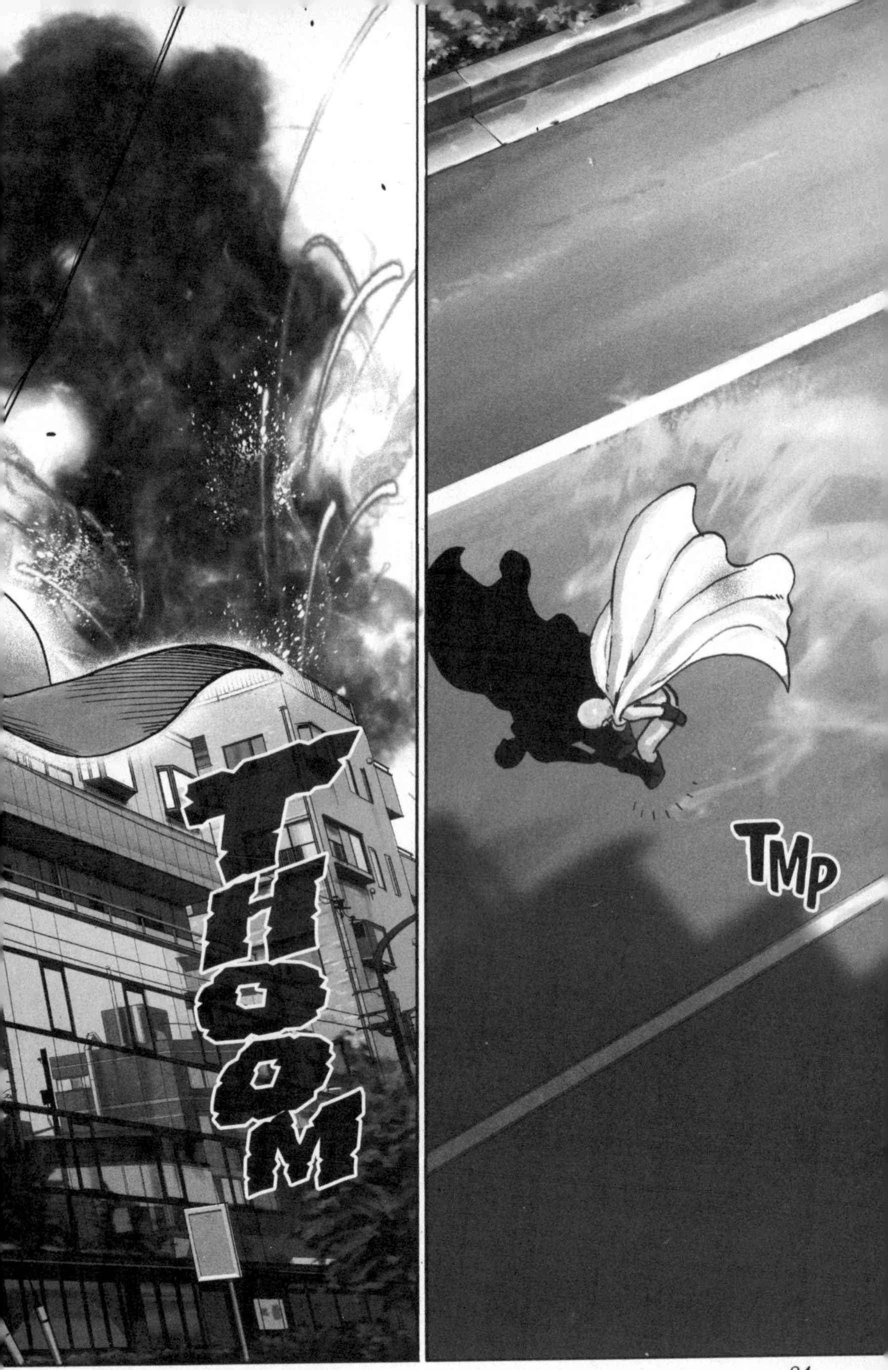
TMP
THOOM

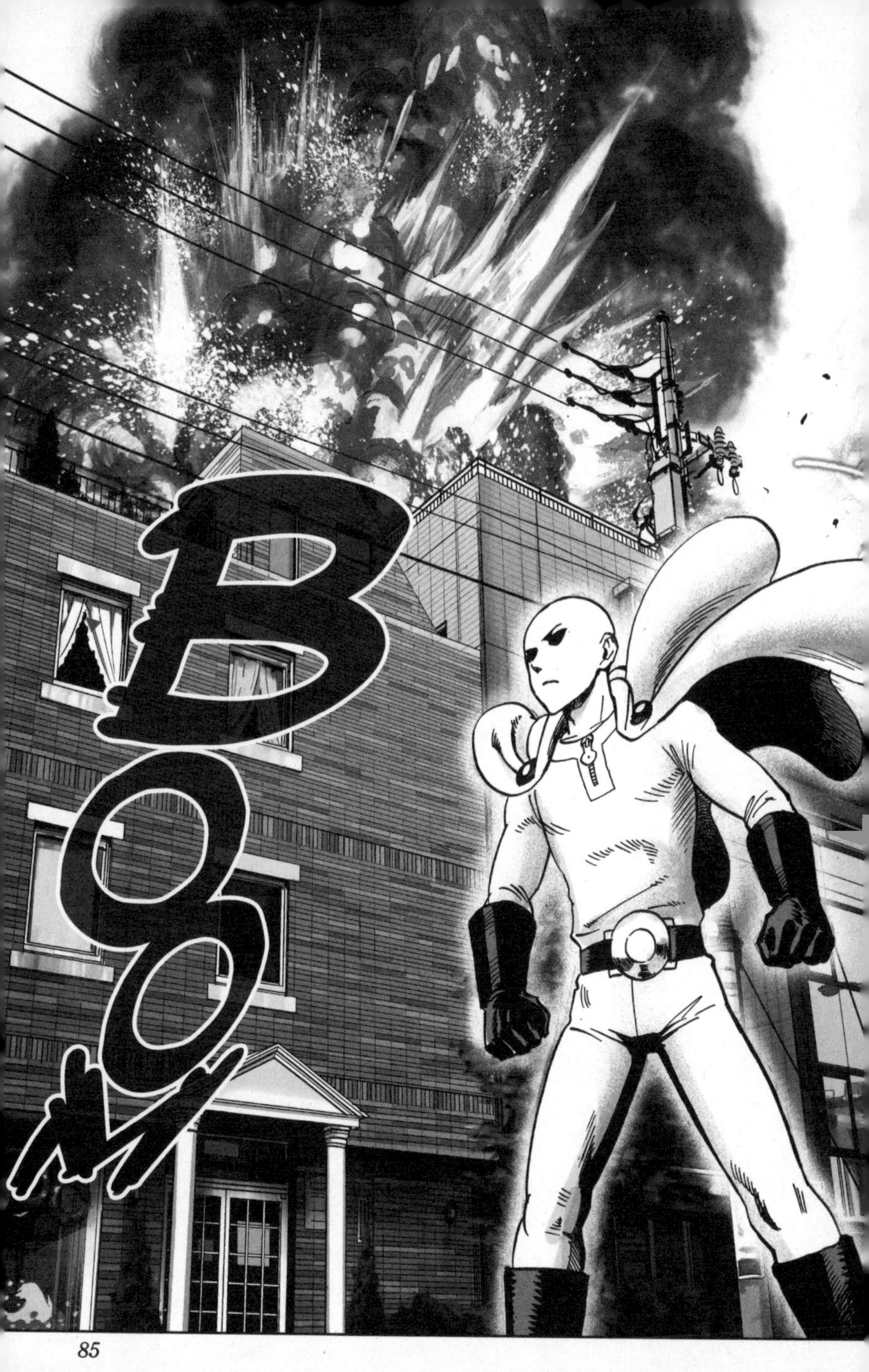
BOOM

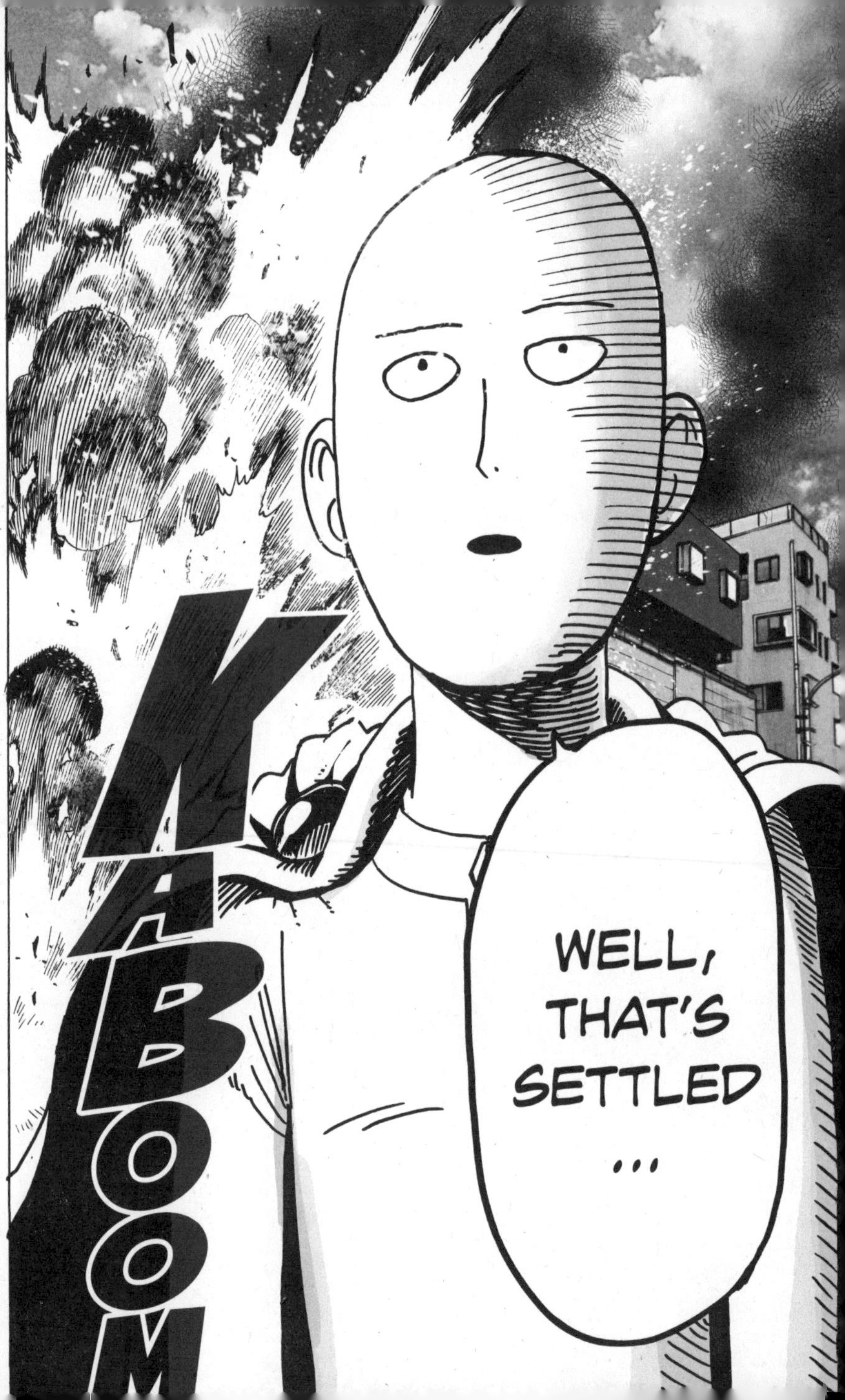
KABOOM
WELL, THAT'S SETTLED ...

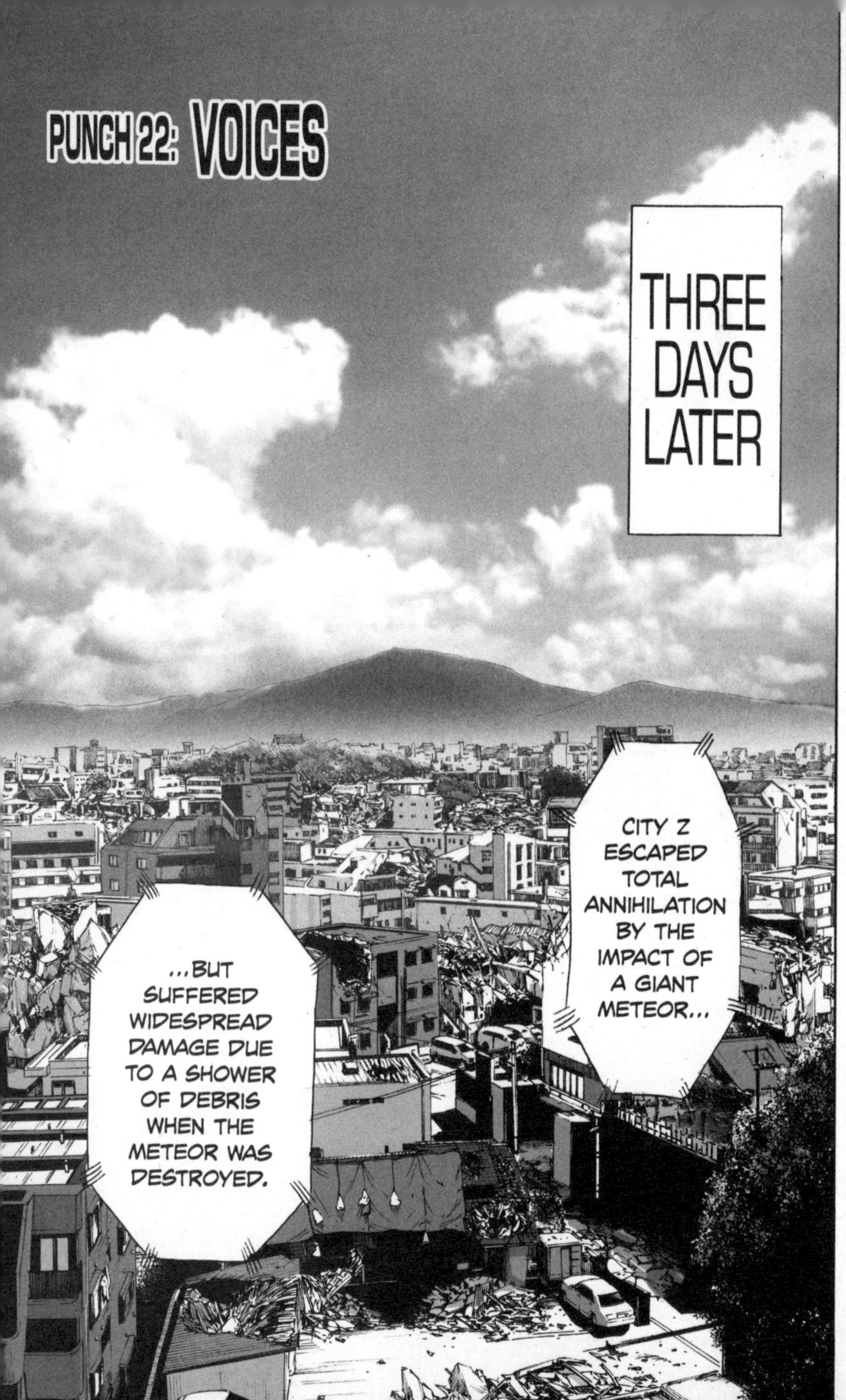
PUNCH 22: VOICES
THREE DAYS LATER
CITY Z ESCAPED TOTAL ANNIHILATION BY THE IMPACT OF A GIANT METEOR...
...BUT SUFFERED WIDESPREAD DAMAGE DUE TO A SHOWER OF DEBRIS WHEN THE METEOR WAS DESTROYED.

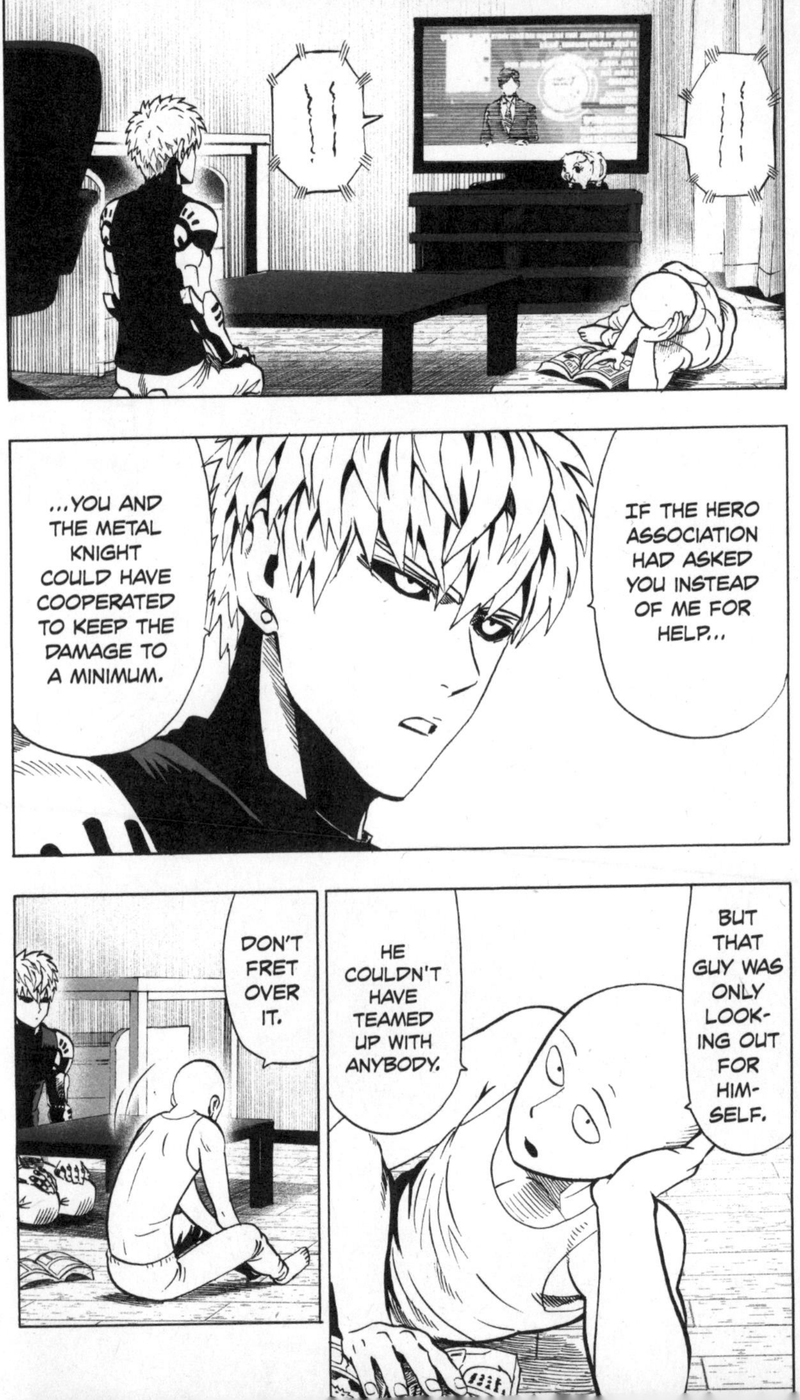
IF THE HERO ASSOCIATION HAD ASKED YOU INSTEAD OF ME FOR HELP...
...YOU AND THE METAL KNIGHT COULD HAVE COOPERATED TO KEEP THE DAMAGE TO A MINIMUM.
BUT THAT GUY WAS ONLY LOOKING OUT FOR HIMSELF.
HE COULDN'T HAVE TEAMED UP WITH ANYBODY.
DON'T FRET OVER IT.

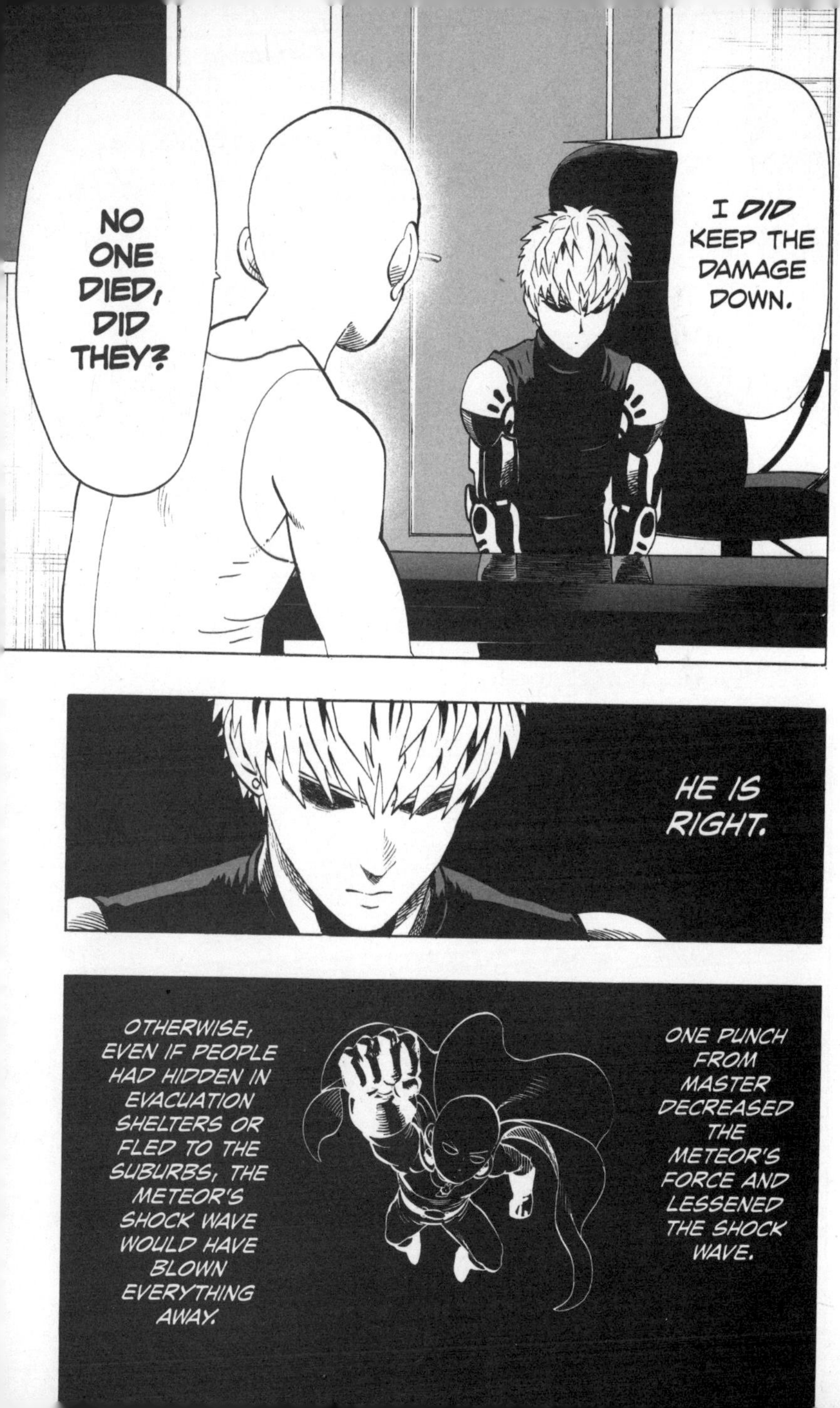
I DID KEEP THE DAMAGE DOWN.
NO ONE DIED, DID THEY?
HE IS RIGHT.
ONE PUNCH FROM MASTER DECREASED THE METEOR'S FORCE AND LESSENED THE SHOCK WAVE.
OTHERWISE, EVEN IF PEOPLE HAD HIDDEN IN EVACUATION SHELTERS OR FLED TO THE SUBURBS, THE METEOR'S SHOCK WAVE WOULD HAVE BLOWN EVERYTHING AWAY.

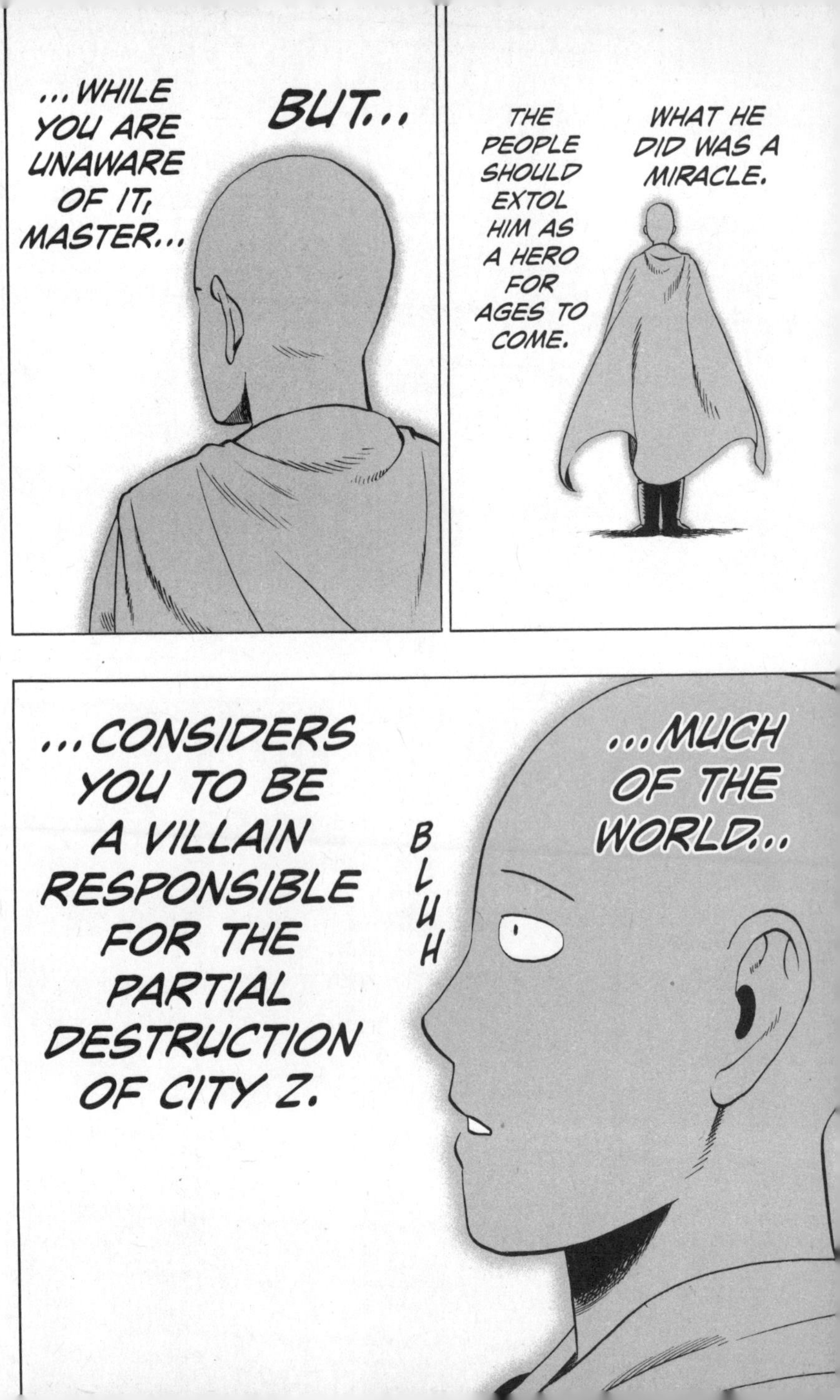
WHAT HE DID WAS A MIRACLE.
THE PEOPLE SHOULD EXTOL HIM AS A HERO FOR AGES TO COME.
BUT...
...WHILE YOU ARE UNAWARE OF IT, MASTER...
...MUCH OF THE WORLD...
BLUH
...CONSIDERS YOU TO BE A VILLAIN RESPONSIBLE FOR THE PARTIAL DESTRUCTION OF CITY Z.

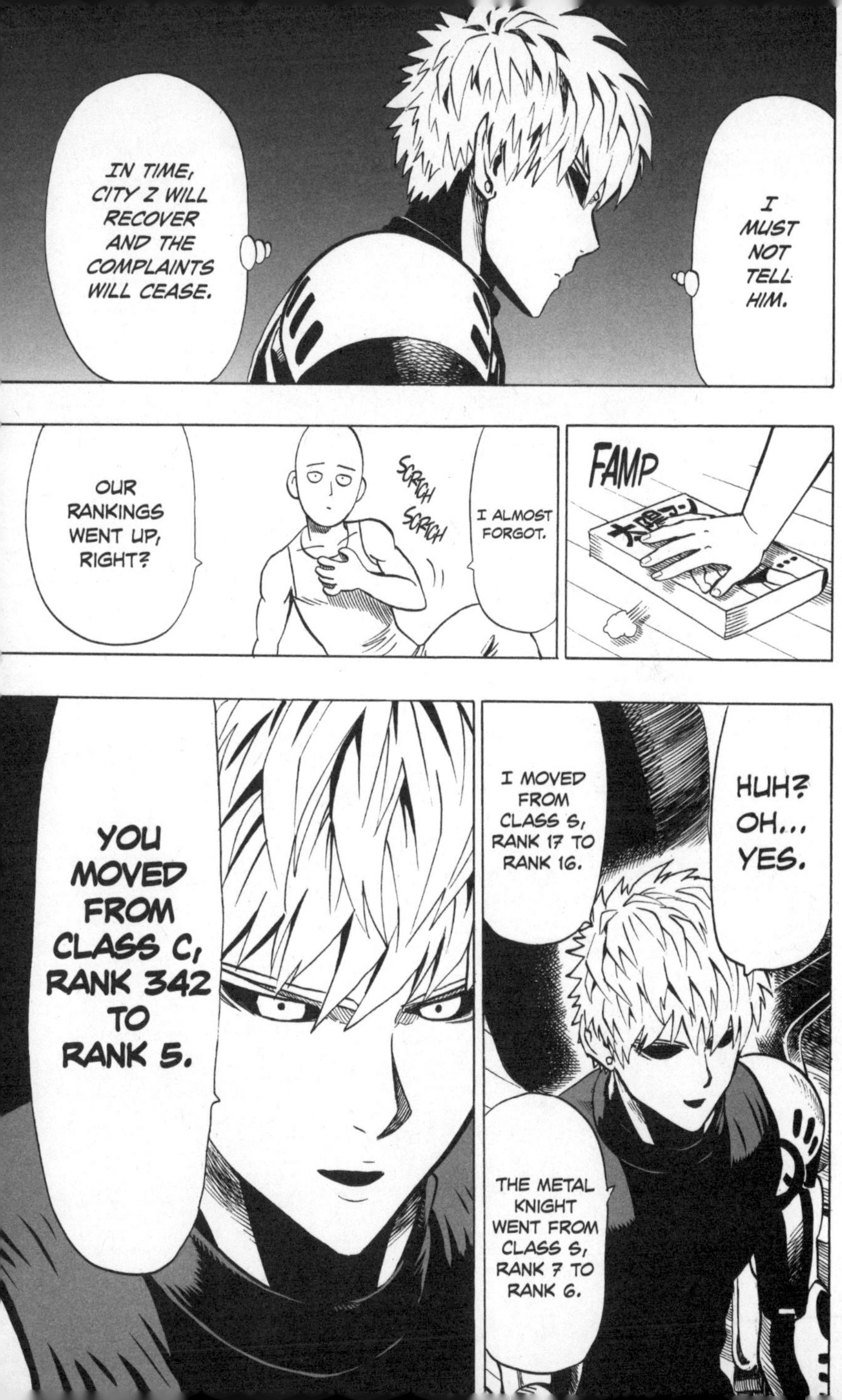
I MUST NOT TELL HIM.
IN TIME, CITY Z WILL RECOVER AND THE COMPLAINTS WILL CEASE.
FAMP
I ALMOST FORGOT.
SCRICH SCRICH
OUR RANKINGS WENT UP, RIGHT?
HUH? OH... YES.
I MOVED FROM CLASS S, RANK 17 TO RANK 16.
THE METAL KNIGHT WENT FROM CLASS S, RANK 7 TO RANK 6.
YOU MOVED FROM CLASS C, RANK 342 TO RANK 5.

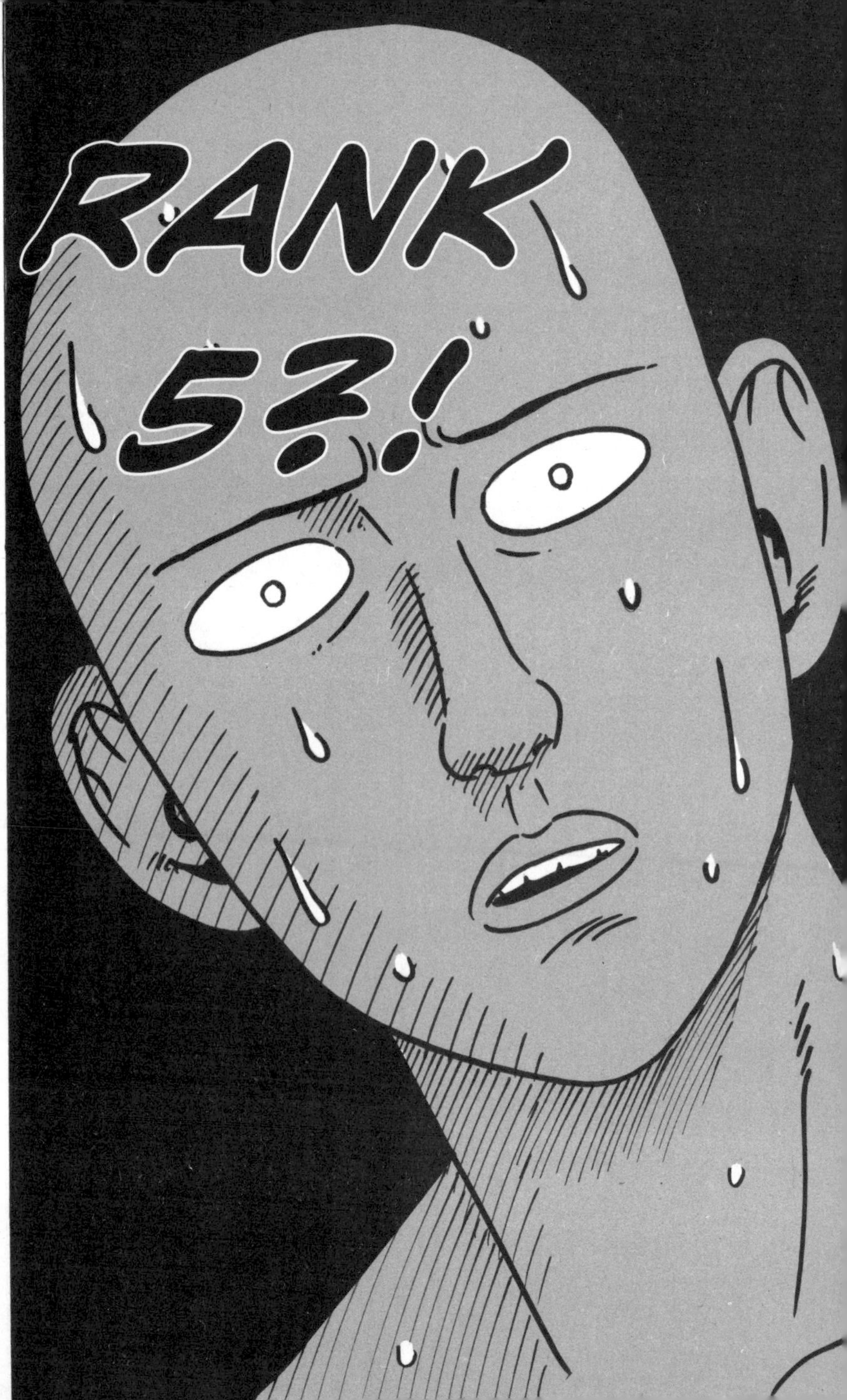
RANK 5?!

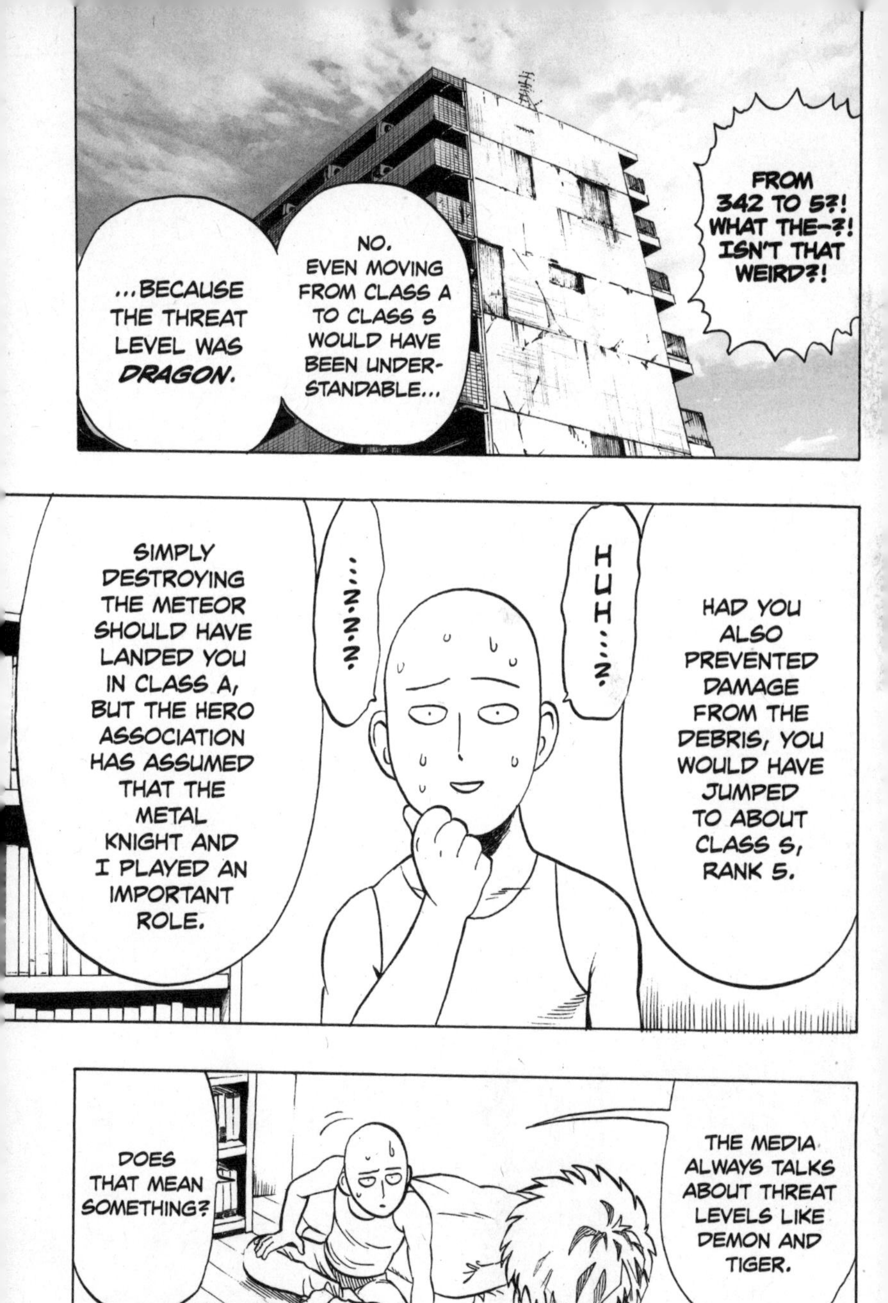
FROM 342 TO 5?! WHAT THE-?! ISN'T THAT WEIRD?!
NO. EVEN MOVING FROM CLASS A TO CLASS S WOULD HAVE BEEN UNDER-STANDABLE...
...BECAUSE THE THREAT LEVEL WAS *DRAGON*.
HAD YOU ALSO PREVENTED DAMAGE FROM THE DEBRIS, YOU WOULD HAVE JUMPED TO ABOUT CLASS S, RANK 5.
HUH...?
...???
SIMPLY DESTROYING THE METEOR SHOULD HAVE LANDED YOU IN CLASS A, BUT THE HERO ASSOCIATION HAS ASSUMED THAT THE METAL KNIGHT AND I PLAYED AN IMPORTANT ROLE.
THE MEDIA ALWAYS TALKS ABOUT THREAT LEVELS LIKE DEMON AND TIGER.
DOES THAT MEAN SOMETHING?

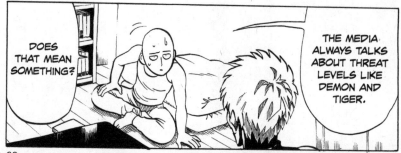

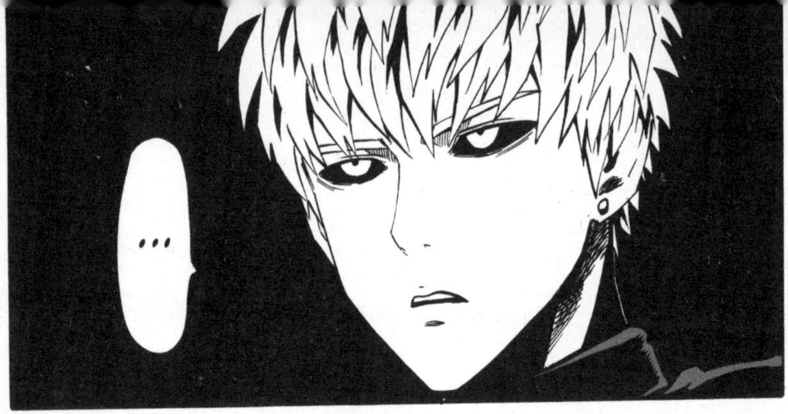
...

Threat Level

God: A crisis threatening the extinction of humankind.

Dragon: A crisis threatening destruction of multiple towns.

Demon: A crisis threatening to interrupt a town's functioning or destroy it altogether.

Tiger: A crisis threatening massive loss of life.

Wolf: Appearance of a life-form or group posing a risk.

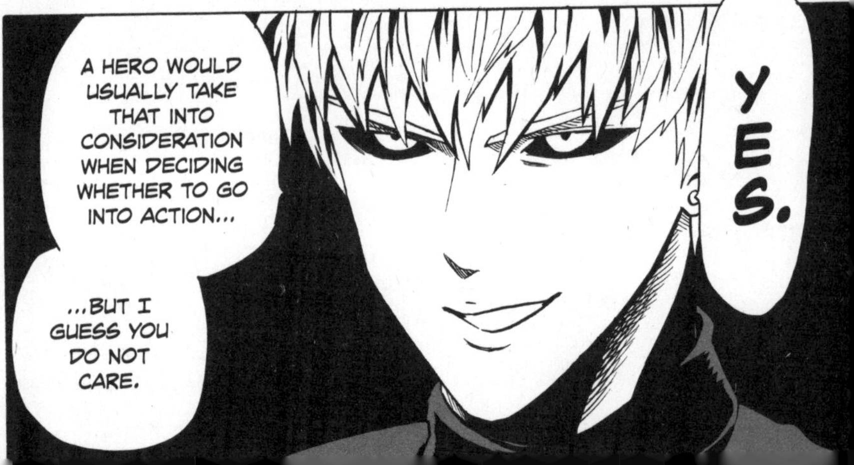
YES.
A HERO WOULD USUALLY TAKE THAT INTO CONSIDERATION WHEN DECIDING WHETHER TO GO INTO ACTION...
...BUT I GUESS YOU DO NOT CARE.

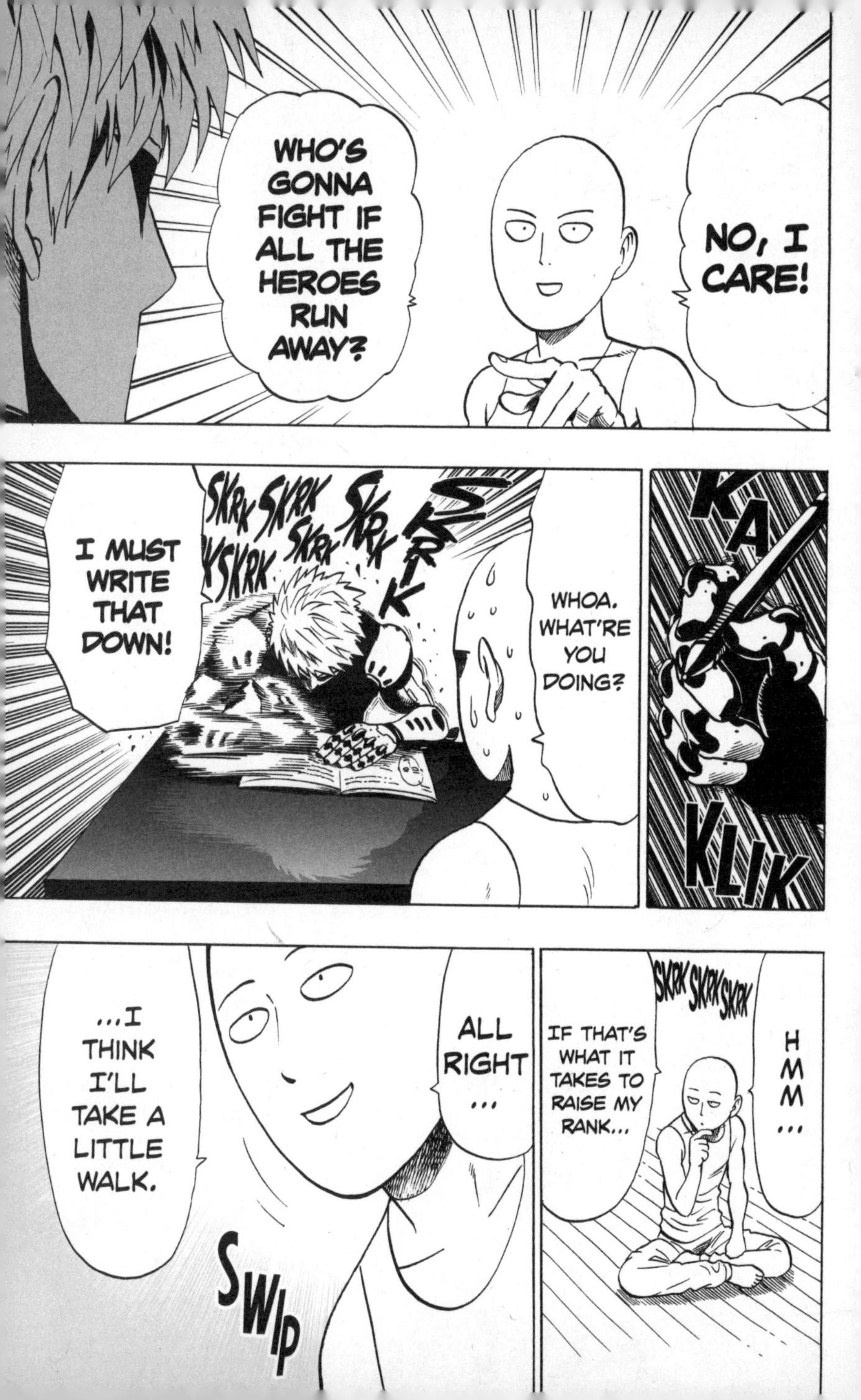
NO, I CARE!
WHO'S GONNA FIGHT IF ALL THE HEROES RUN AWAY?
KA
KLIK
WHOA. WHAT'RE YOU DOING?
SKRIK
SKRK SKRK SKRK SKRK SKRK SKRK
I MUST WRITE THAT DOWN!
SKRK SKRK SKRK
HMM...
IF THAT'S WHAT IT TAKES TO RAISE MY RANK...
ALL RIGHT...
...I THINK I'LL TAKE A LITTLE WALK.
SWIP

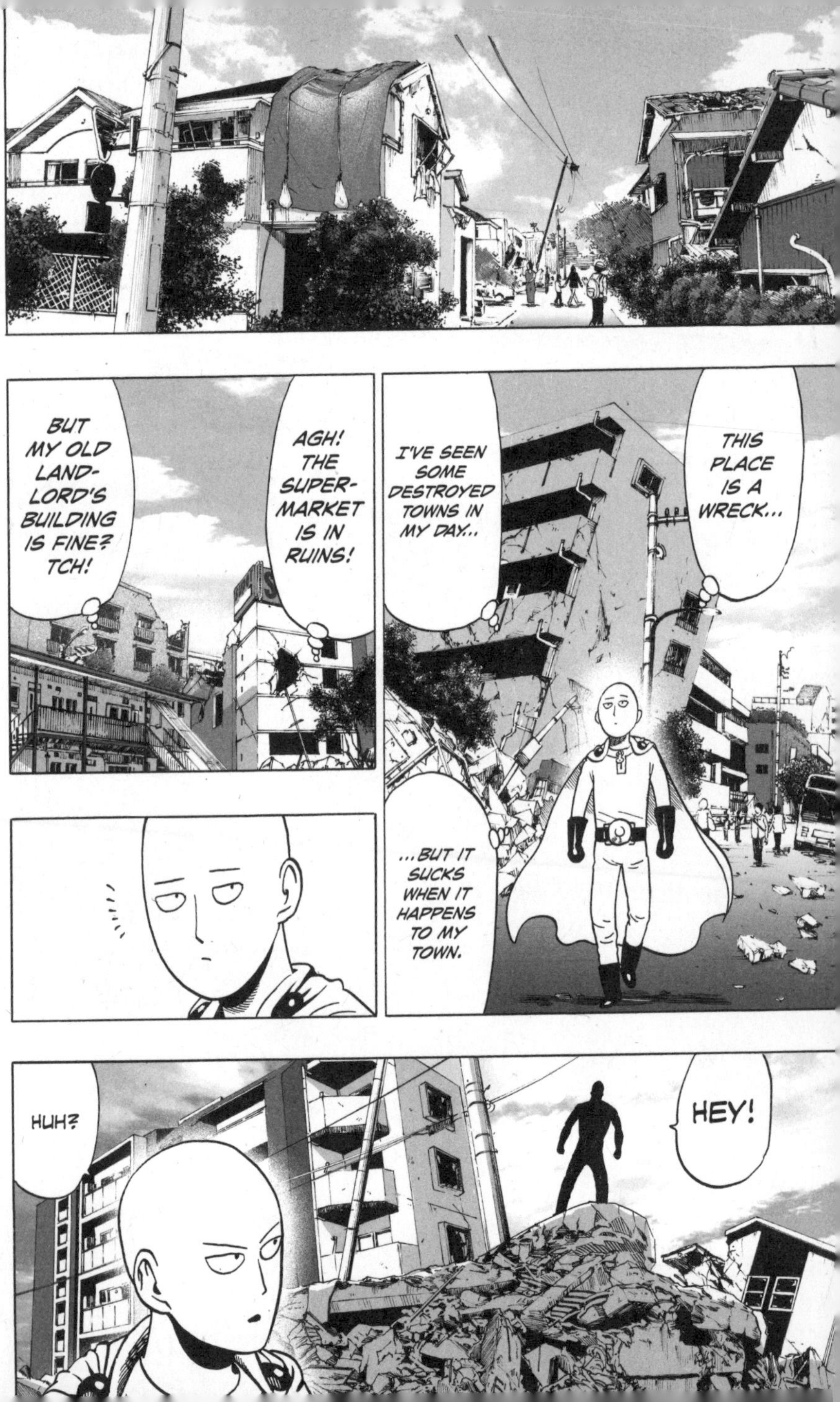
THIS PLACE IS A WRECK...
I'VE SEEN SOME DESTROYED TOWNS IN MY DAY...
...BUT IT SUCKS WHEN IT HAPPENS TO MY TOWN.
AGH! THE SUPER-MARKET IS IN RUINS!
BUT MY OLD LAND-LORD'S BUILDING IS FINE? TCH!
HEY!
HUH?

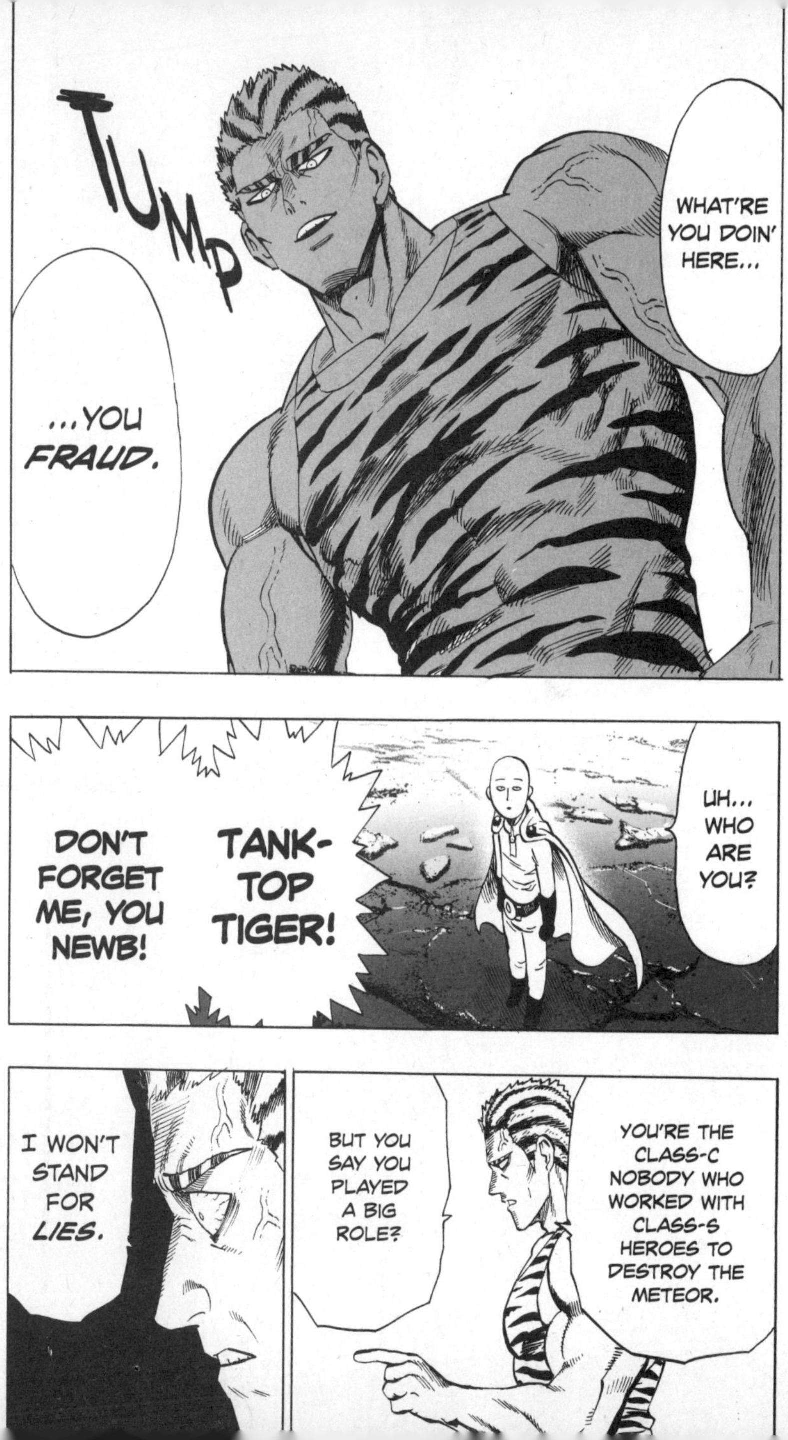
WHAT'RE YOU DOIN' HERE...
TUMP
...YOU *FRAUD.*
UH... WHO ARE YOU?
TANK-TOP TIGER!
DON'T FORGET ME, YOU NEWB!
YOU'RE THE CLASS-C NOBODY WHO WORKED WITH CLASS-S HEROES TO DESTROY THE METEOR.
BUT YOU SAY YOU PLAYED A BIG ROLE?
I WON'T STAND FOR *LIES.*

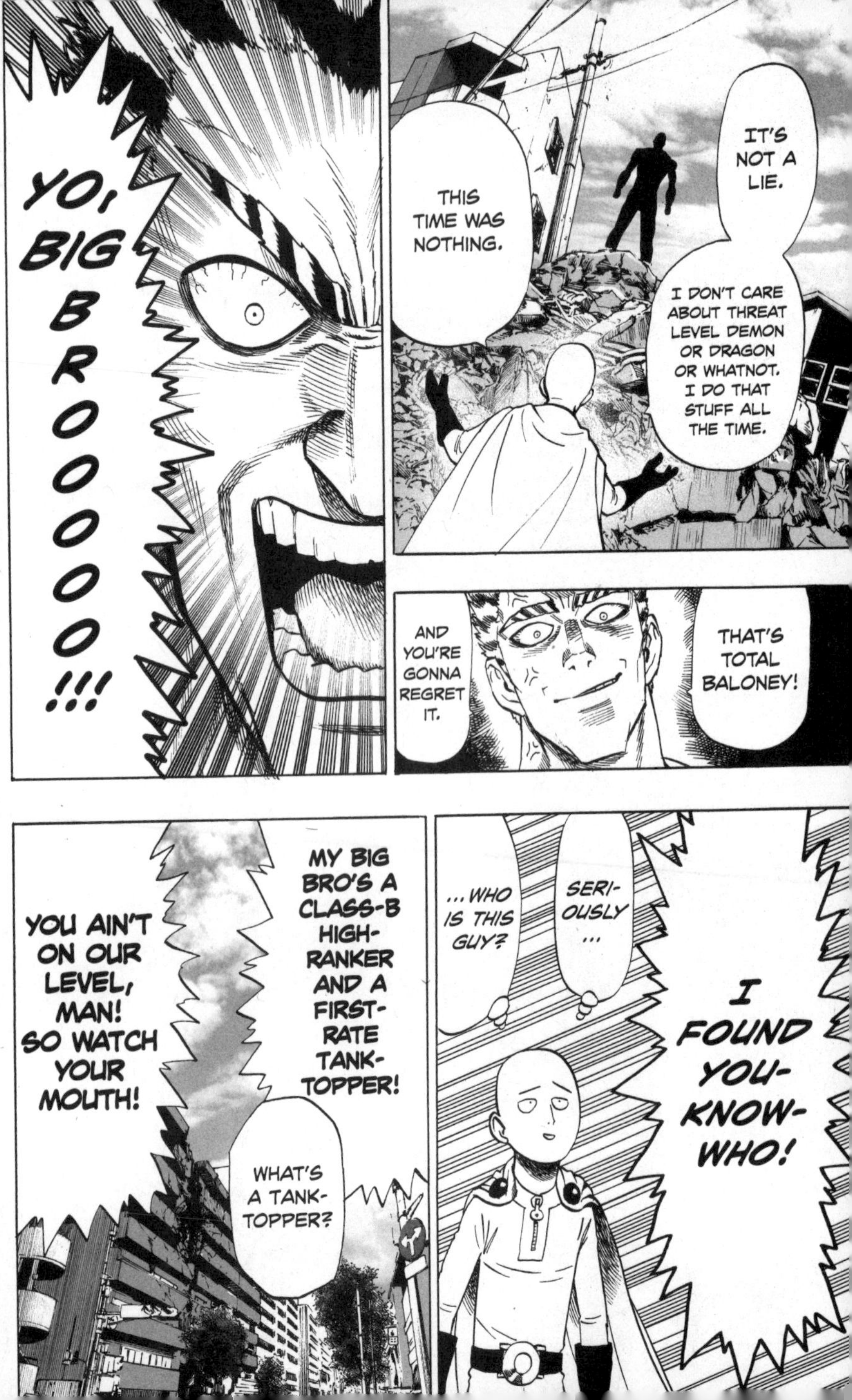
IT'S NOT A LIE.
I DON'T CARE ABOUT THREAT LEVEL DEMON OR DRAGON OR WHATNOT. I DO THAT STUFF ALL THE TIME.
THIS TIME WAS NOTHING.
THAT'S TOTAL BALONEY!
AND YOU'RE GONNA REGRET IT.
YO, BIG BROOOOOOO!!!
I FOUND YOU-KNOW-WHO!
SERIOUSLY...
...WHO IS THIS GUY?
MY BIG BRO'S A CLASS-B HIGH-RANKER AND A FIRST-RATE TANK-TOPPER!
YOU AIN'T ON OUR LEVEL, MAN! SO WATCH YOUR MOUTH!
WHAT'S A TANK-TOPPER?

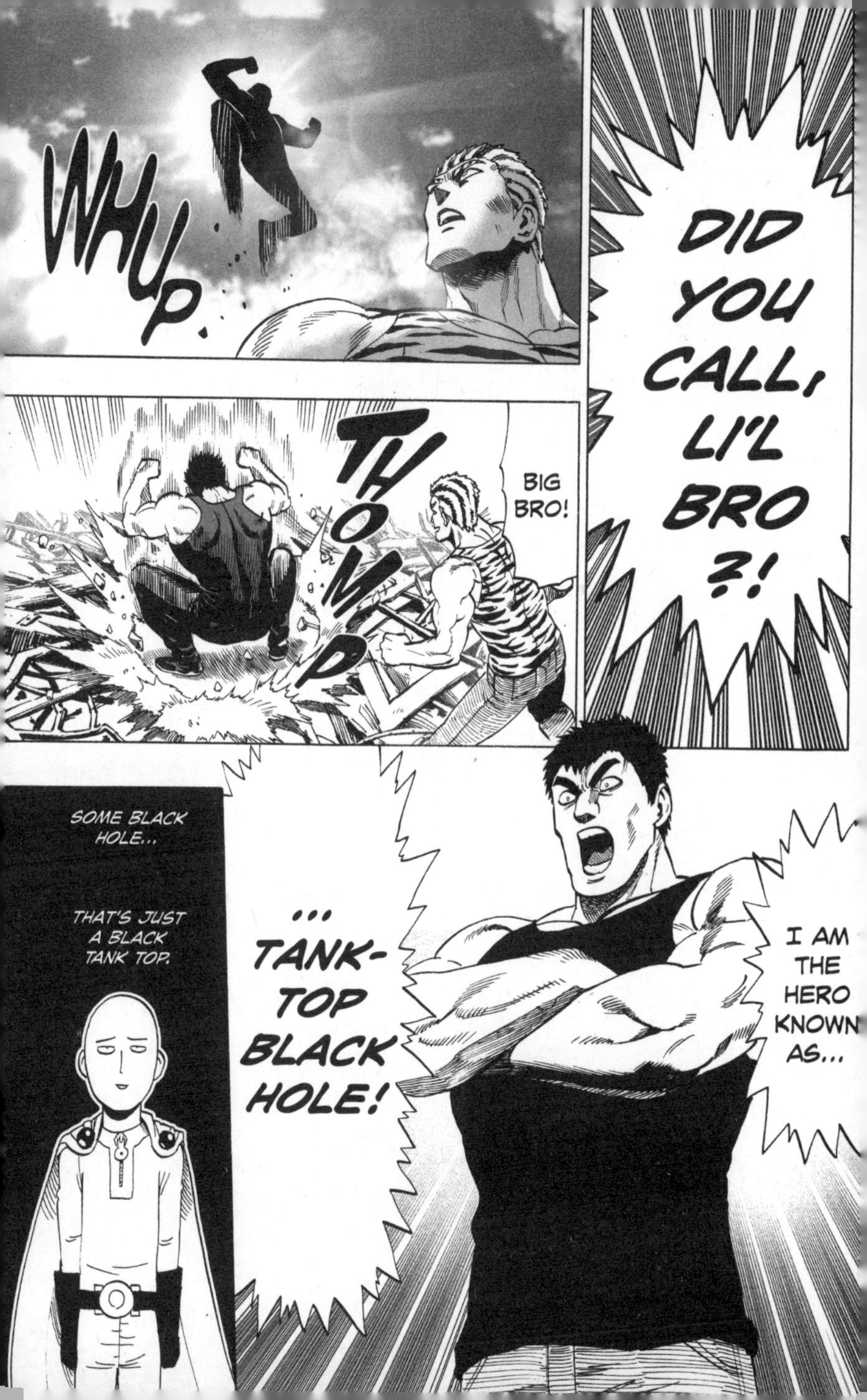
DID YOU CALL, LI'L BRO?!
WHUP
BIG BRO!
THOMP
I AM THE HERO KNOWN AS...
...TANK-TOP BLACK HOLE!
SOME BLACK HOLE...
THAT'S JUST A BLACK TANK TOP.

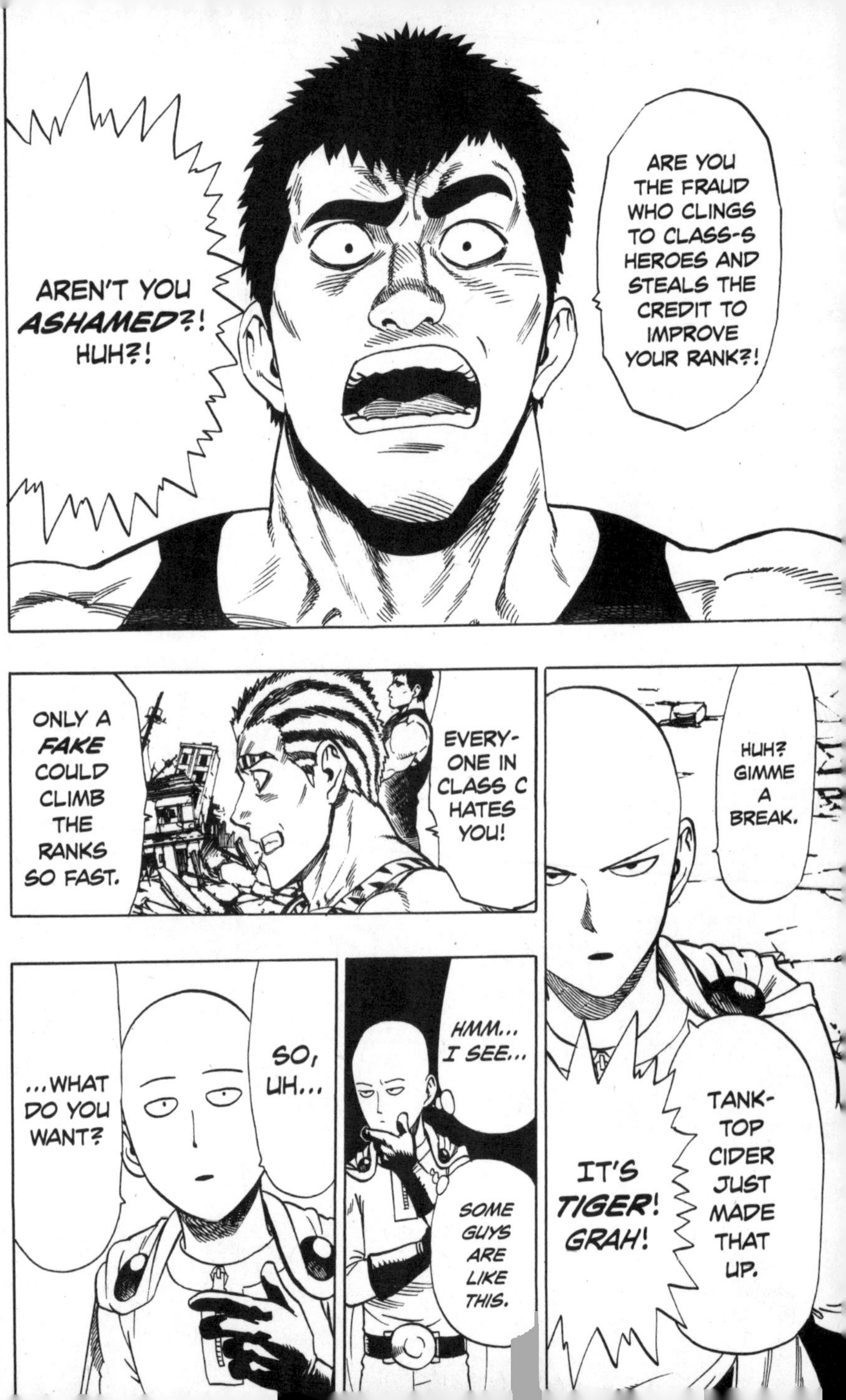
ARE YOU THE FRAUD WHO CLINGS TO CLASS-S HEROES AND STEALS THE CREDIT TO IMPROVE YOUR RANK?!
AREN'T YOU *ASHAMED*?! HUH?!
HUH? GIMME A BREAK.
TANK-TOP CIDER JUST MADE THAT UP.
IT'S *TIGER*! *GRAH*!
EVERY-ONE IN CLASS C HATES YOU!
ONLY A *FAKE* COULD CLIMB THE RANKS SO FAST.
HMM... I SEE...
SOME GUYS ARE LIKE THIS.
SO, UH...
...WHAT DO YOU WANT?

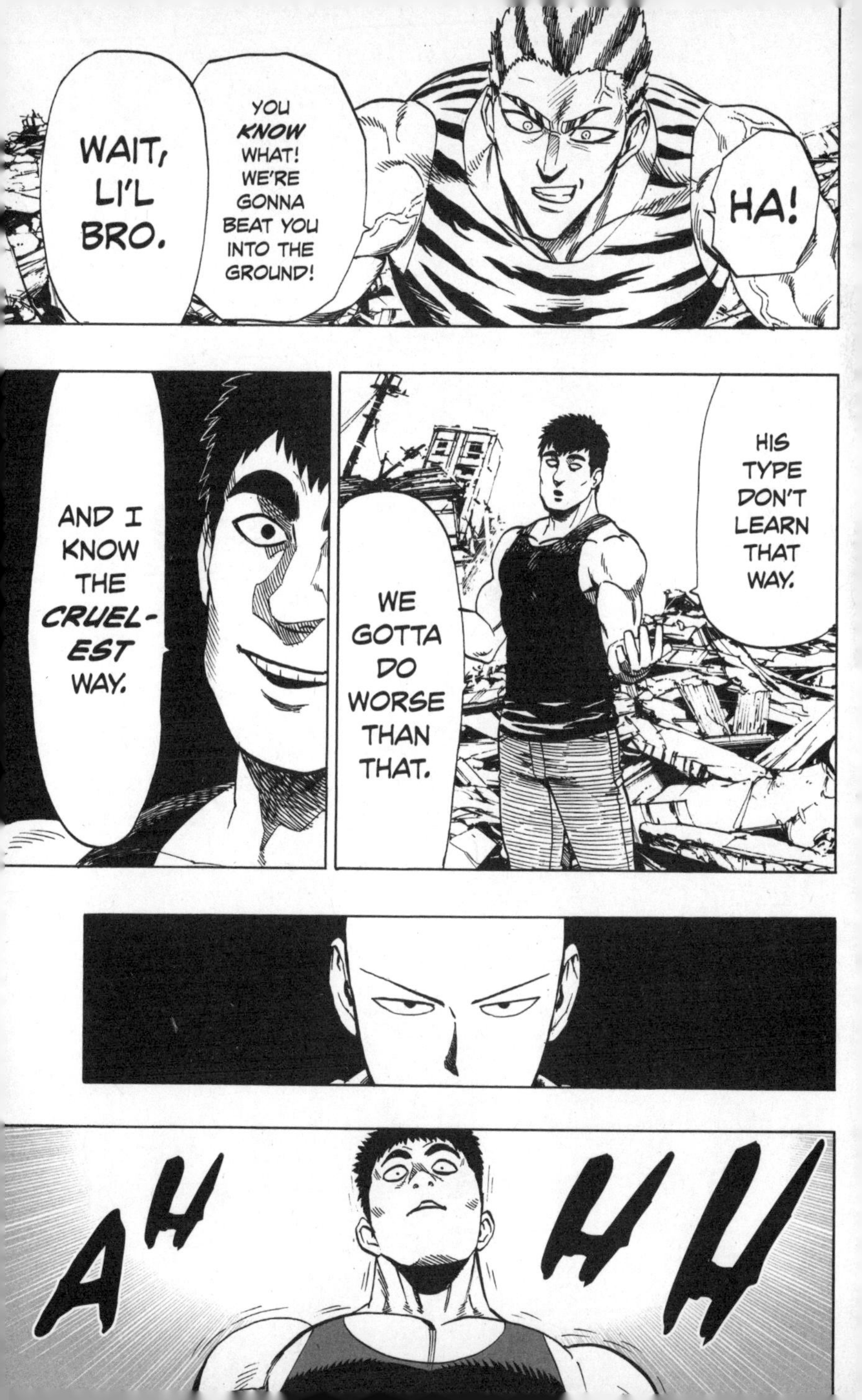
HA!
YOU KNOW WHAT! WE'RE GONNA BEAT YOU INTO THE GROUND!
WAIT, LI'L BRO.
HIS TYPE DON'T LEARN THAT WAY.
WE GOTTA DO WORSE THAN THAT.
AND I KNOW THE CRUEL-EST WAY.
AHHHHH

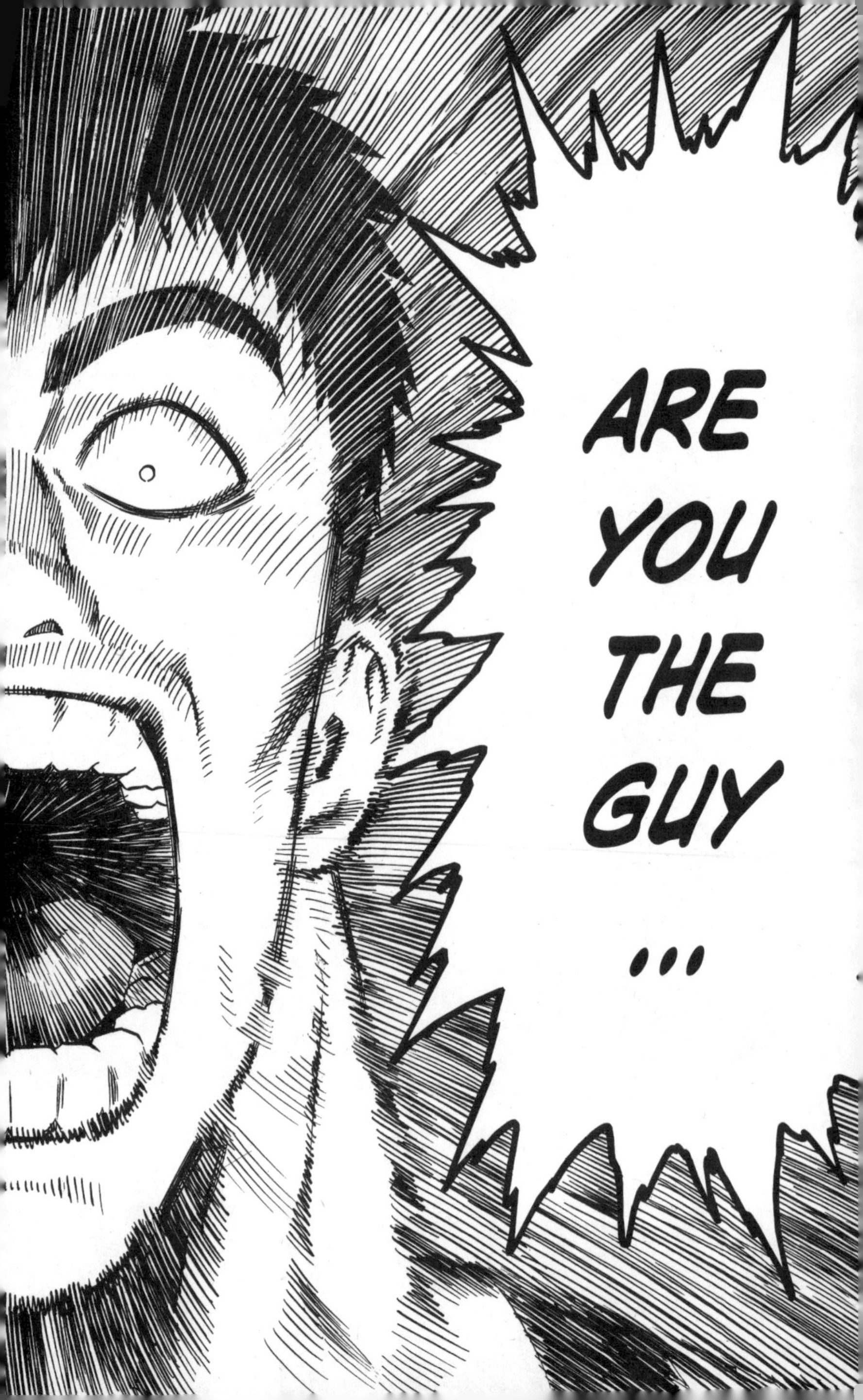
ARE YOU THE GUY ...

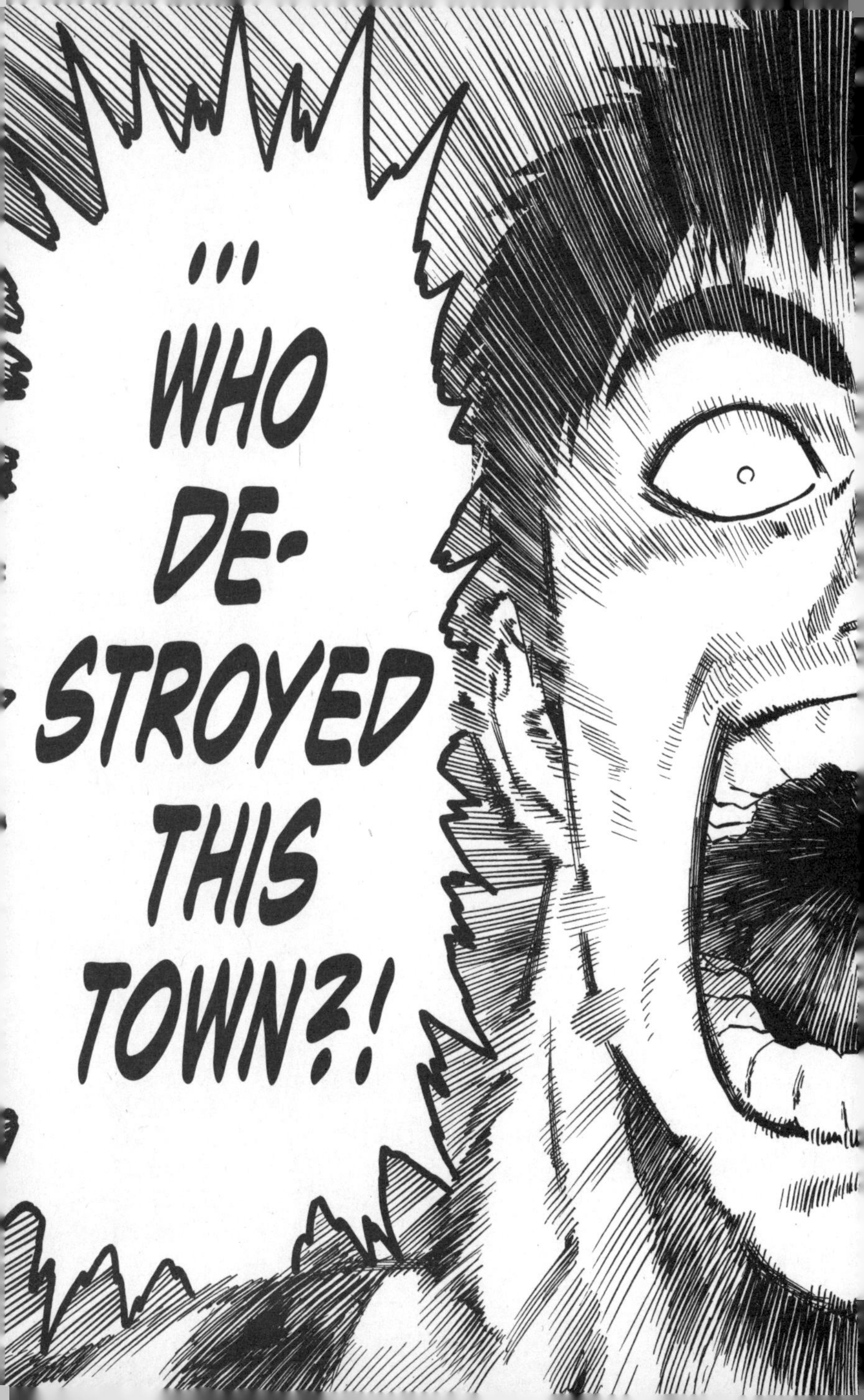
...WHO DE-STROYED THIS TOWN?!

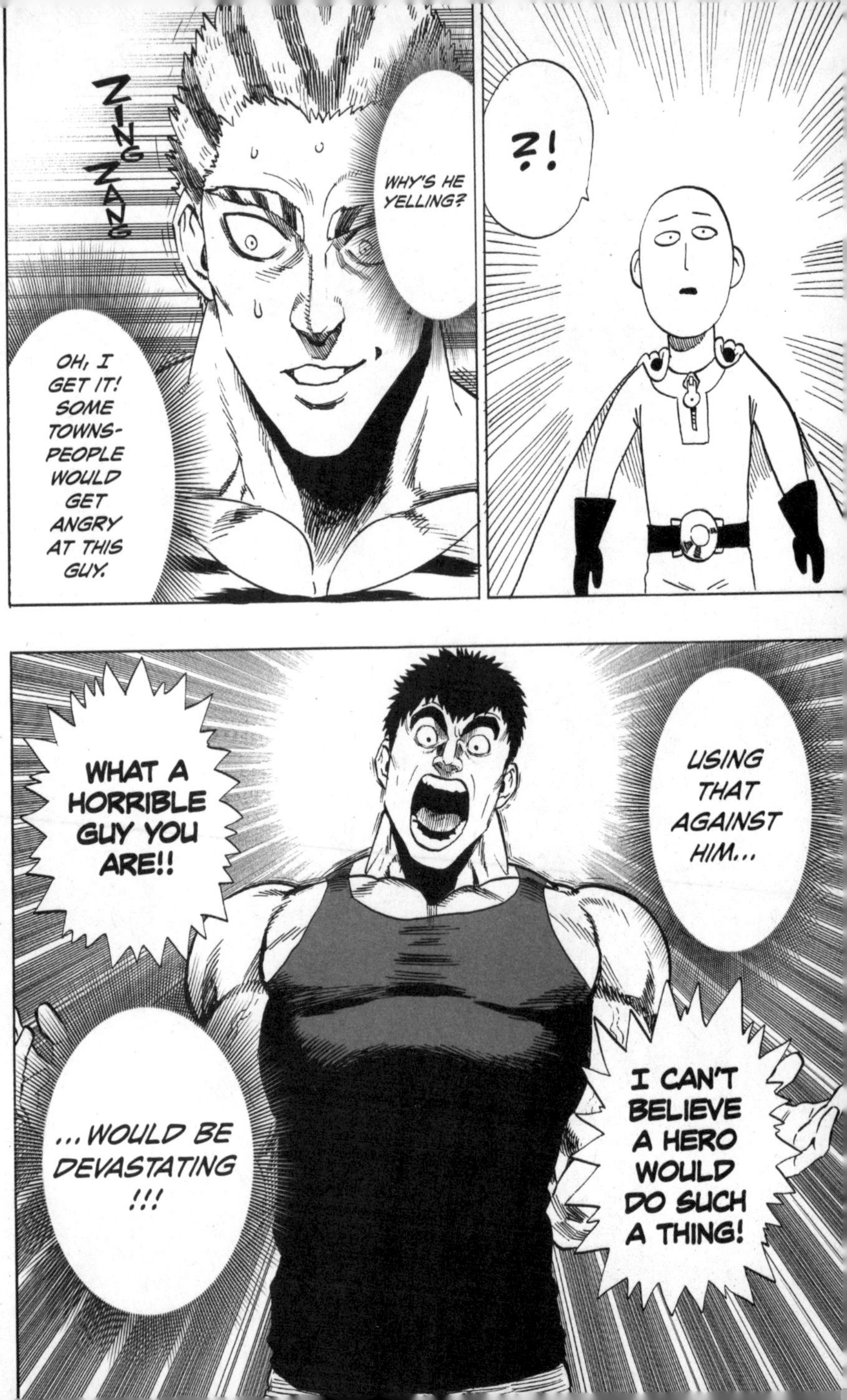
?!
WHY'S HE YELLING?
ZING ZANG
OH, I GET IT! SOME TOWNS-PEOPLE WOULD GET ANGRY AT THIS GUY.
USING THAT AGAINST HIM...
WHAT A HORRIBLE GUY YOU ARE!!
I CAN'T BELIEVE A HERO WOULD DO SUCH A THING!
...WOULD BE DEVASTATING!!!

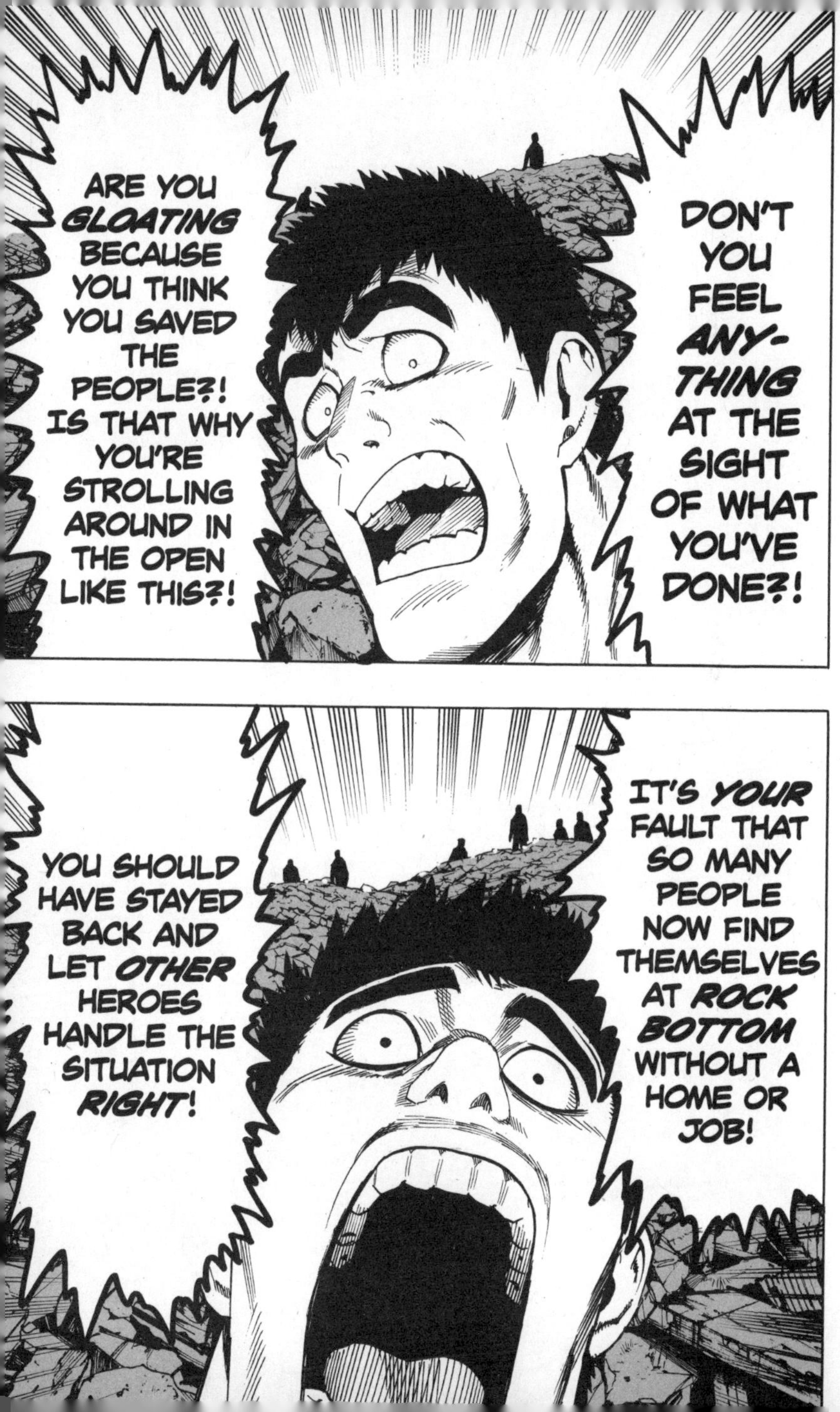
DON'T YOU FEEL ANYTHING AT THE SIGHT OF WHAT YOU'VE DONE?!
ARE YOU GLOATING BECAUSE YOU THINK YOU SAVED THE PEOPLE?! IS THAT WHY YOU'RE STROLLING AROUND IN THE OPEN LIKE THIS?!
IT'S YOUR FAULT THAT SO MANY PEOPLE NOW FIND THEMSELVES AT ROCK BOTTOM WITHOUT A HOME OR JOB!
YOU SHOULD HAVE STAYED BACK AND LET OTHER HEROES HANDLE THE SITUATION RIGHT!

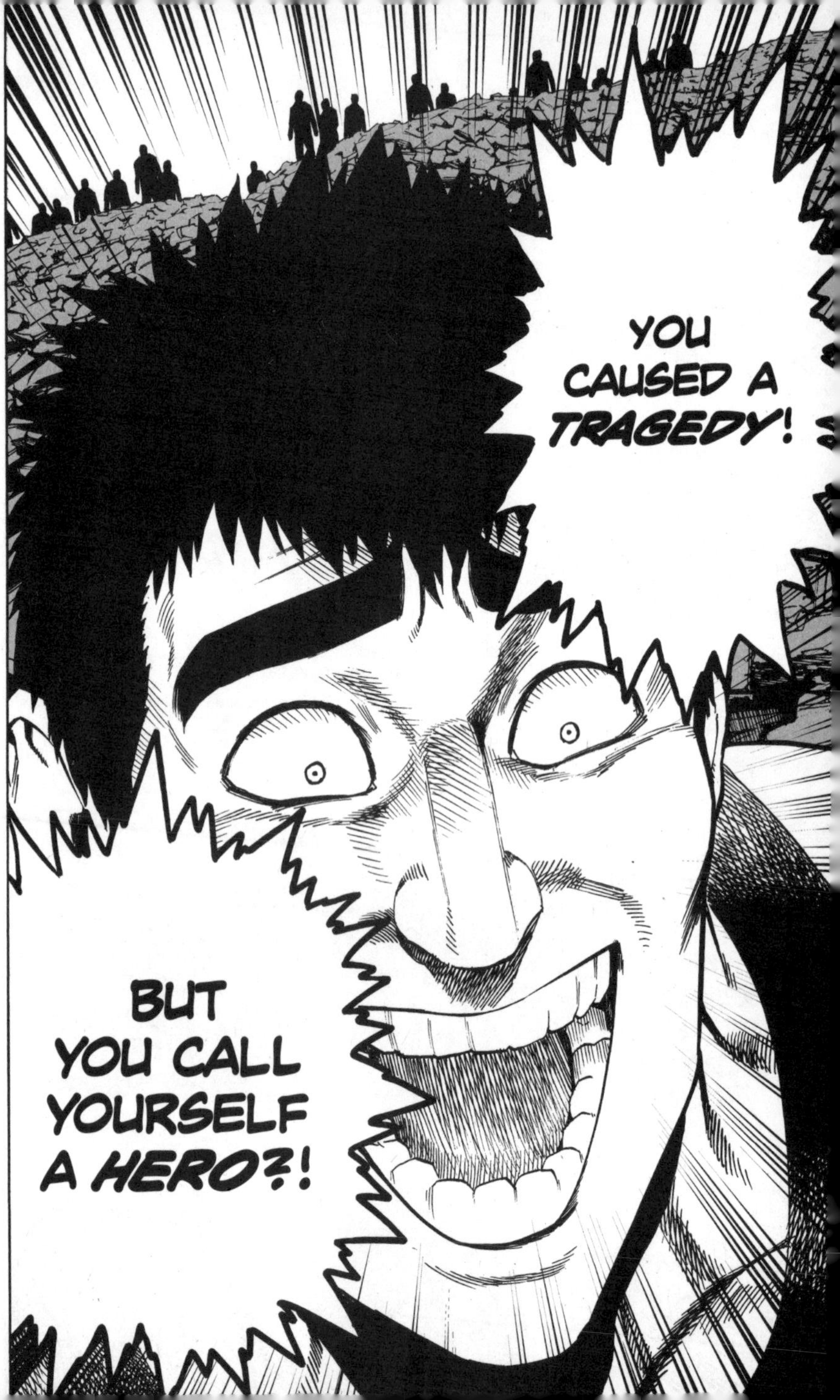
YOU CAUSED A TRAGEDY!
BUT YOU CALL YOURSELF A HERO?!

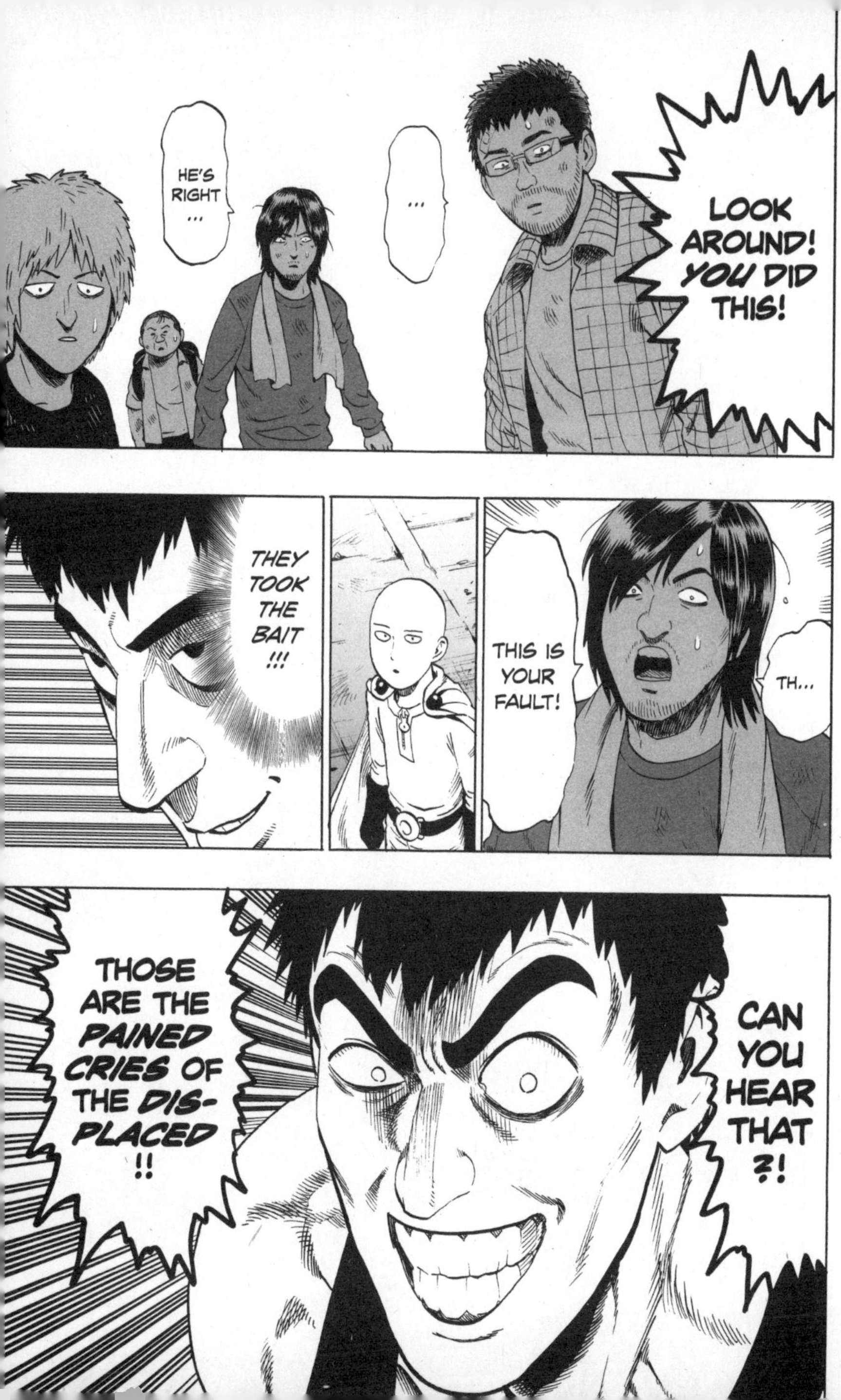
LOOK AROUND! YOU DID THIS!
...
HE'S RIGHT ...
TH...
THIS IS YOUR FAULT!
THEY TOOK THE BAIT!!!
CAN YOU HEAR THAT?!
THOSE ARE THE PAINED CRIES OF THE DIS-PLACED!!

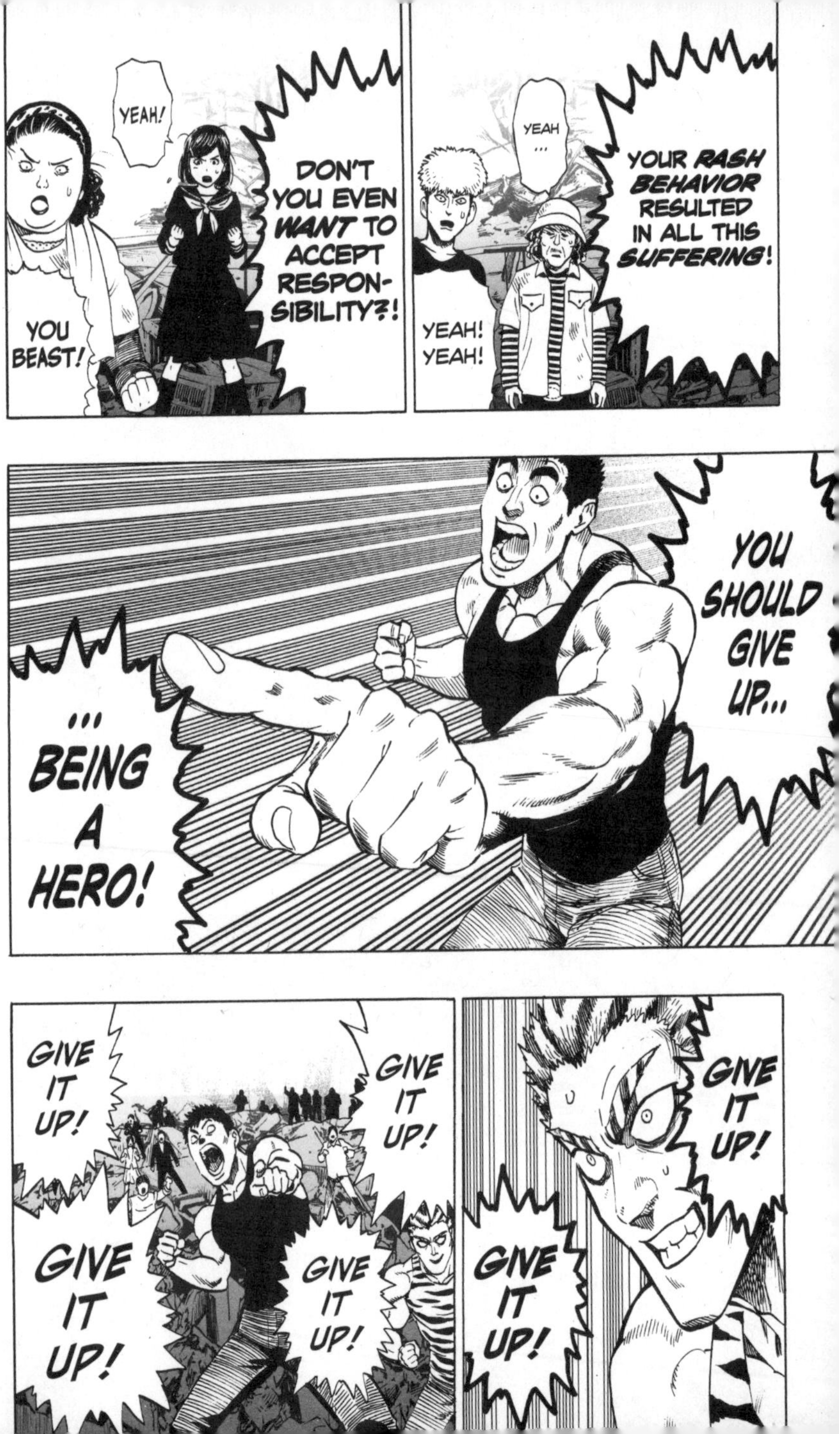
YOUR RASH BEHAVIOR RESULTED IN ALL THIS SUFFERING!
YEAH ...
YEAH! YEAH!
DON'T YOU EVEN WANT TO ACCEPT RESPONSIBILITY?!
YEAH!
YOU BEAST!
YOU SHOULD GIVE UP...
... BEING A HERO!
GIVE IT UP!
GIVE IT UP!
GIVE IT UP!
GIVE IT UP!
GIVE IT UP!
GIVE IT UP!

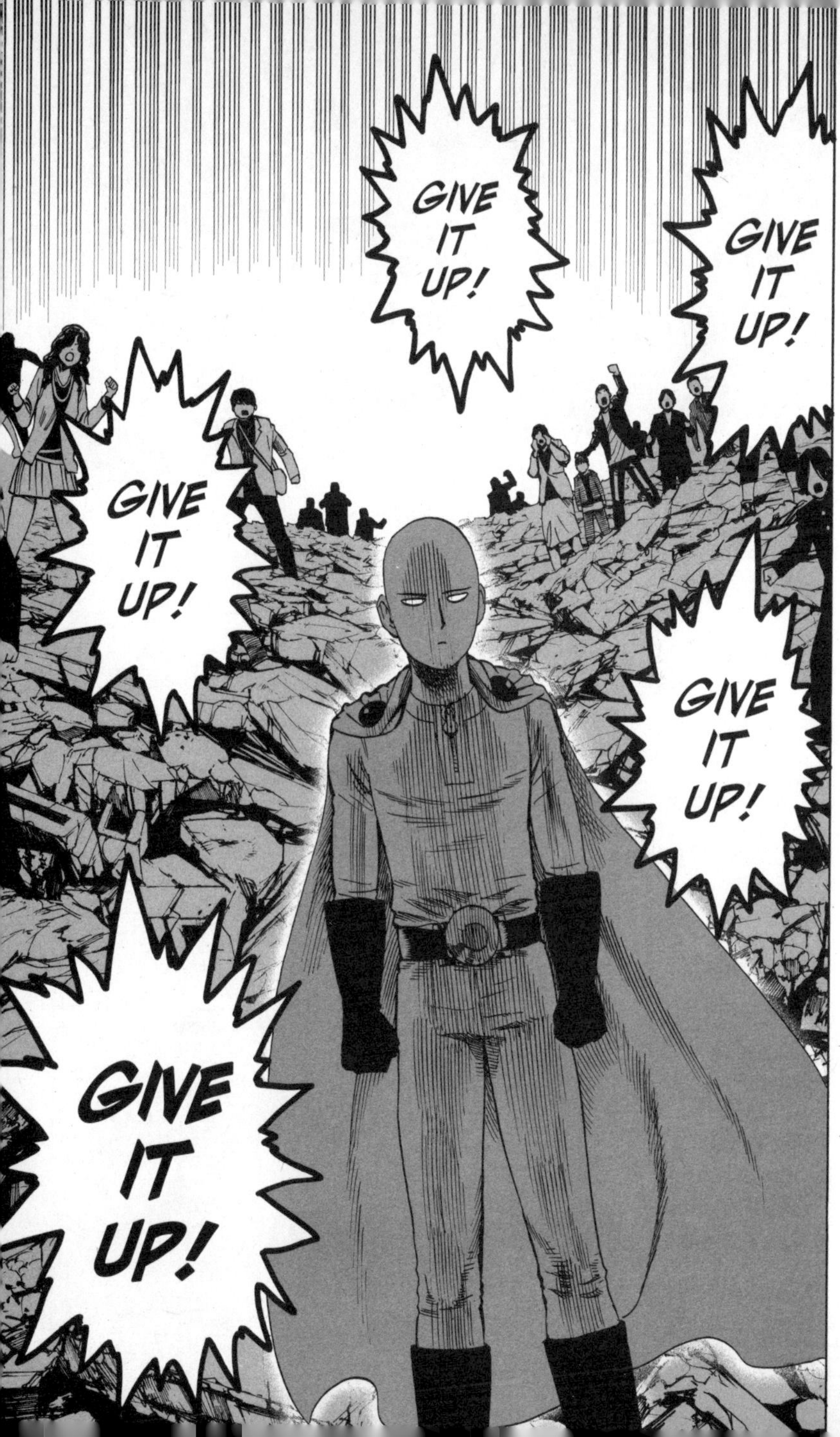
GIVE IT UP!
GIVE IT UP!
GIVE IT UP!
GIVE IT UP!
GIVE IT UP!

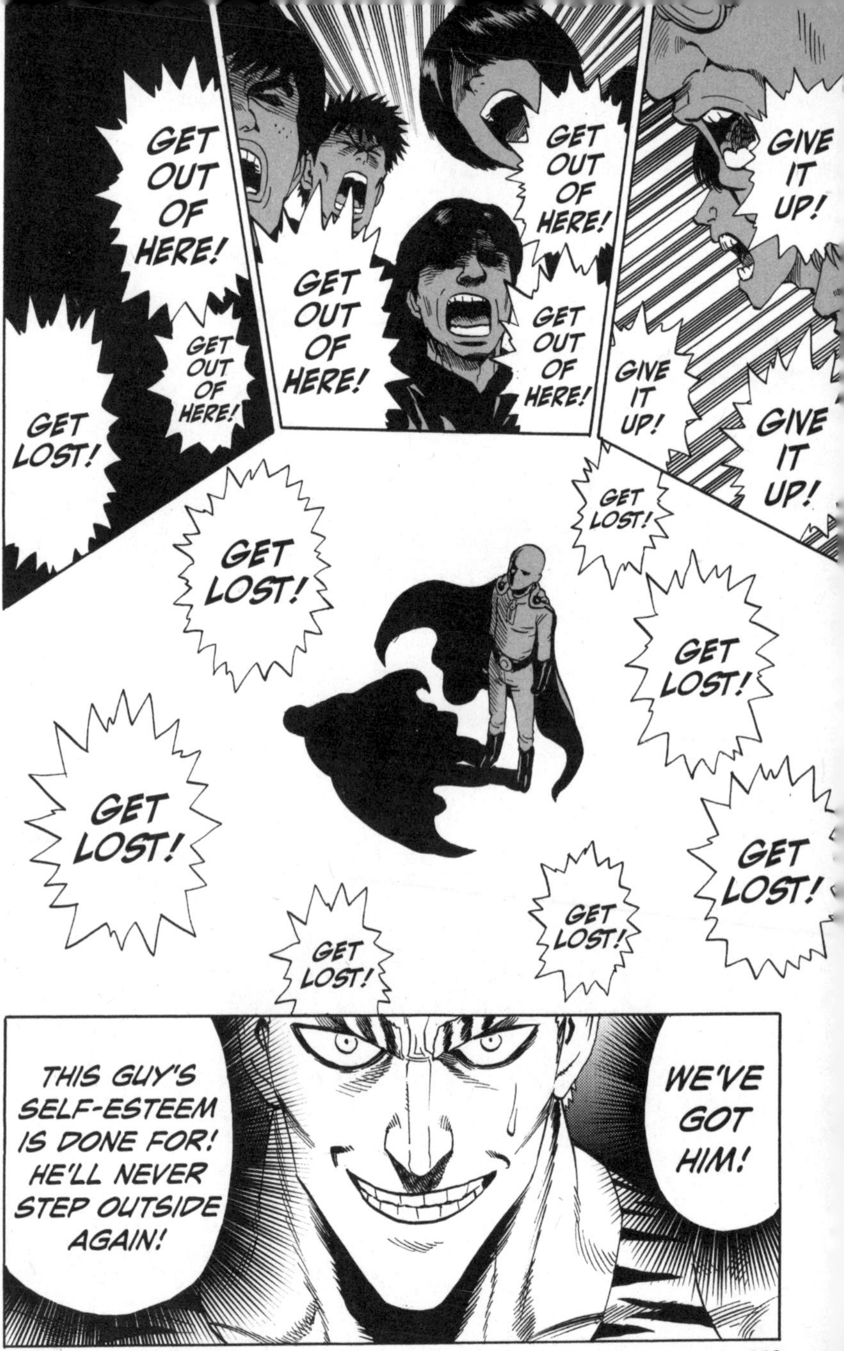
GIVE IT UP!
GIVE IT UP!
GIVE IT UP!
GET OUT OF HERE!
GET OUT OF HERE!
GET OUT OF HERE!
GET OUT OF HERE!
GET OUT OF HERE!
GET LOST!
GET LOST!
GET LOST!
GET LOST!
GET LOST!
GET LOST!
GET LOST!
GET LOST!
WE'VE GOT HIM!
THIS GUY'S SELF-ESTEEM IS DONE FOR! HE'LL NEVER STEP OUTSIDE AGAIN!

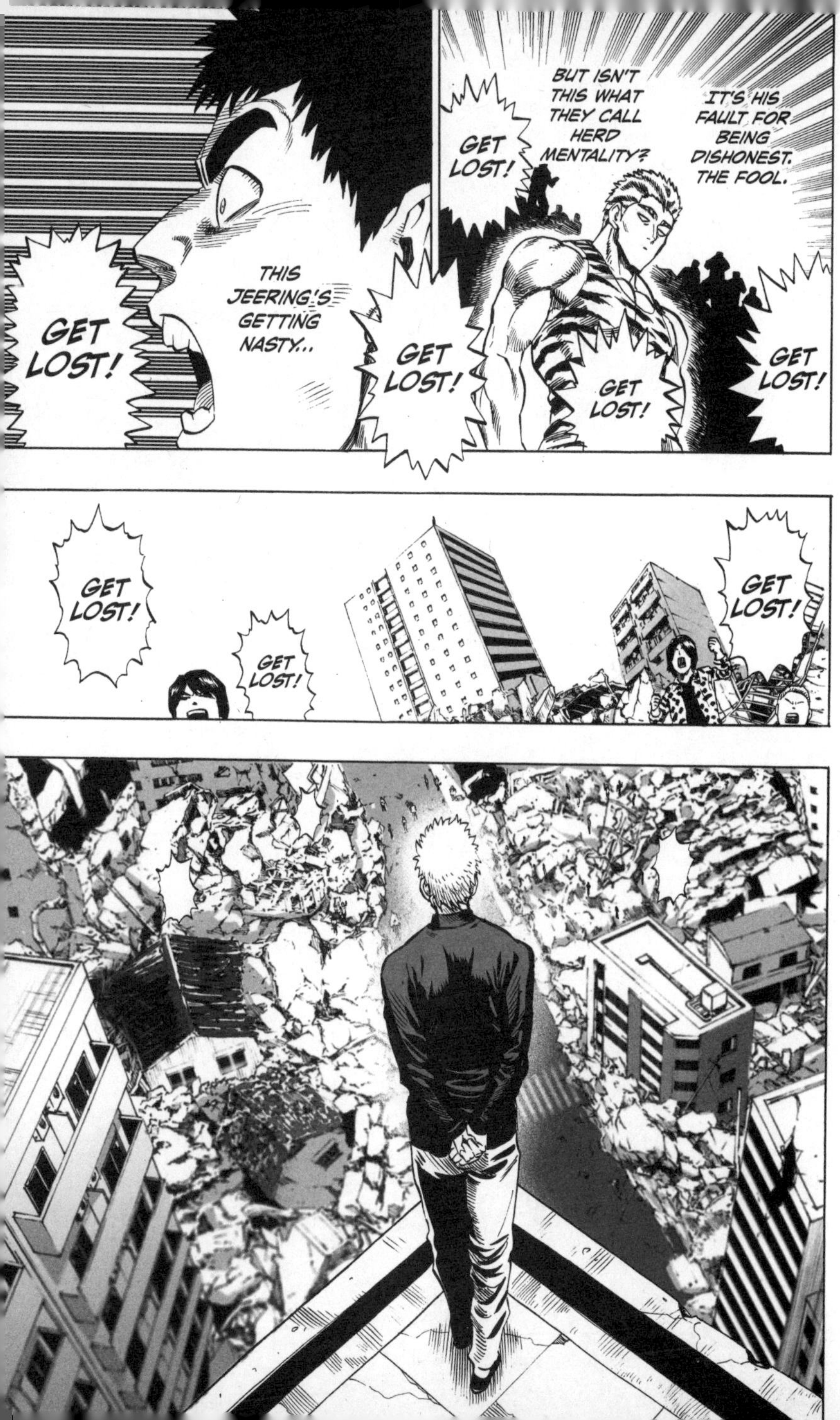
IT'S HIS FAULT FOR BEING DISHONEST. THE FOOL.
BUT ISN'T THIS WHAT THEY CALL HERD MENTALITY?
GET LOST!
GET LOST!
GET LOST!
GET LOST!
THIS JEERING'S GETTING NASTY...
GET LOST!
GET LOST!
GET LOST!
GET LOST!

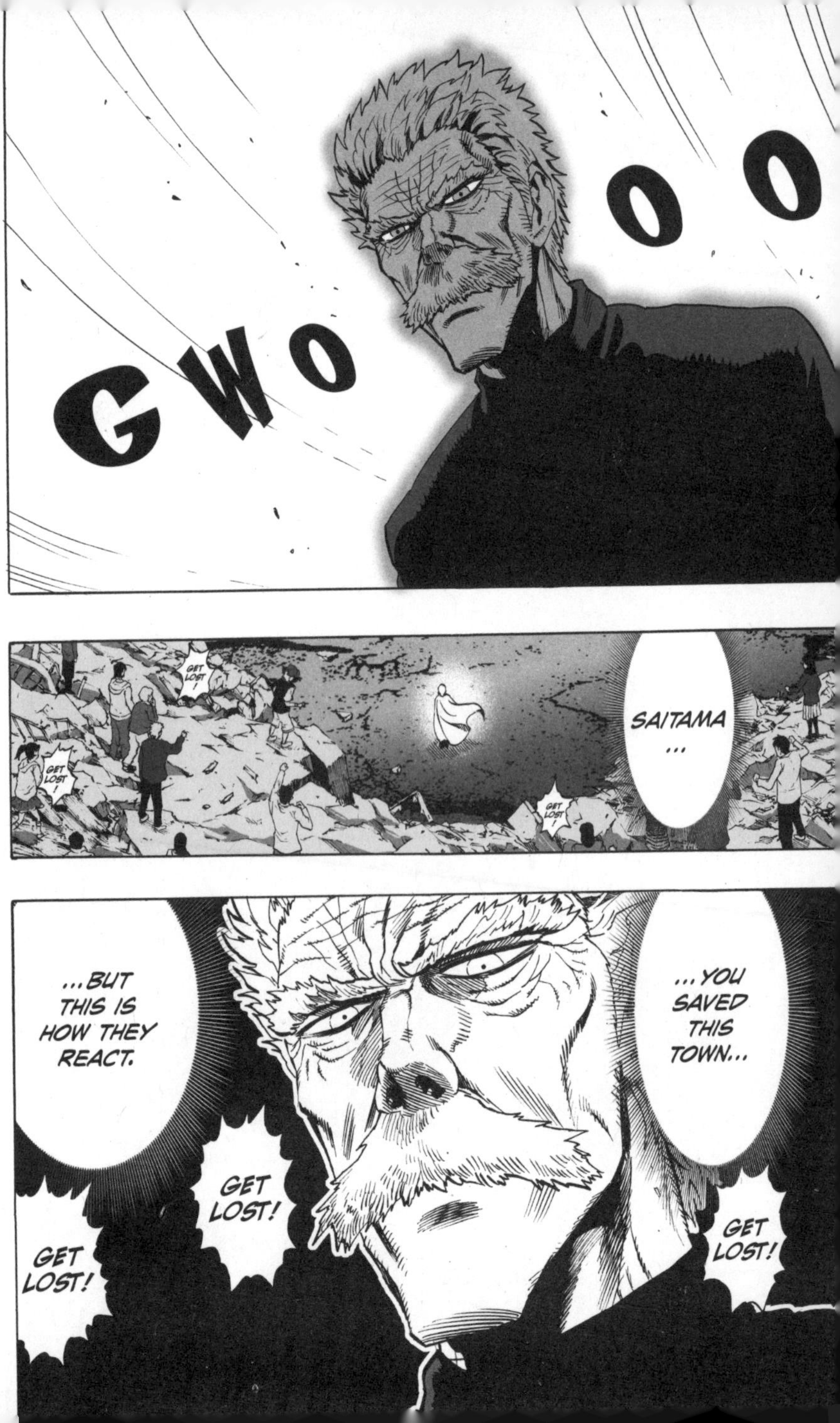
GWOOOO
SAITAMA...
GET LOST!
GET LOST!
GET LOST!
...YOU SAVED THIS TOWN...
GET LOST!
...BUT THIS IS HOW THEY REACT.
GET LOST!
GET LOST!

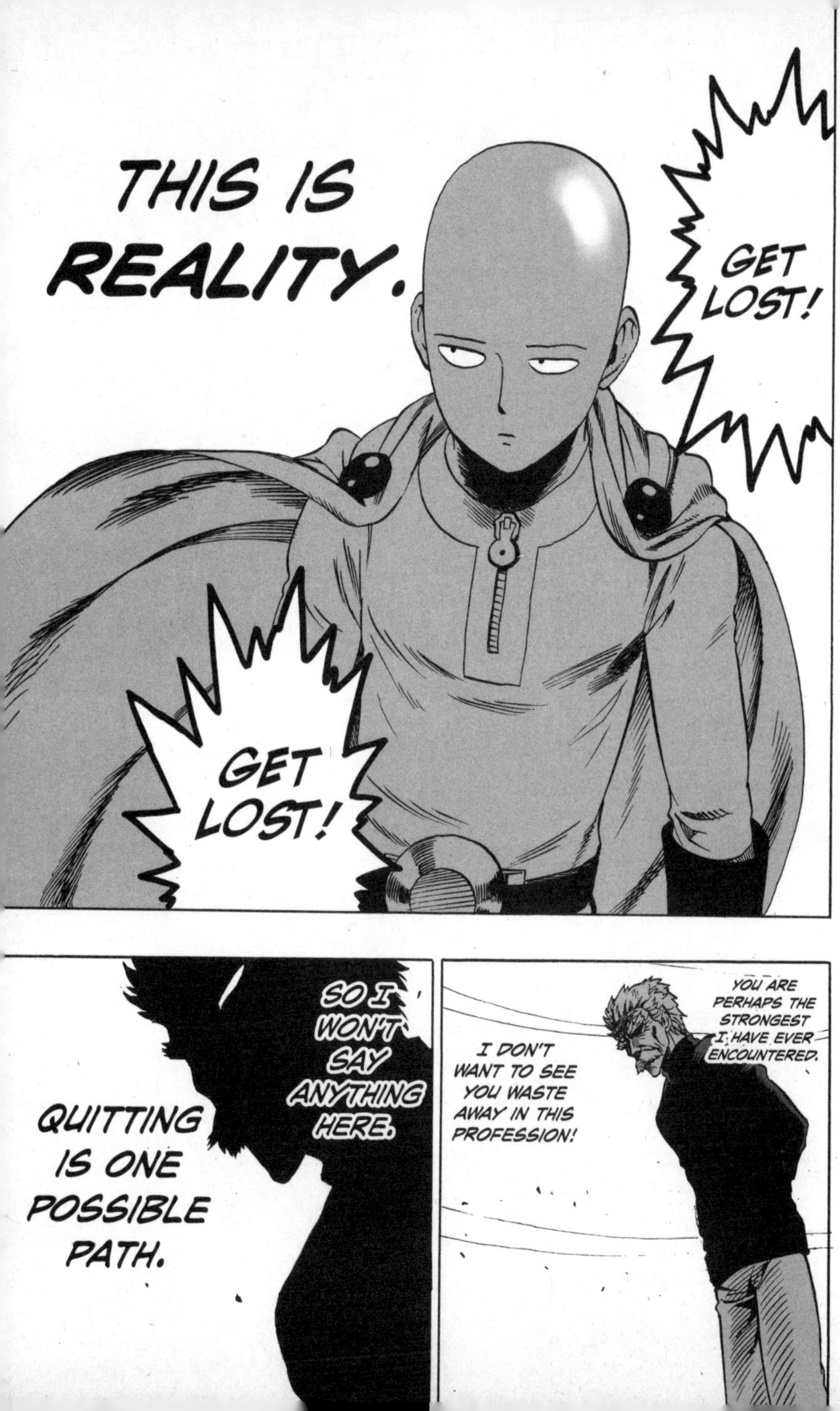
GET LOST!
THIS IS REALITY.
GET LOST!
YOU ARE PERHAPS THE STRONGEST I HAVE EVER ENCOUNTERED.
I DON'T WANT TO SEE YOU WASTE AWAY IN THIS PROFESSION!
SO I WON'T SAY ANYTHING HERE.
QUITTING IS ONE POSSIBLE PATH.

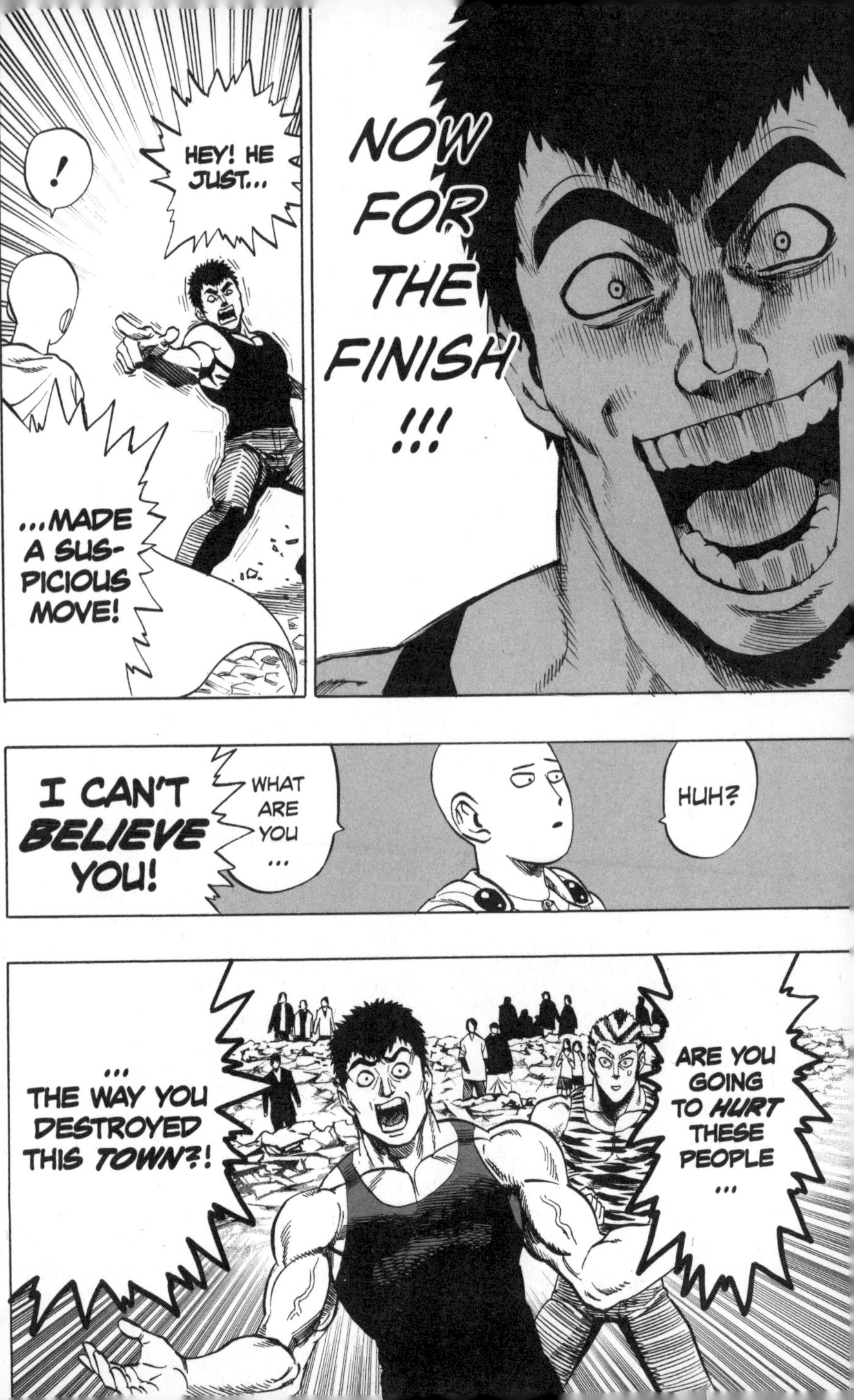
NOW FOR THE FINISH !!!
!
HEY! HE JUST...
...MADE A SUS-PICIOUS MOVE!
HUH?
WHAT ARE YOU ...
I CAN'T BELIEVE YOU!
ARE YOU GOING TO HURT THESE PEOPLE ...
... THE WAY YOU DESTROYED THIS TOWN?!

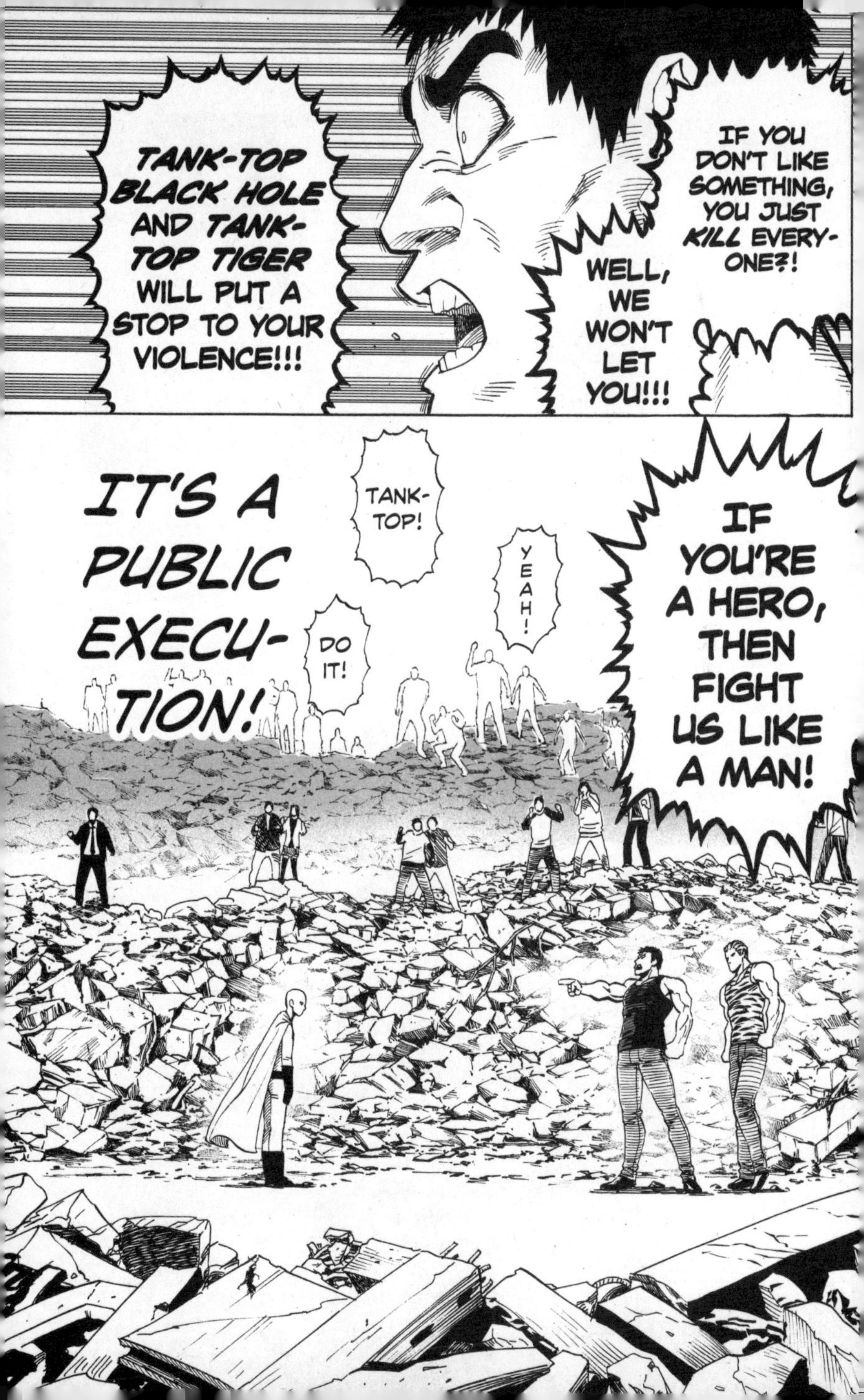
IF YOU DON'T LIKE SOMETHING, YOU JUST KILL EVERYONE?!
WELL, WE WON'T LET YOU!!!
TANK-TOP BLACK HOLE AND TANK-TOP TIGER WILL PUT A STOP TO YOUR VIOLENCE!!!
IF YOU'RE A HERO, THEN FIGHT US LIKE A MAN!
TANK-TOP!
YEAH!
DO IT!
IT'S A PUBLIC EXECUTION!

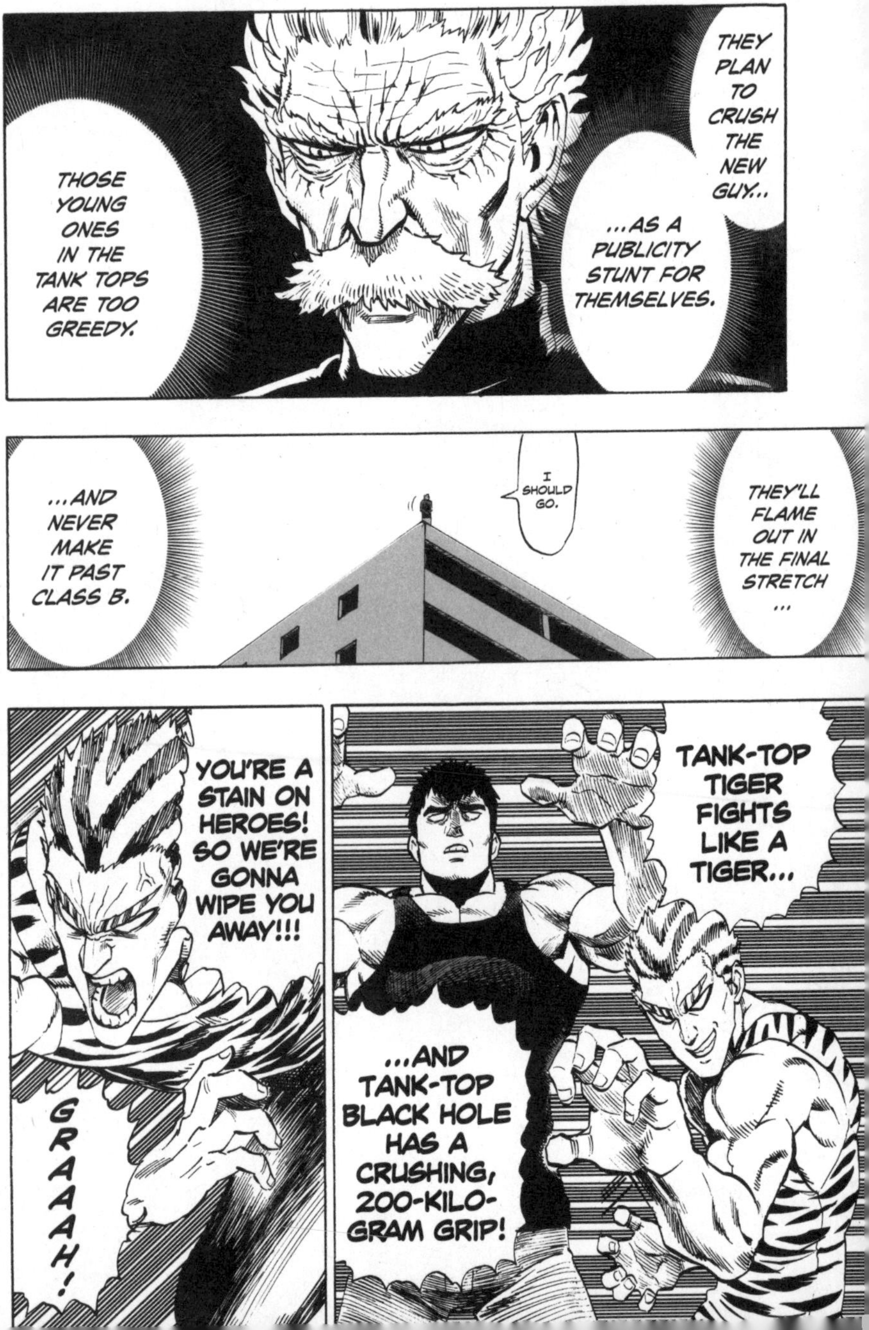
THEY PLAN TO CRUSH THE NEW GUY...
...AS A PUBLICITY STUNT FOR THEMSELVES.
THOSE YOUNG ONES IN THE TANK TOPS ARE TOO GREEDY.
THEY'LL FLAME OUT IN THE FINAL STRETCH ...
I SHOULD GO.
...AND NEVER MAKE IT PAST CLASS B.
TANK-TOP TIGER FIGHTS LIKE A TIGER...
...AND TANK-TOP BLACK HOLE HAS A CRUSHING, 200-KILO-GRAM GRIP!
YOU'RE A STAIN ON HEROES! SO WE'RE GONNA WIPE YOU AWAY!!!
GRAAAAH!

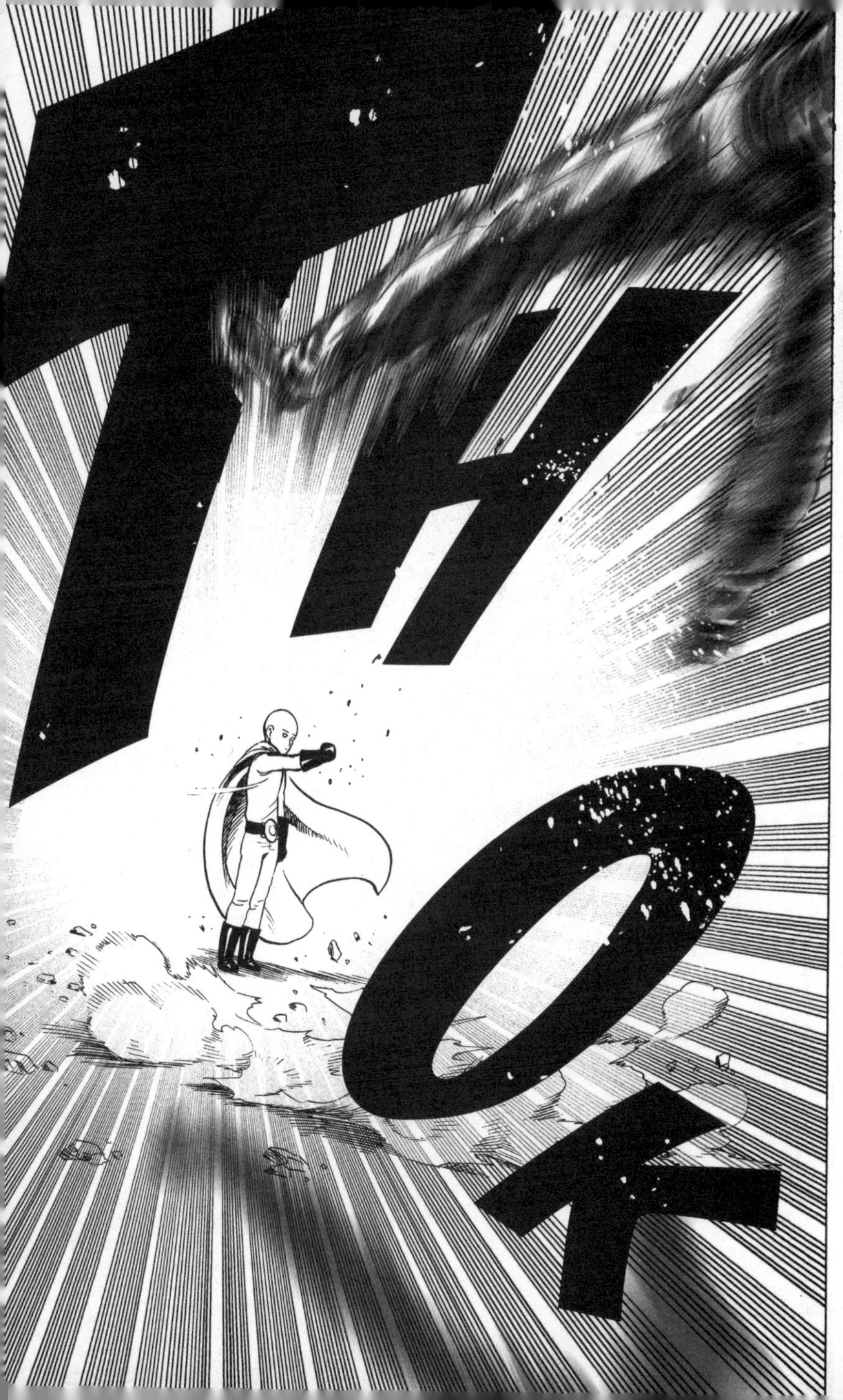
THOK

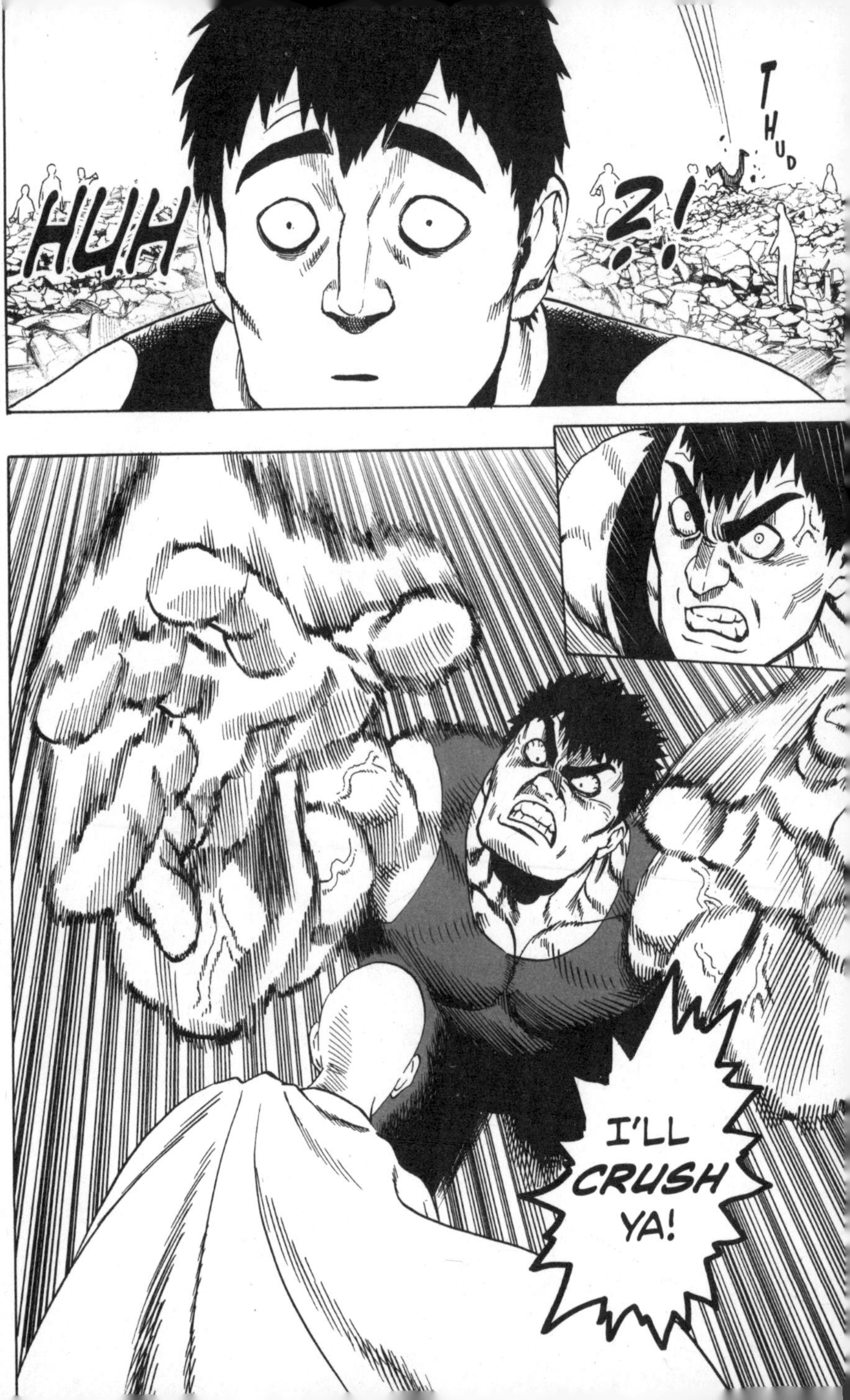
THUD
?!
HUH
I'LL CRUSH YA!

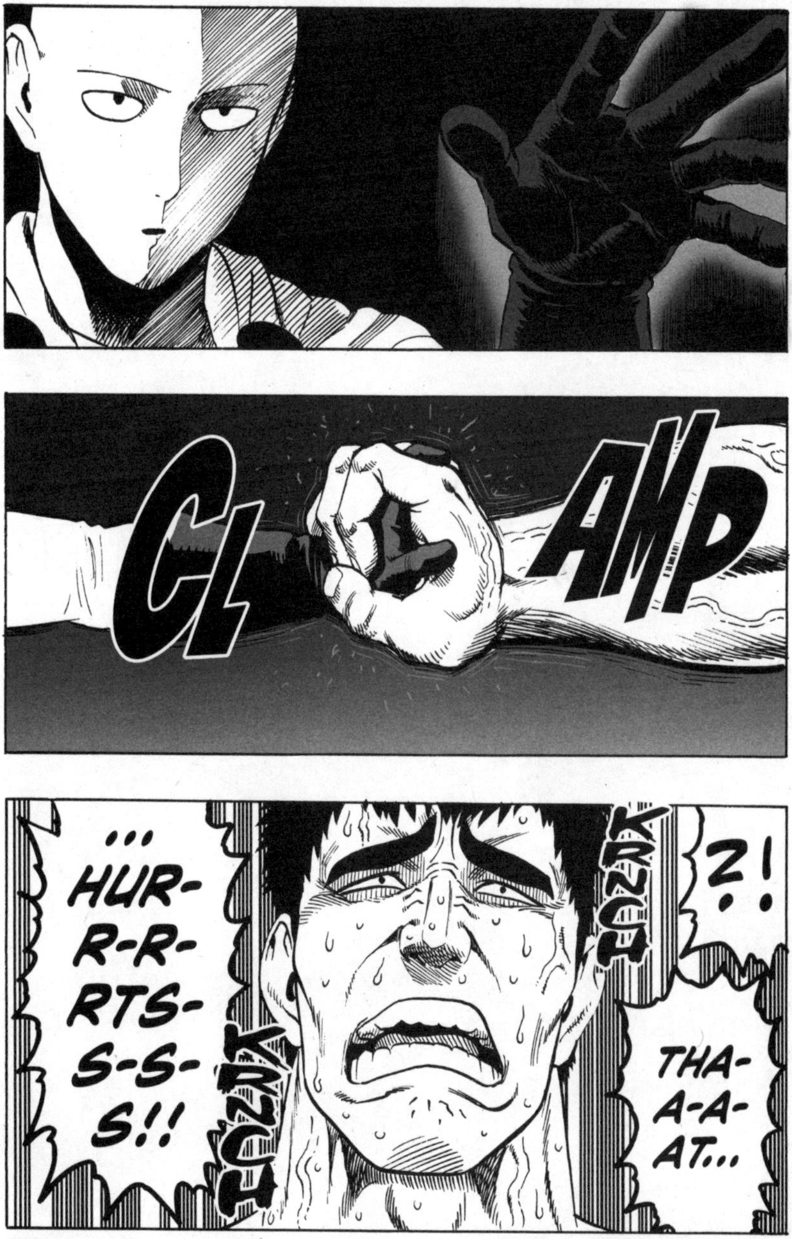
CLAMP
?!
KRNCH
THA-A-A-AT...
...HURR-R-RTS-S-S-S!!
KRNCH

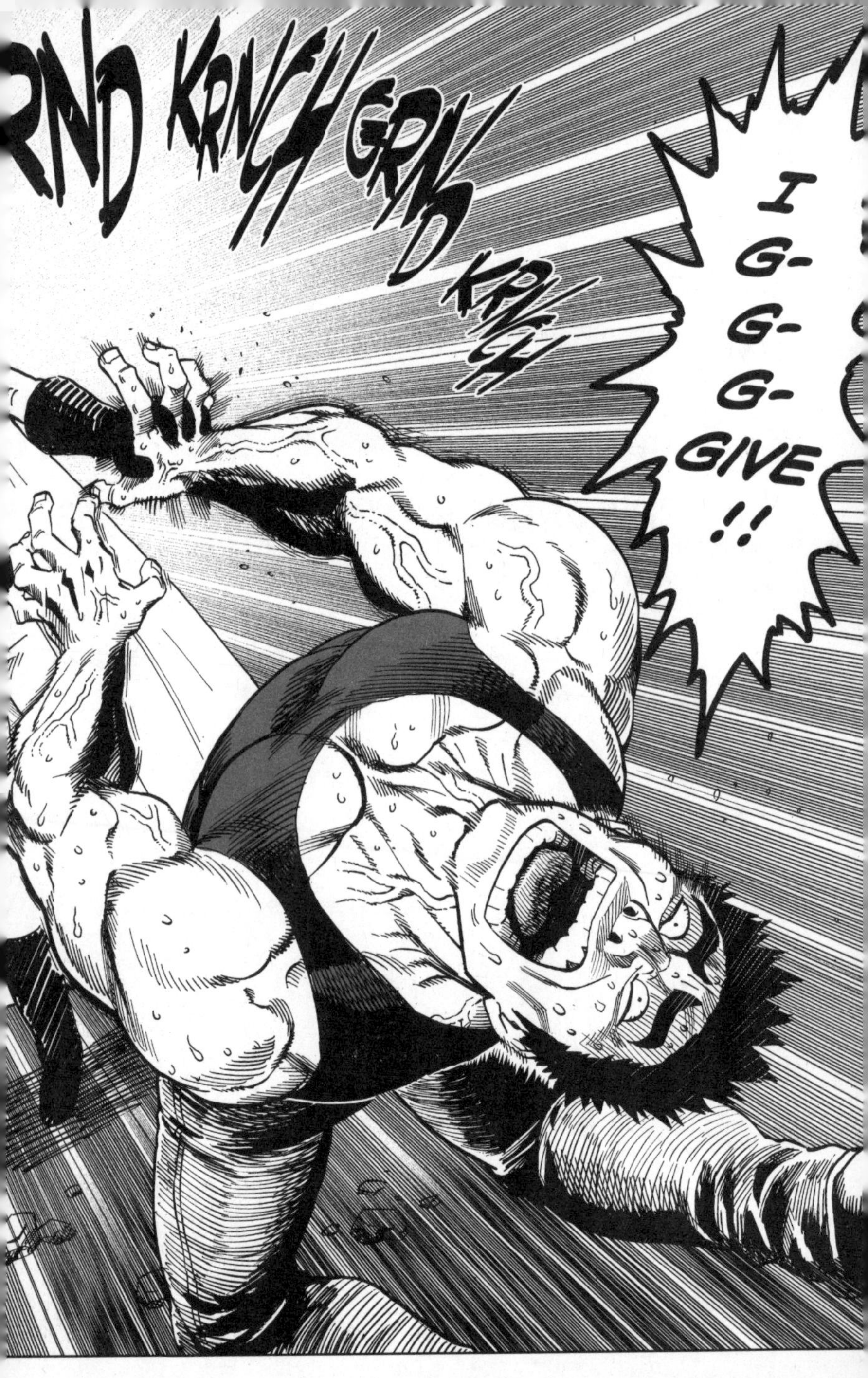
I G- G- G- GIVE !!
RND KRNCH GRND KRNCH

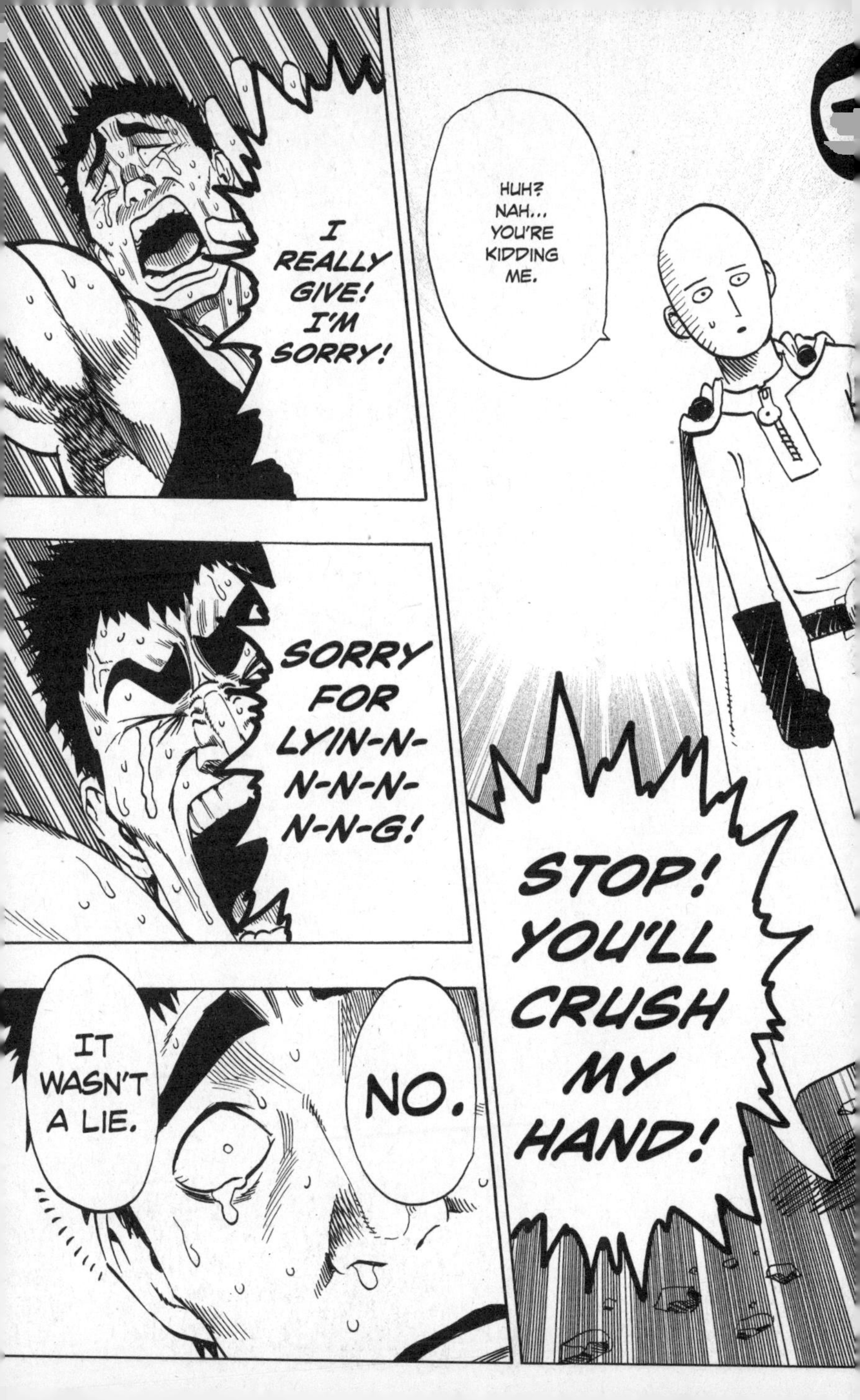
HUH? NAH... YOU'RE KIDDING ME.
STOP! YOU'LL CRUSH MY HAND!
I REALLY GIVE! I'M SORRY!
SORRY FOR LYIN-N-N-N-N-N-N-G!
NO.
IT WASN'T A LIE.

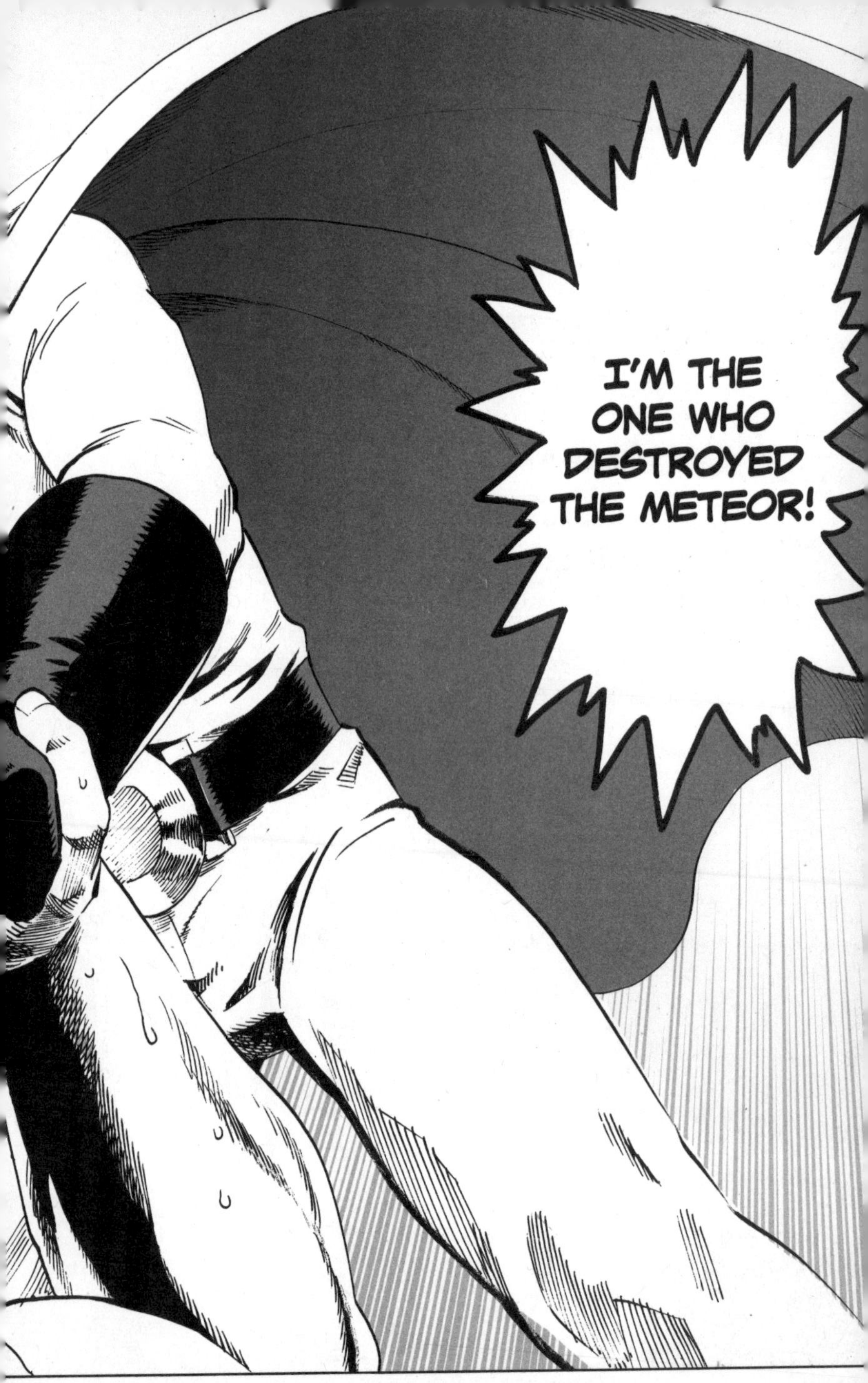
I'M THE ONE WHO DESTROYED THE METEOR!

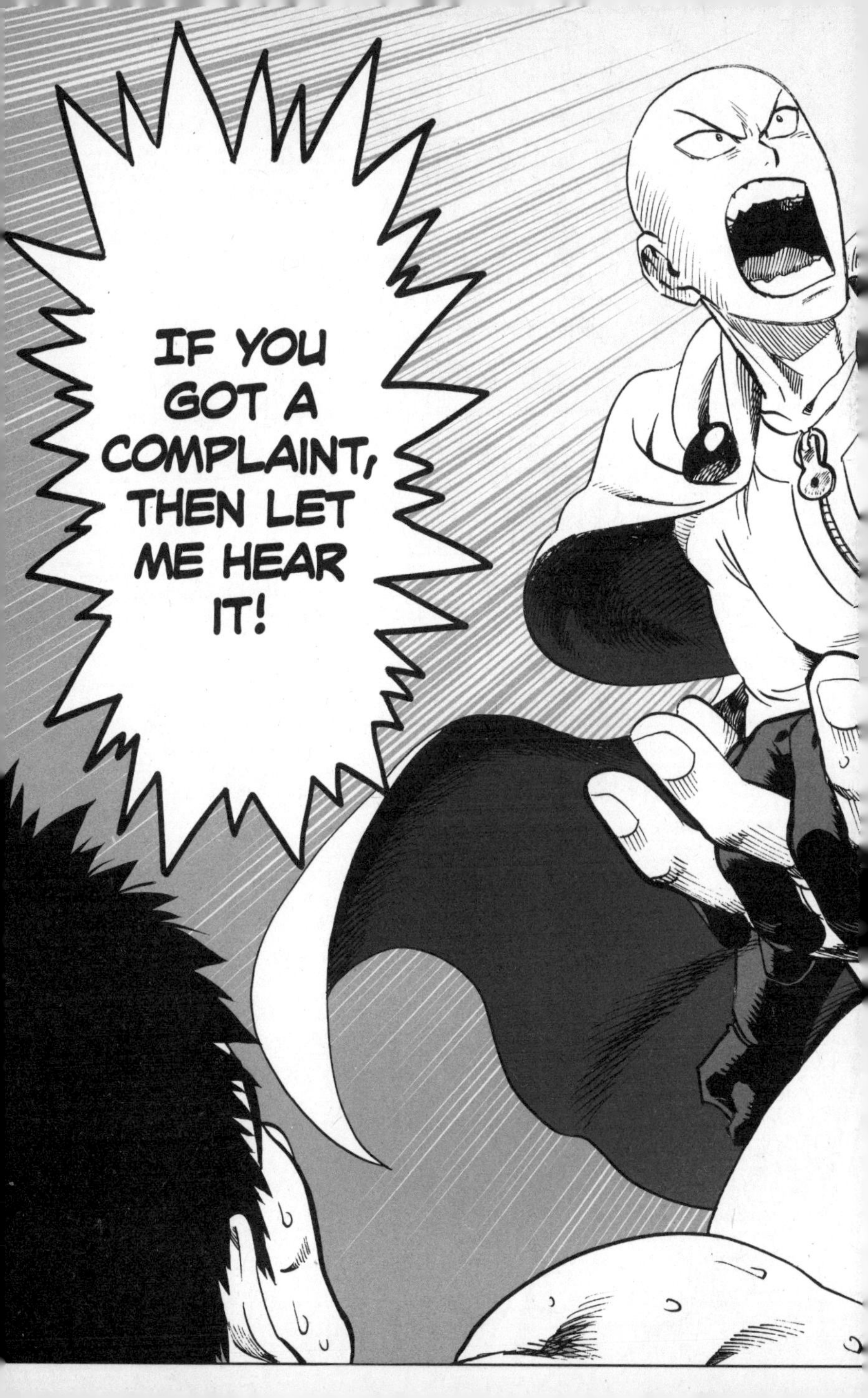
IF YOU GOT A COMPLAINT, THEN LET ME HEAR IT!

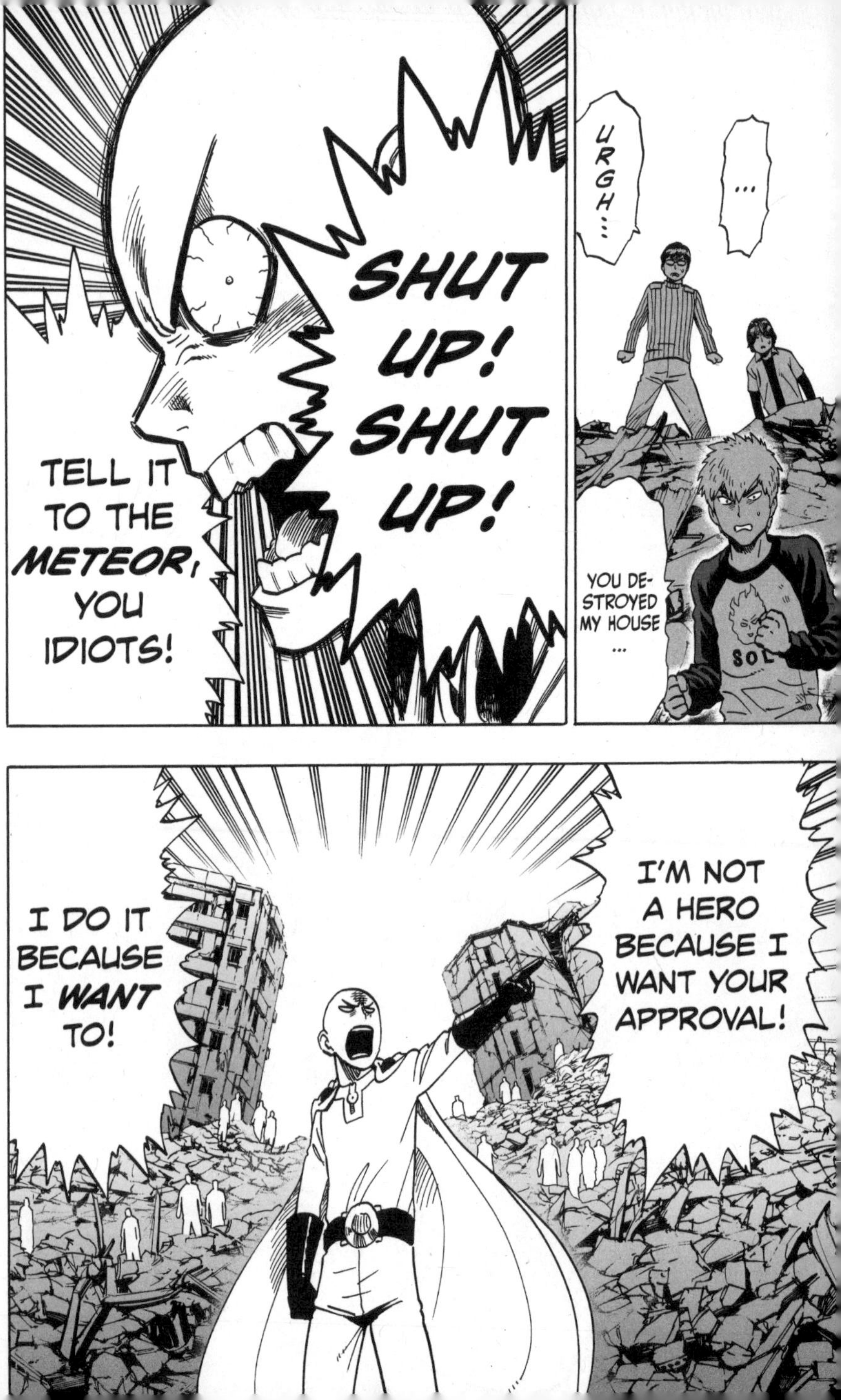
...
URGH...
YOU DESTROYED MY HOUSE ...
SHUT UP! SHUT UP!
TELL IT TO THE *METEOR*, YOU IDIOTS!
I'M NOT A HERO BECAUSE I WANT YOUR APPROVAL!
I DO IT BECAUSE I *WANT* TO!

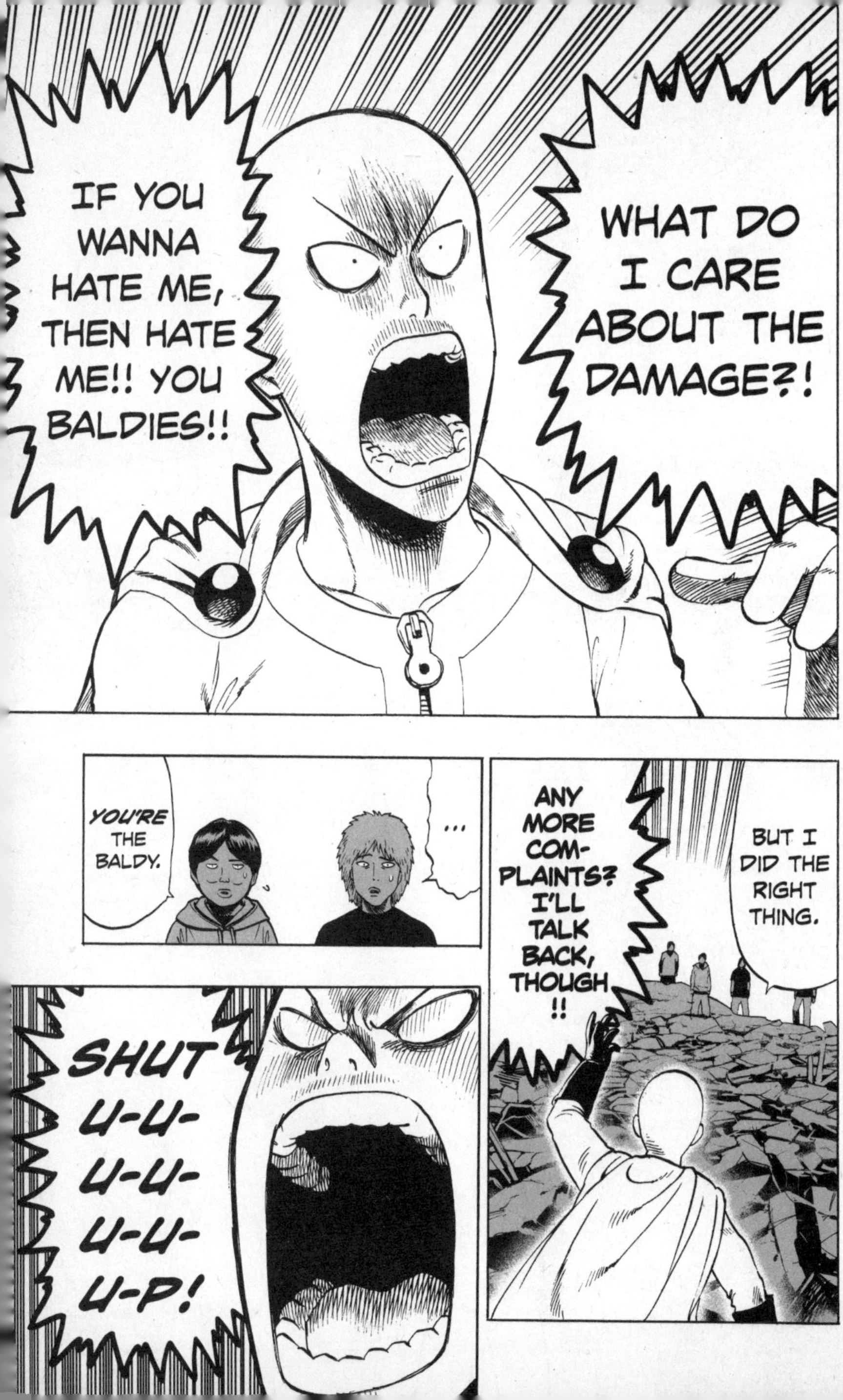
WHAT DO I CARE ABOUT THE DAMAGE?!
IF YOU WANNA HATE ME, THEN HATE ME!! YOU BALDIES!!
BUT I DID THE RIGHT THING.
ANY MORE COM-PLAINTS? I'LL TALK BACK, THOUGH!!
...
YOU'RE THE BALDY.
SHUT U-U-U-U-U-U-U-P!

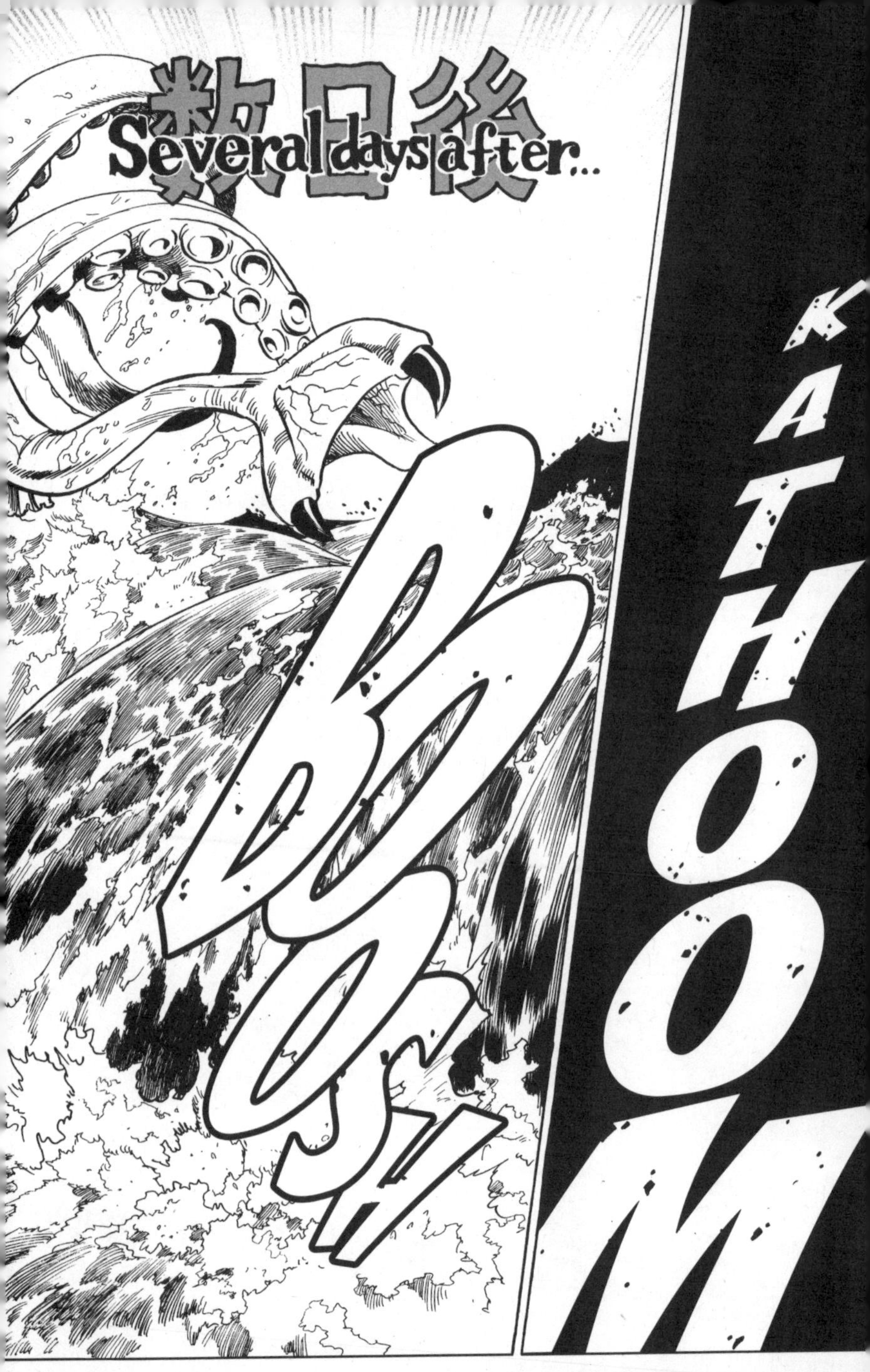
KATHOOM
数日後
Several days after...

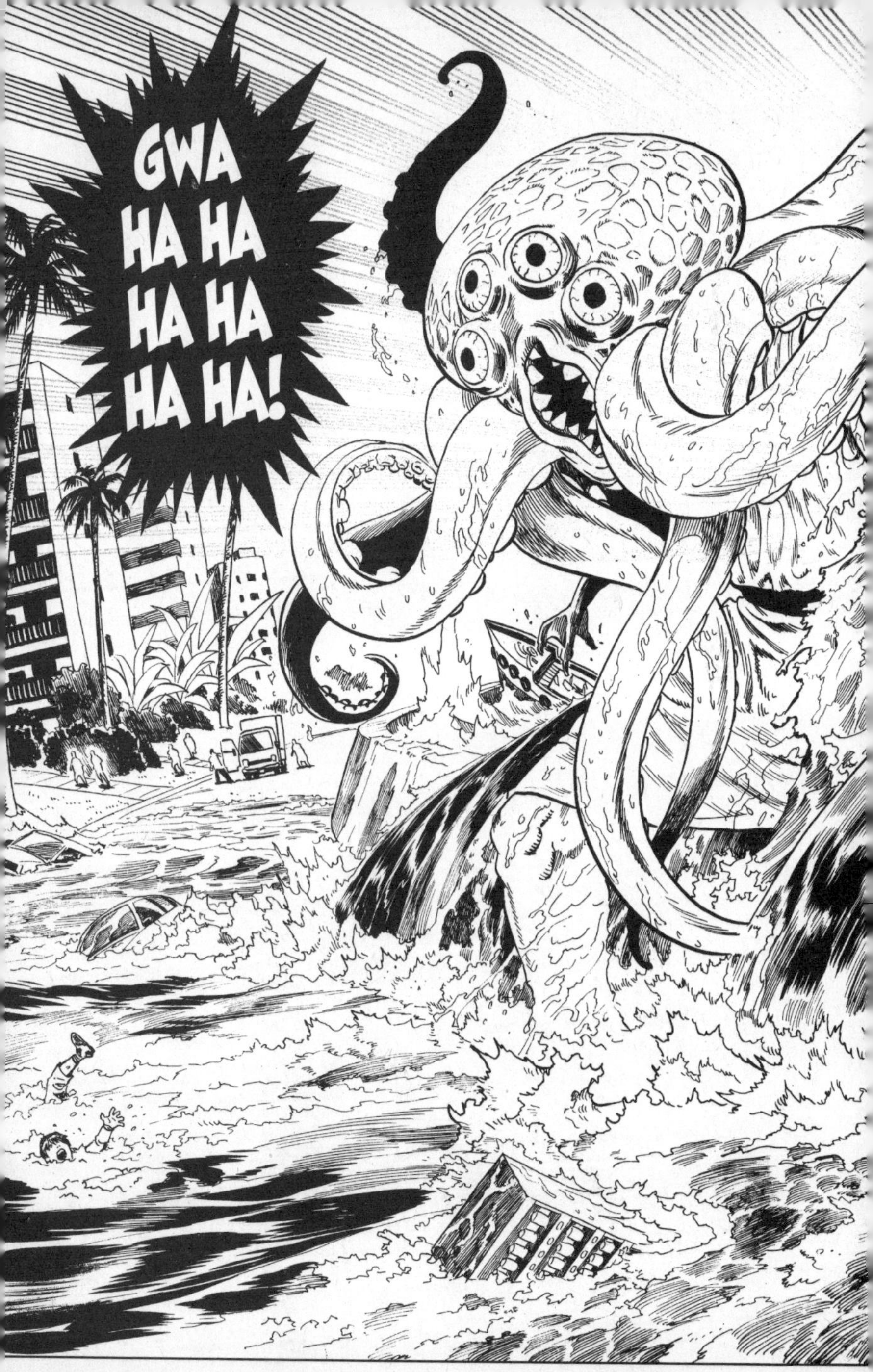
GWA HA HA HA HA HA HA!

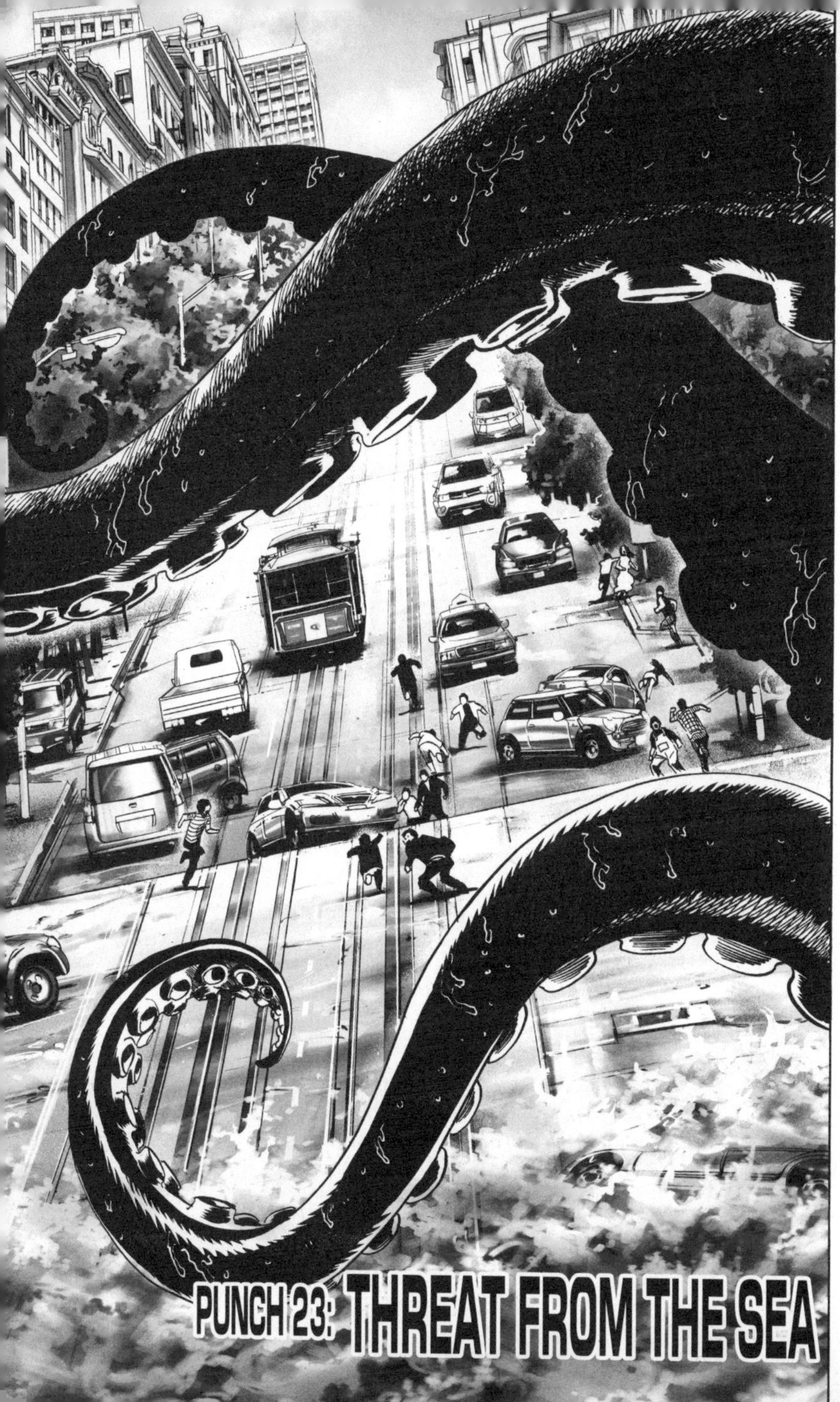
PUNCH 23: THREAT FROM THE SEA

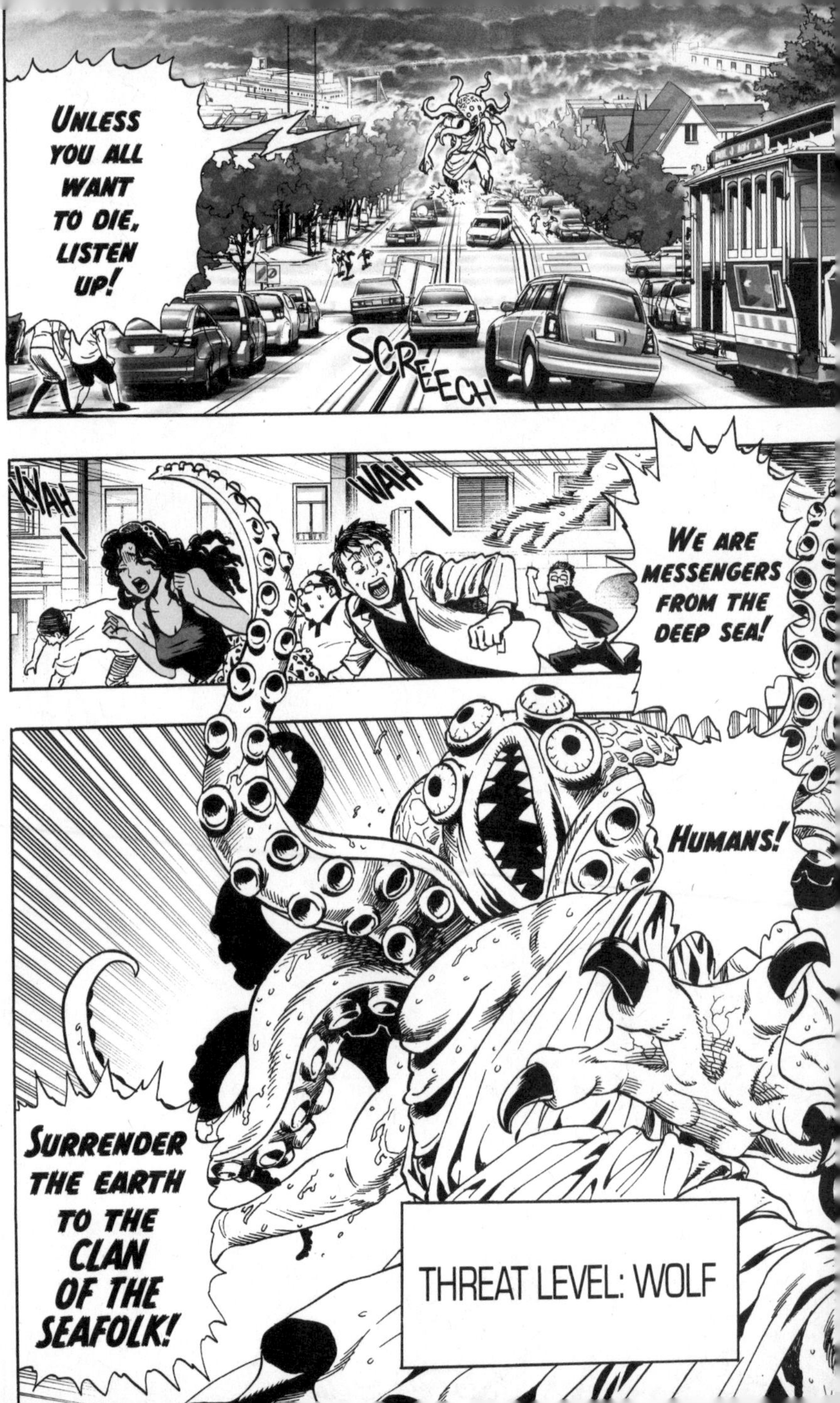
UNLESS YOU ALL WANT TO DIE, LISTEN UP!
SCREEECH
WE ARE MESSENGERS FROM THE DEEP SEA!
WAH!
KYAH!
HUMANS!
SURRENDER THE EARTH TO THE CLAN OF THE SEAFOLK!
THREAT LEVEL: WOLF

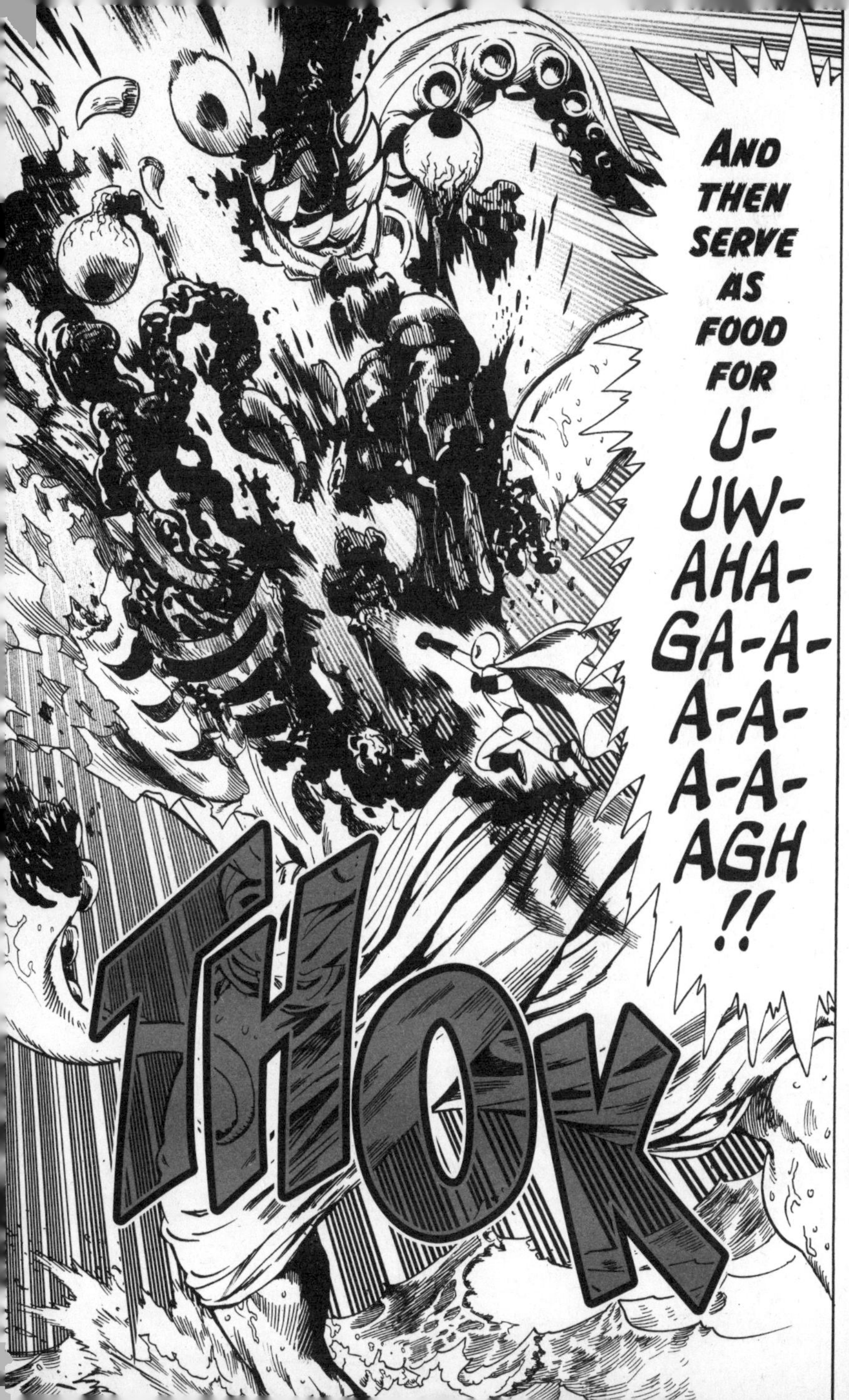

AND THEN SERVE AS FOOD FOR U- UW- AHA- GA-A- A-A- A-A- AGH!!
THOK

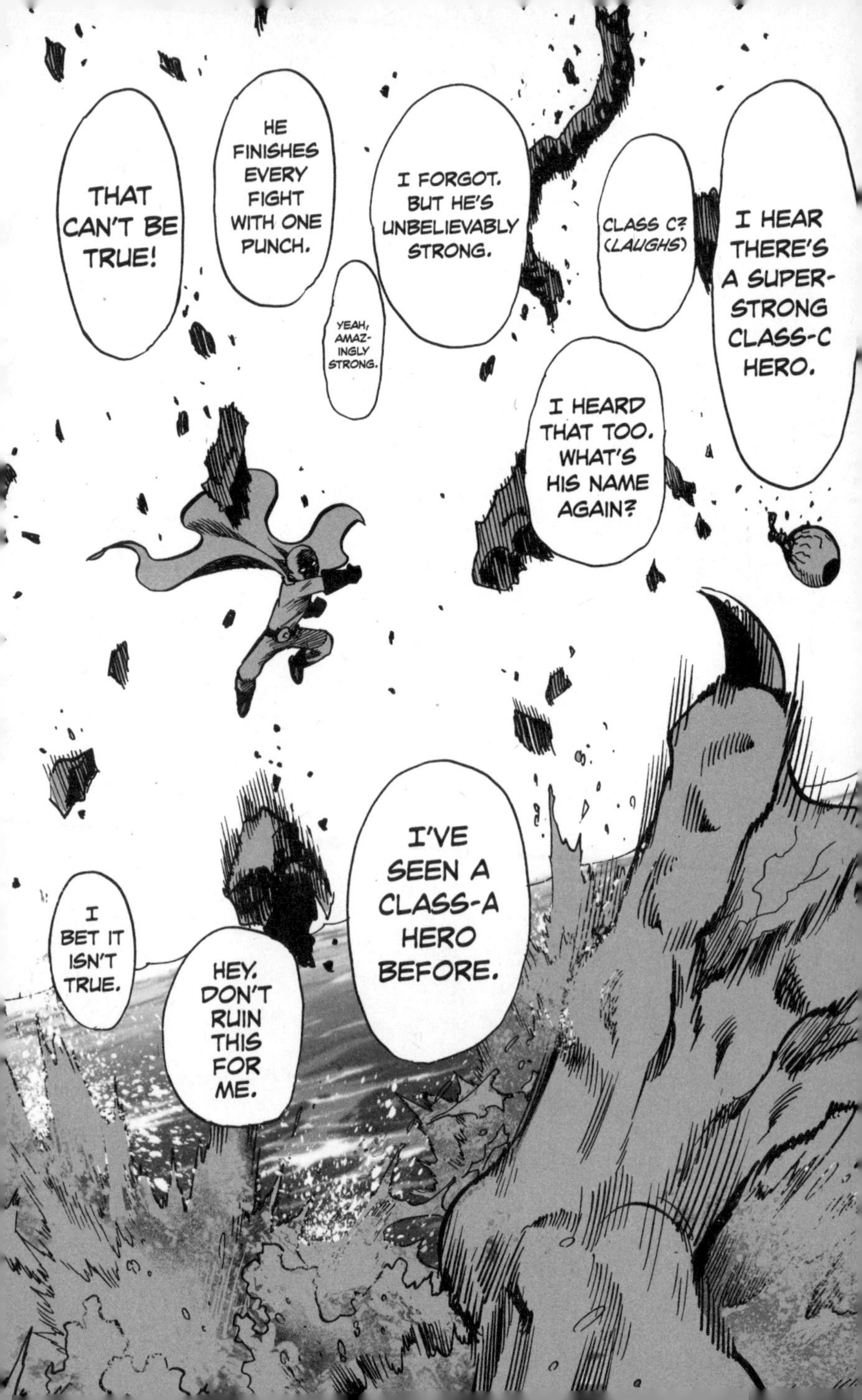
I HEAR THERE'S A SUPER-STRONG CLASS-C HERO.
CLASS C? (LAUGHS)
I HEARD THAT TOO. WHAT'S HIS NAME AGAIN?
I FORGOT. BUT HE'S UNBELIEVABLY STRONG.
YEAH, AMAZINGLY STRONG.
HE FINISHES EVERY FIGHT WITH ONE PUNCH.
THAT CAN'T BE TRUE!
I'VE SEEN A CLASS-A HERO BEFORE.
I BET IT ISN'T TRUE.
HEY. DON'T RUIN THIS FOR ME.

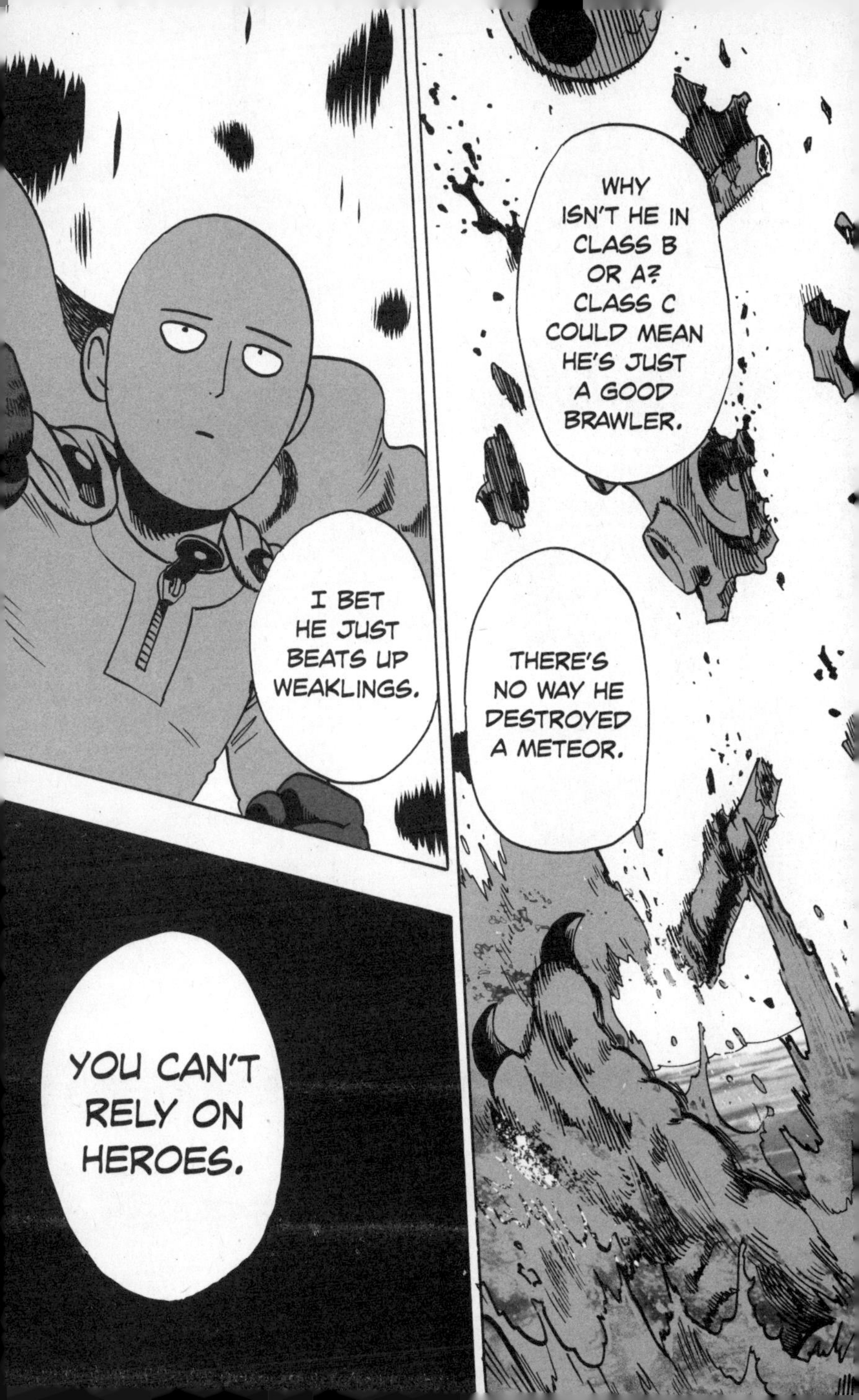
WHY ISN'T HE IN CLASS B OR A? CLASS C COULD MEAN HE'S JUST A GOOD BRAWLER.
THERE'S NO WAY HE DESTROYED A METEOR.
I BET HE JUST BEATS UP WEAKLINGS.
YOU CAN'T RELY ON HEROES.

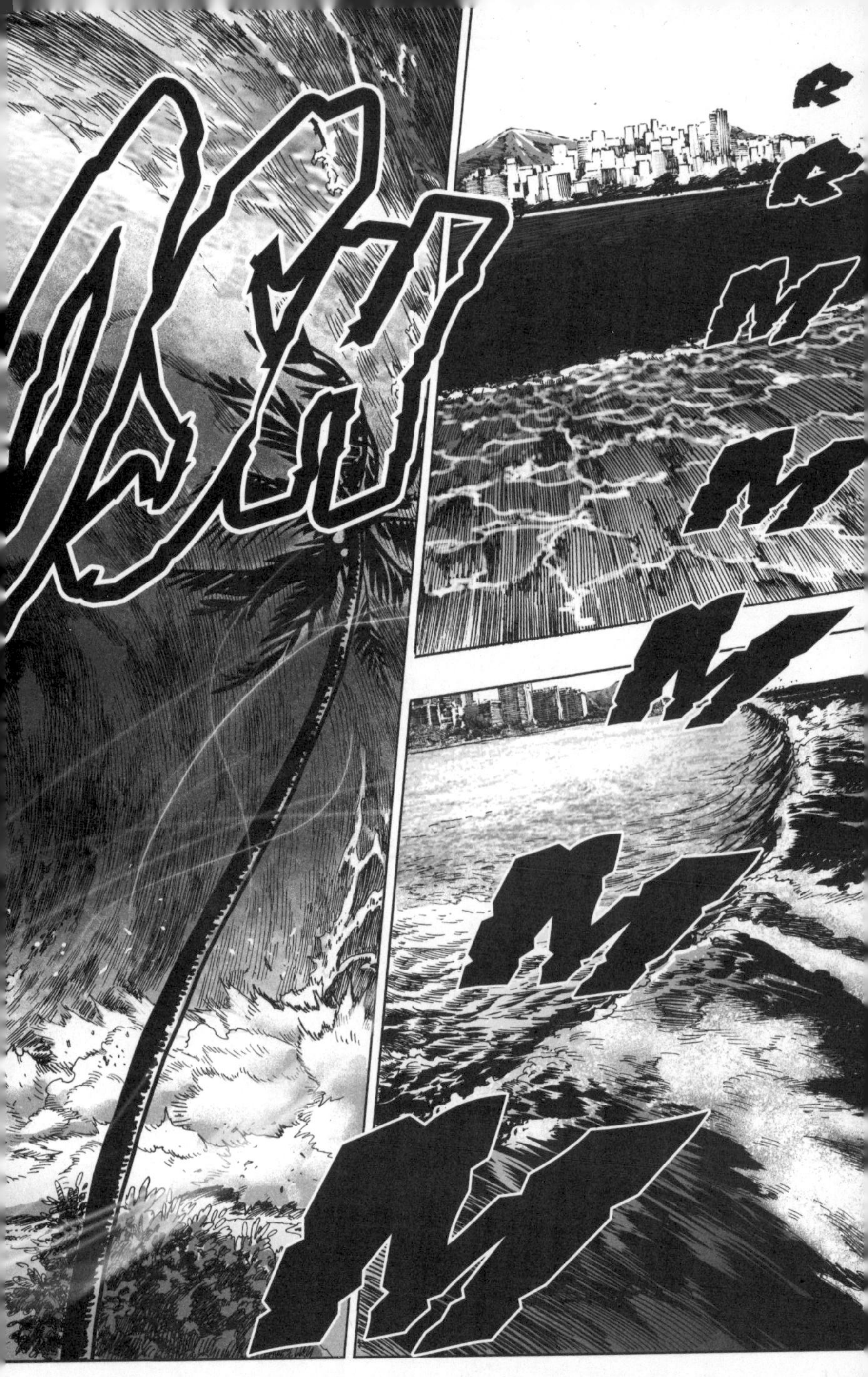
RRMMMMM

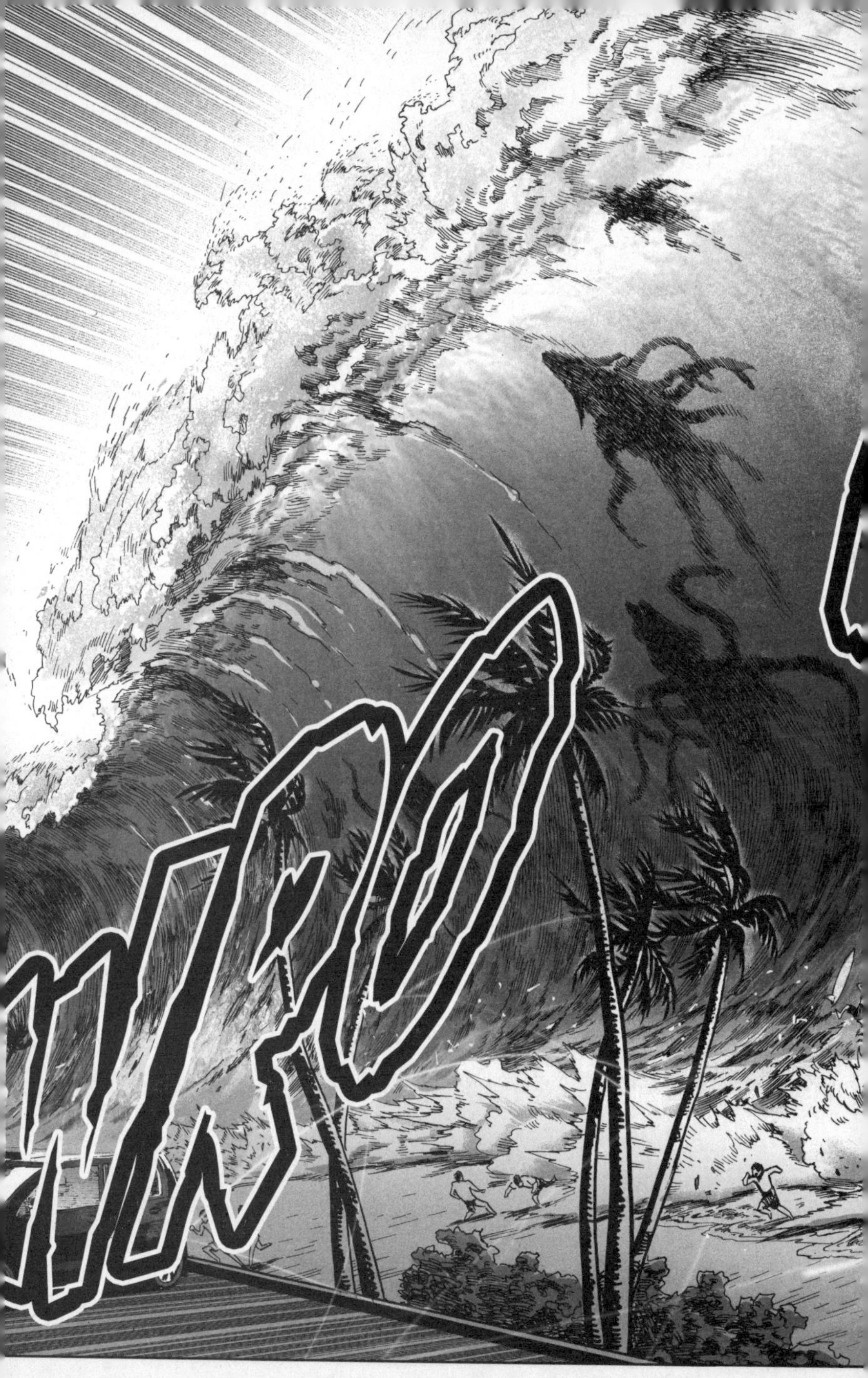

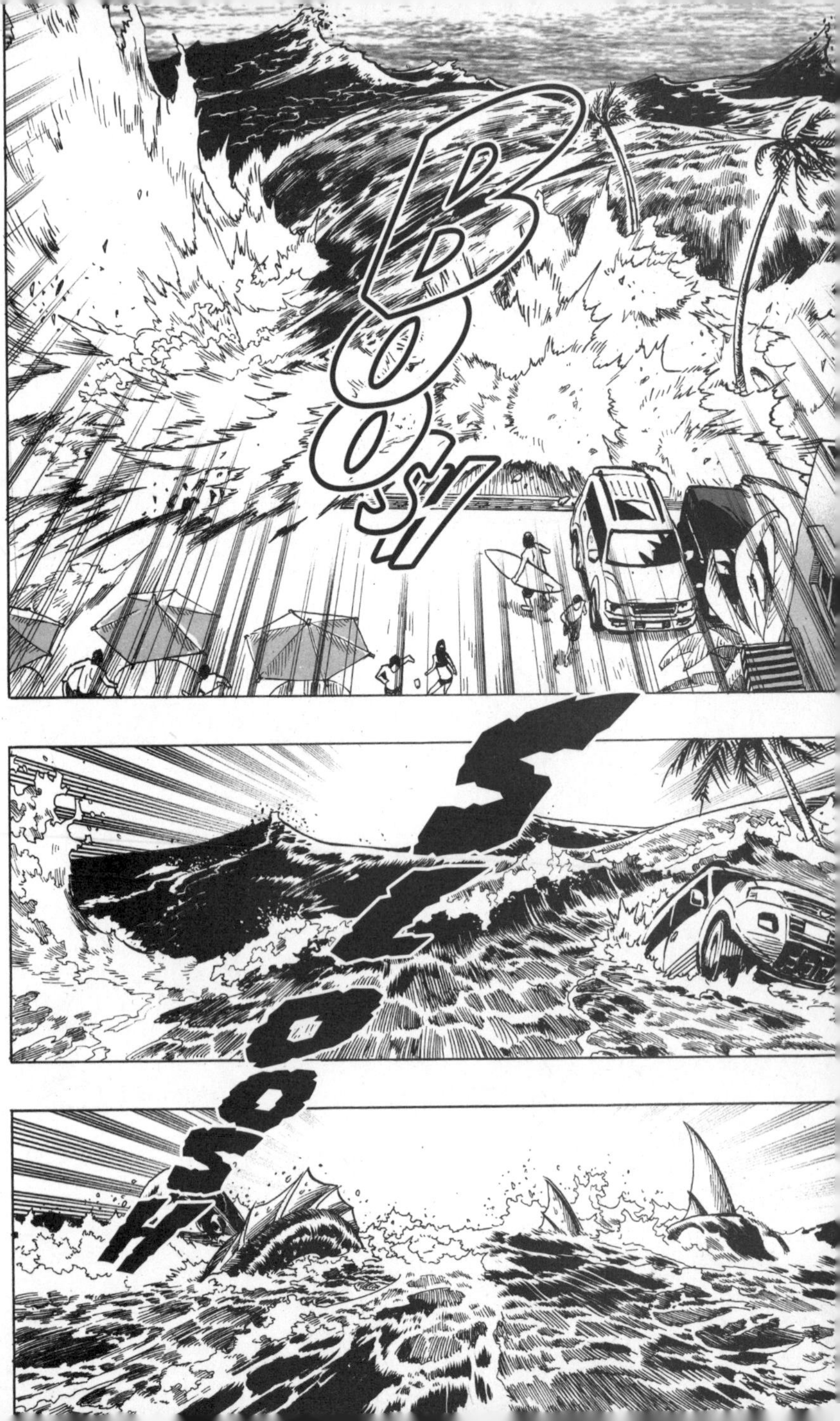
BOOSH!
SLOOSH

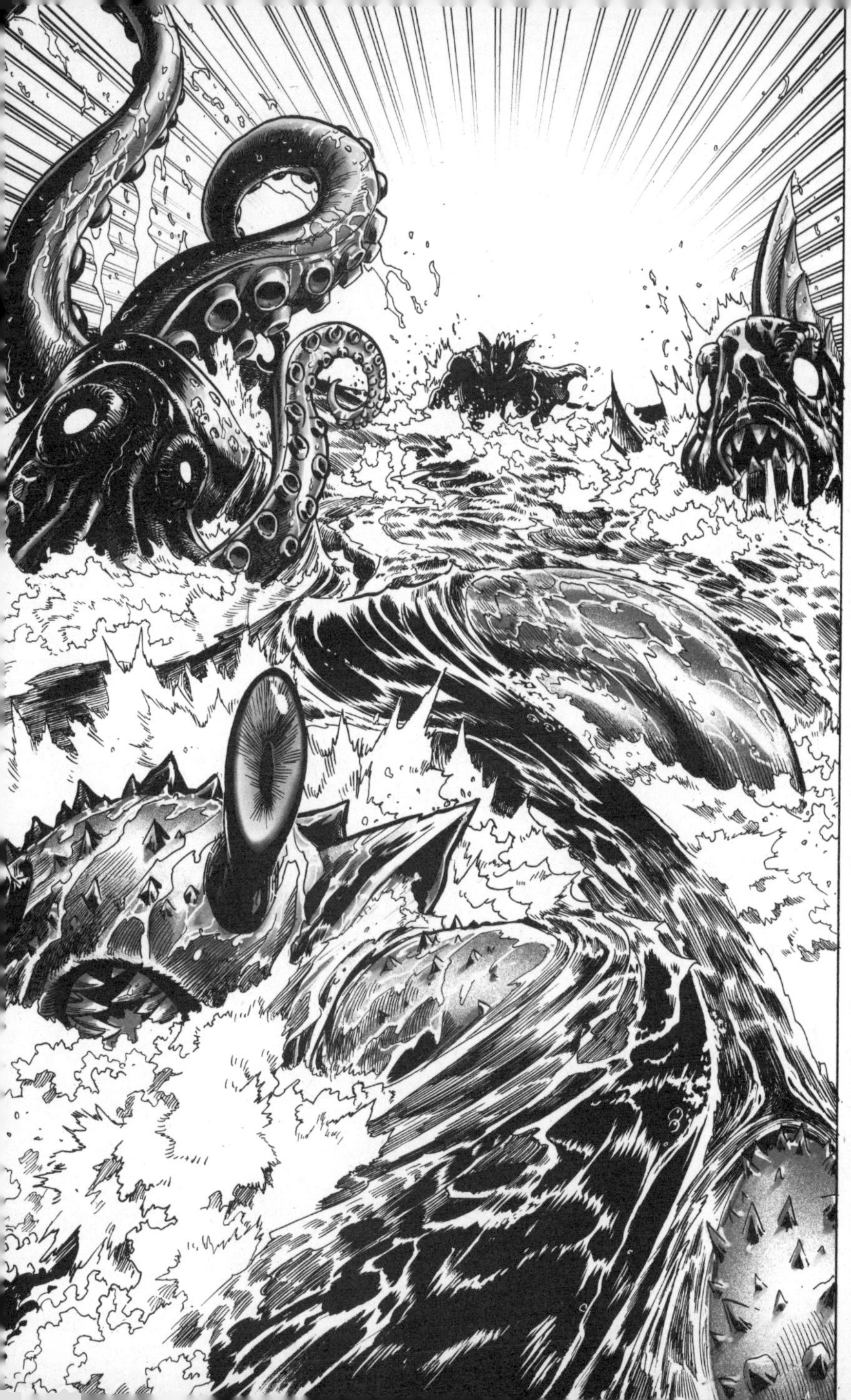

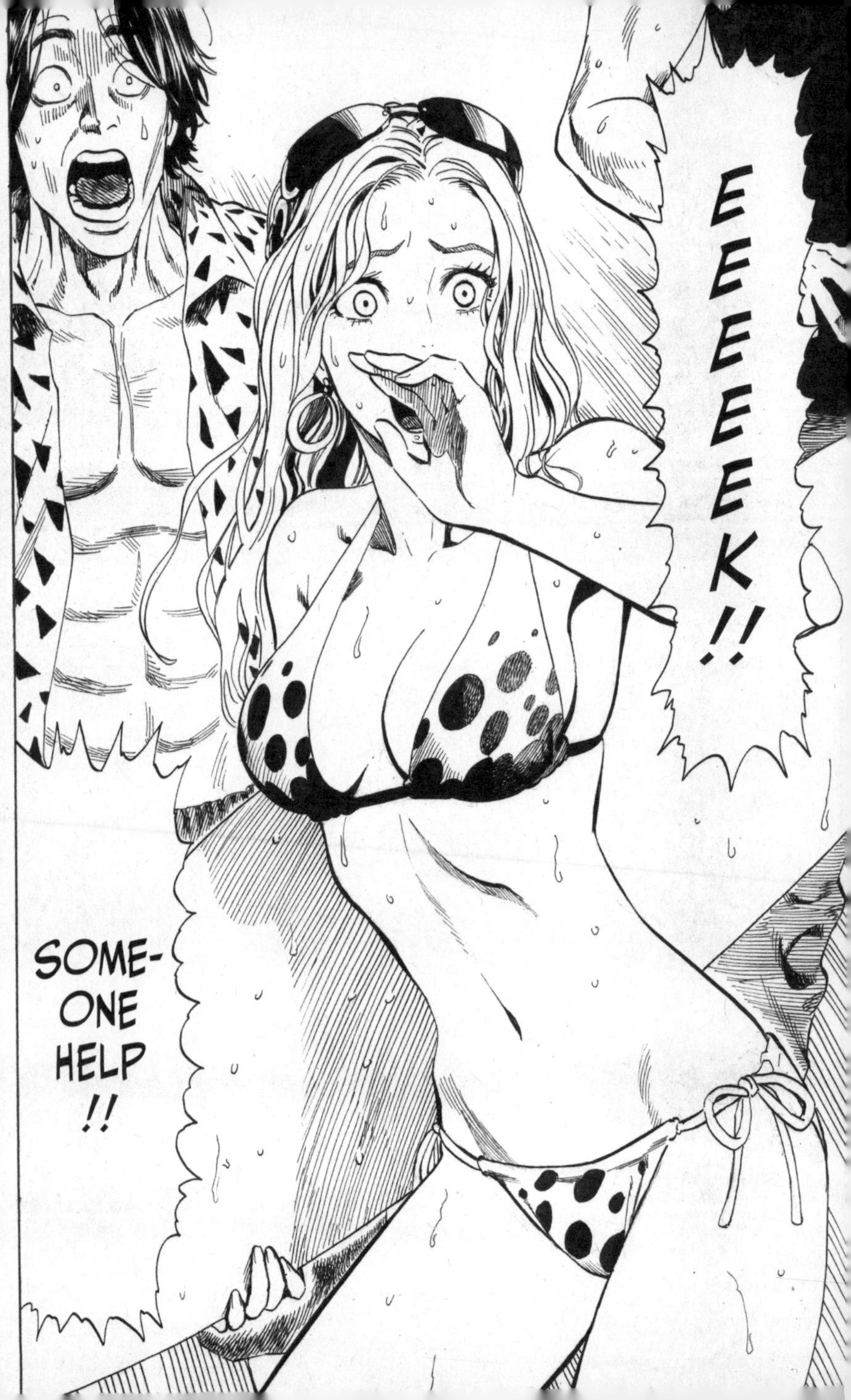
EEEEEK!!
SOME-
ONE
HELP
!!

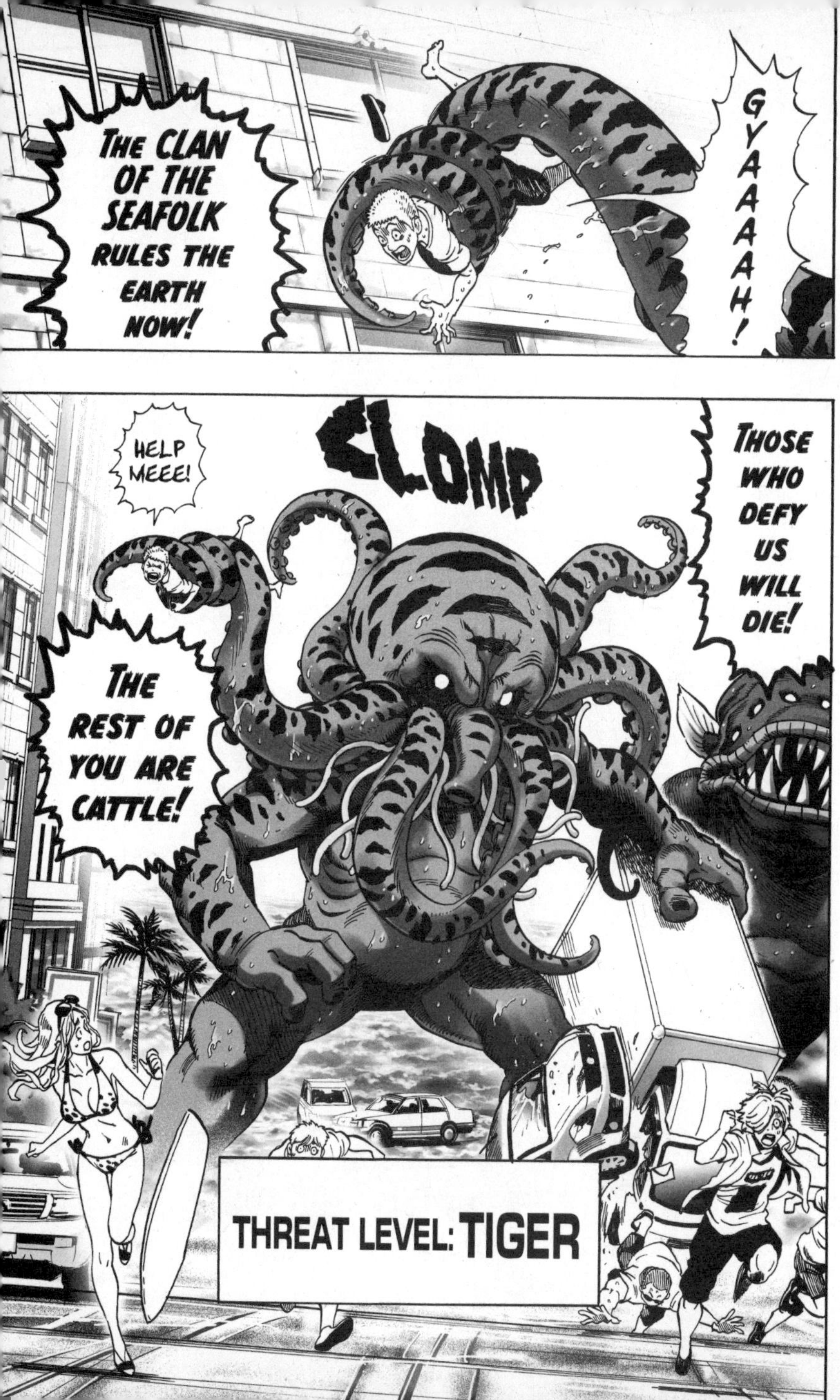
GYAAAAAH!
The CLAN OF THE SEAFOLK RULES THE EARTH NOW!
THOSE WHO DEFY US WILL DIE!
CLOMP
HELP MEEE!
THE REST OF YOU ARE CATTLE!
THREAT LEVEL: TIGER

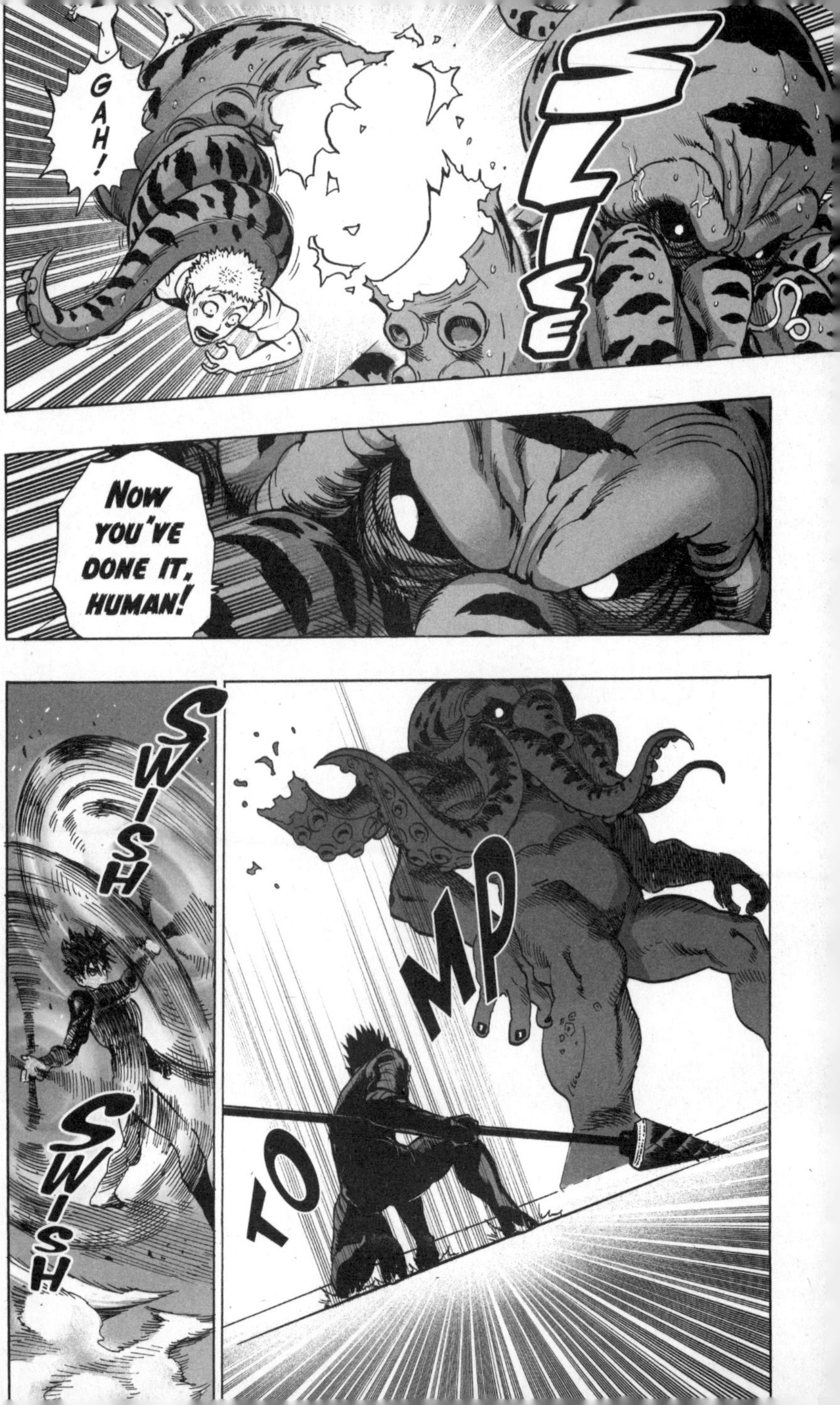
SLICE
GAH!
Now you've done it, human!
TOMP
SWISH
SWISH

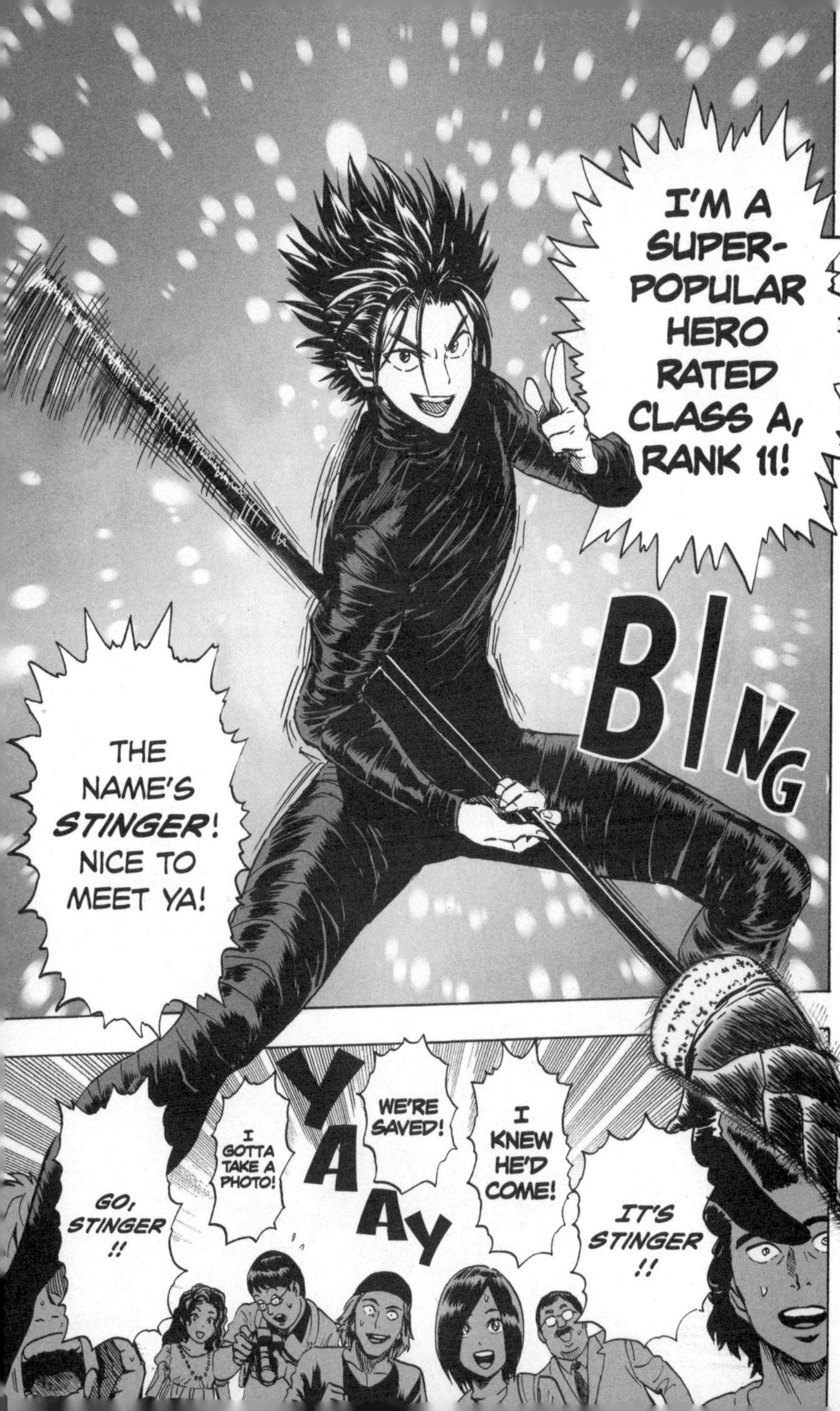
I'M A SUPER-POPULAR HERO RATED CLASS A, RANK 11!
BING
THE NAME'S *STINGER*! NICE TO MEET YA!
IT'S STINGER!!
I KNEW HE'D COME!
WE'RE SAVED!
YAAAY
I GOTTA TAKE A PHOTO!
GO, STINGER!!

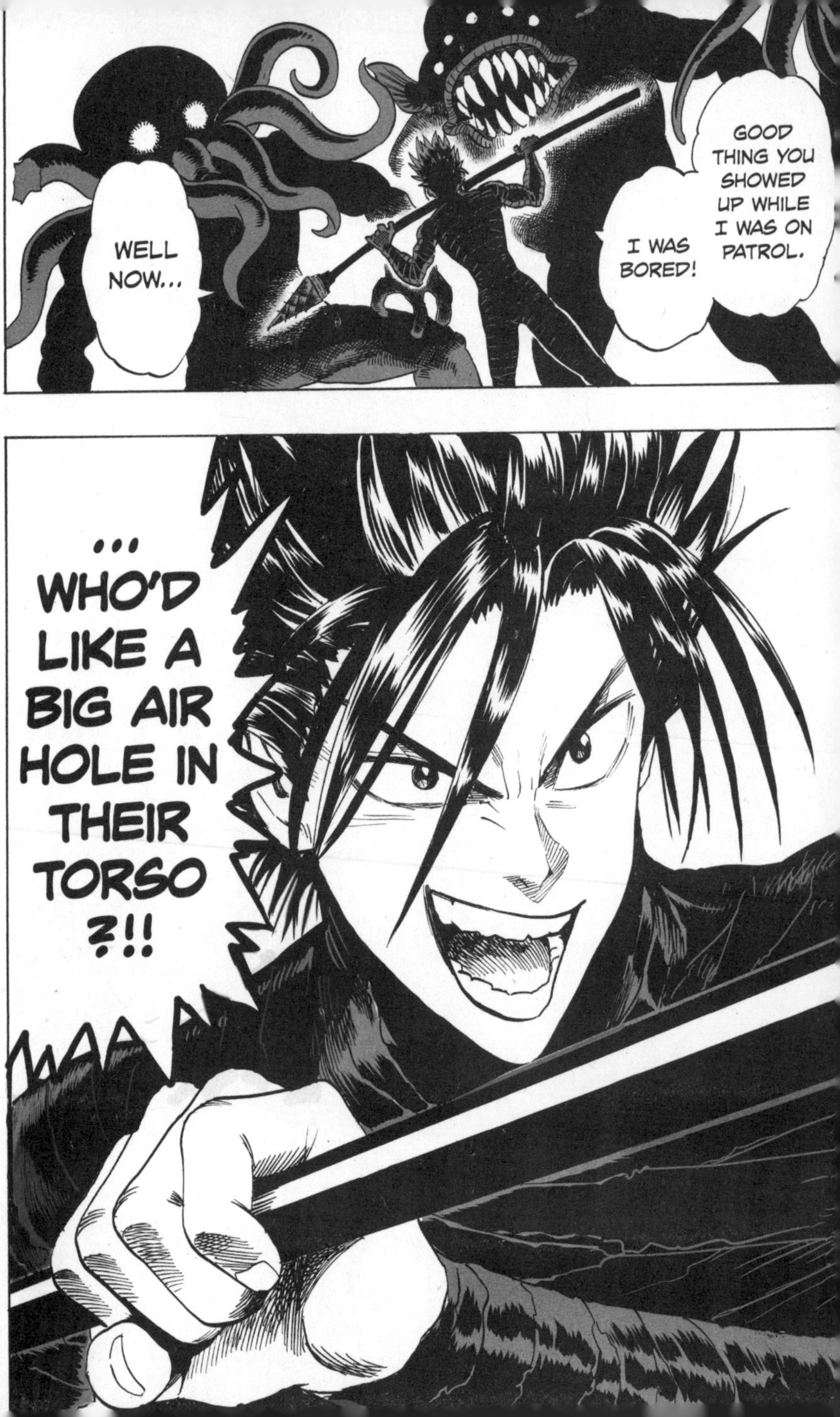
GOOD THING YOU SHOWED UP WHILE I WAS ON PATROL.
I WAS BORED!
WELL NOW...
...WHO'D LIKE A BIG AIR HOLE IN THEIR TORSO?!!

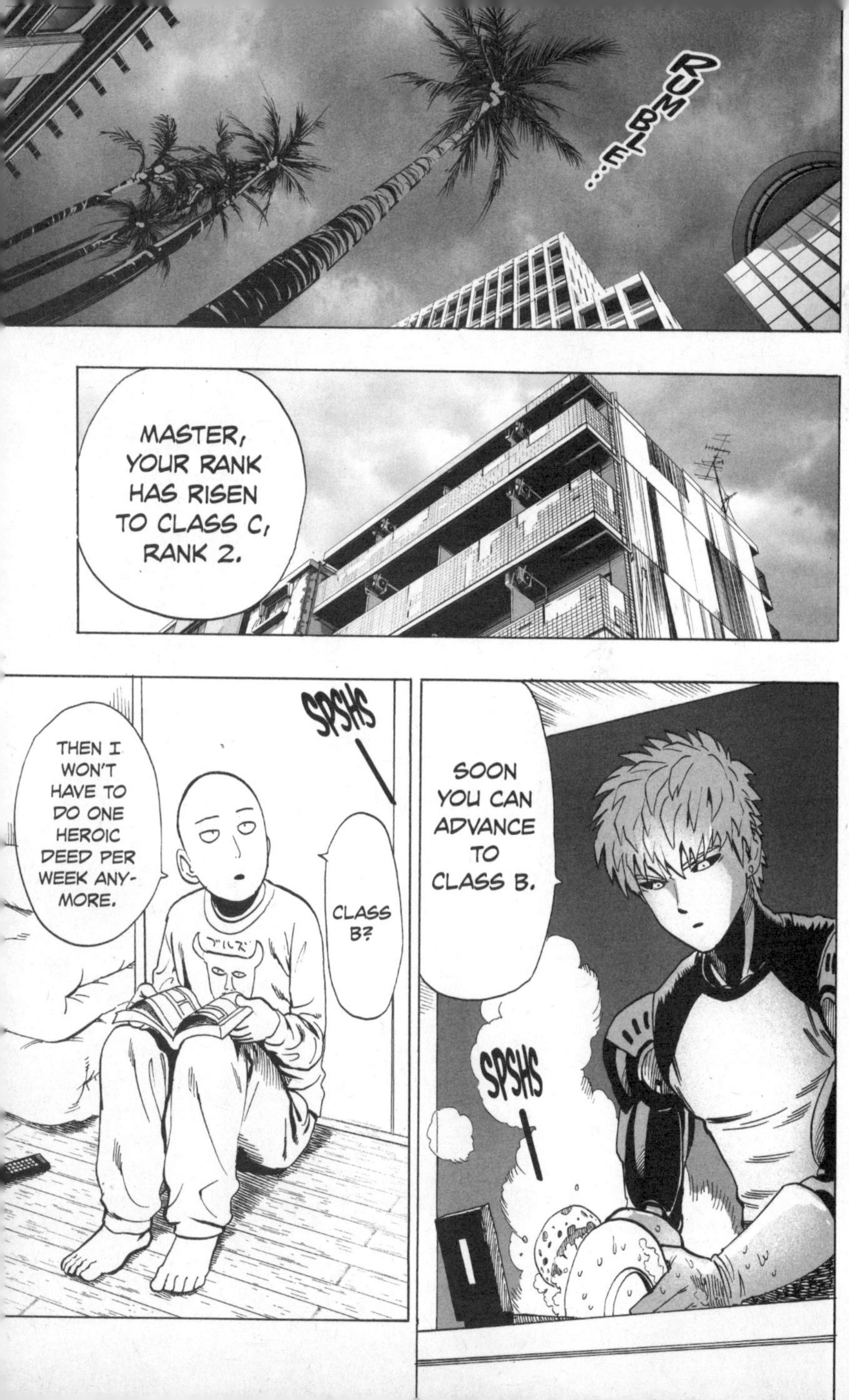
RUMBLE...
MASTER, YOUR RANK HAS RISEN TO CLASS C, RANK 2.
SOON YOU CAN ADVANCE TO CLASS B.
SPSHS
SPSHS
CLASS B?
THEN I WON'T HAVE TO DO ONE HEROIC DEED PER WEEK ANY-MORE.

IF YOU REACH CLASS C, RANK 1, YOU CAN BECOME A B-RANKER...

...BUT YOU COULD ALSO REMAIN AT CLASS C, RANK 1.

VWOO

CLINK

COR-RECT.

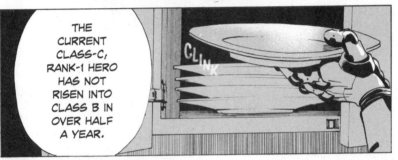

THE CURRENT CLASS-C, RANK-1 HERO HAS NOT RISEN INTO CLASS B IN OVER HALF A YEAR.

CLINK

RRING

THAT HERO...

EVEN WORSE IS THE CURRENT CLASS-B, RANK-1 HERO.

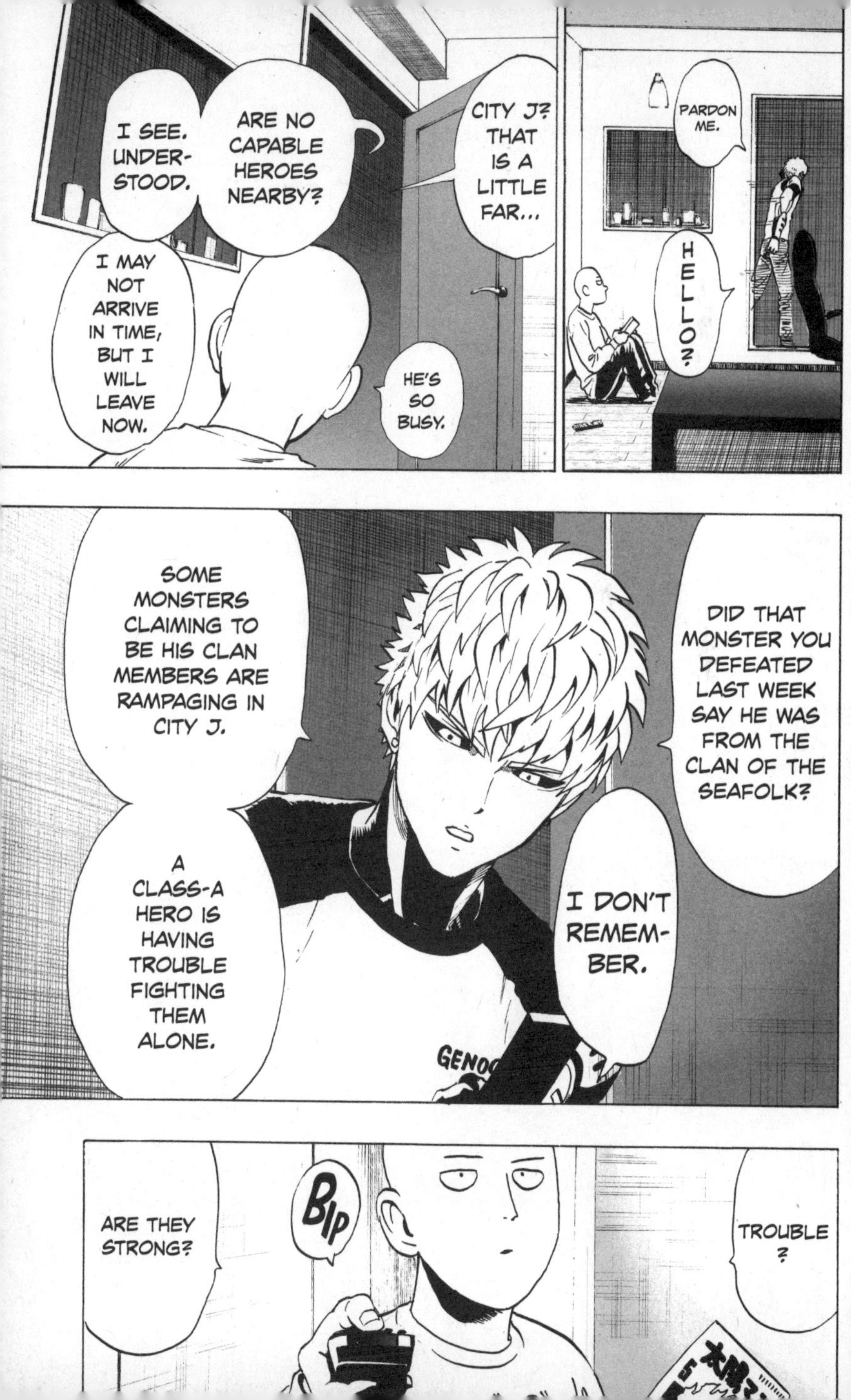
PARDON ME.
HELLO?
CITY J? THAT IS A LITTLE FAR...
ARE NO CAPABLE HEROES NEARBY?
I SEE. UNDER-STOOD.
I MAY NOT ARRIVE IN TIME, BUT I WILL LEAVE NOW.
HE'S SO BUSY.
DID THAT MONSTER YOU DEFEATED LAST WEEK SAY HE WAS FROM THE CLAN OF THE SEAFOLK?
I DON'T REMEM-BER.
SOME MONSTERS CLAIMING TO BE HIS CLAN MEMBERS ARE RAMPAGING IN CITY J.
A CLASS-A HERO IS HAVING TROUBLE FIGHTING THEM ALONE.
TROUBLE?
BIP
ARE THEY STRONG?

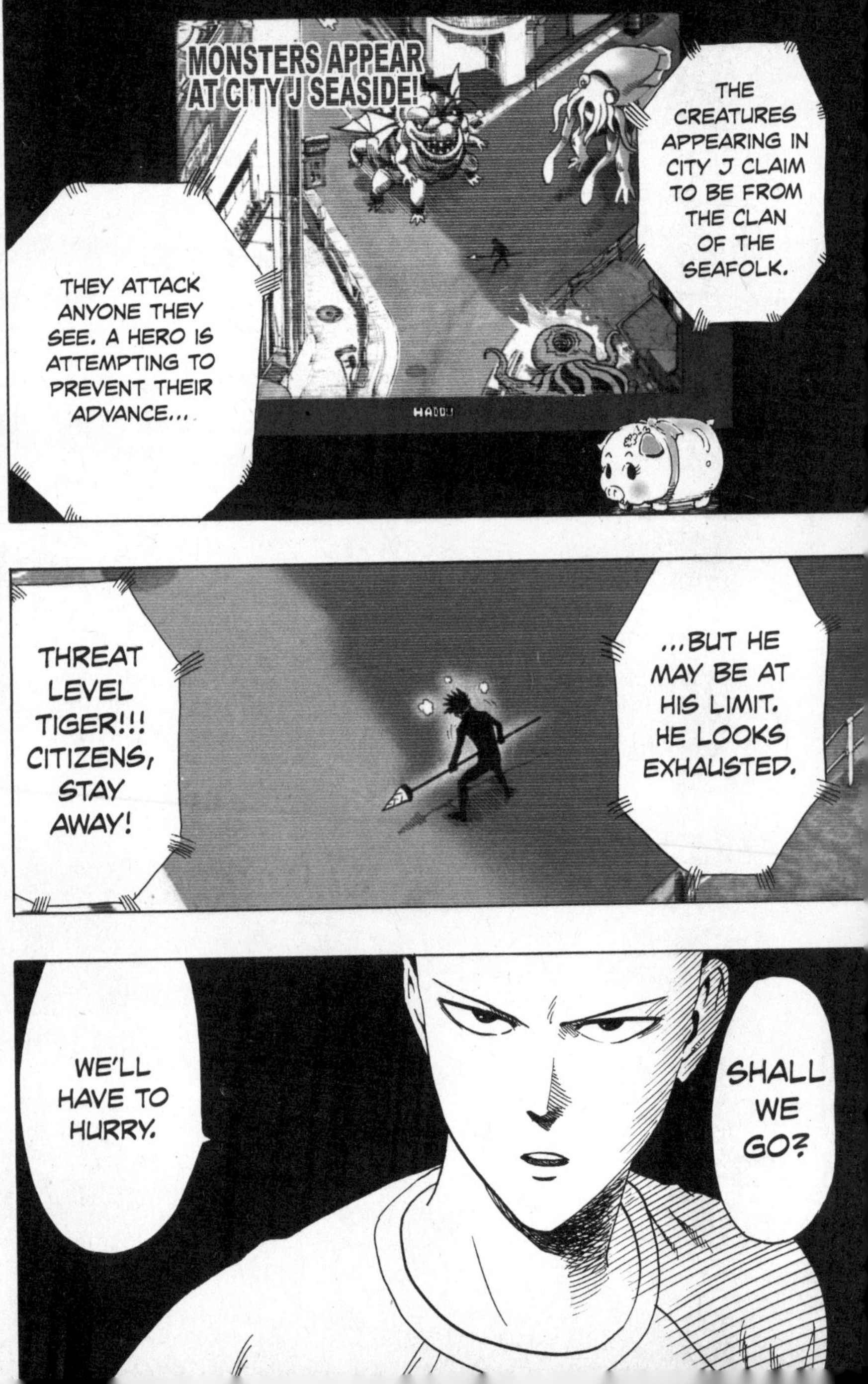
MONSTERS APPEAR AT CITY J SEASIDE!
THE CREATURES APPEARING IN CITY J CLAIM TO BE FROM THE CLAN OF THE SEAFOLK.
THEY ATTACK ANYONE THEY SEE. A HERO IS ATTEMPTING TO PREVENT THEIR ADVANCE...
...BUT HE MAY BE AT HIS LIMIT. HE LOOKS EXHAUSTED.
THREAT LEVEL TIGER!!! CITIZENS, STAY AWAY!
SHALL WE GO?
WE'LL HAVE TO HURRY.

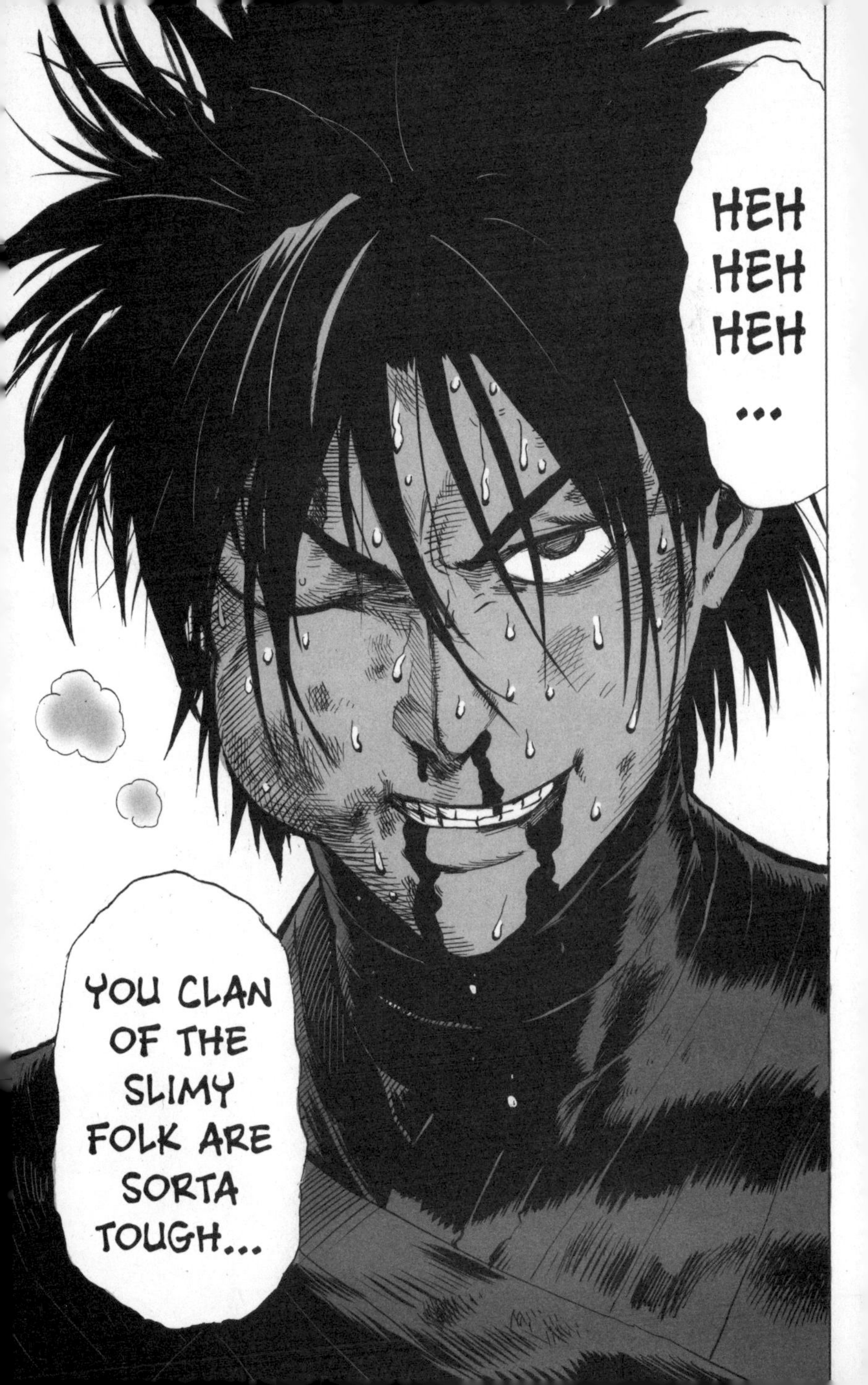
HEH HEH HEH ...
YOU CLAN OF THE SLIMY FOLK ARE SORTA TOUGH...

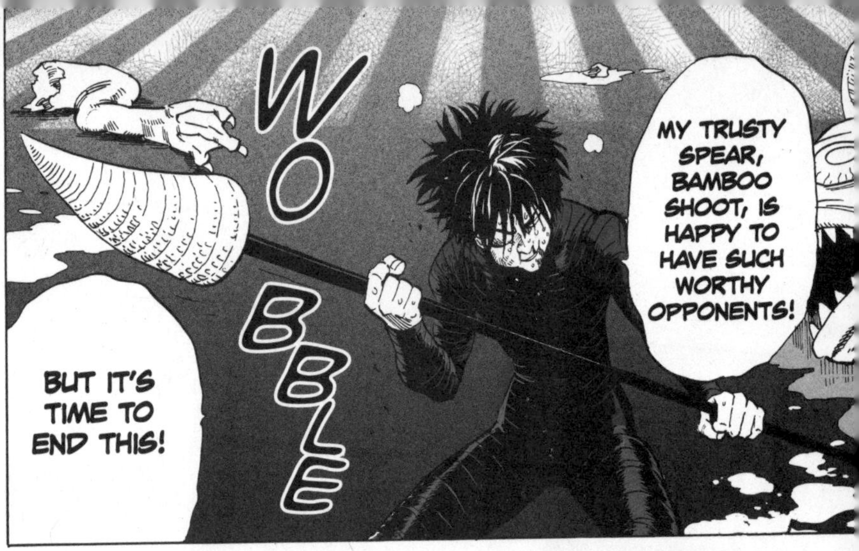
MY TRUSTY SPEAR, BAMBOO SHOOT, IS HAPPY TO HAVE SUCH WORTHY OPPONENTS!
WOBBLE
BUT IT'S TIME TO END THIS!
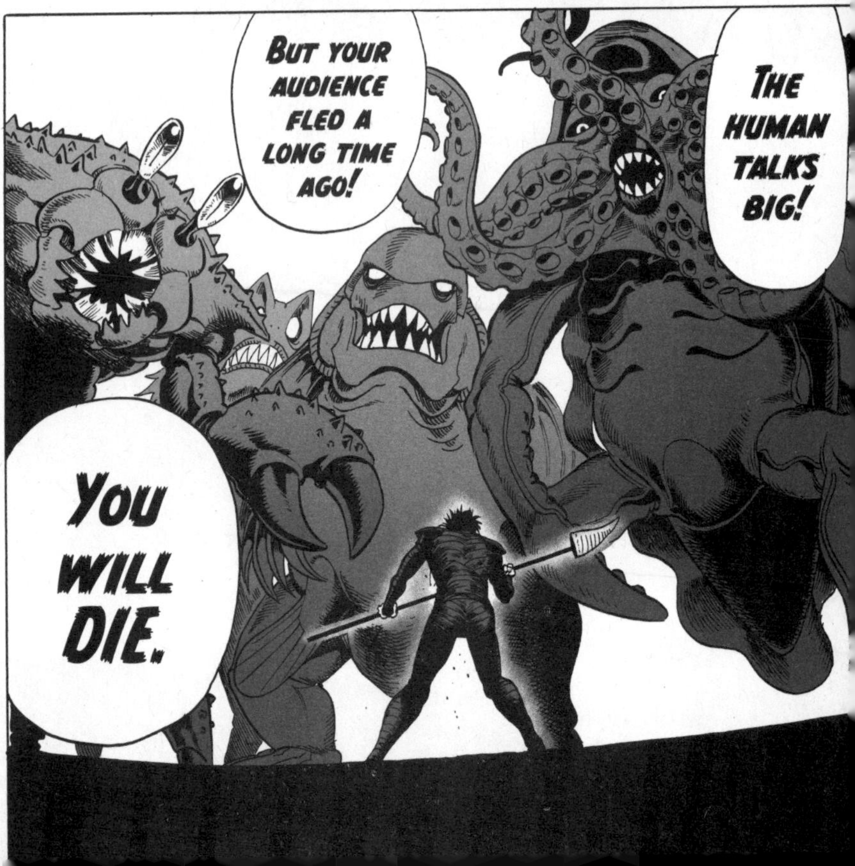
THE HUMAN TALKS BIG!
BUT YOUR AUDIENCE FLED A LONG TIME AGO!
YOU WILL DIE.

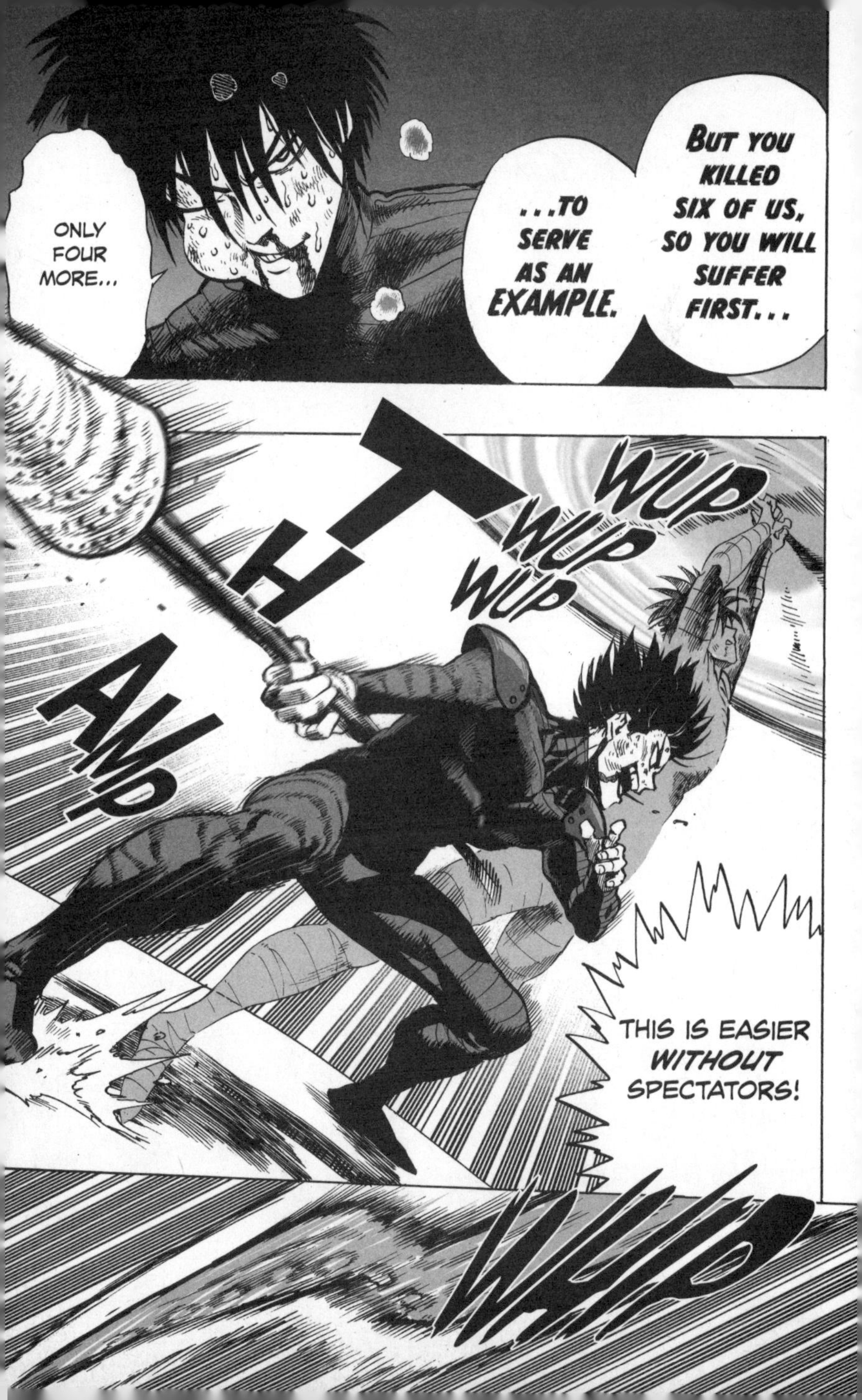
BUT YOU KILLED SIX OF US, SO YOU WILL SUFFER FIRST...
...TO SERVE AS AN EXAMPLE.
ONLY FOUR MORE...
WUP WUP WUP
THAMP
THIS IS EASIER WITHOUT SPECTATORS!
WHUP

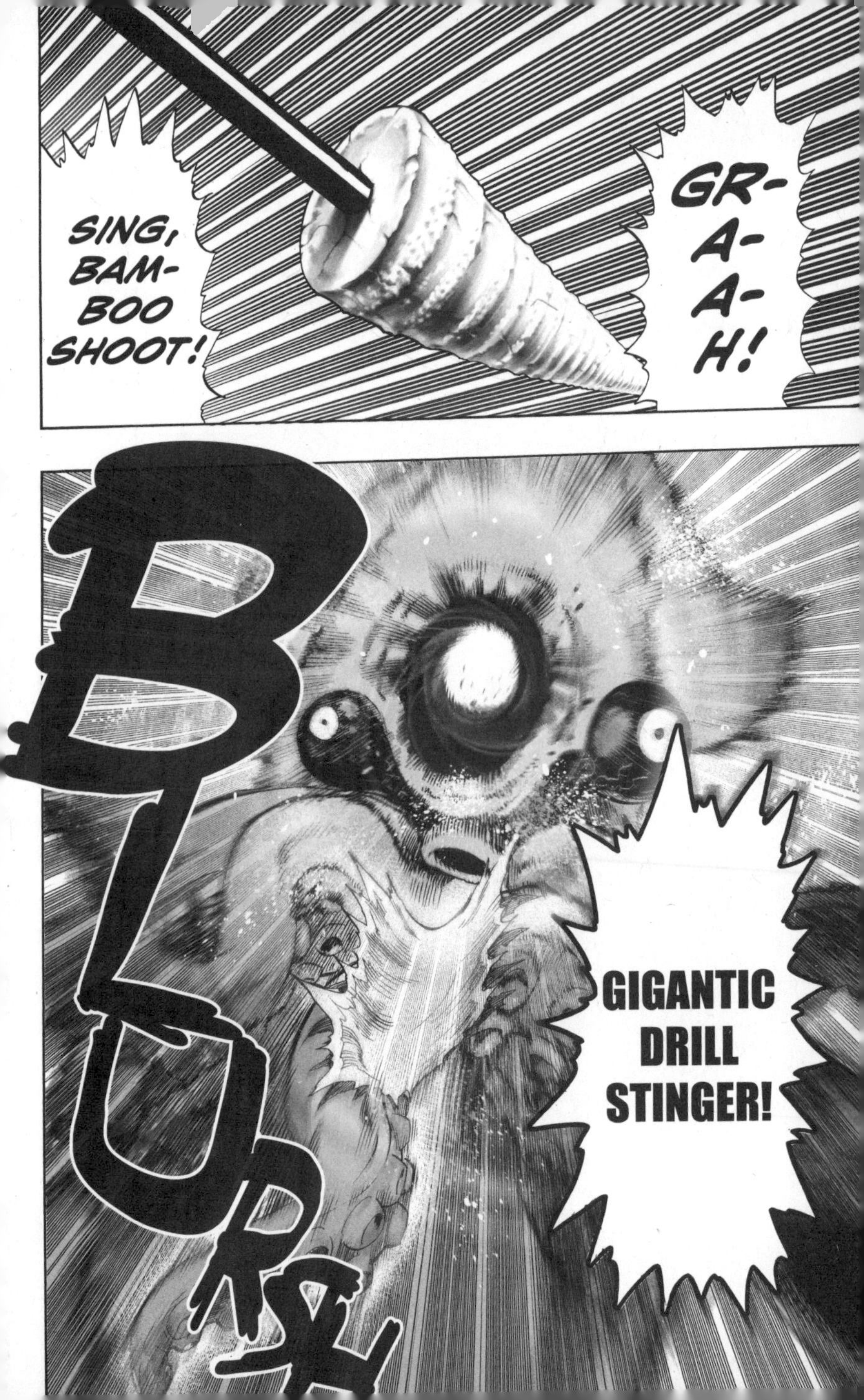
GR-A-A-H!
SING, BAM-BOO SHOOT!
GIGANTIC DRILL STINGER!

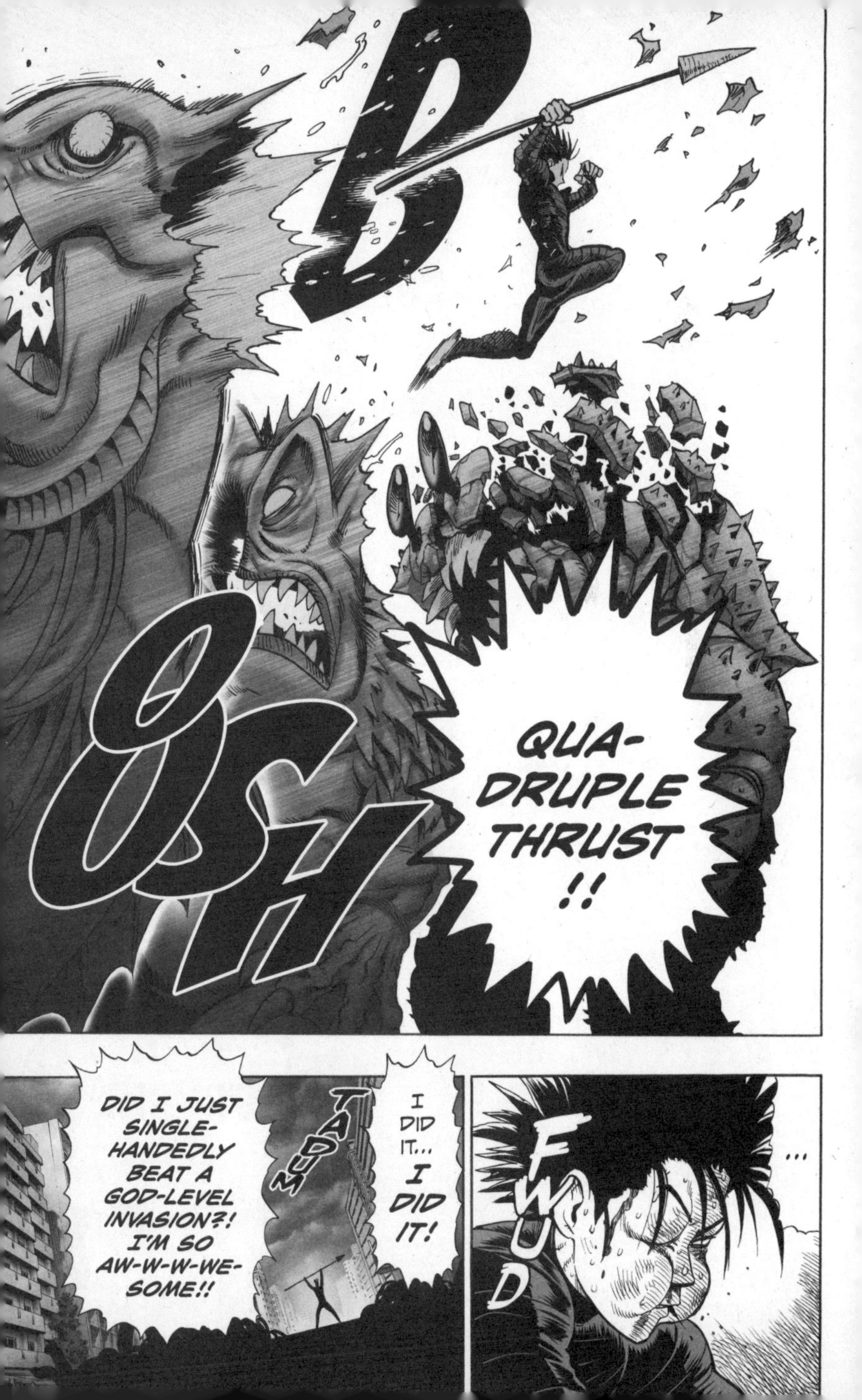
BOOSH
QUA-DRUPLE THRUST!!
FWUD
...
I DID IT... I DID IT!
TADUM
DID I JUST SINGLE-HANDEDLY BEAT A GOD-LEVEL INVASION?! I'M SO AW-W-W-WE-SOME!!

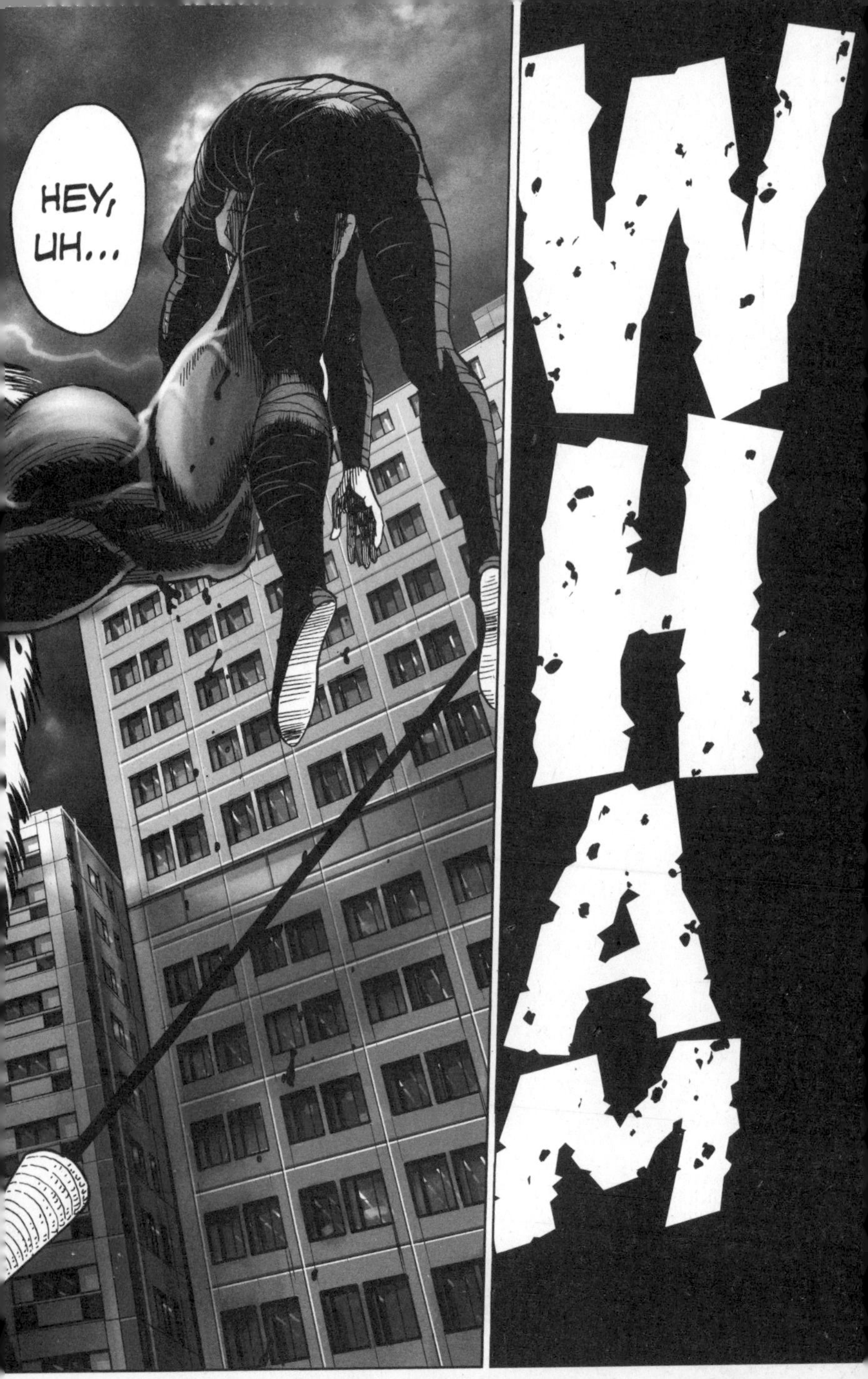
WHAM
HEY, UH...

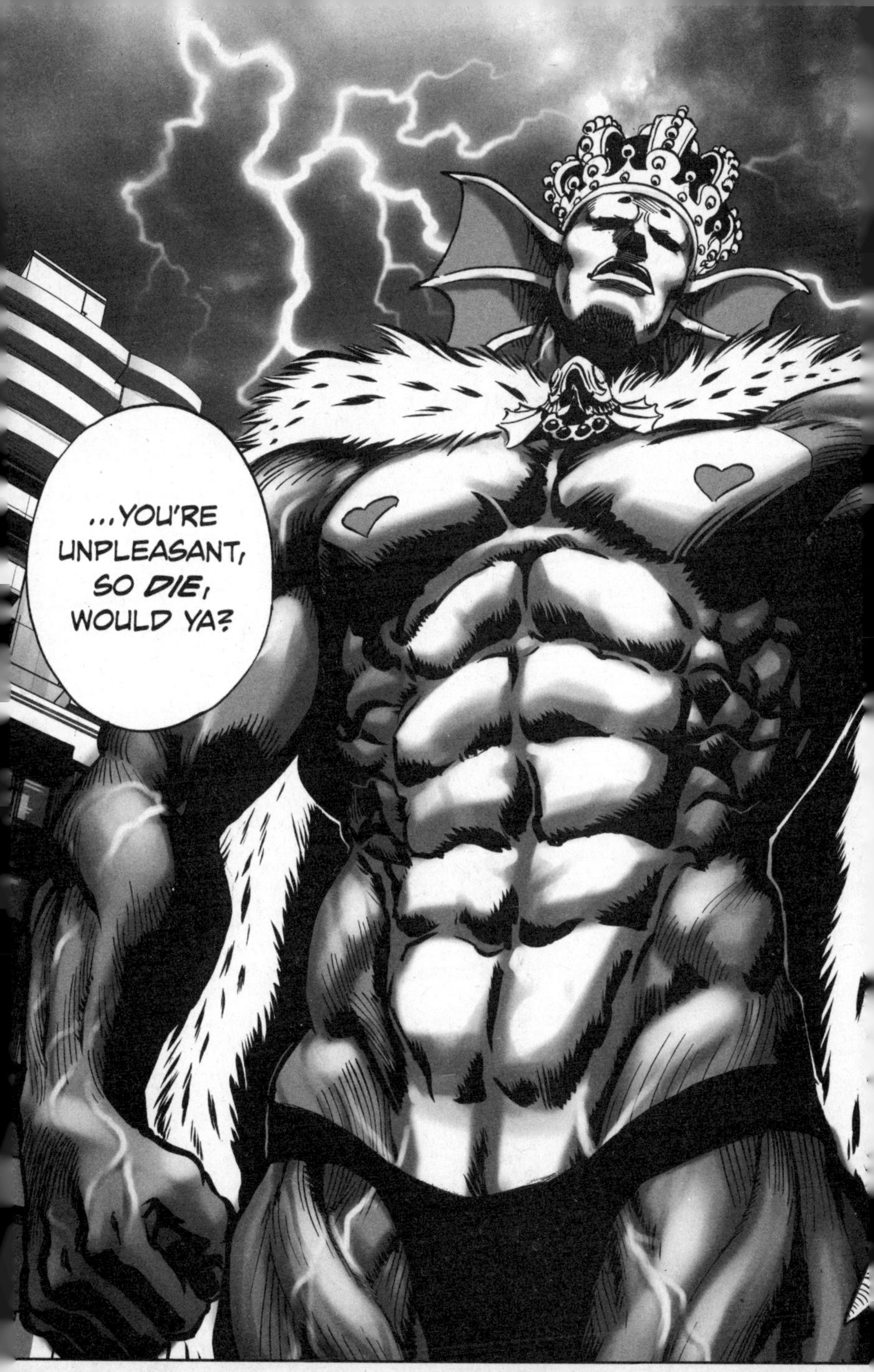
...YOU'RE UNPLEASANT, SO *DIE*, WOULD YA?

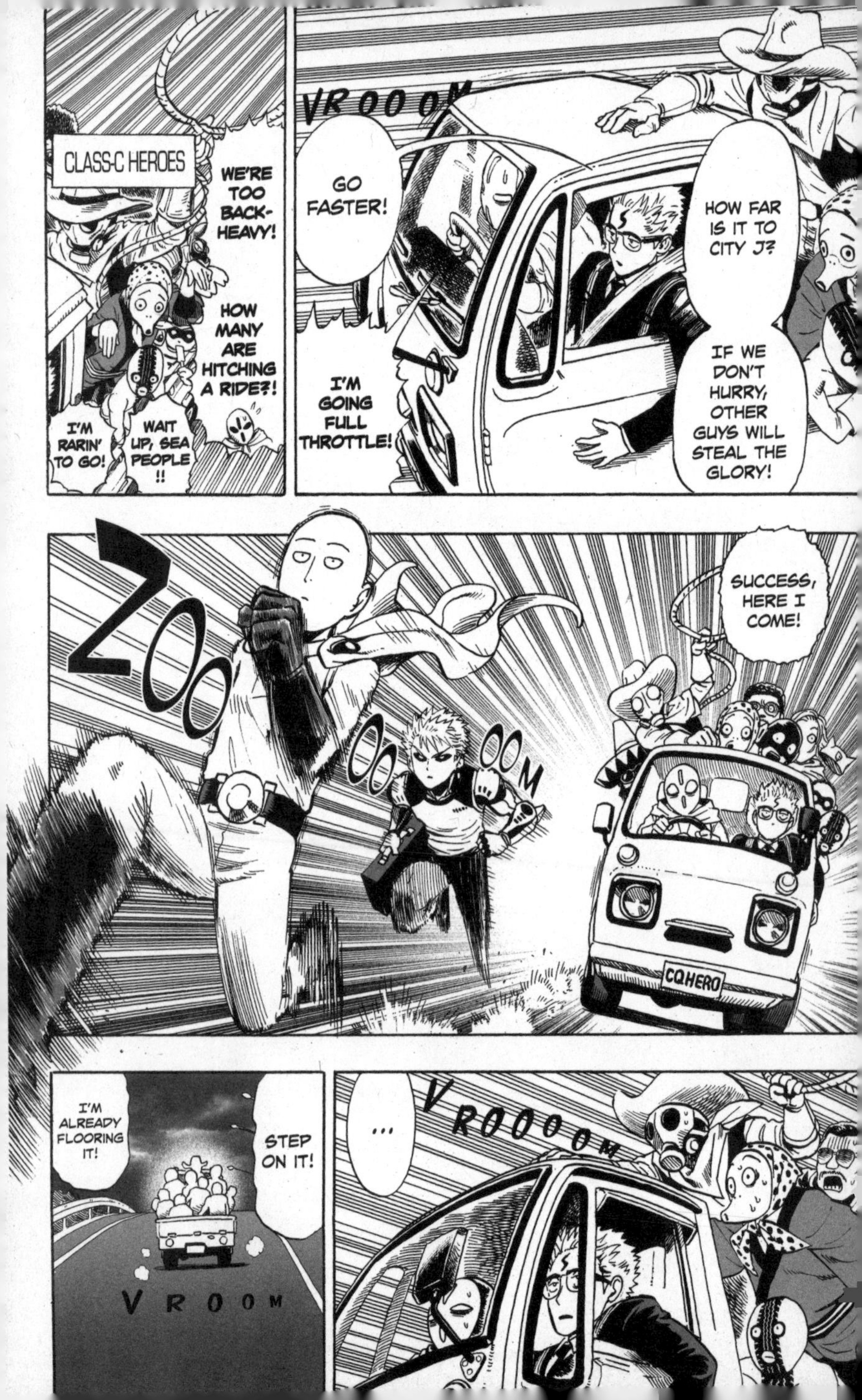
HOW FAR IS IT TO CITY J?
IF WE DON'T HURRY, OTHER GUYS WILL STEAL THE GLORY!
VROOOM
GO FASTER!
I'M GOING FULL THROTTLE!
CLASS-C HEROES
WE'RE TOO BACK-HEAVY!
HOW MANY ARE HITCHING A RIDE?!
WAIT UP, SEA PEOPLE!!
I'M RARIN' TO GO!
SUCCESS, HERE I COME!
ZOOOOOOM
CQHERO
VROOOOOM
...
STEP ON IT!
I'M ALREADY FLOORING IT!
VROOM

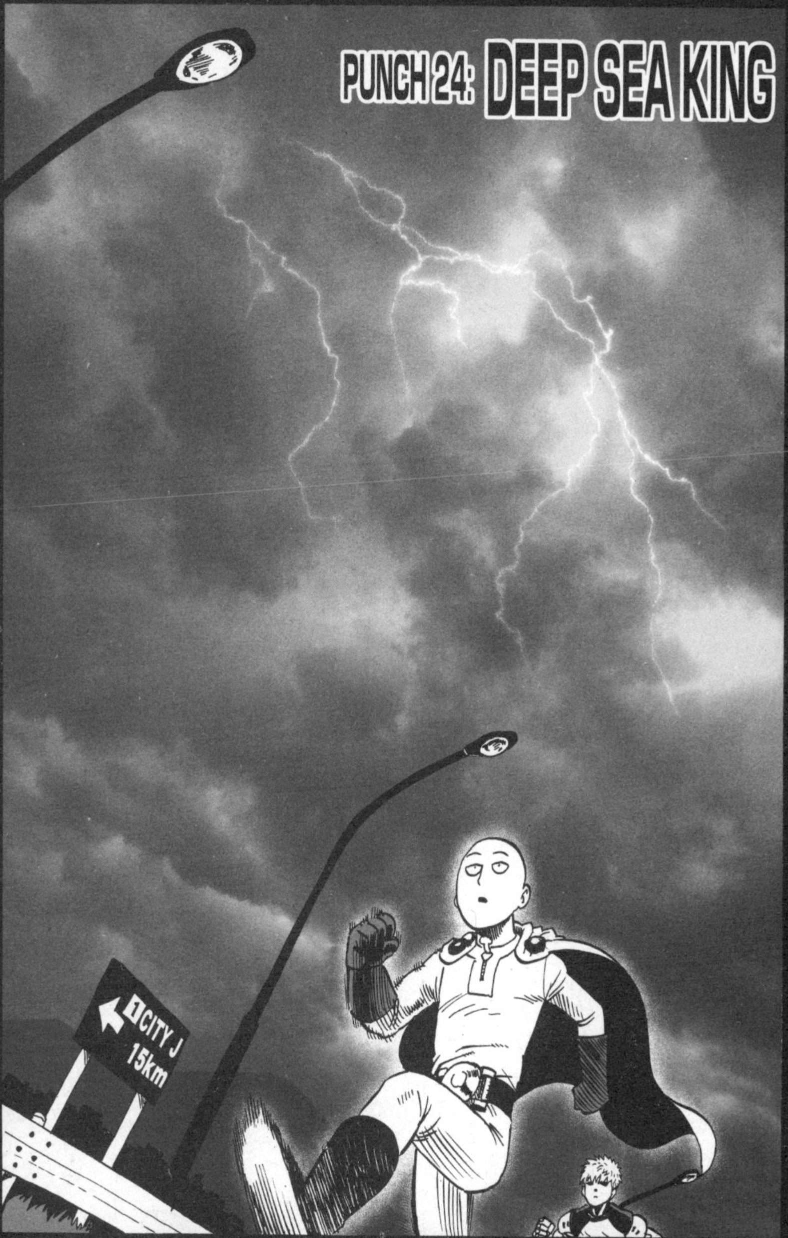
PUNCH 24: DEEP SEA KING
1 CITY J
15km

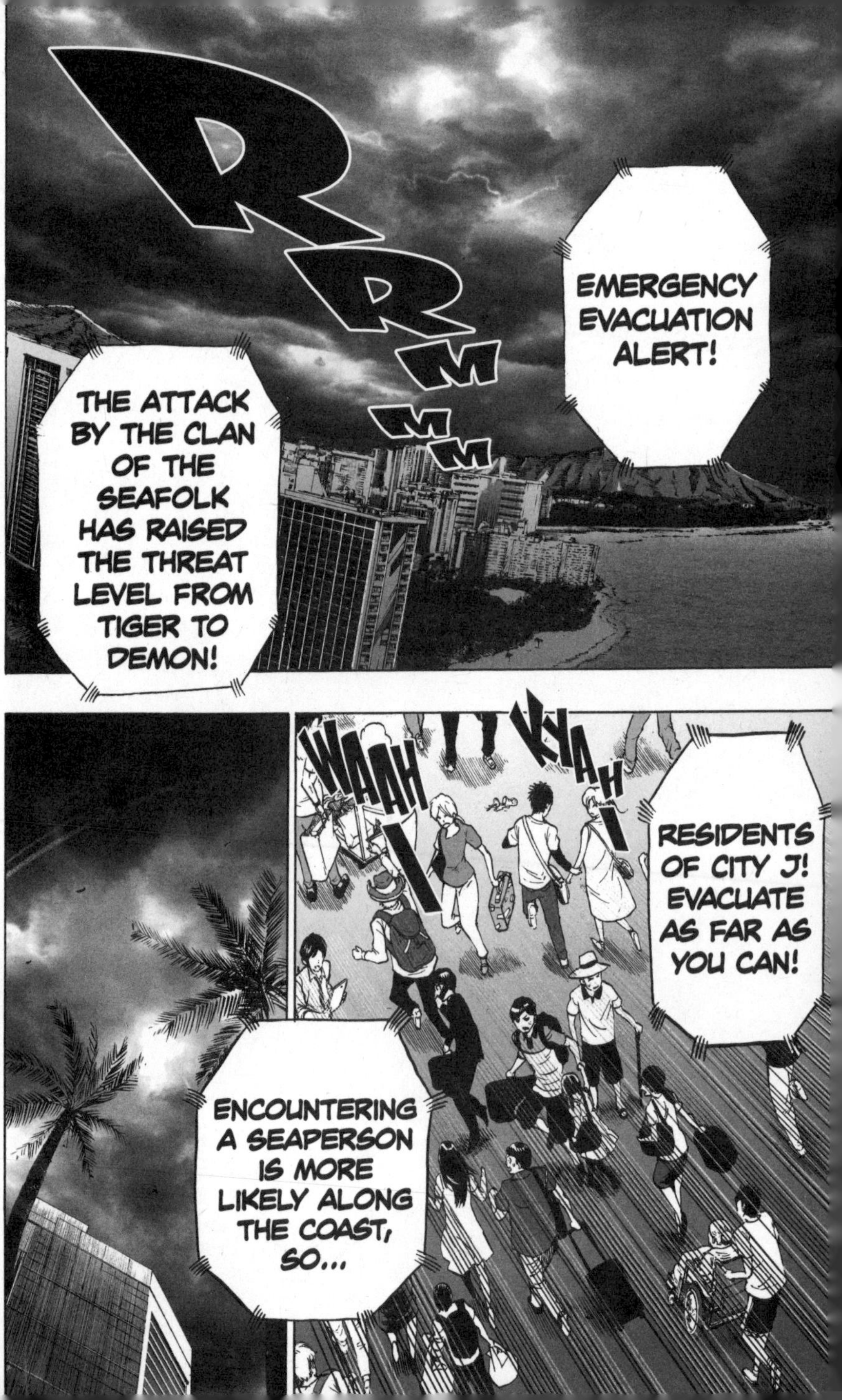
RRMMM
EMERGENCY EVACUATION ALERT!
THE ATTACK BY THE CLAN OF THE SEAFOLK HAS RAISED THE THREAT LEVEL FROM TIGER TO DEMON!
KYAH!
WAAH!!
RESIDENTS OF CITY J! EVACUATE AS FAR AS YOU CAN!
ENCOUNTERING A SEAPERSON IS MORE LIKELY ALONG THE COAST, SO...

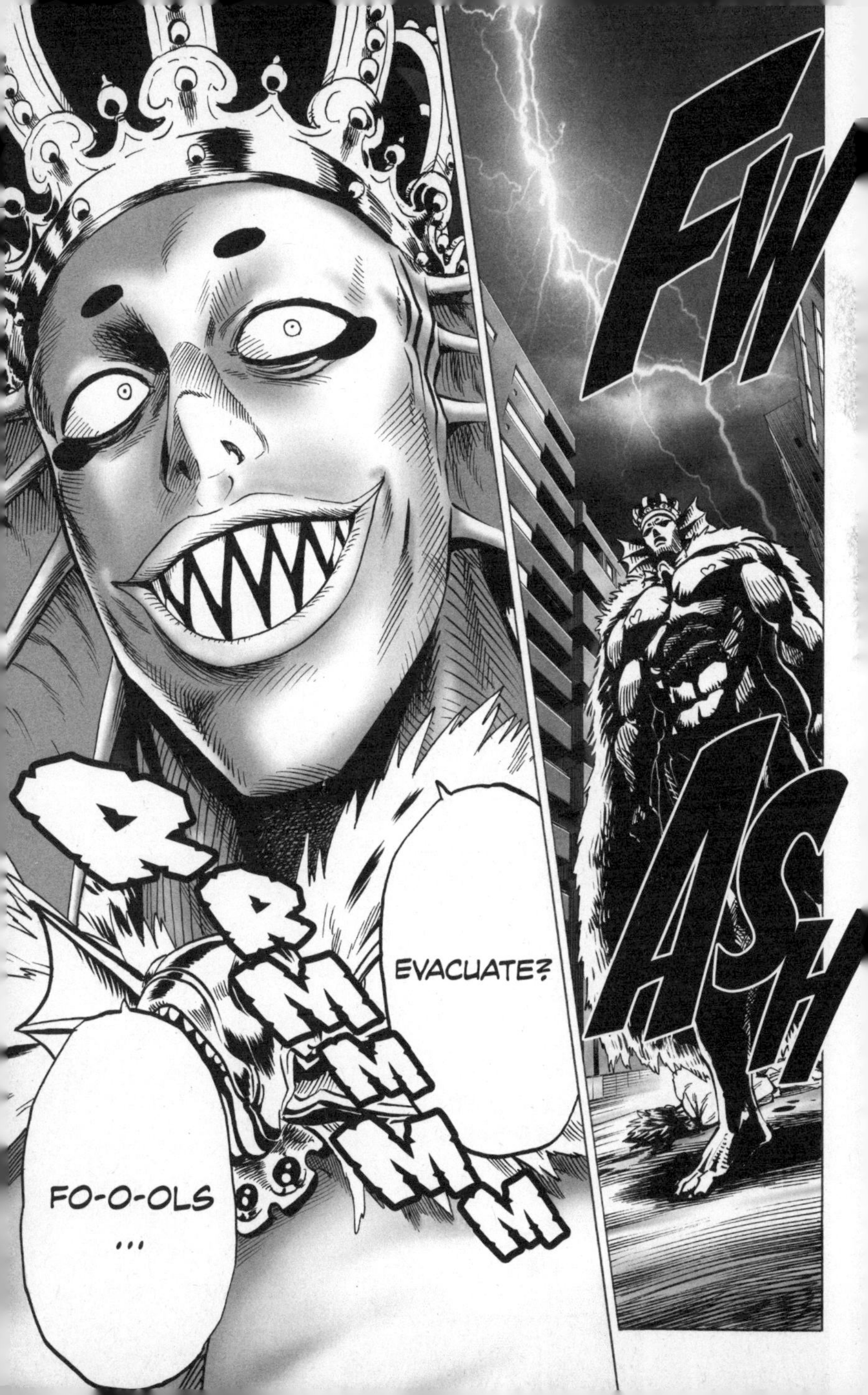
FWASH
EVACUATE?
RRMMMM
FO-O-OLS
...

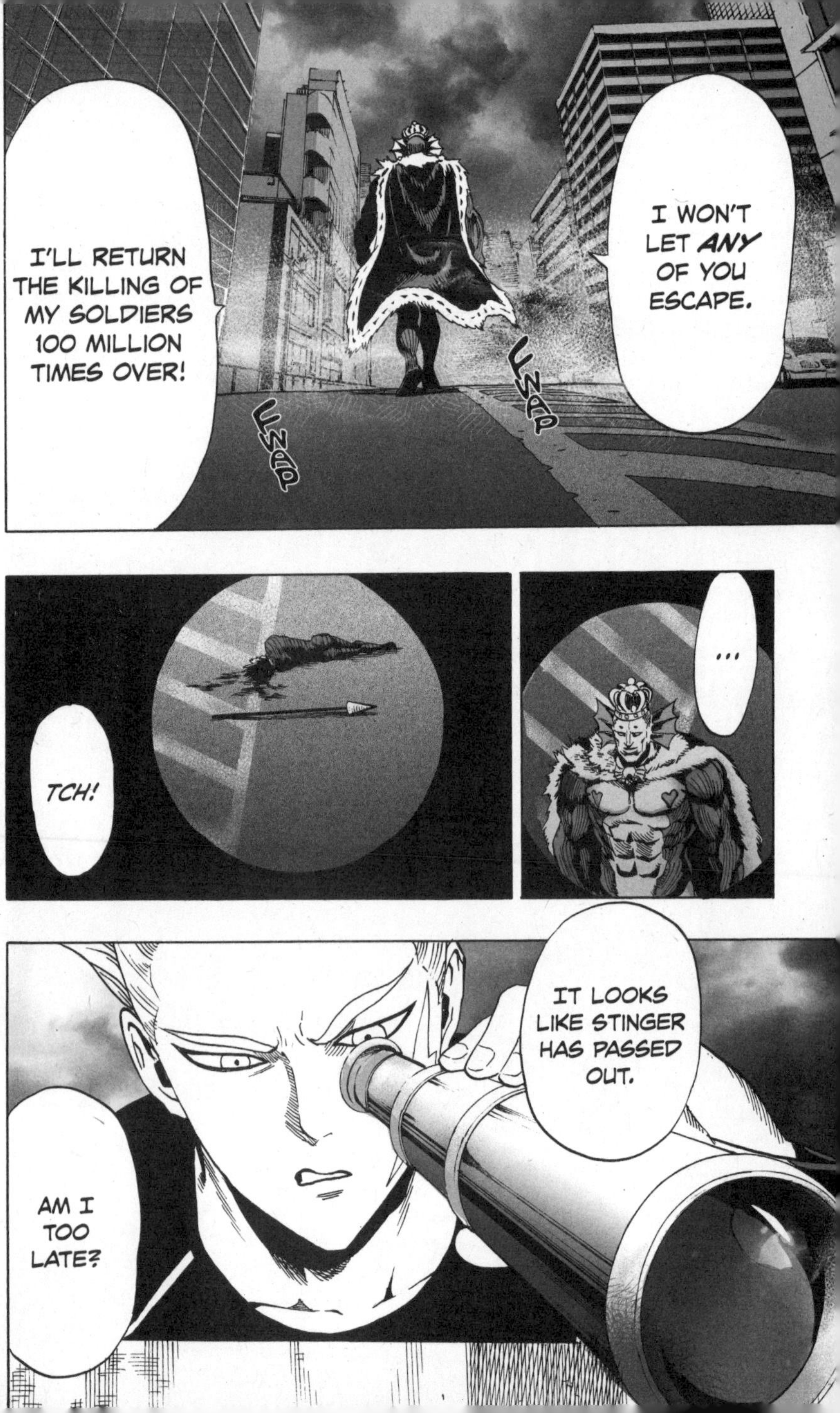
I WON'T LET ANY OF YOU ESCAPE.
I'LL RETURN THE KILLING OF MY SOLDIERS 100 MILLION TIMES OVER!
FWAP
FWAP
...
TCH!
IT LOOKS LIKE STINGER HAS PASSED OUT.
AM I TOO LATE?

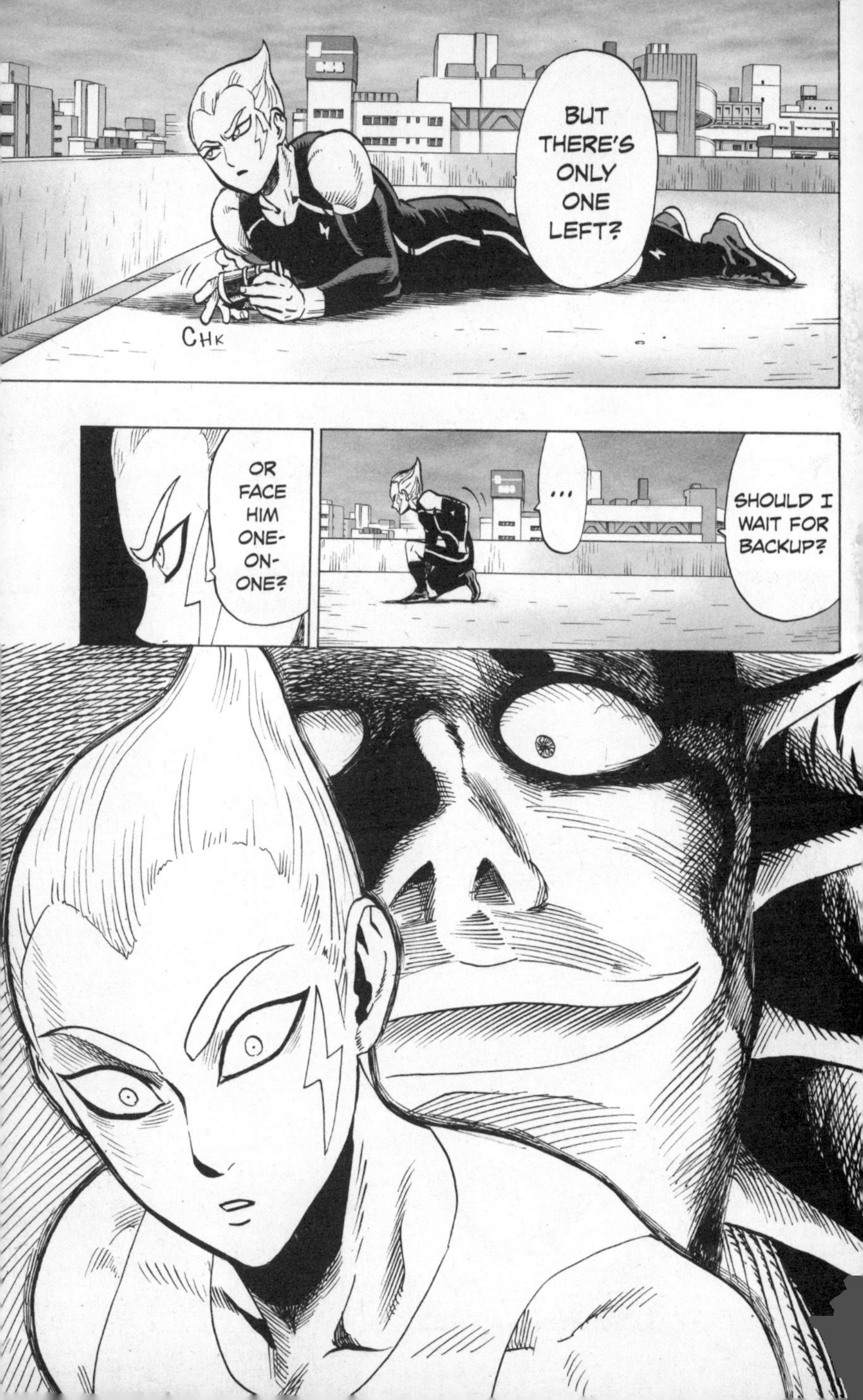
BUT THERE'S ONLY ONE LEFT?
CHK
SHOULD I WAIT FOR BACKUP?
...
OR FACE HIM ONE-ON-ONE?

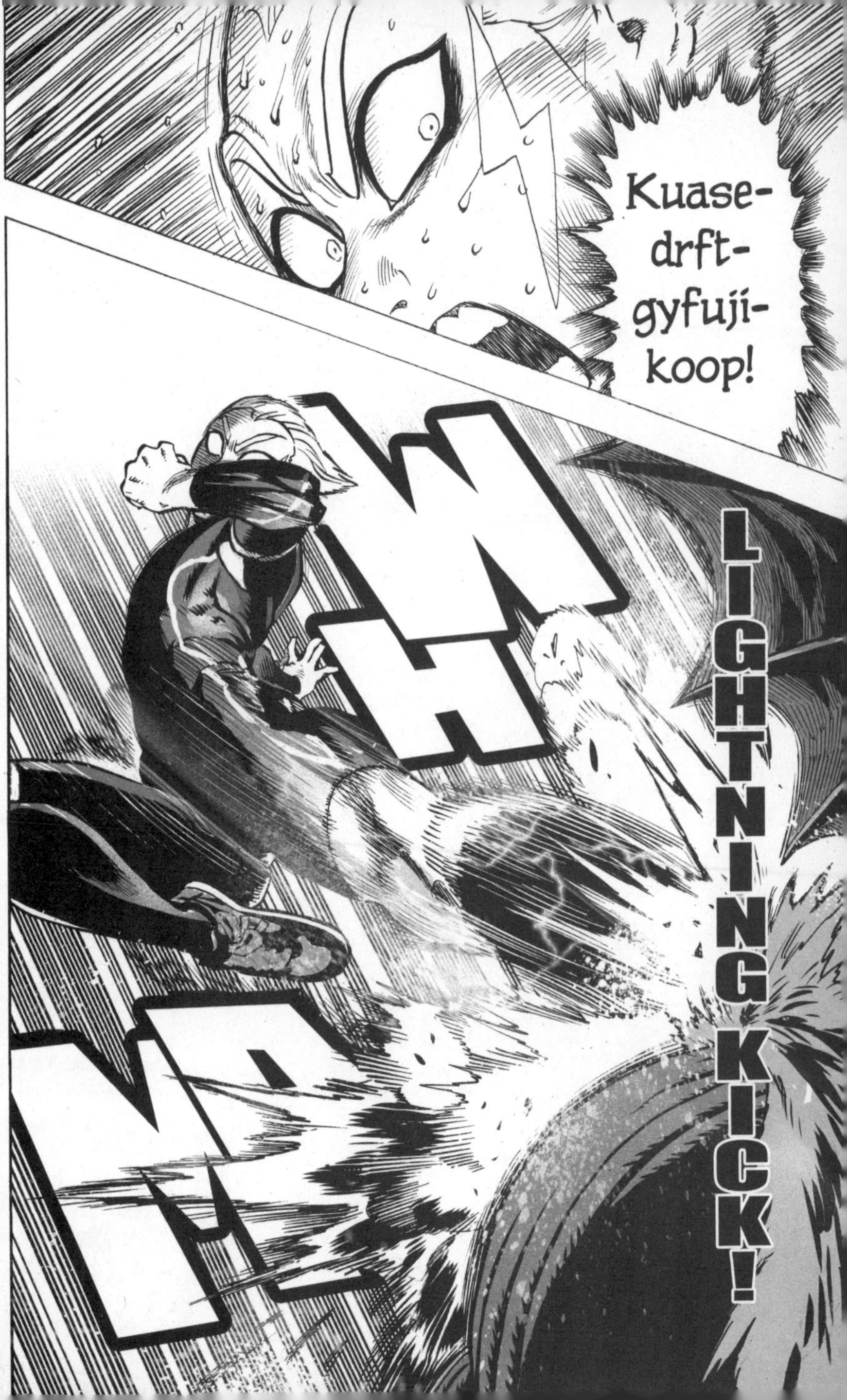
Kuase-drft-gyfuji-koop!
LIGHTNING KICK!

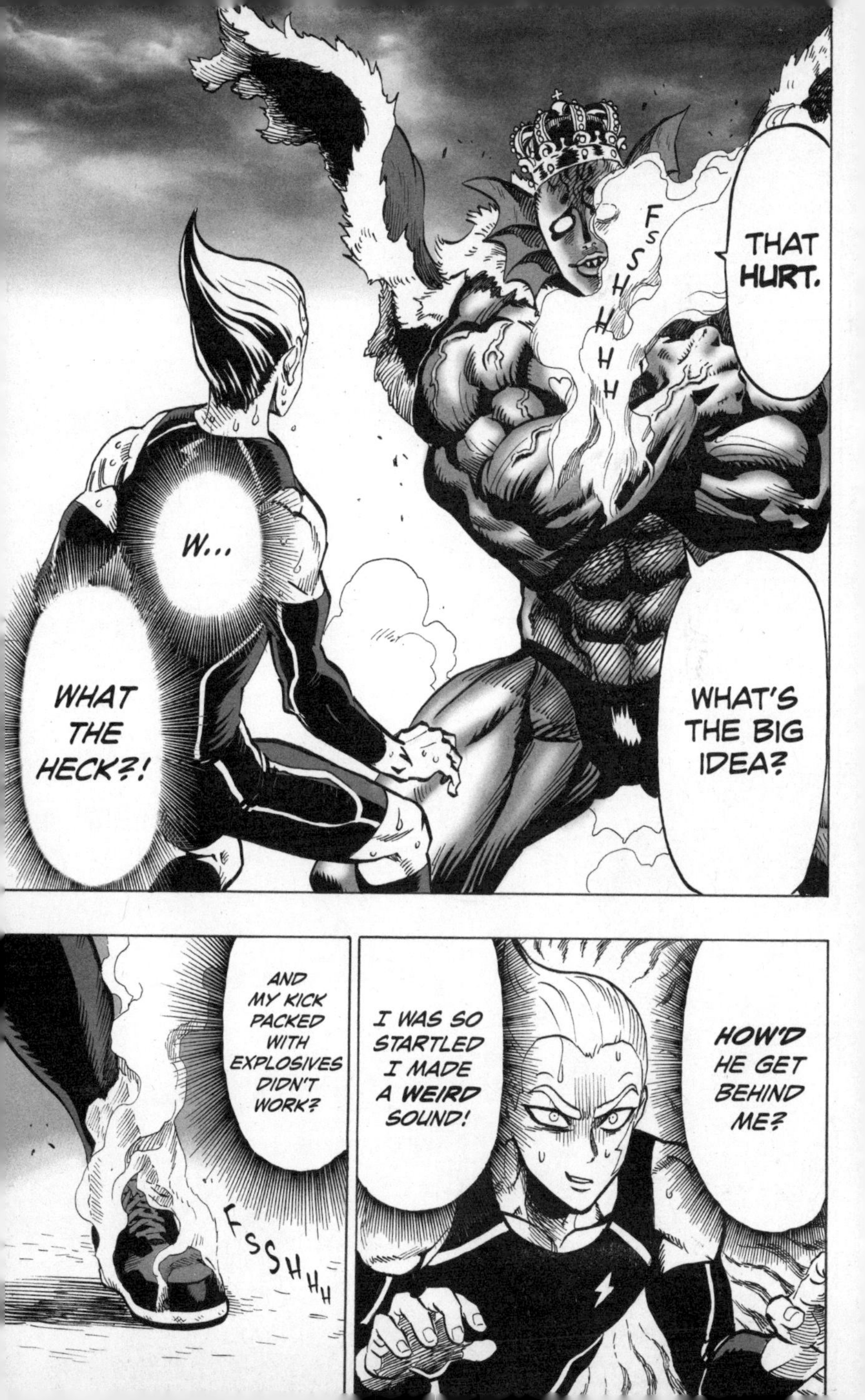
THAT HURT.
FSSHHHHH
WHAT'S THE BIG IDEA?
W...
WHAT THE HECK?!
HOW'D HE GET BEHIND ME?
I WAS SO STARTLED I MADE A WEIRD SOUND!
AND MY KICK PACKED WITH EXPLOSIVES DIDN'T WORK?
FSSHHH

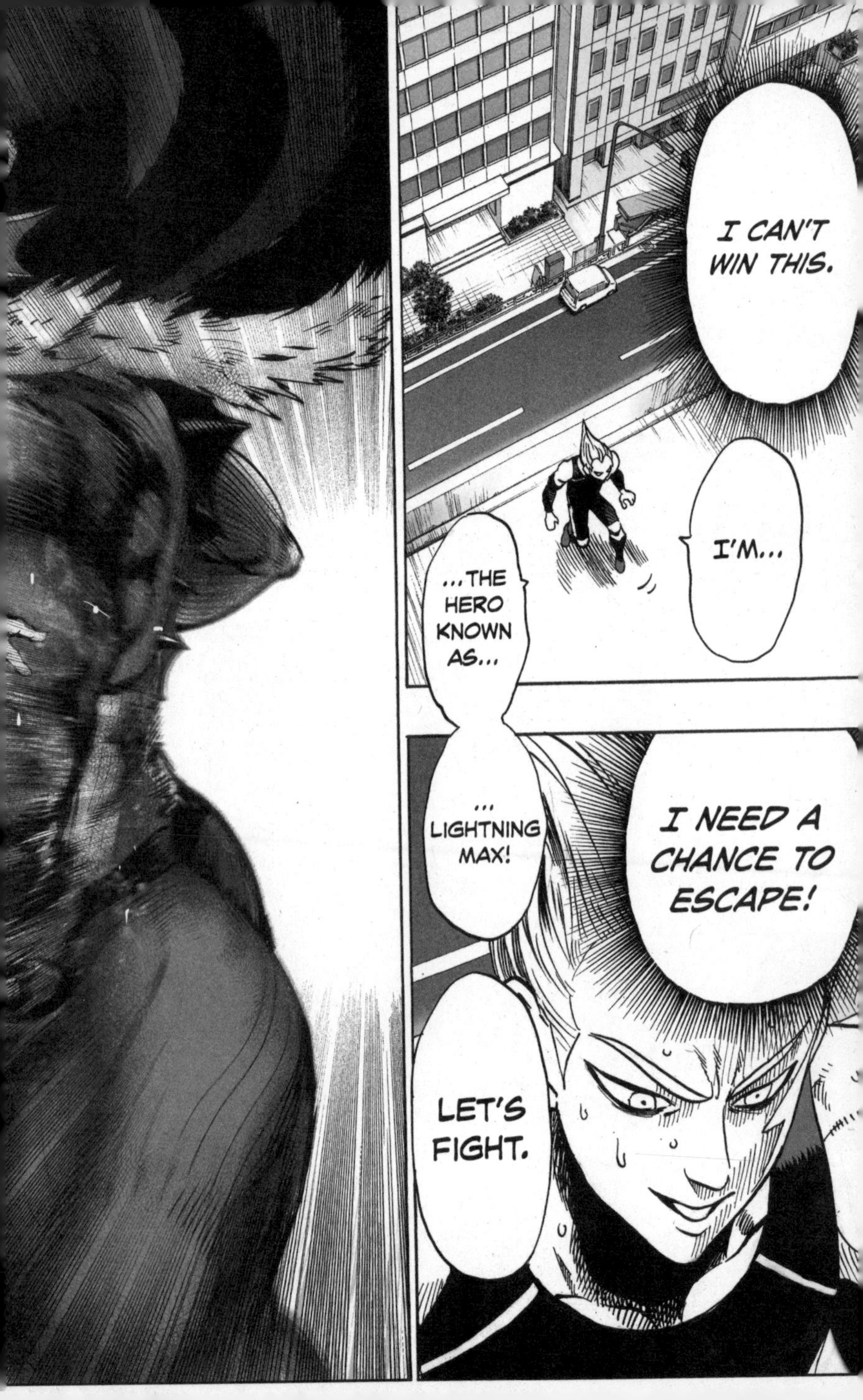
I CAN'T WIN THIS.
I'M...
...THE HERO KNOWN AS...
I NEED A CHANCE TO ESCAPE!
...LIGHTNING MAX!
LET'S FIGHT.

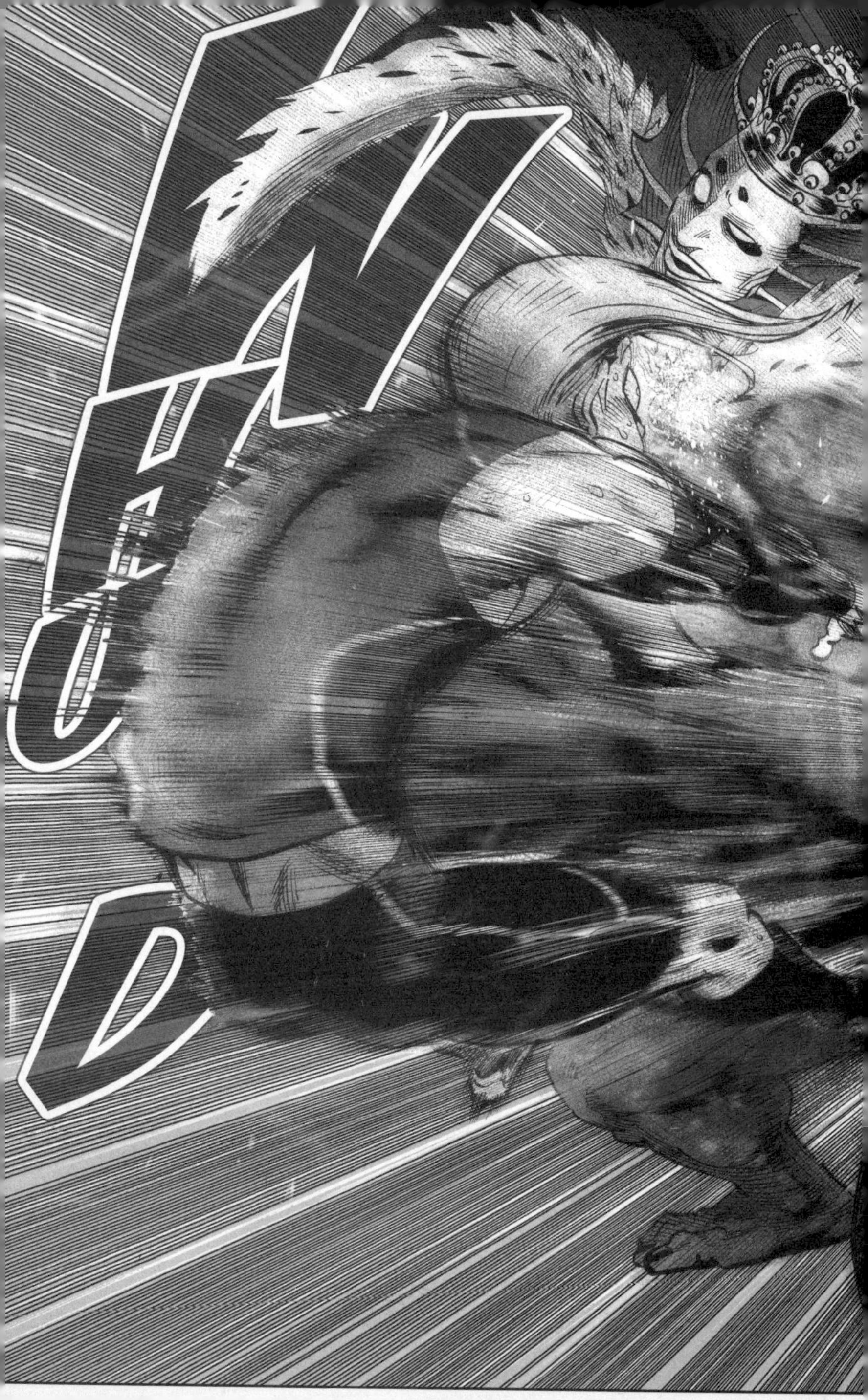

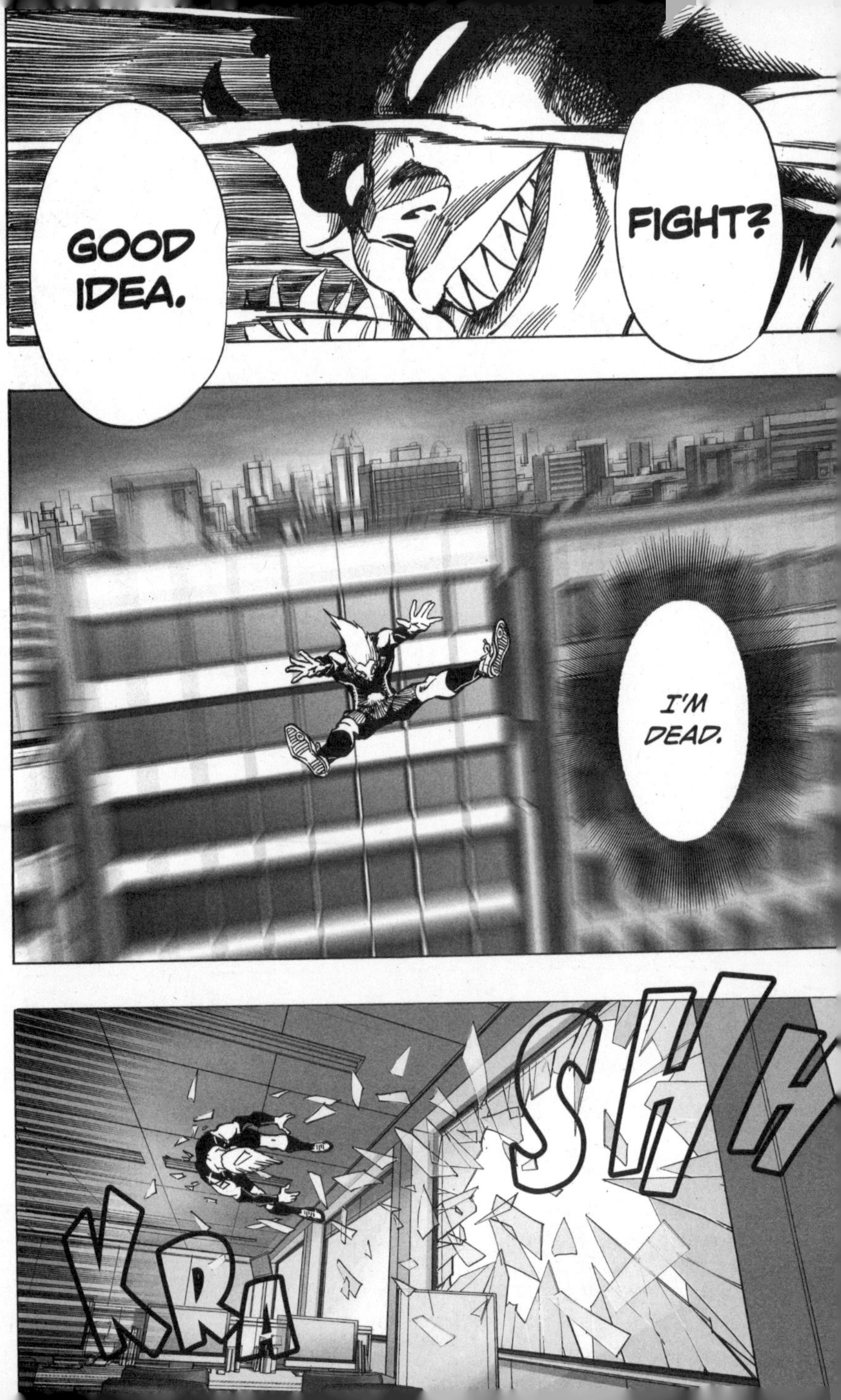
FIGHT?
GOOD IDEA.
I'M DEAD.
KRASH

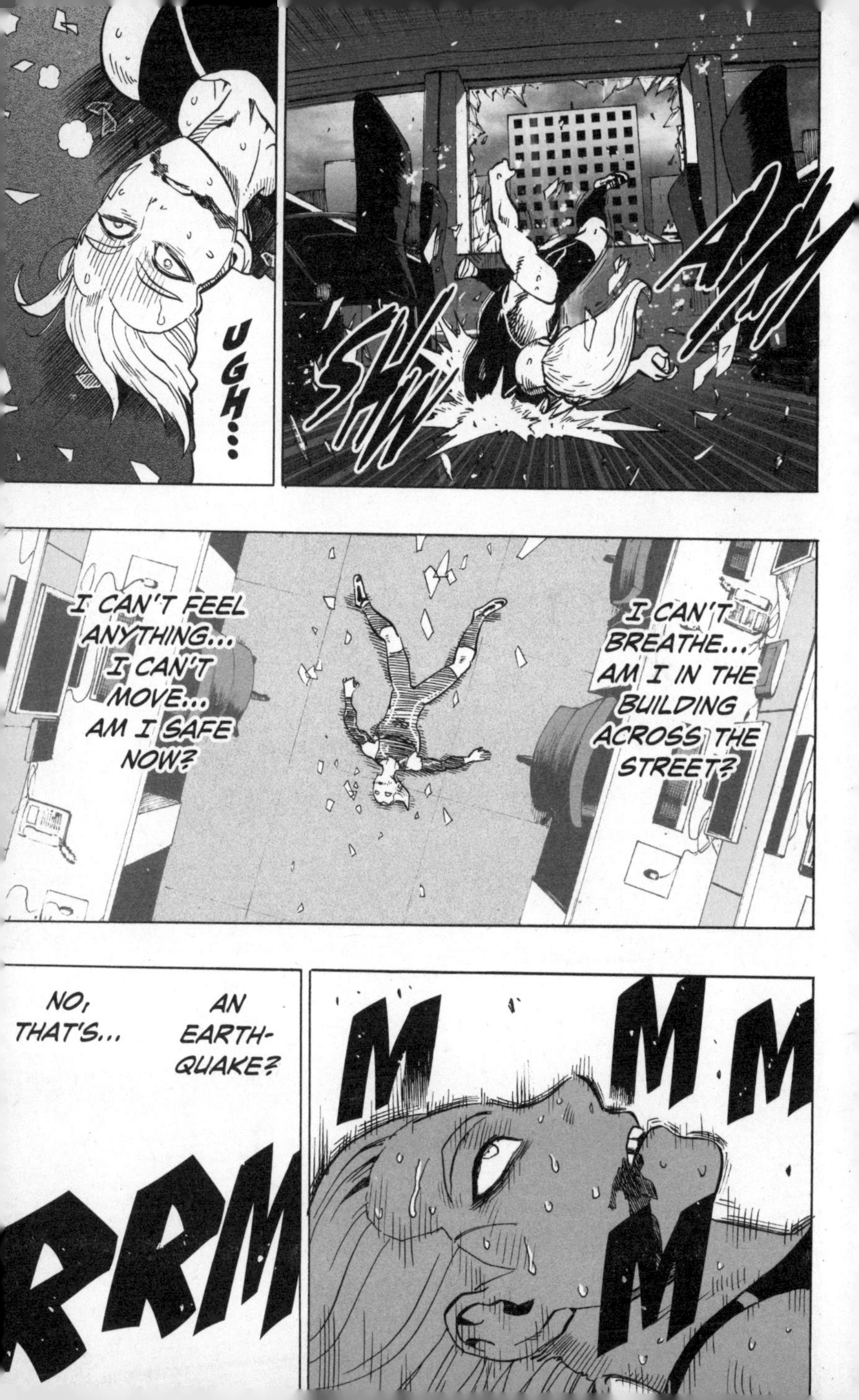
SHW
AM
UGH...
I CAN'T BREATHE... AM I IN THE BUILDING ACROSS THE STREET?
I CAN'T FEEL ANYTHING... I CAN'T MOVE... AM I SAFE NOW?
M M M
M
RRM
AN EARTH-QUAKE?
NO, THAT'S...

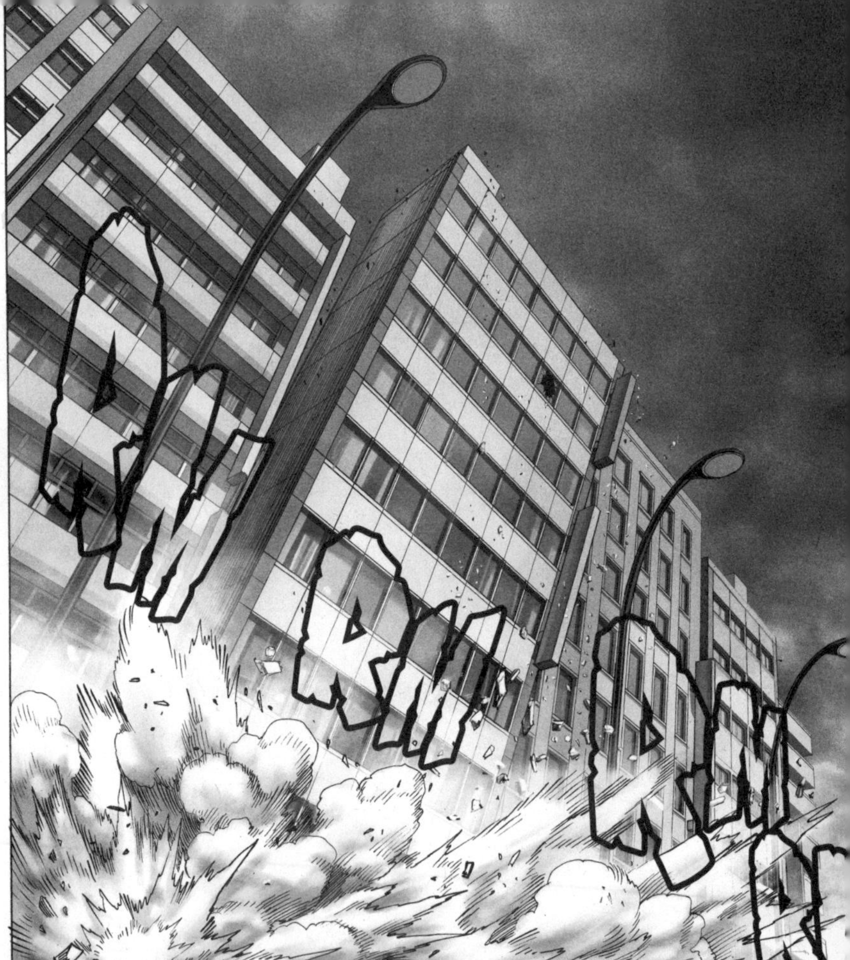

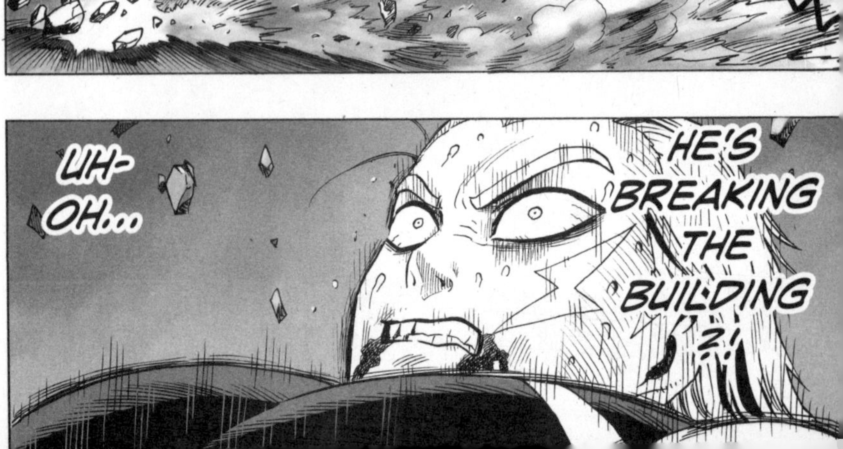
HE'S BREAKING THE BUILDING?!
UH-OH...

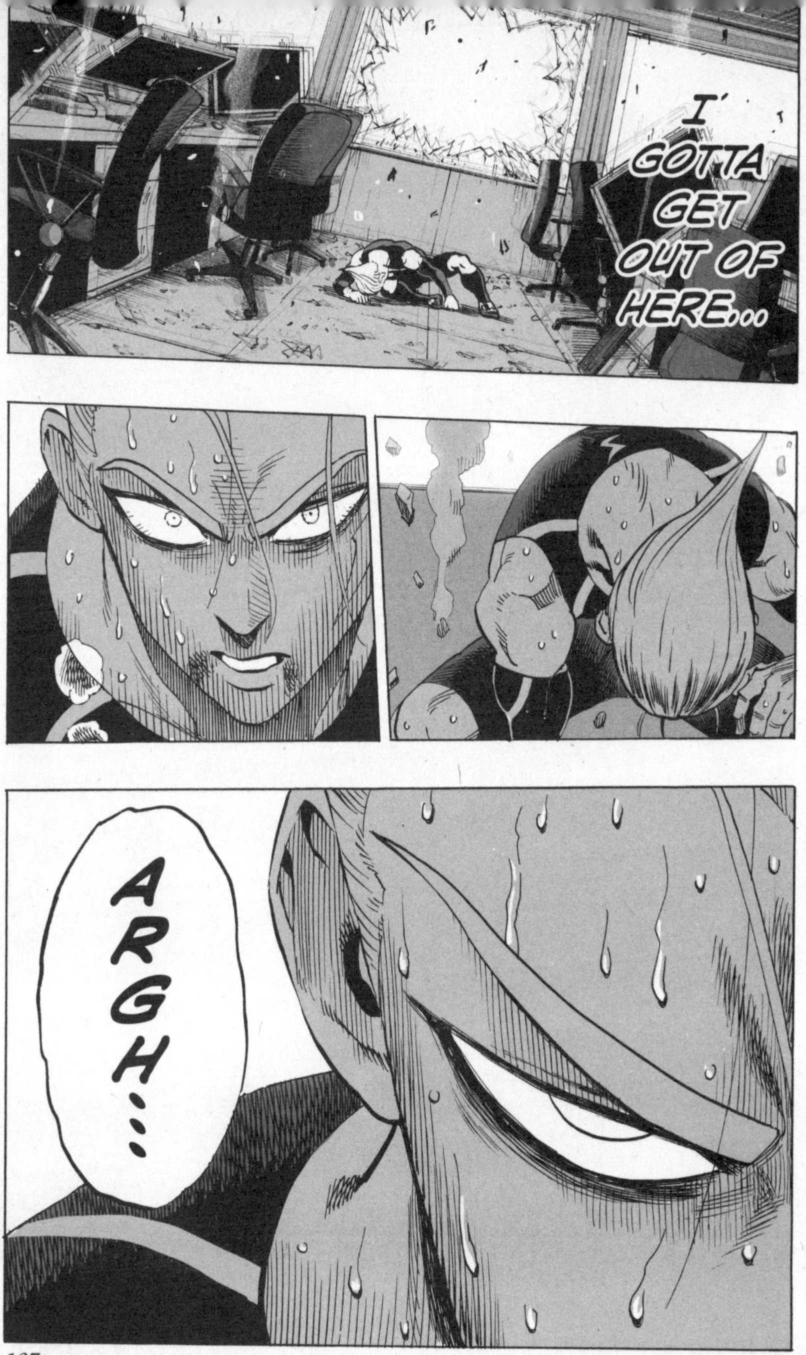
I' GOTTA GET OUT OF HERE...
ARGH...

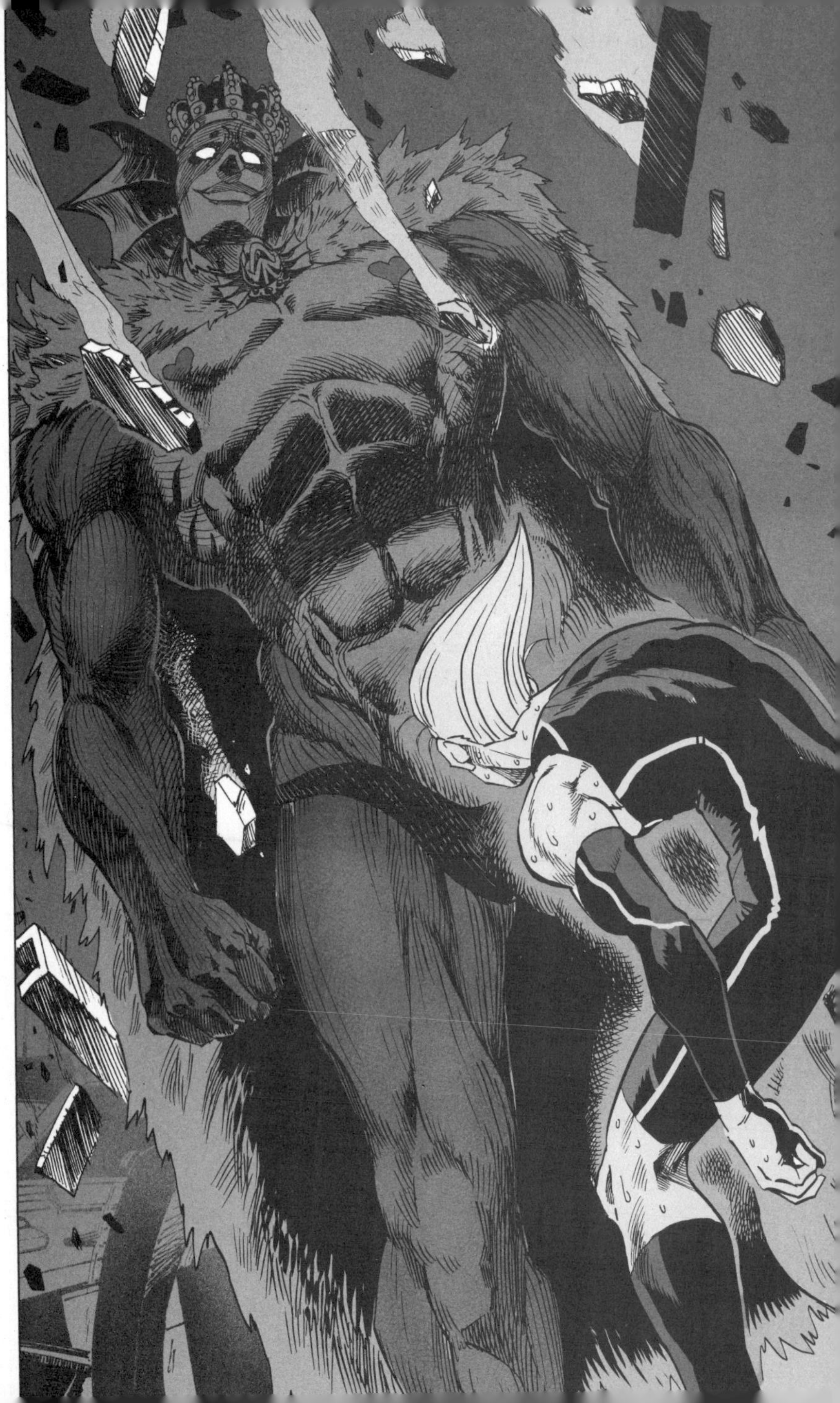

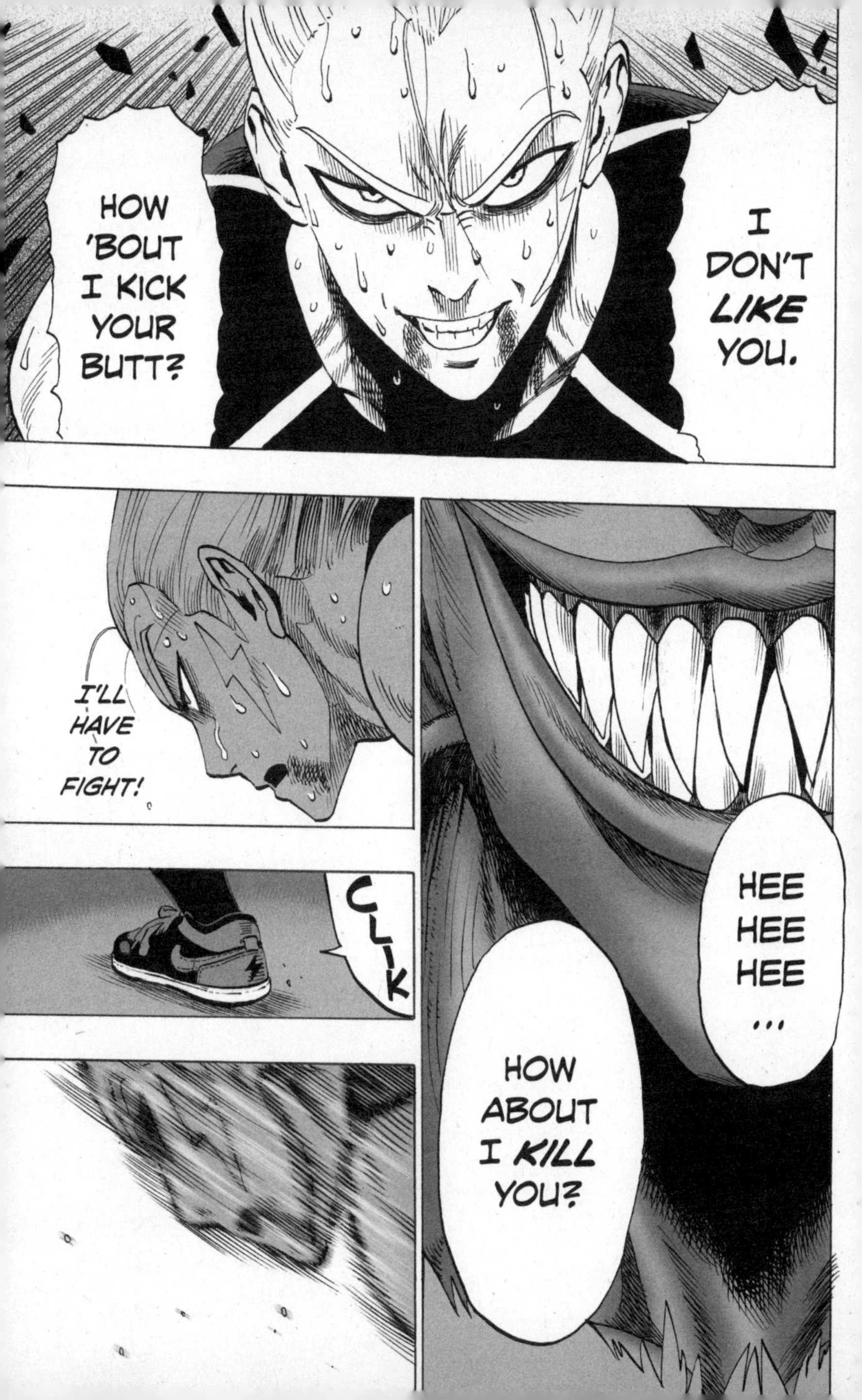
I DON'T *LIKE* YOU.
HOW 'BOUT I KICK YOUR BUTT?
HEE HEE HEE ...
HOW ABOUT I *KILL* YOU?
I'LL HAVE TO FIGHT!
CLIK

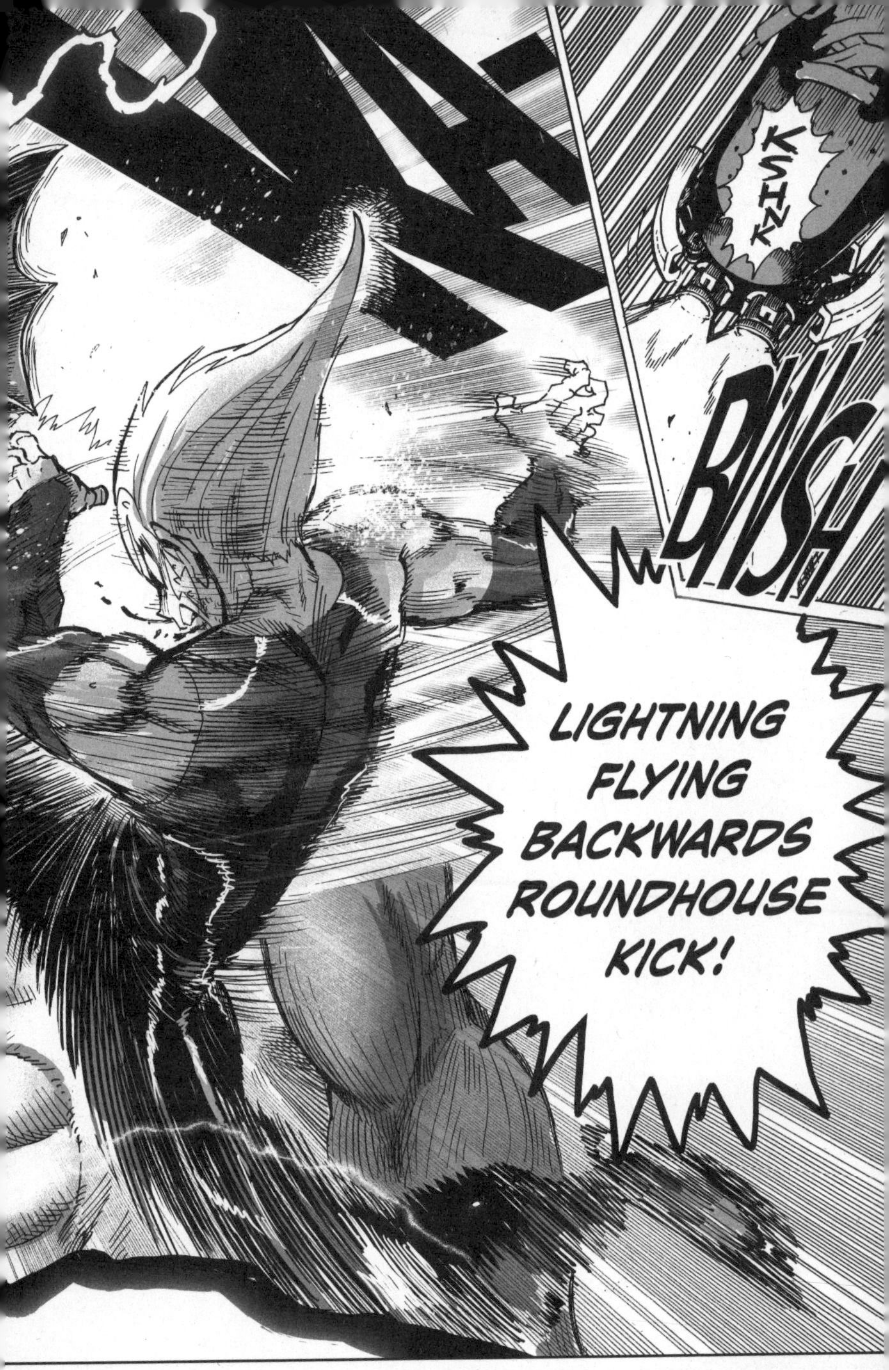
KSHNK
BISH
LIGHTNING FLYING BACKWARDS ROUNDHOUSE KICK!

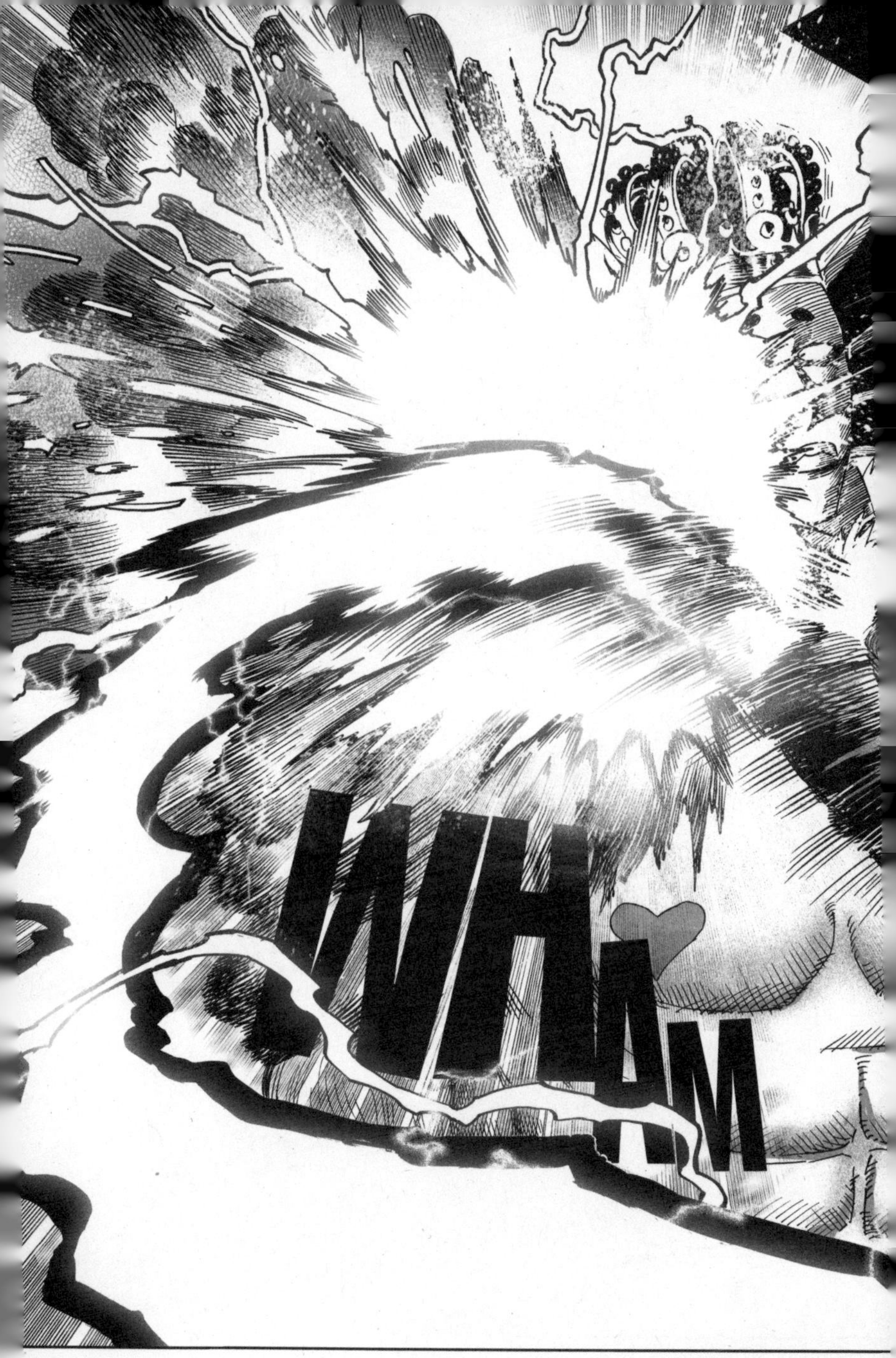
WHAM

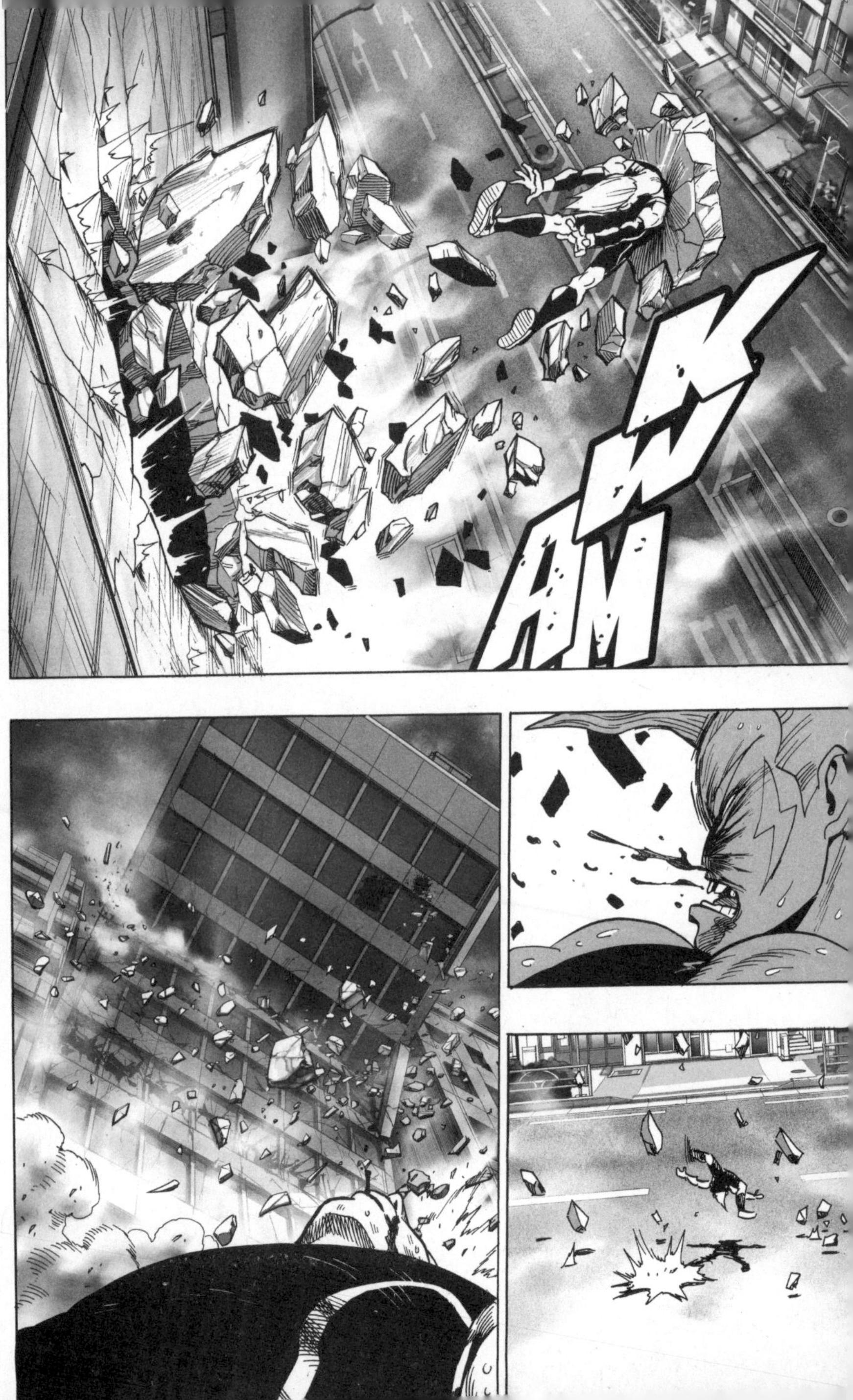
KWAM

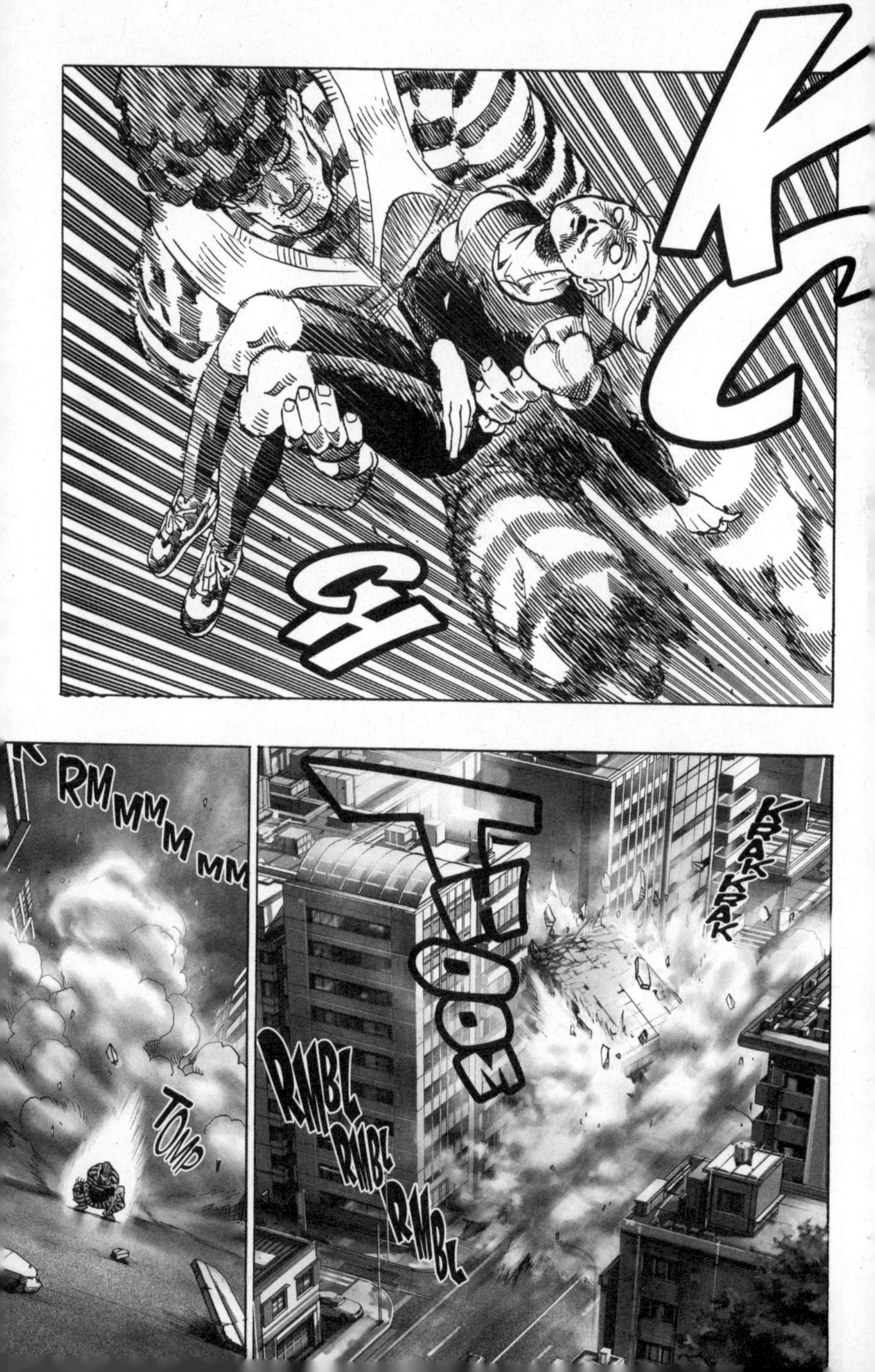
KRG
GH
TOOOM
KRAK KRAK KRAK
RMBL RMBL RMBL
RMMMMM MM
TOMP

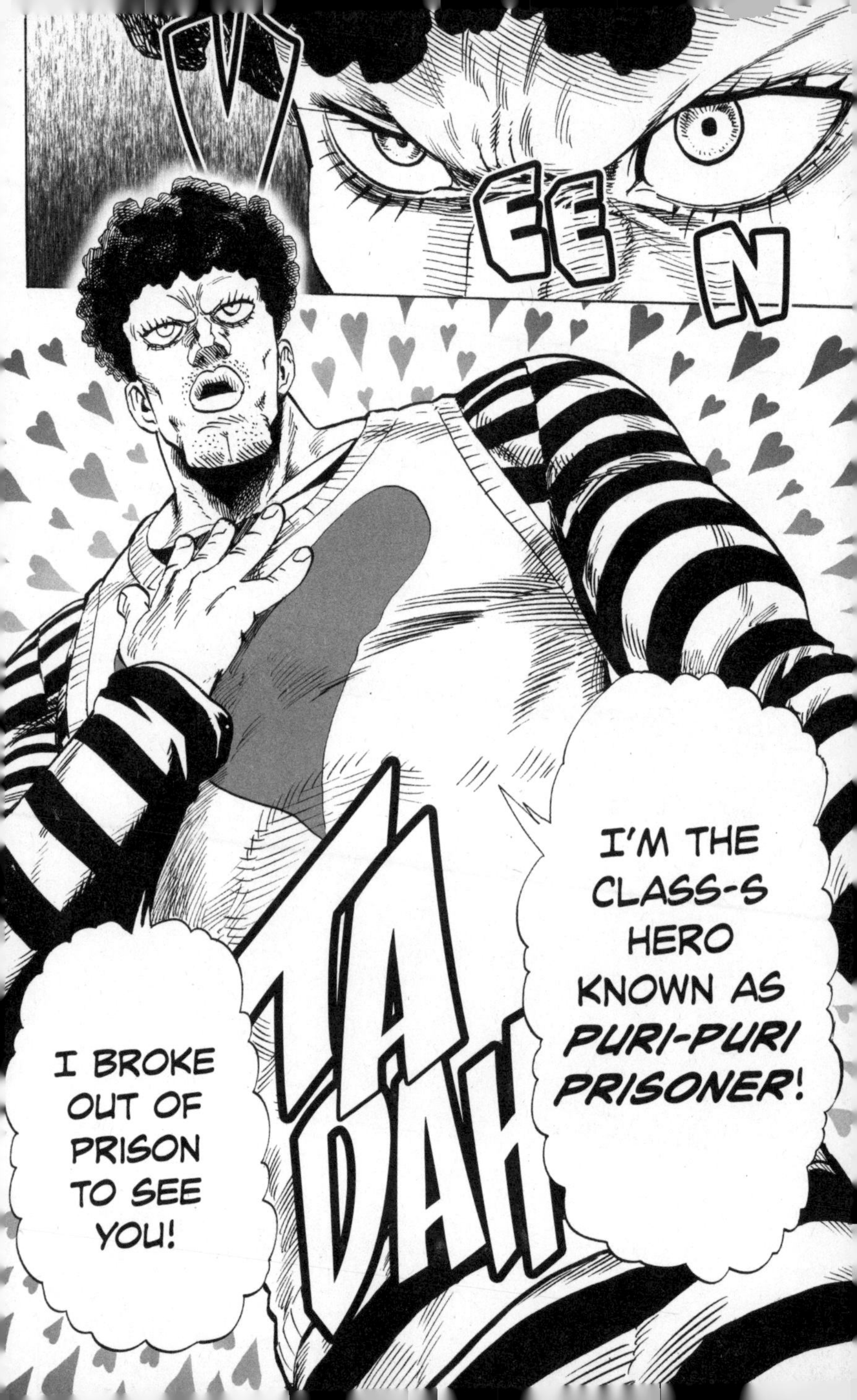

VEEN
I'M THE CLASS-S HERO KNOWN AS *PURI-PURI PRISONER*!
TA DAH
I BROKE OUT OF PRISON TO SEE YOU!

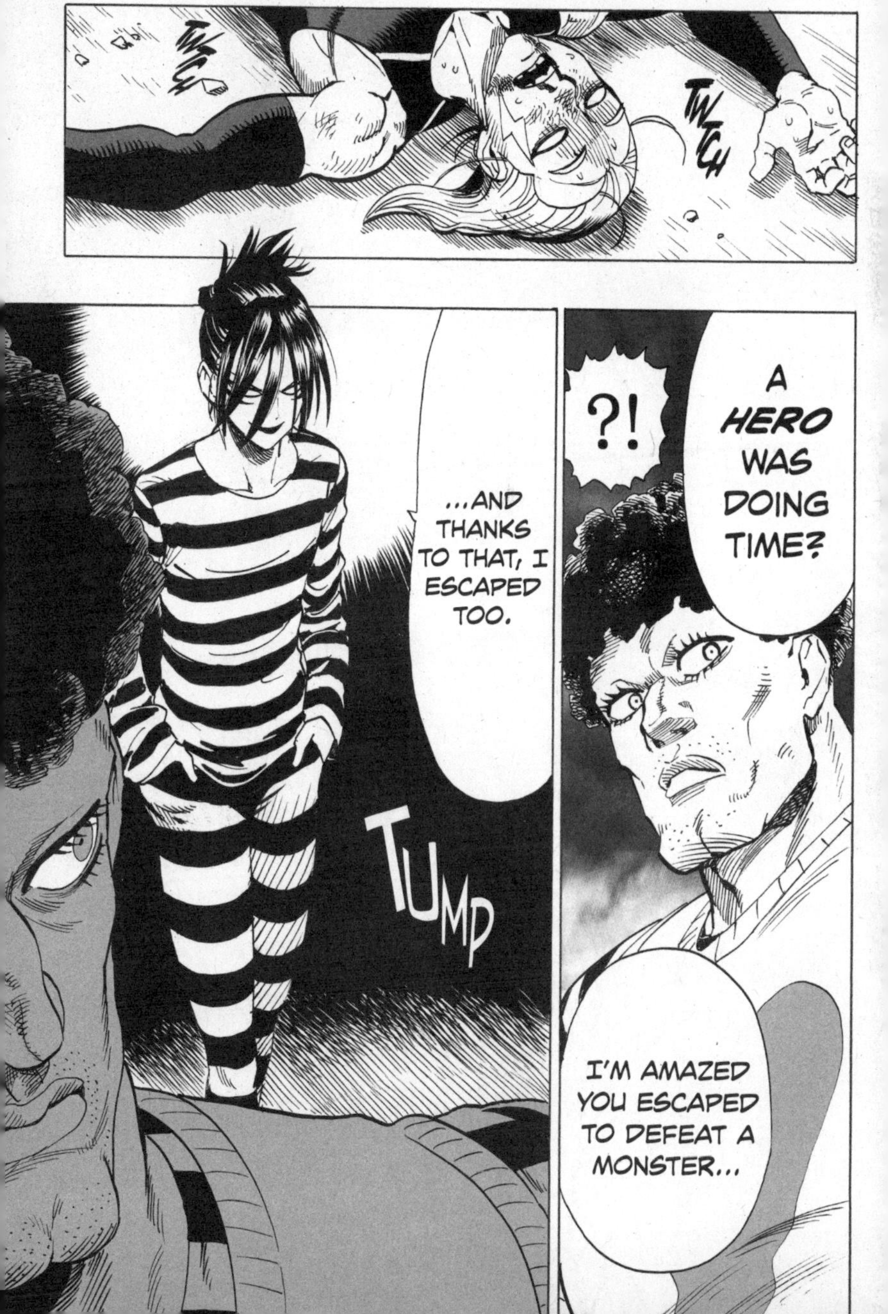
TWITCH
TWITCH
?!
A HERO WAS DOING TIME?
I'M AMAZED YOU ESCAPED TO DEFEAT A MONSTER...
...AND THANKS TO THAT, I ESCAPED TOO.
TUMP

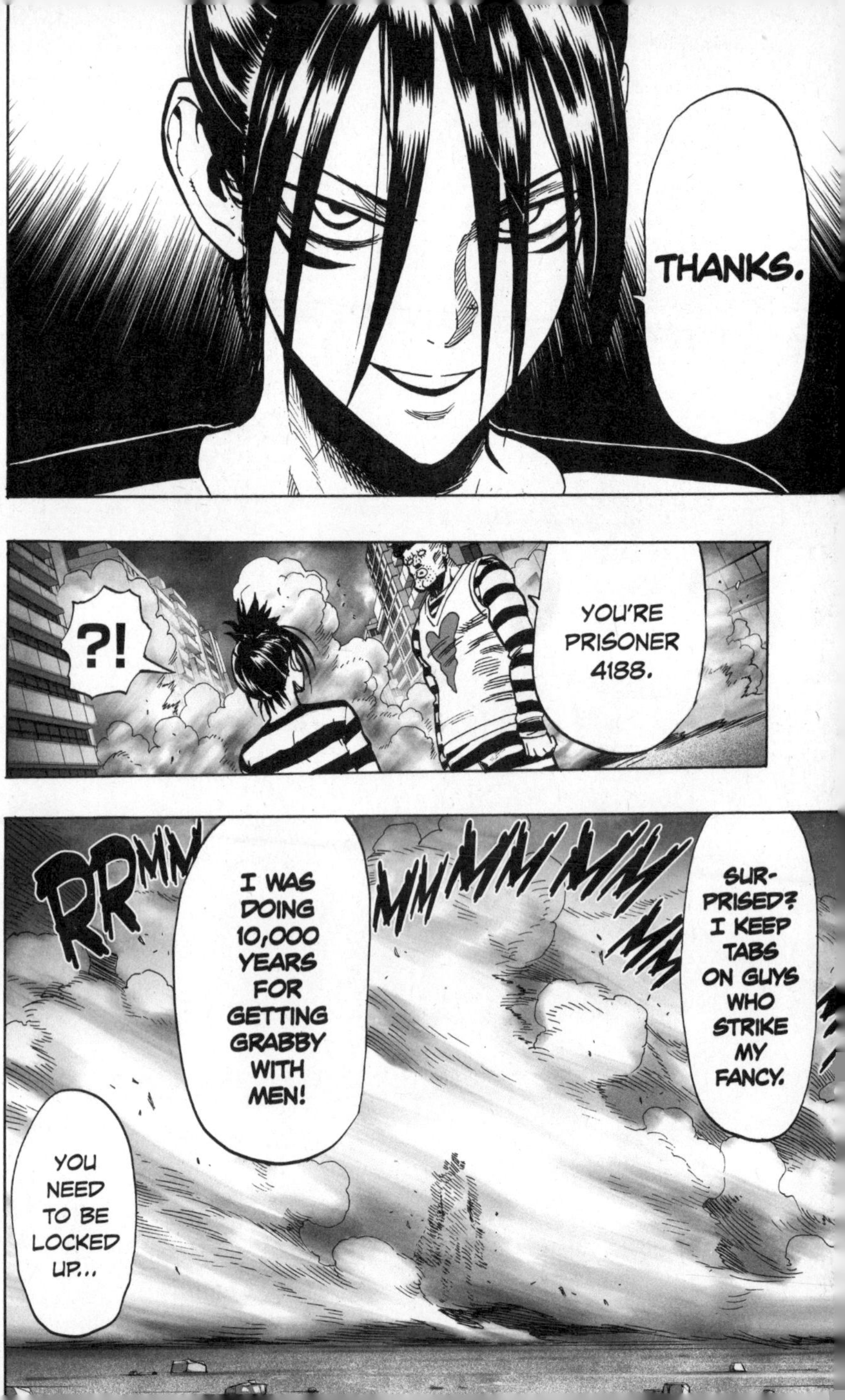
THANKS.
YOU'RE PRISONER 4188.
?!
SUR-PRISED? I KEEP TABS ON GUYS WHO STRIKE MY FANCY.
I WAS DOING 10,000 YEARS FOR GETTING GRABBY WITH MEN!
RRMMMMMMMMMMMM
YOU NEED TO BE LOCKED UP...

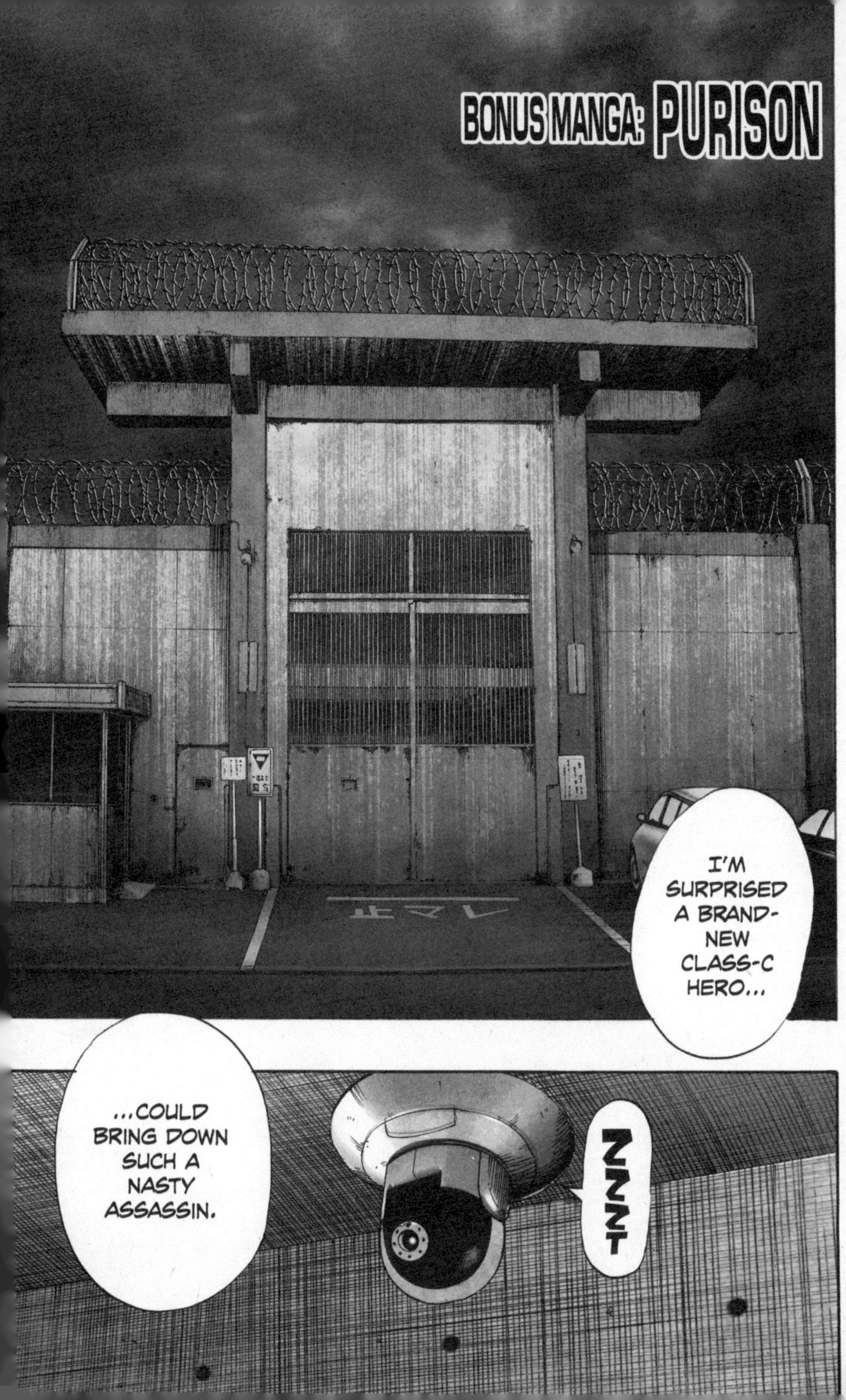
BONUS MANGA: PURISON
I'M SURPRISED A BRAND-NEW CLASS-C HERO...
...COULD BRING DOWN SUCH A NASTY ASSASSIN.
NZZT

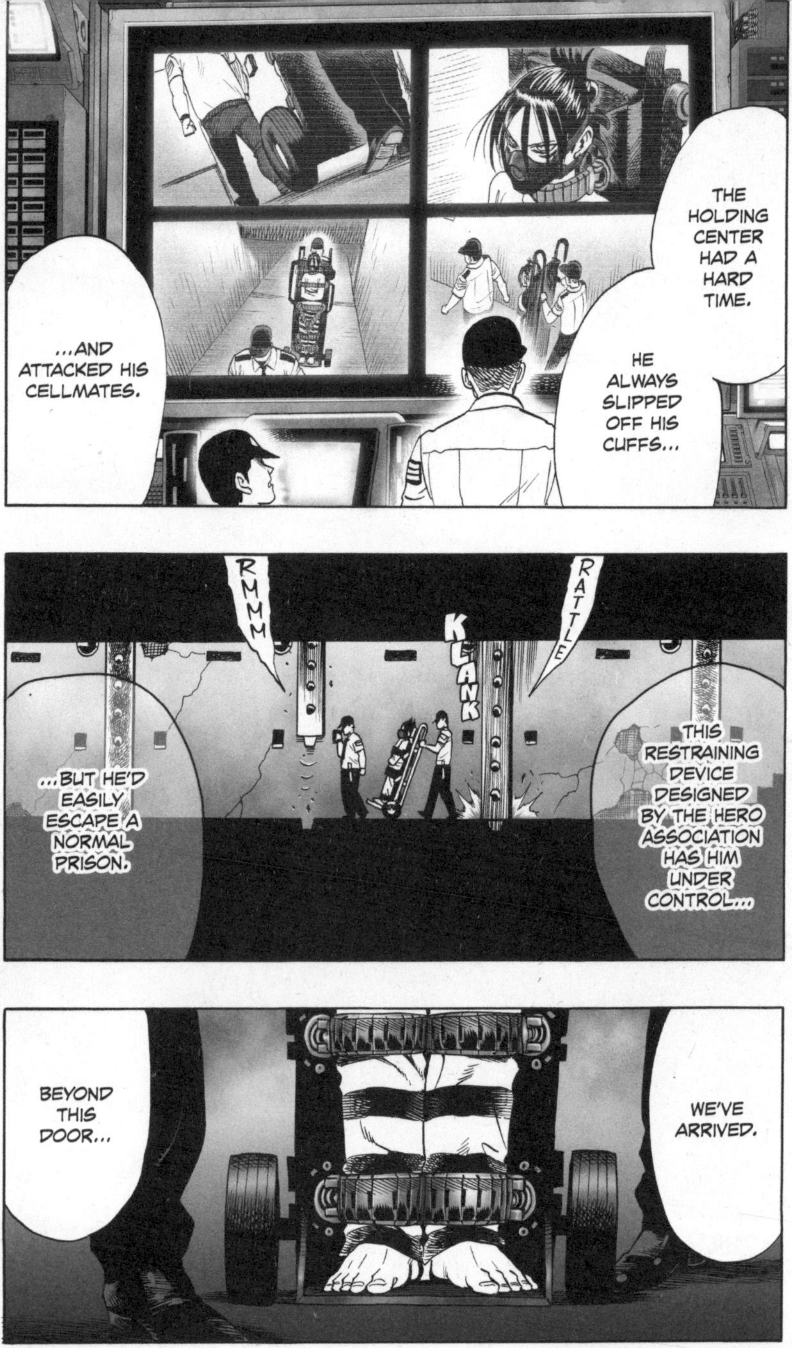
THE HOLDING CENTER HAD A HARD TIME.
HE ALWAYS SLIPPED OFF HIS CUFFS...
...AND ATTACKED HIS CELLMATES.
RATTLE
KLANK
RMMM
THIS RESTRAINING DEVICE DESIGNED BY THE HERO ASSOCIATION HAS HIM UNDER CONTROL...
...BUT HE'D EASILY ESCAPE A NORMAL PRISON.
WE'VE ARRIVED.
BEYOND THIS DOOR...

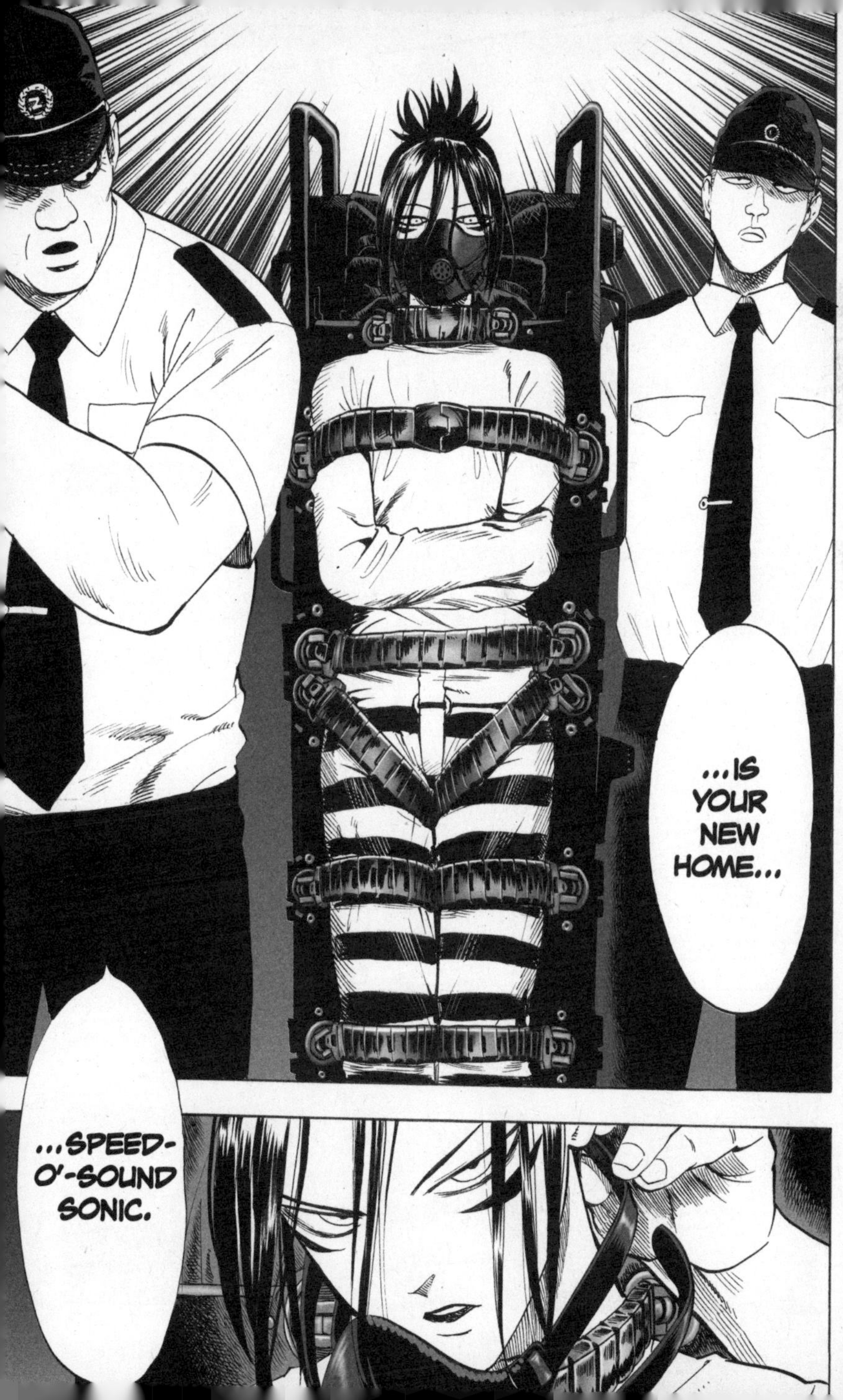
...IS YOUR NEW HOME...
...SPEED-O'-SOUND SONIC.

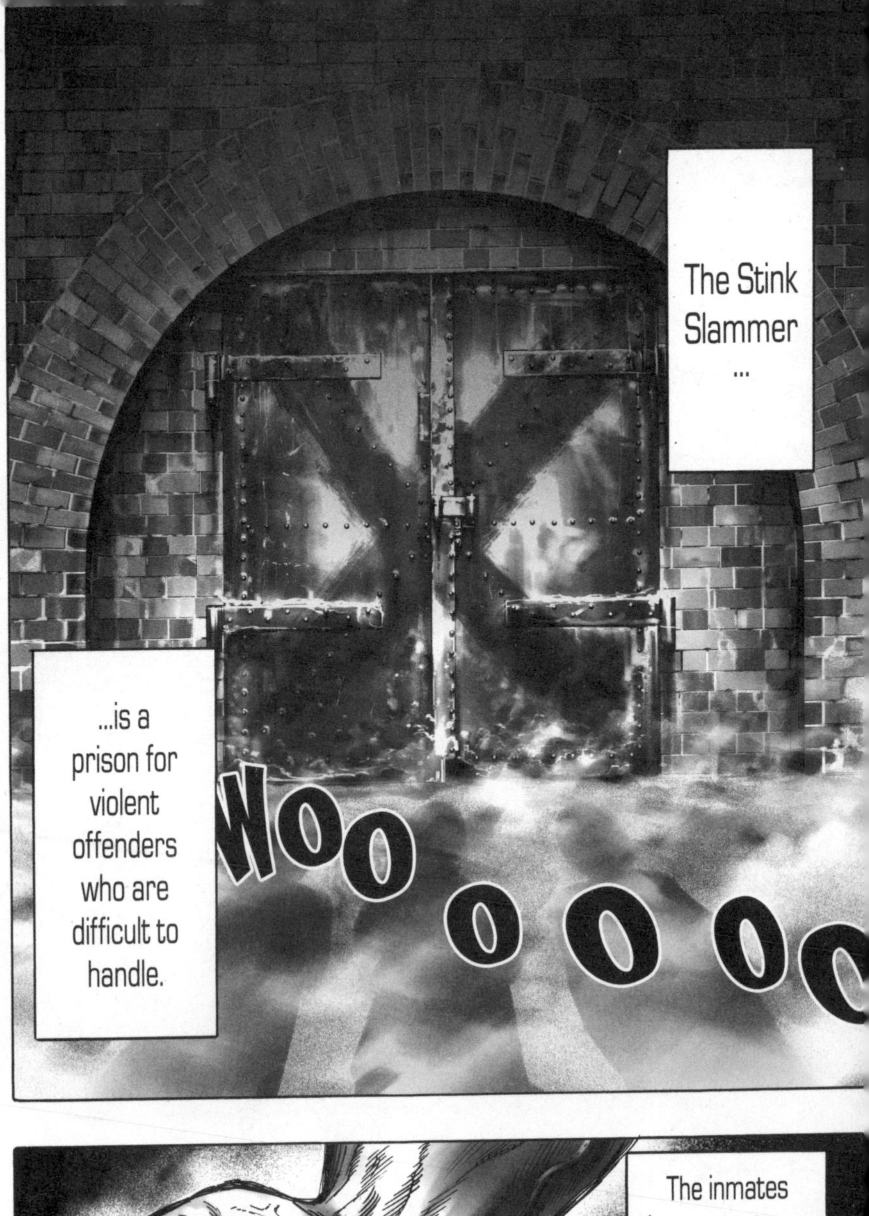
The Stink Slammer ...
...is a prison for violent offenders who are difficult to handle.
WOOOOOO

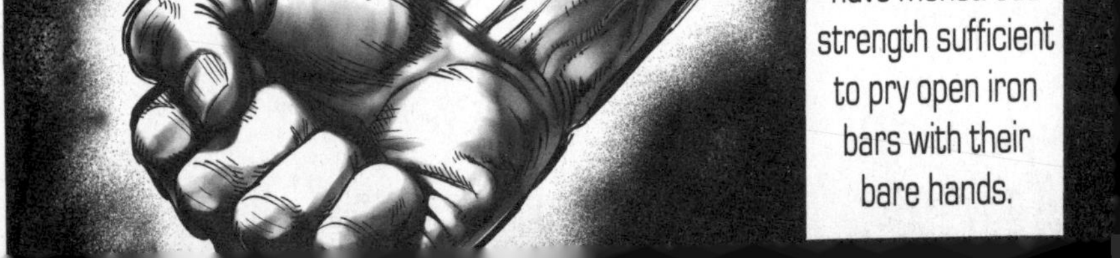
The inmates have monstrous strength sufficient to pry open iron bars with their bare hands.

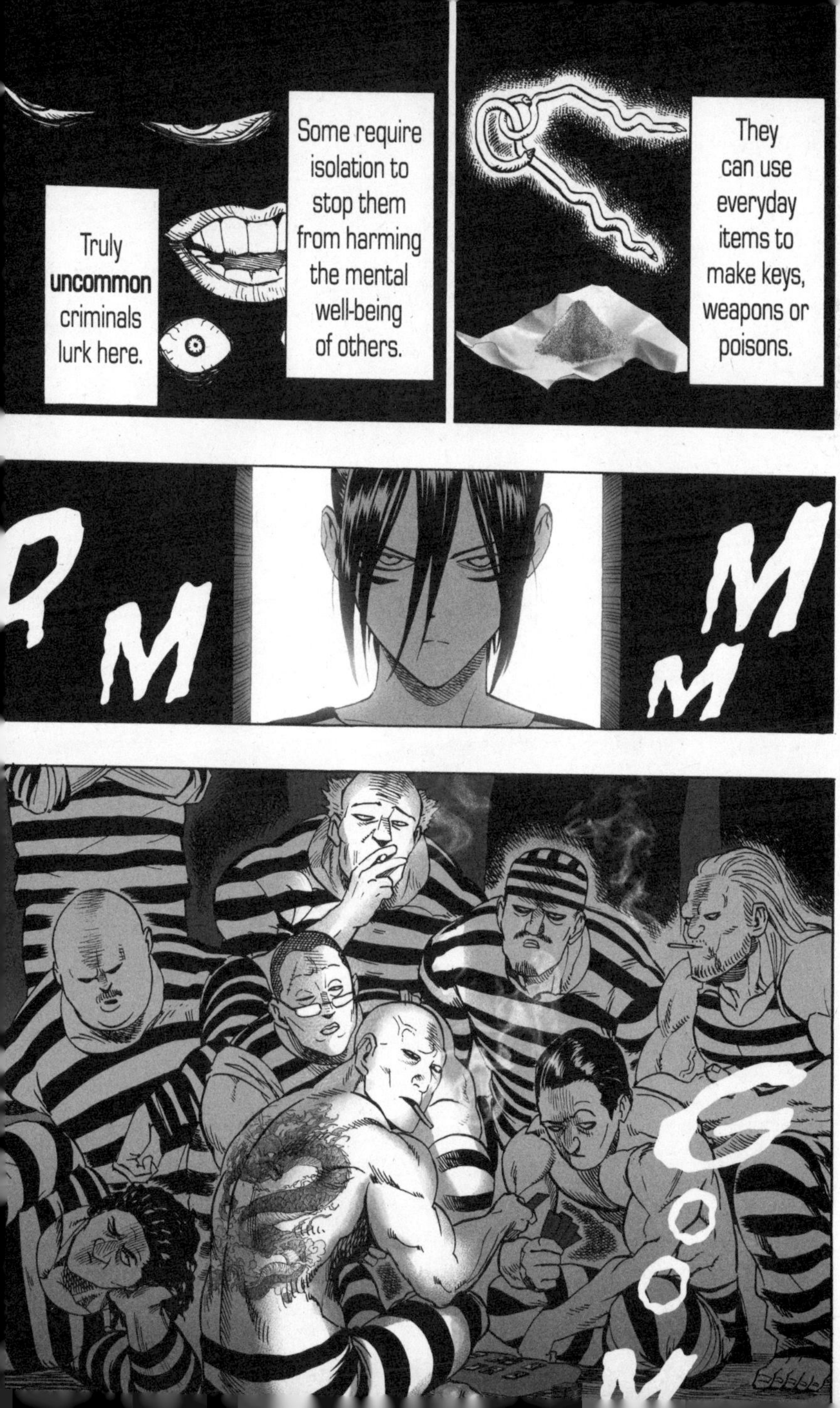

They can use everyday items to make keys, weapons or poisons.
Some require isolation to stop them from harming the mental well-being of others.
Truly **uncommon** criminals lurk here.
MM
M
GOOOM

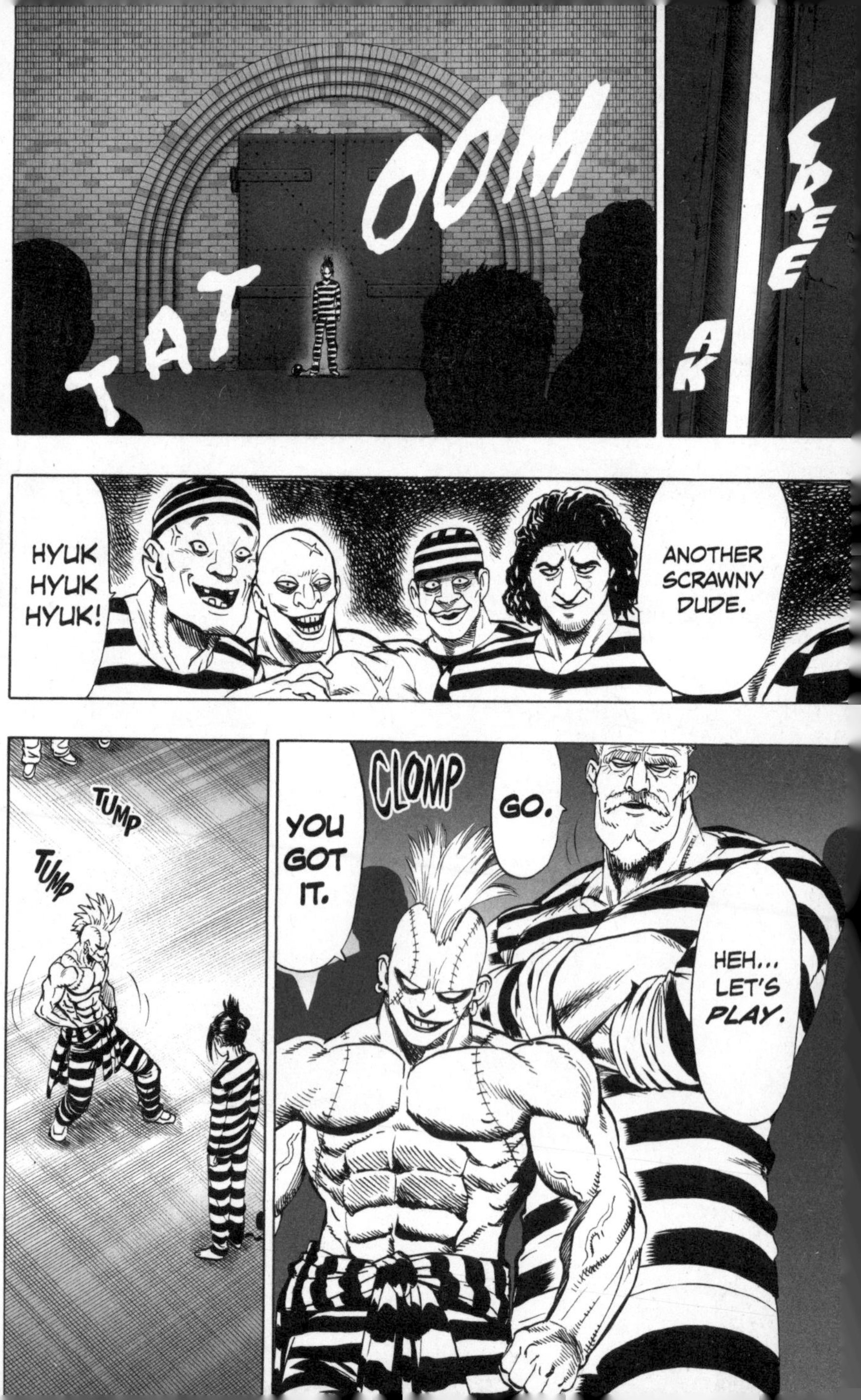
CREEAK
TATOOM
ANOTHER SCRAWNY DUDE.
HYUK HYUK HYUK!
GO.
CLOMP
YOU GOT IT.
HEH... LET'S *PLAY*.
TUMP
TUMP

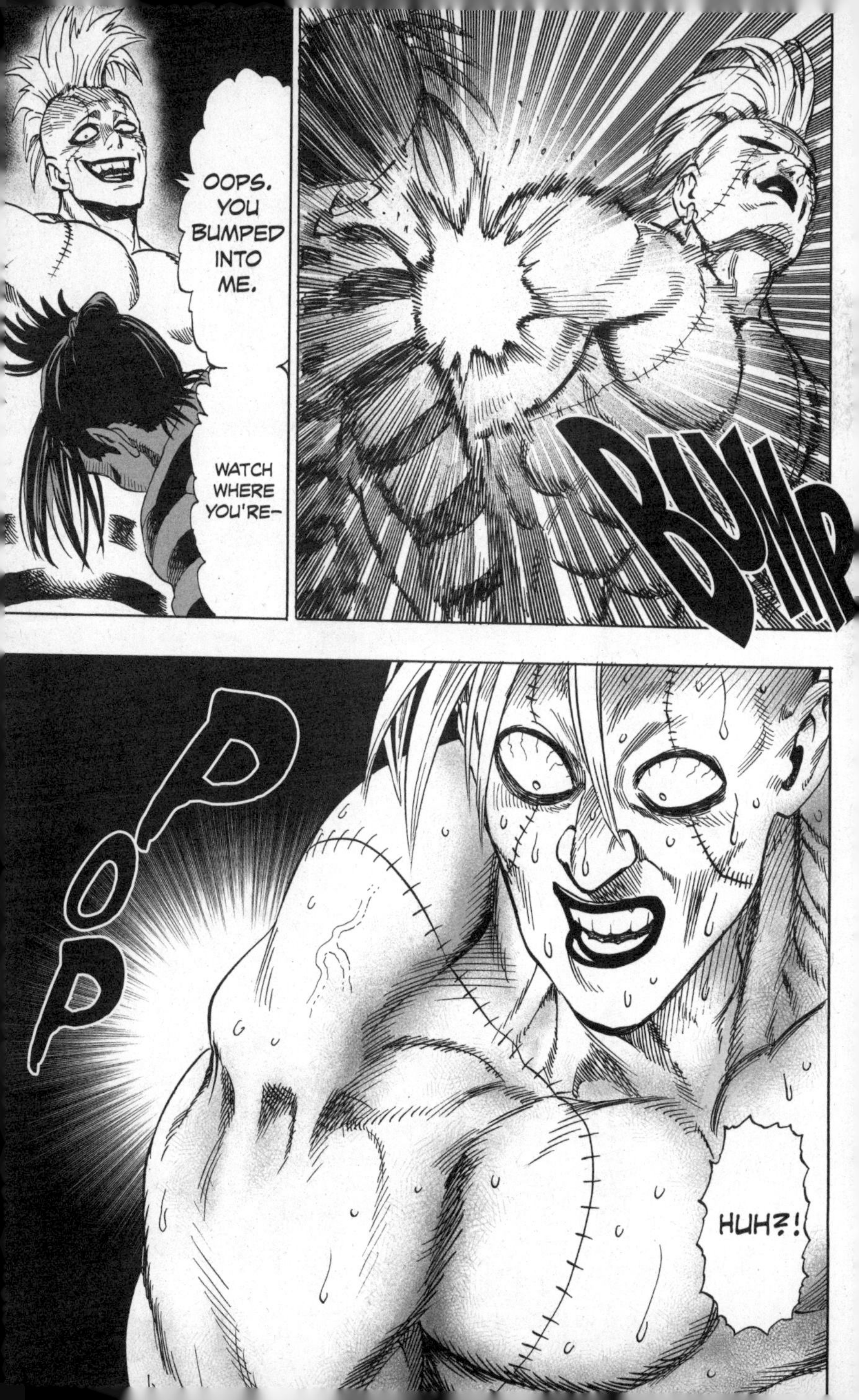
BUMP
OOPS. YOU BUMPED INTO ME.
WATCH WHERE YOU'RE-
HUH?!
POP

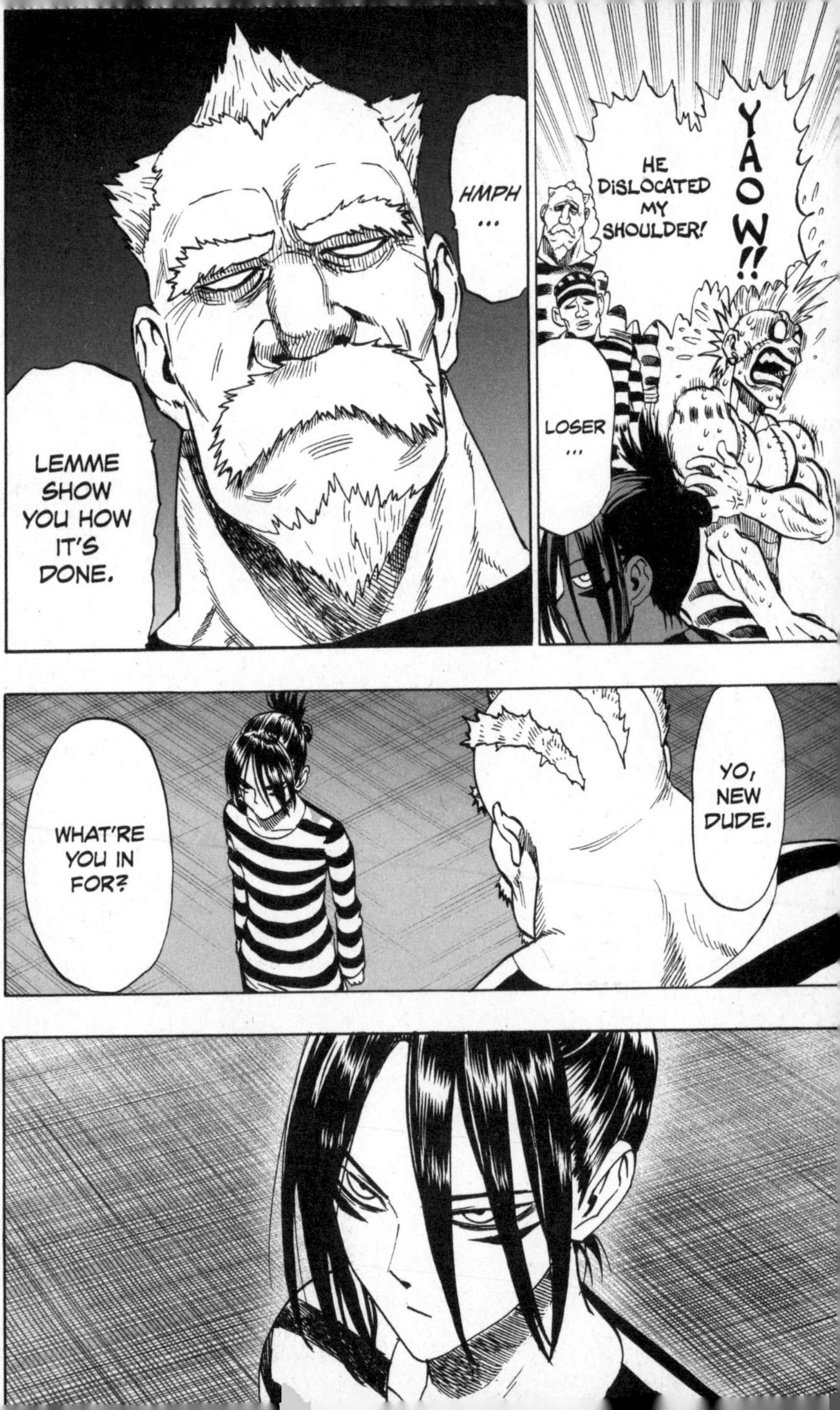
YAOW!!
HE DISLOCATED MY SHOULDER!
LOSER ...
HMPH ...
LEMME SHOW YOU HOW IT'S DONE.
YO, NEW DUDE.
WHAT'RE YOU IN FOR?

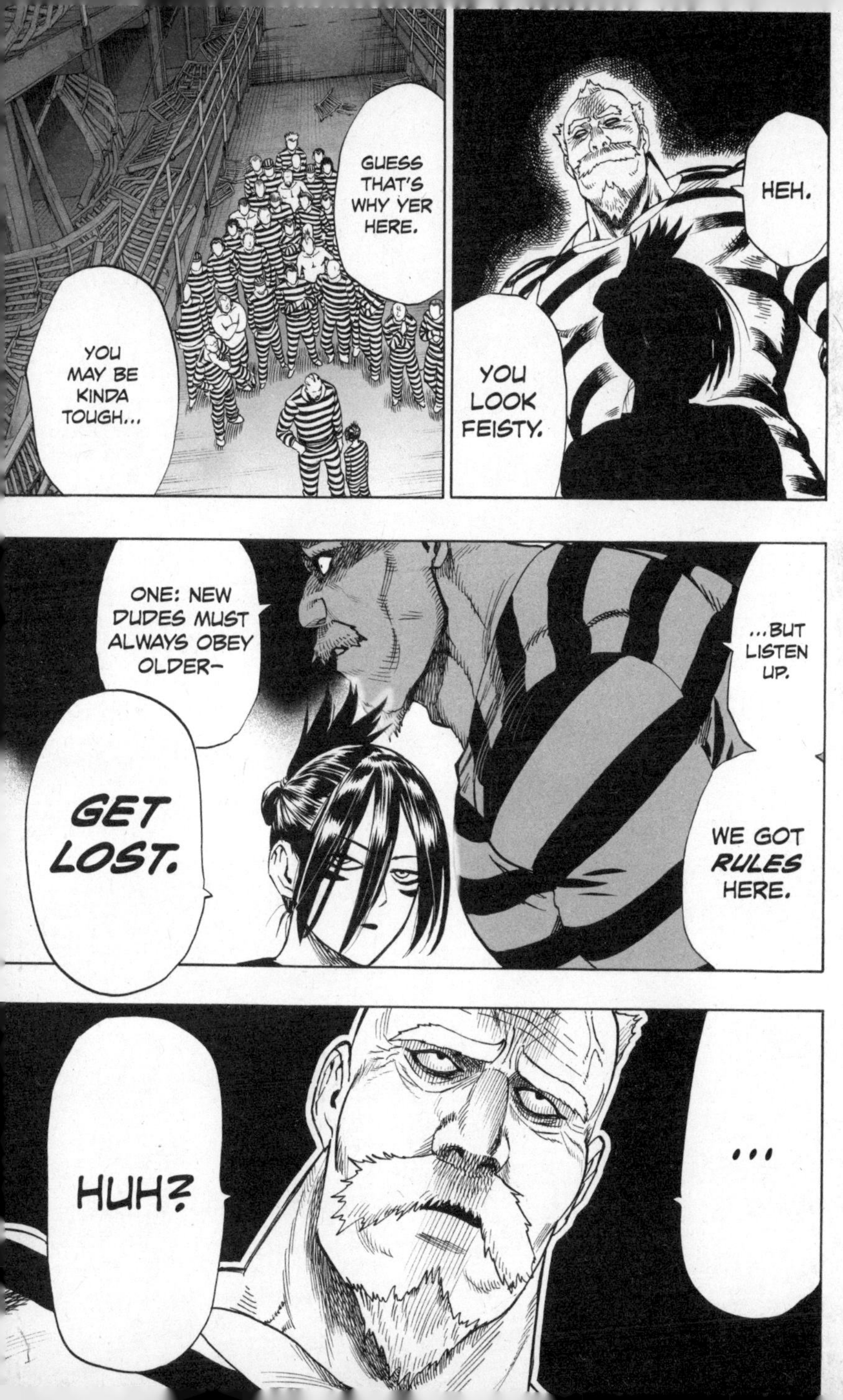
HEH.
YOU LOOK FEISTY.
GUESS THAT'S WHY YER HERE.
YOU MAY BE KINDA TOUGH...
...BUT LISTEN UP.
WE GOT *RULES* HERE.
ONE: NEW DUDES MUST ALWAYS OBEY OLDER-
GET LOST.
...
HUH?

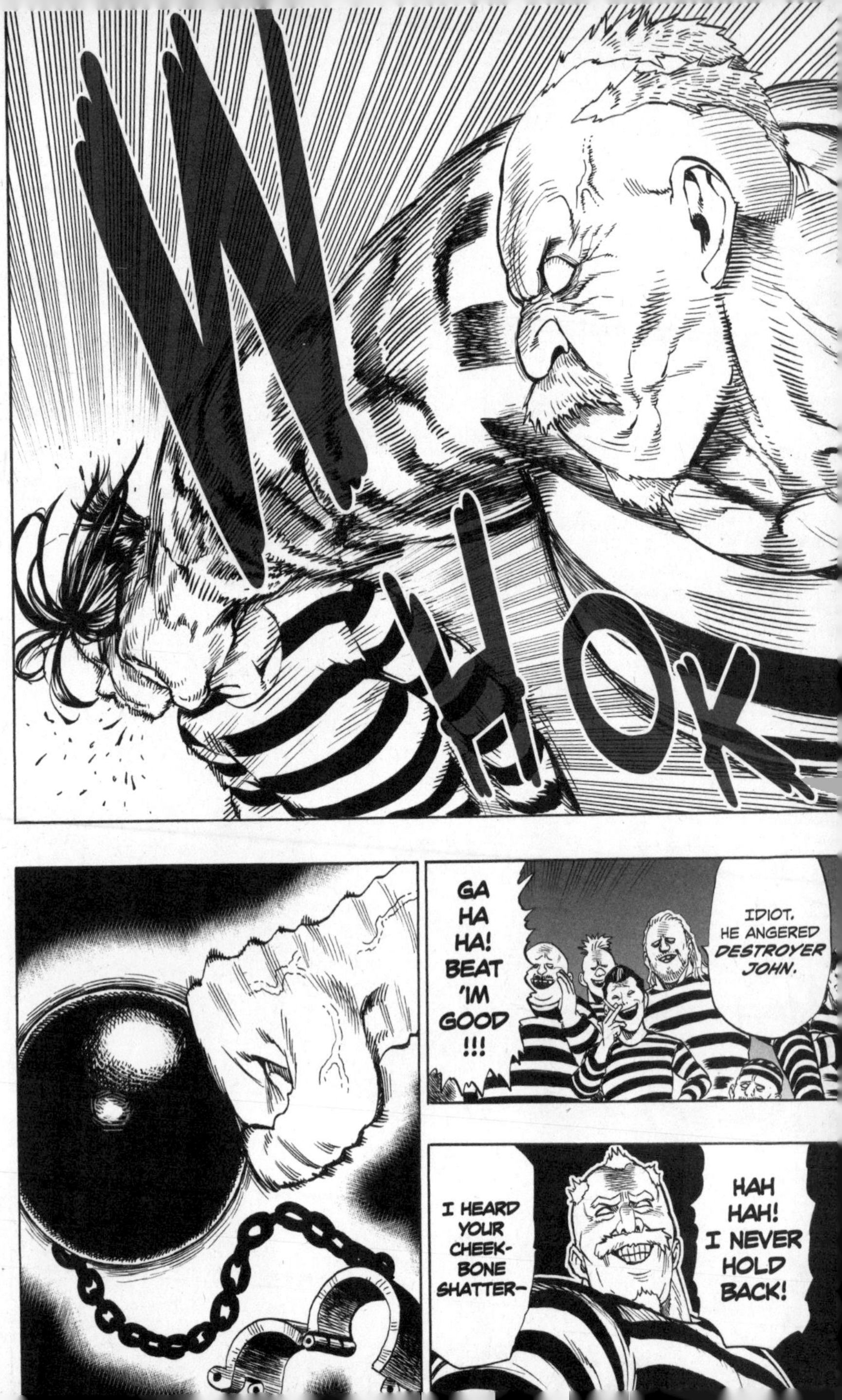
WHOK
IDIOT. HE ANGERED *DESTROYER JOHN.*
GA HA HA! BEAT 'IM GOOD!!!
HAH HAH! I NEVER HOLD BACK!
I HEARD YOUR CHEEK-BONE SHATTER-

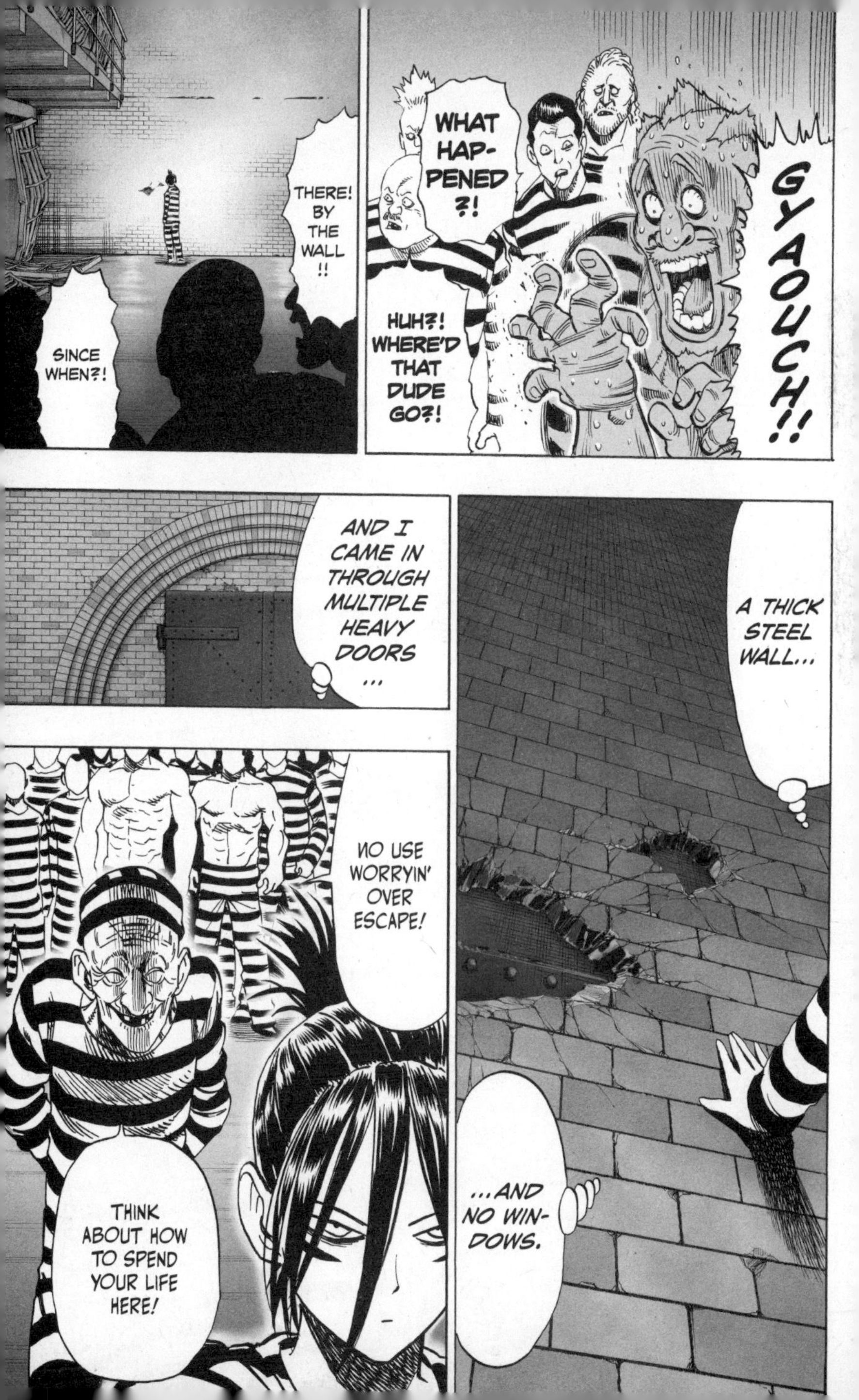
GYAOUCH!!
WHAT HAPPENED?!
HUH?! WHERE'D THAT DUDE GO?!
THERE! BY THE WALL!!
SINCE WHEN?!
A THICK STEEL WALL...
...AND NO WINDOWS.
AND I CAME IN THROUGH MULTIPLE HEAVY DOORS...
NO USE WORRYIN' OVER ESCAPE!
THINK ABOUT HOW TO SPEND YOUR LIFE HERE!

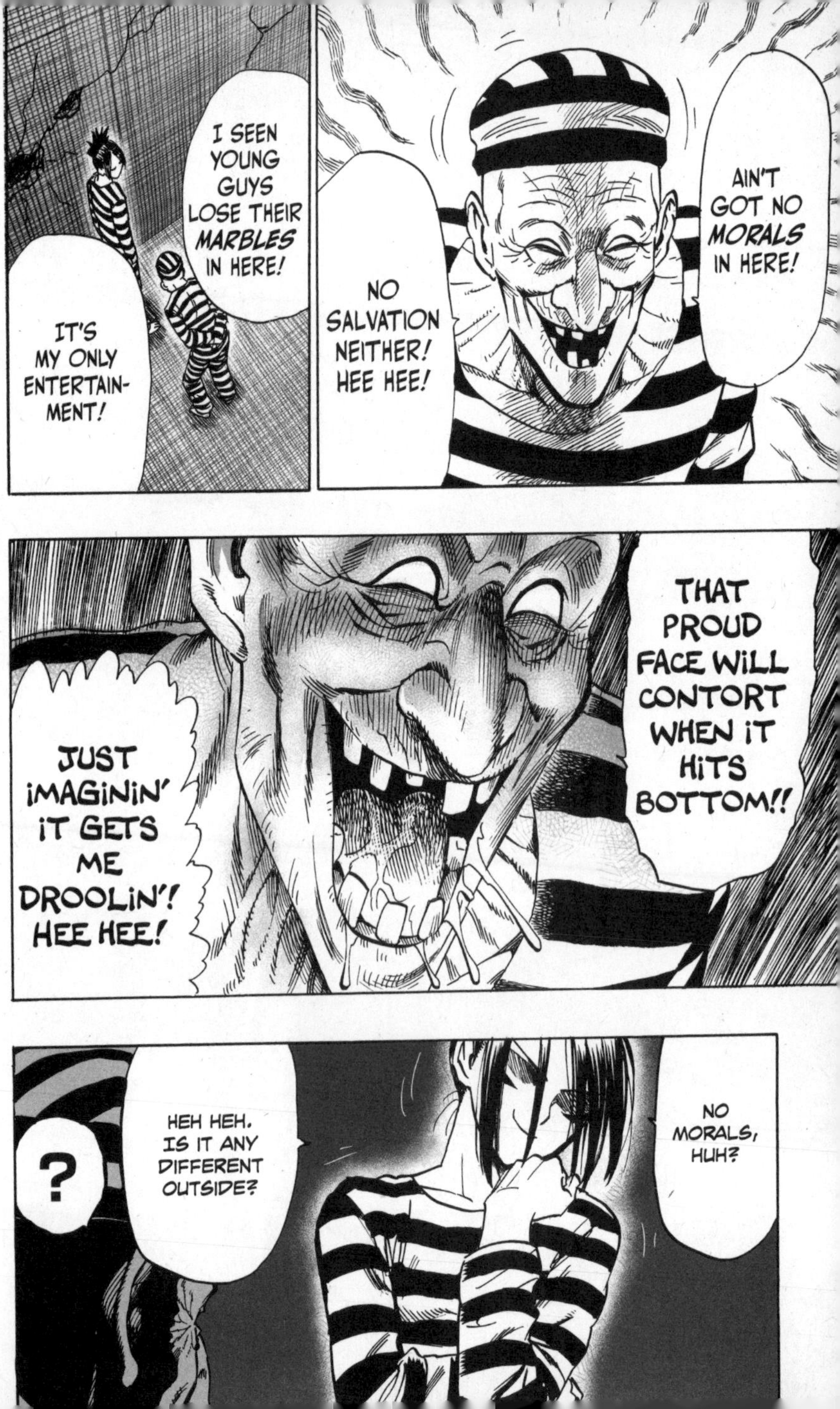
AIN'T GOT NO MORALS IN HERE!
NO SALVATION NEITHER! HEE HEE!
I SEEN YOUNG GUYS LOSE THEIR MARBLES IN HERE!
IT'S MY ONLY ENTERTAIN-MENT!
THAT PROUD FACE WILL CONTORT WHEN IT HITS BOTTOM!!
JUST IMAGININ' IT GETS ME DROOLIN'! HEE HEE!
NO MORALS, HUH?
HEH HEH. IS IT ANY DIFFERENT OUTSIDE?
?

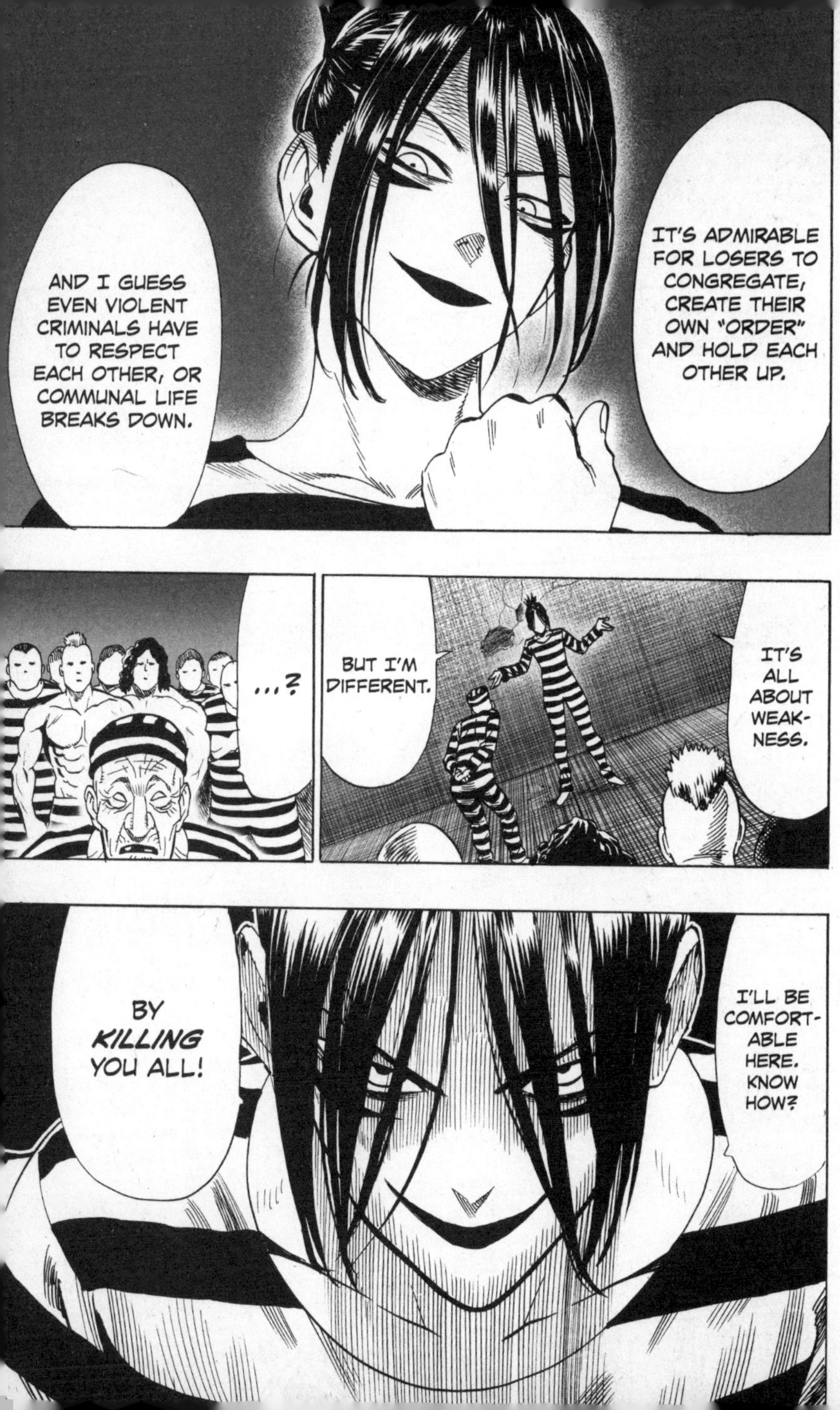
IT'S ADMIRABLE FOR LOSERS TO CONGREGATE, CREATE THEIR OWN "ORDER" AND HOLD EACH OTHER UP.
AND I GUESS EVEN VIOLENT CRIMINALS HAVE TO RESPECT EACH OTHER, OR COMMUNAL LIFE BREAKS DOWN.
IT'S ALL ABOUT WEAK-NESS.
BUT I'M DIFFERENT.
...?
I'LL BE COMFORT-ABLE HERE. KNOW HOW?
BY *KILLING* YOU ALL!

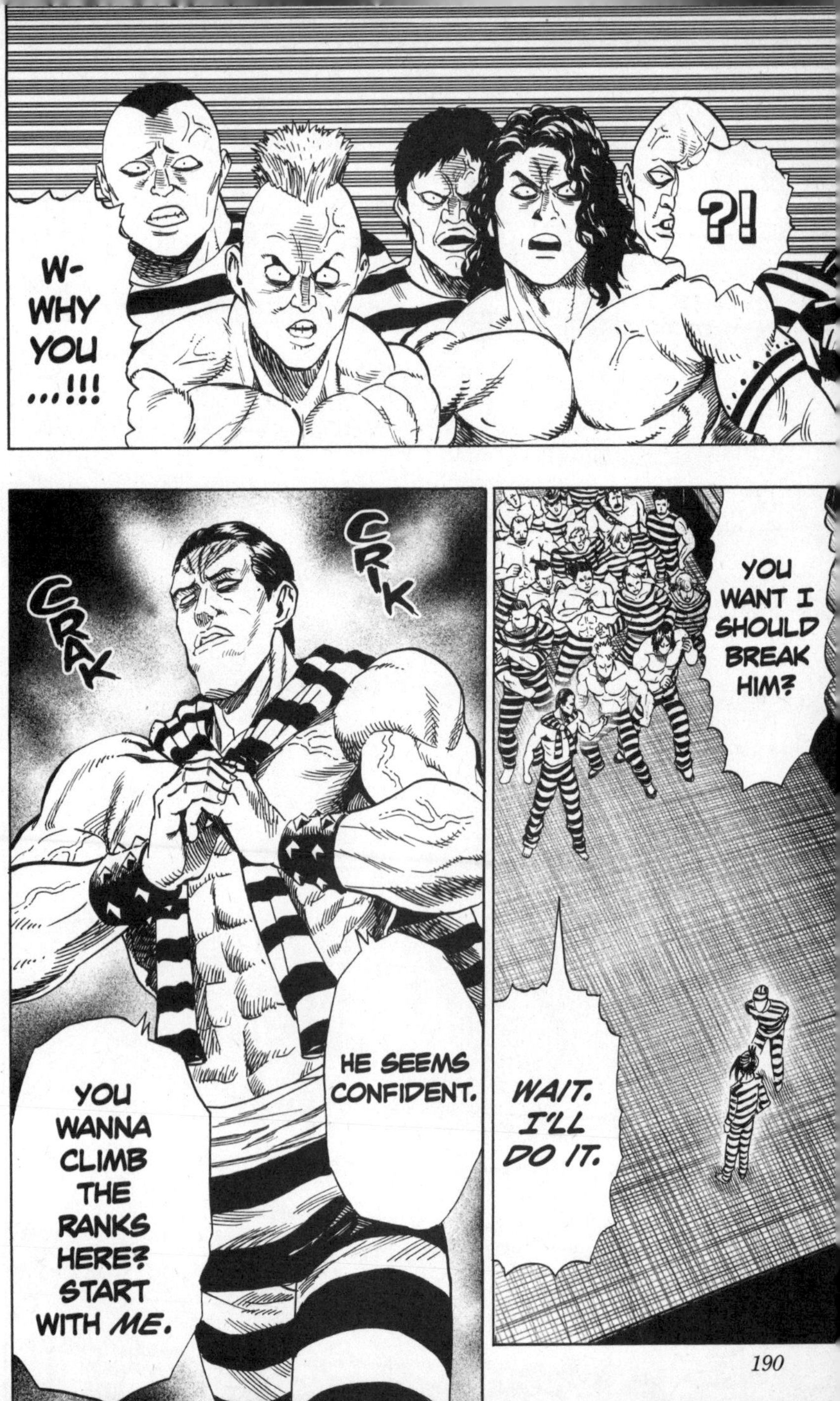
?!
W-WHY YOU ...!!!
YOU WANT I SHOULD BREAK HIM?
WAIT. I'LL DO IT.
CRIK
CRAK
HE SEEMS CONFIDENT.
YOU WANNA CLIMB THE RANKS HERE? START WITH ME.

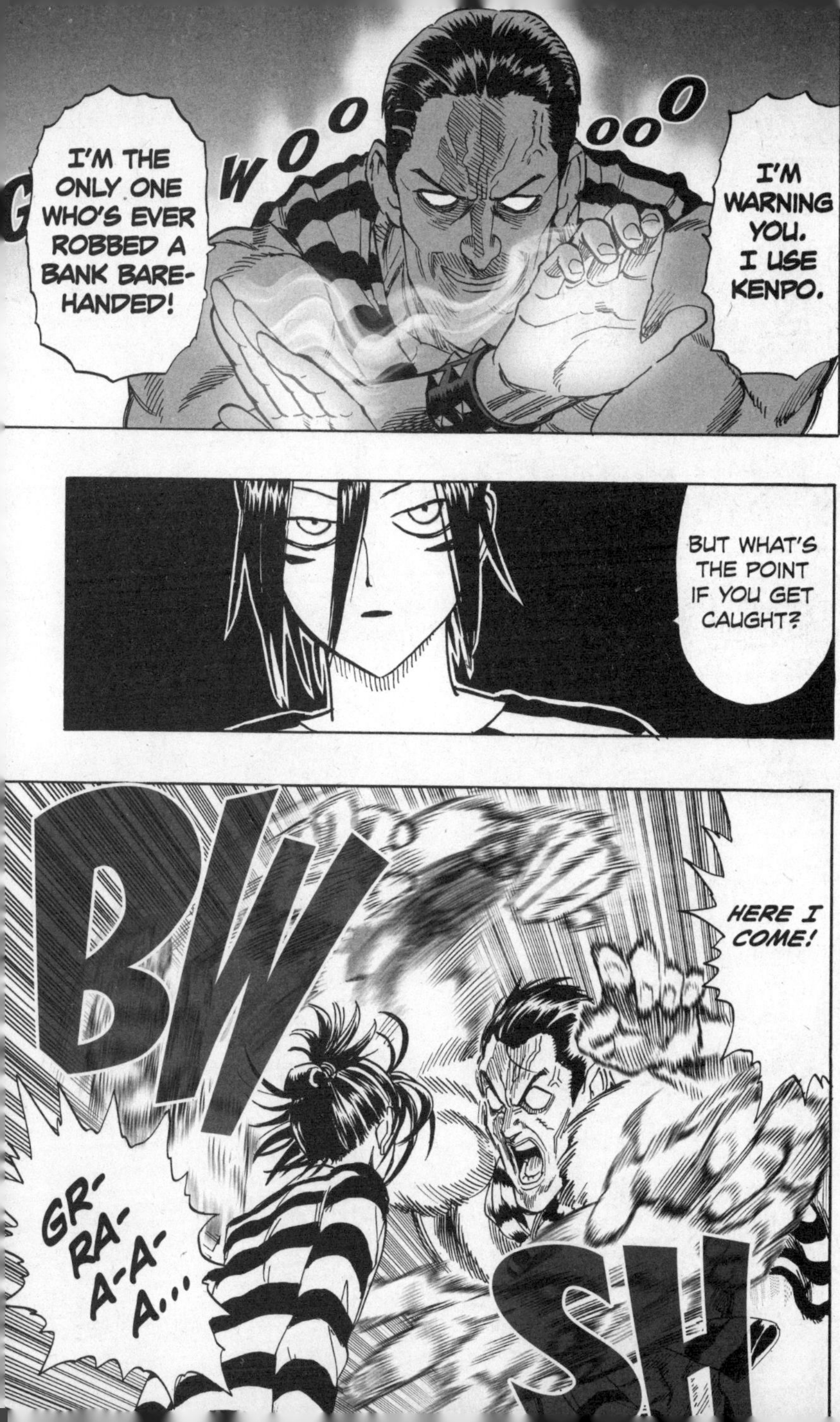
I'M WARNING YOU. I USE KENPO.
GWOOOOOOO
I'M THE ONLY ONE WHO'S EVER ROBBED A BANK BARE-HANDED!
BUT WHAT'S THE POINT IF YOU GET CAUGHT?
HERE I COME!
BWSH
GR-RA-A-A-A...

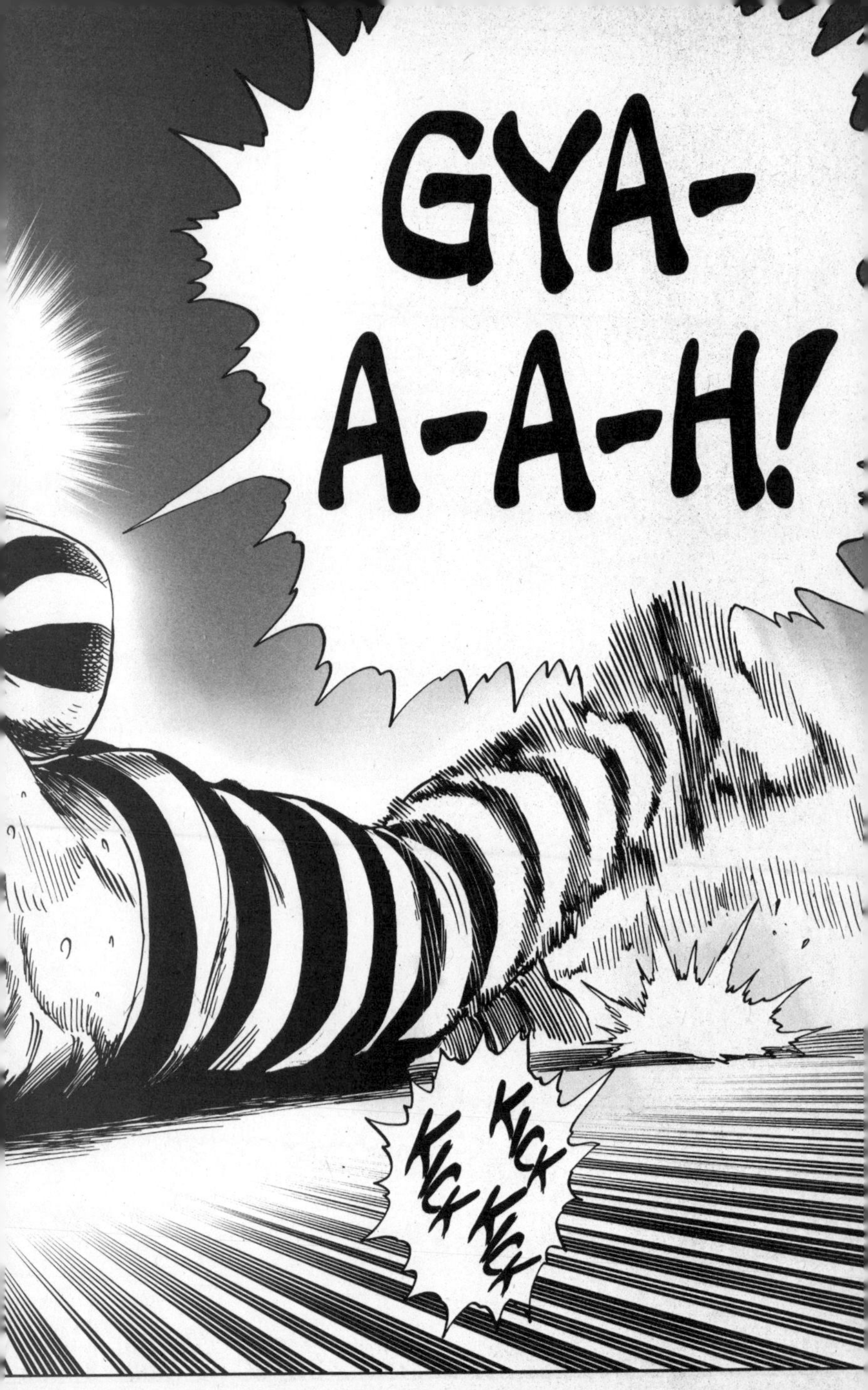
GYA-A-A-H!
KICK KICK
KICK KICK

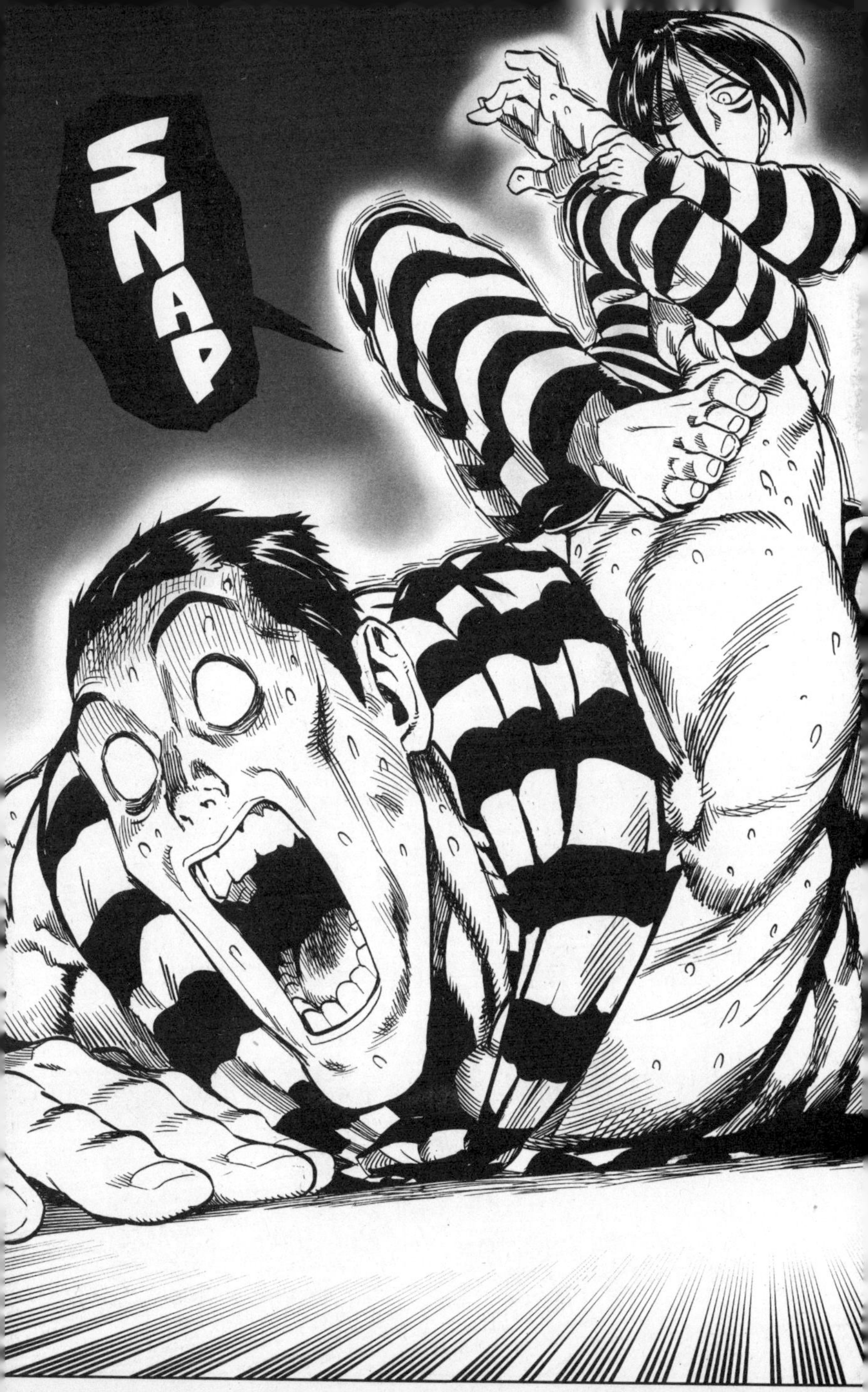
SNAP

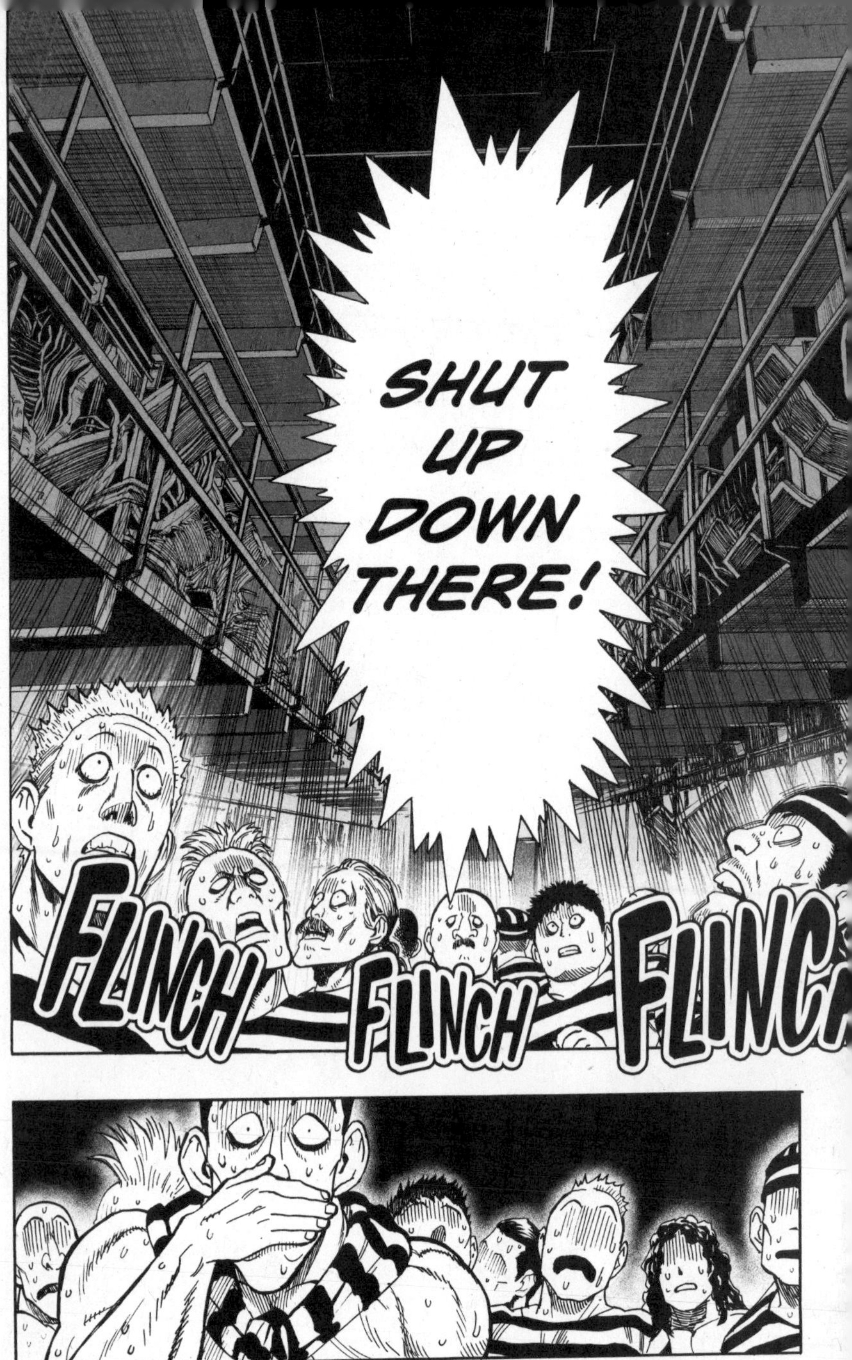
SHUT UP DOWN THERE!
FLINC
FLINCH
FLINCH

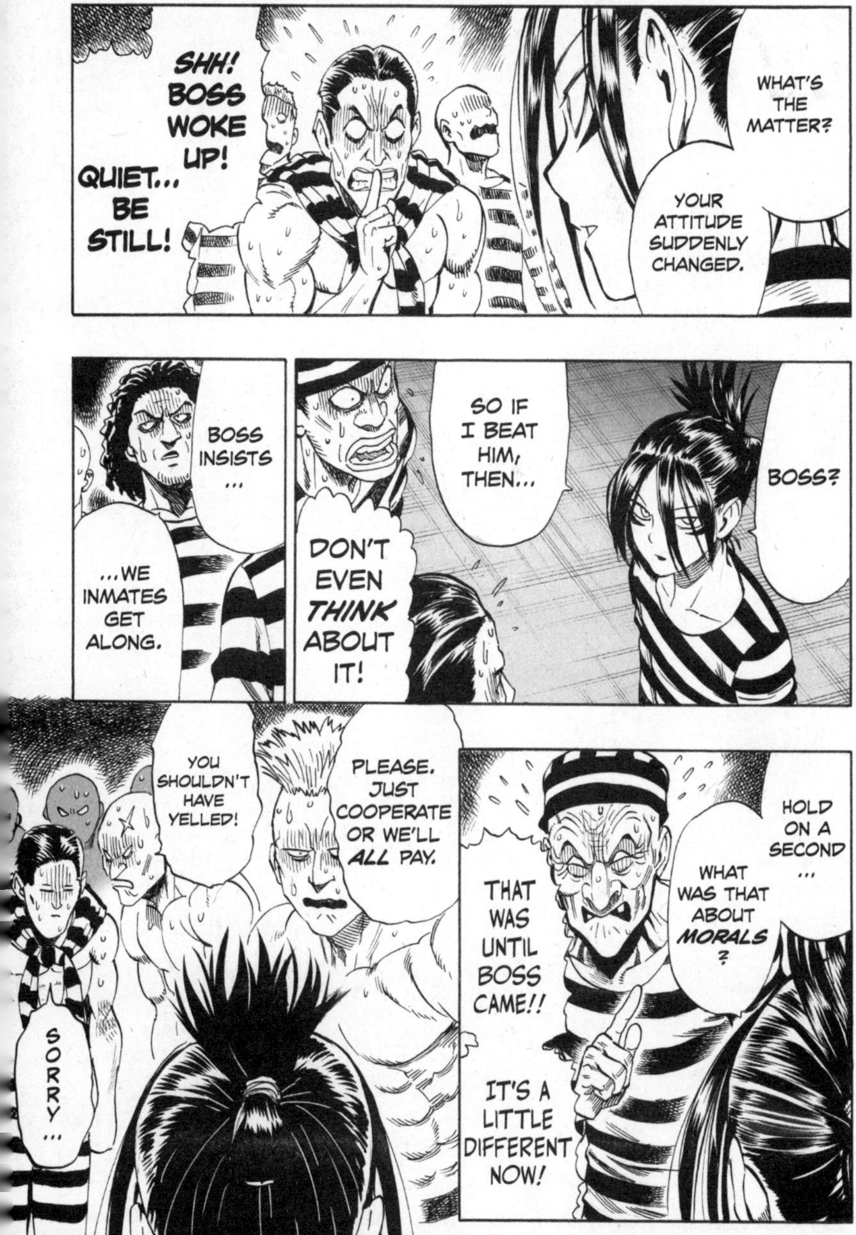
WHAT'S THE MATTER?
YOUR ATTITUDE SUDDENLY CHANGED.
SHH! BOSS WOKE UP!
QUIET... BE STILL!
BOSS?
SO IF I BEAT HIM, THEN...
DON'T EVEN *THINK* ABOUT IT!
BOSS INSISTS ...
...WE INMATES GET ALONG.
HOLD ON A SECOND ...
WHAT WAS THAT ABOUT *MORALS*?
THAT WAS UNTIL BOSS CAME!!
IT'S A LITTLE DIFFERENT NOW!
PLEASE. JUST COOPERATE OR WE'LL *ALL* PAY.
YOU SHOULDN'T HAVE YELLED!
SORRY...

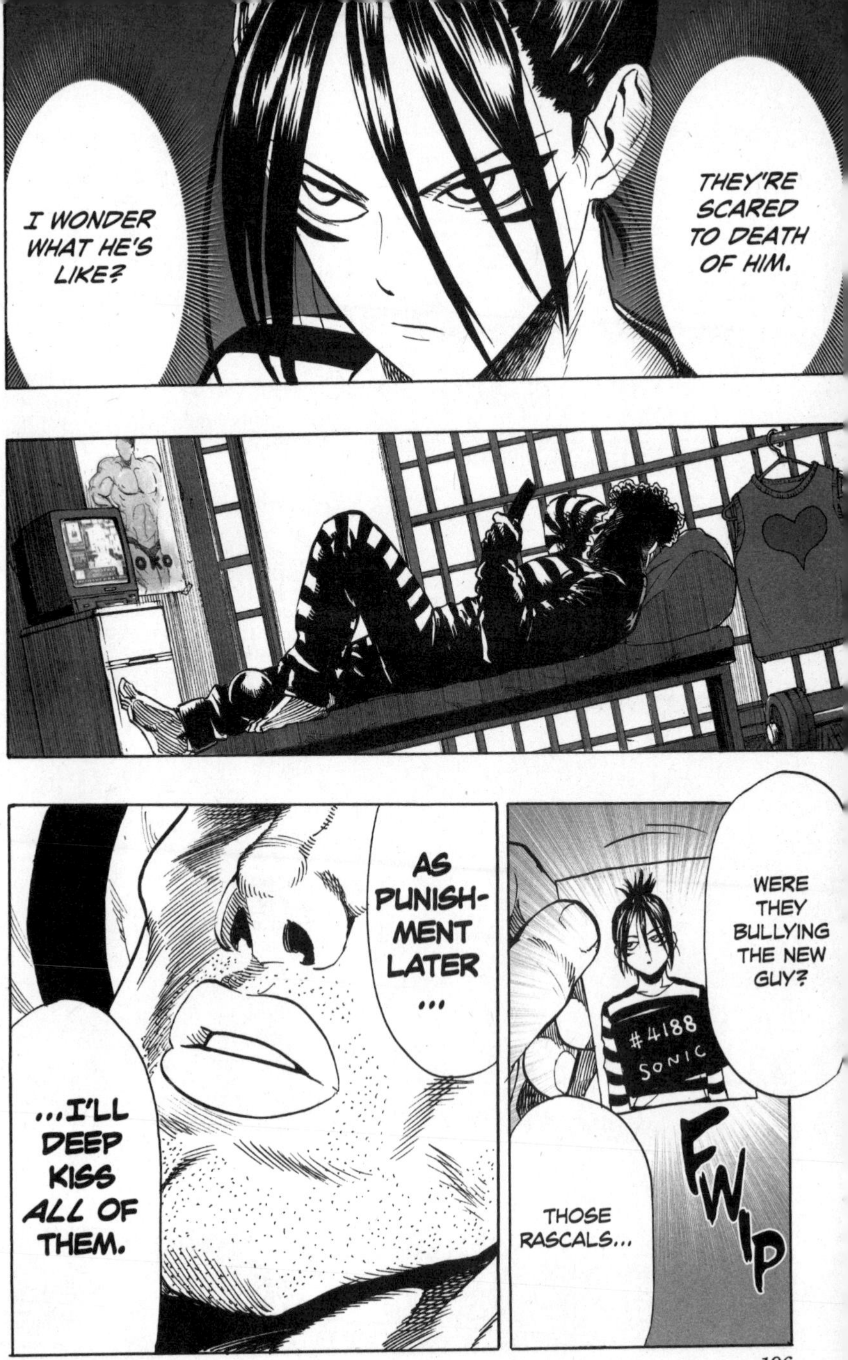
THEY'RE SCARED TO DEATH OF HIM.
I WONDER WHAT HE'S LIKE?
WERE THEY BULLYING THE NEW GUY?
#4188 SONIC
FWIP
THOSE RASCALS...
AS PUNISH-MENT LATER ...
...I'LL DEEP KISS ALL OF THEM.

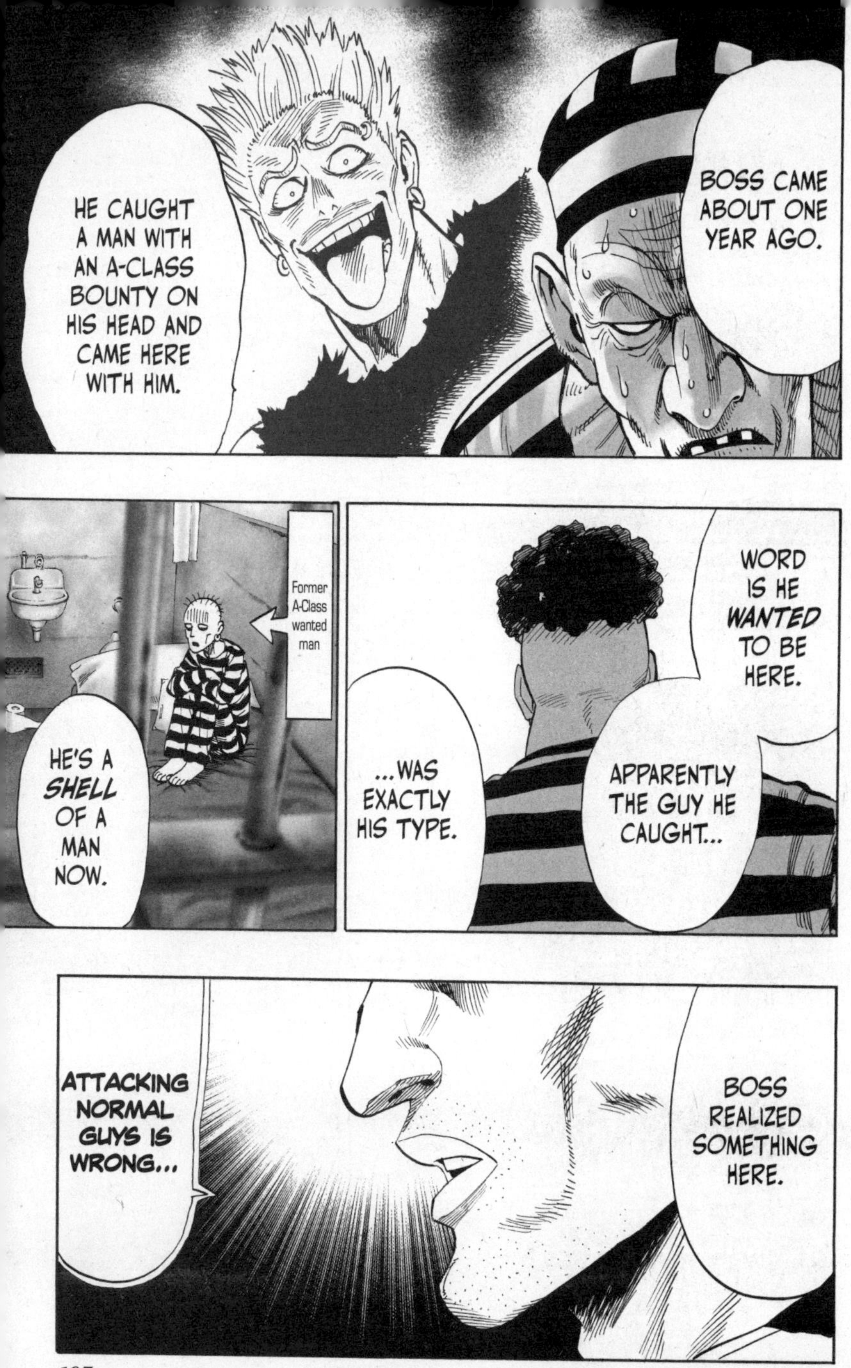
BOSS CAME ABOUT ONE YEAR AGO.
HE CAUGHT A MAN WITH AN A-CLASS BOUNTY ON HIS HEAD AND CAME HERE WITH HIM.
WORD IS HE *WANTED* TO BE HERE.
APPARENTLY THE GUY HE CAUGHT...
...WAS EXACTLY HIS TYPE.
Former A-Class wanted man
HE'S A *SHELL* OF A MAN NOW.
BOSS REALIZED SOMETHING HERE.
ATTACKING NORMAL GUYS IS WRONG...

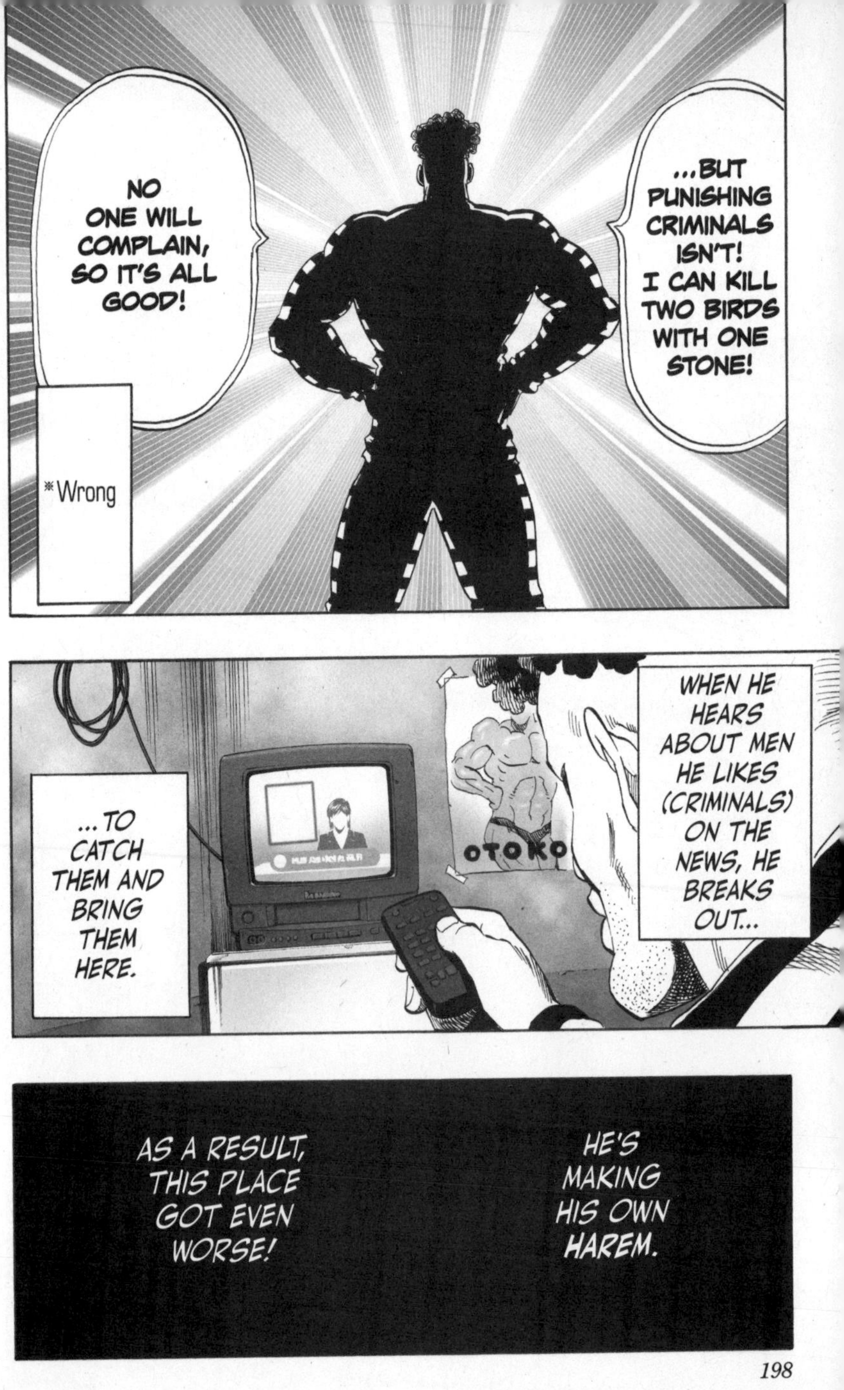
...BUT PUNISHING CRIMINALS ISN'T! I CAN KILL TWO BIRDS WITH ONE STONE!
NO ONE WILL COMPLAIN, SO IT'S ALL GOOD!
※Wrong
WHEN HE HEARS ABOUT MEN HE LIKES (CRIMINALS) ON THE NEWS, HE BREAKS OUT...
OTOKO
...TO CATCH THEM AND BRING THEM HERE.
HE'S MAKING HIS OWN HAREM.
AS A RESULT, THIS PLACE GOT EVEN WORSE!

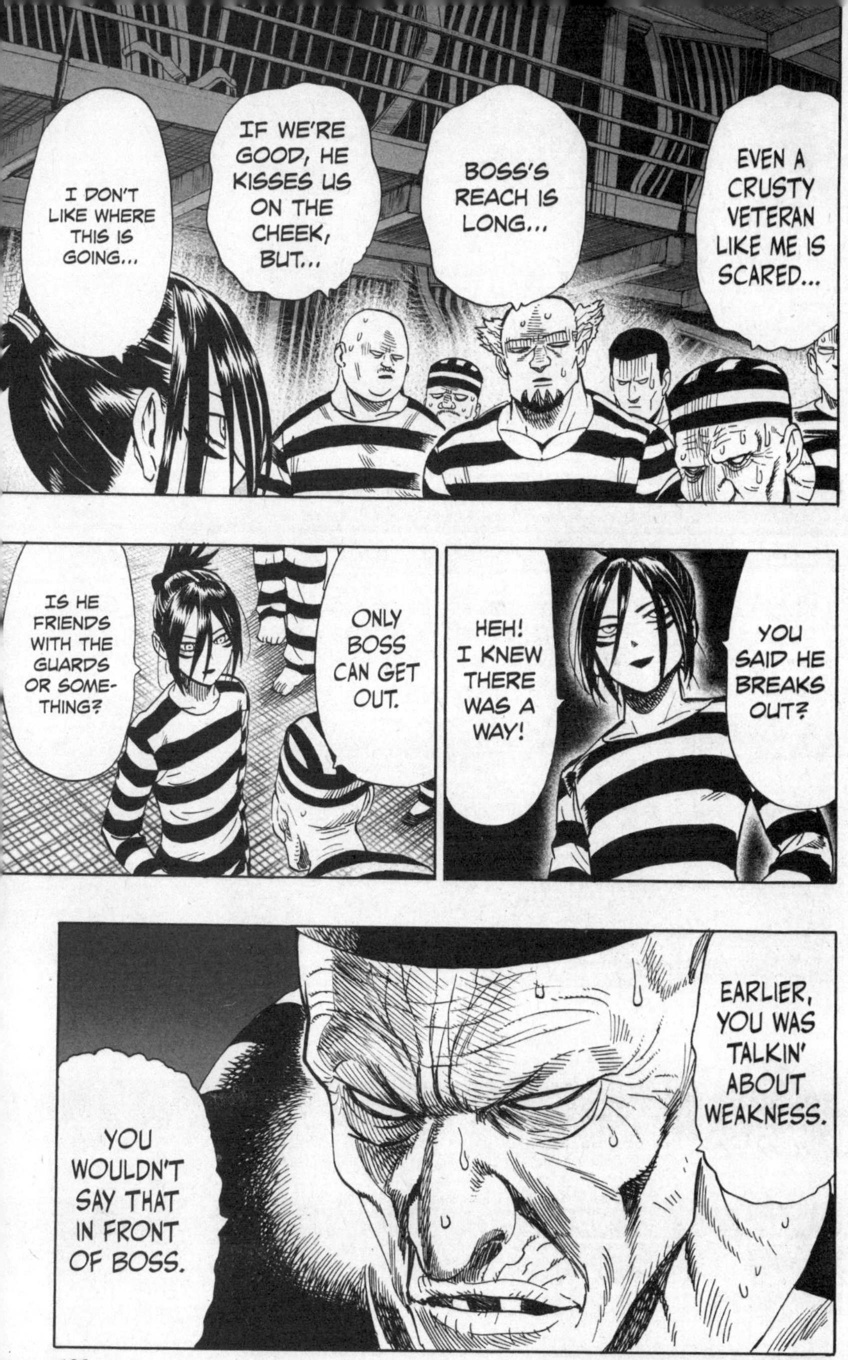
EVEN A CRUSTY VETERAN LIKE ME IS SCARED...
BOSS'S REACH IS LONG...
IF WE'RE GOOD, HE KISSES US ON THE CHEEK, BUT...
I DON'T LIKE WHERE THIS IS GOING...
YOU SAID HE BREAKS OUT?
HEH! I KNEW THERE WAS A WAY!
ONLY BOSS CAN GET OUT.
IS HE FRIENDS WITH THE GUARDS OR SOME-THING?
EARLIER, YOU WAS TALKIN' ABOUT WEAKNESS.
YOU WOULDN'T SAY THAT IN FRONT OF BOSS.

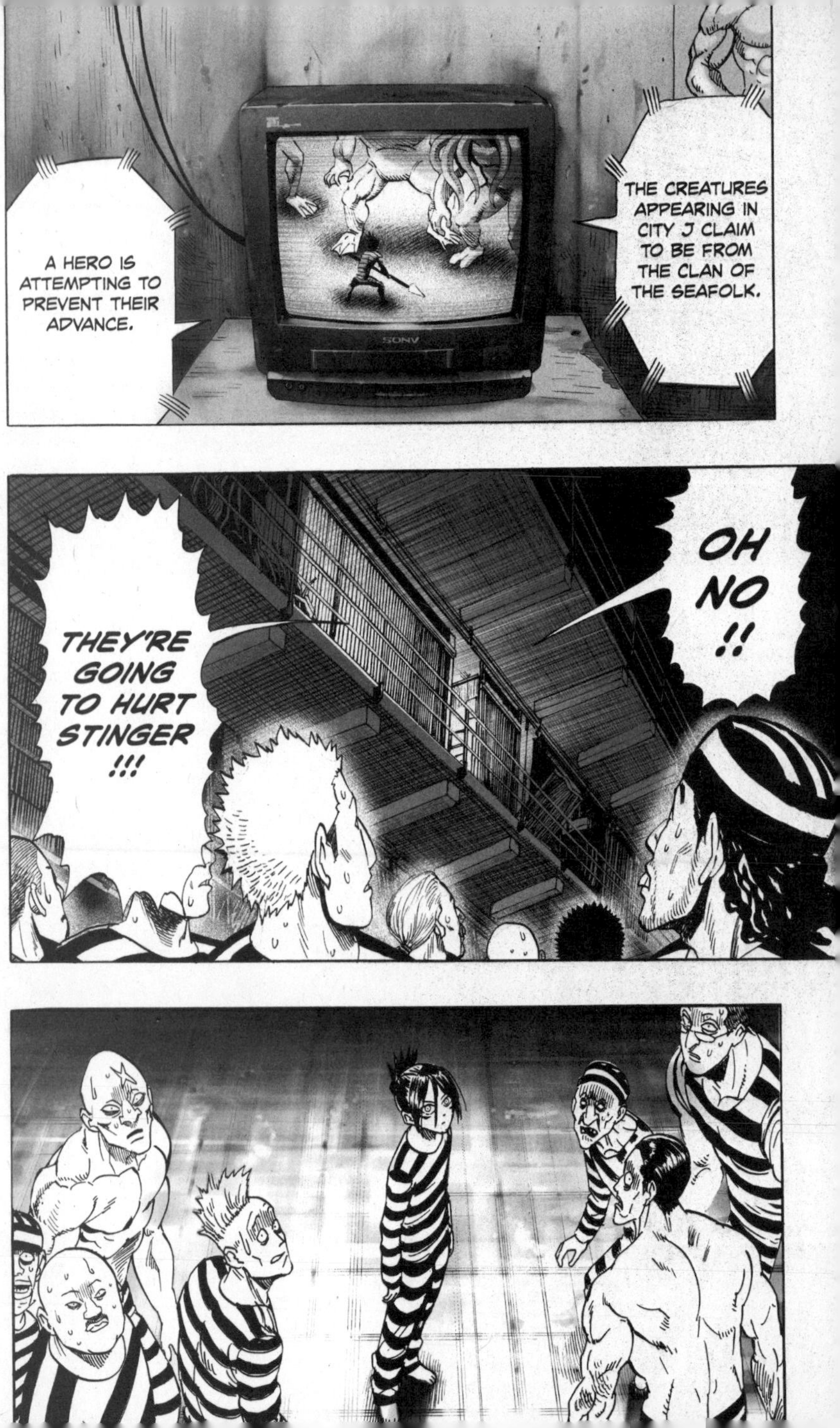
THE CREATURES APPEARING IN CITY J CLAIM TO BE FROM THE CLAN OF THE SEAFOLK.
A HERO IS ATTEMPTING TO PREVENT THEIR ADVANCE.
OH NO !!
THEY'RE GOING TO HURT STINGER !!!

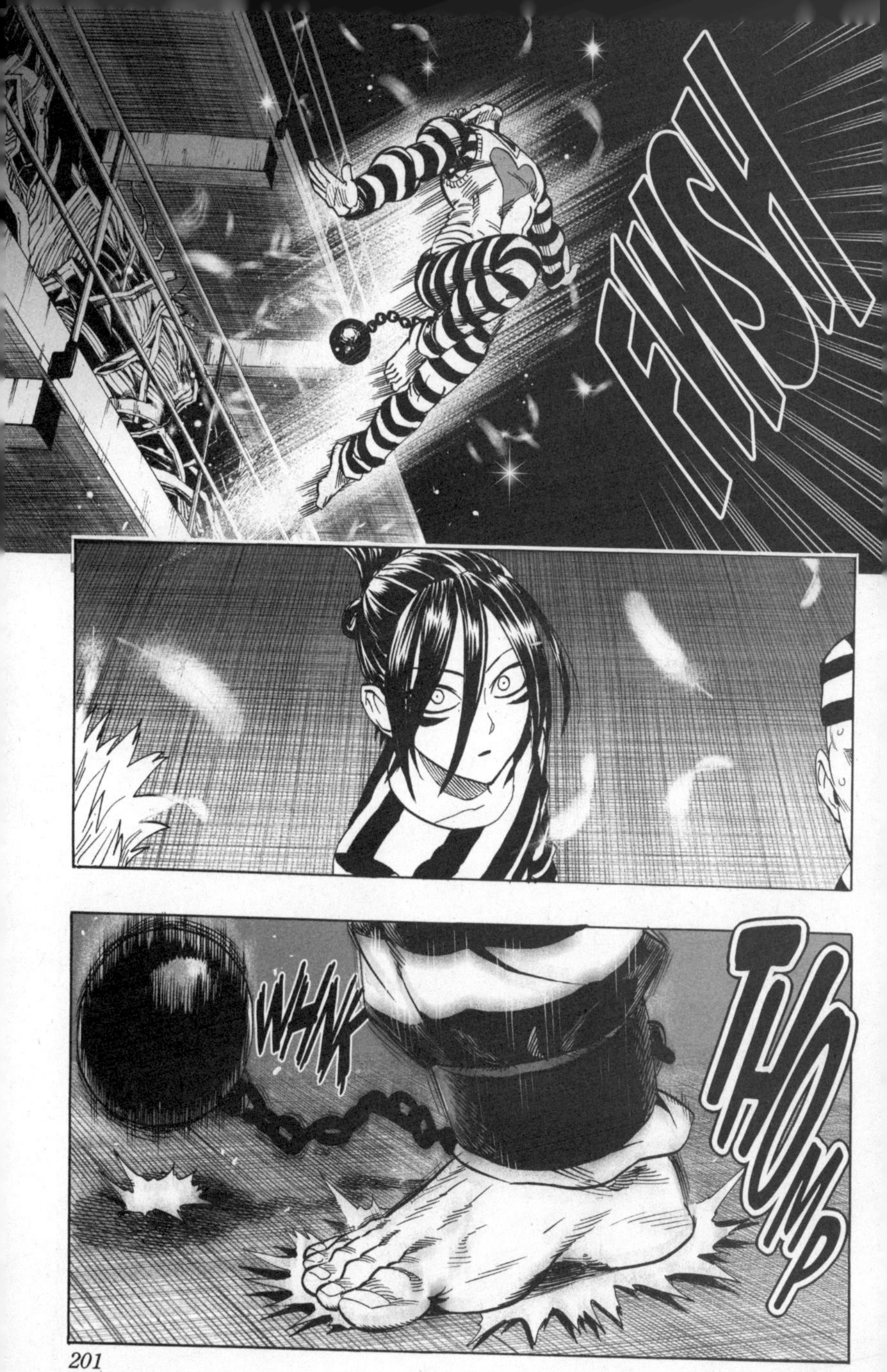
FWISH
THUMP
WHNK

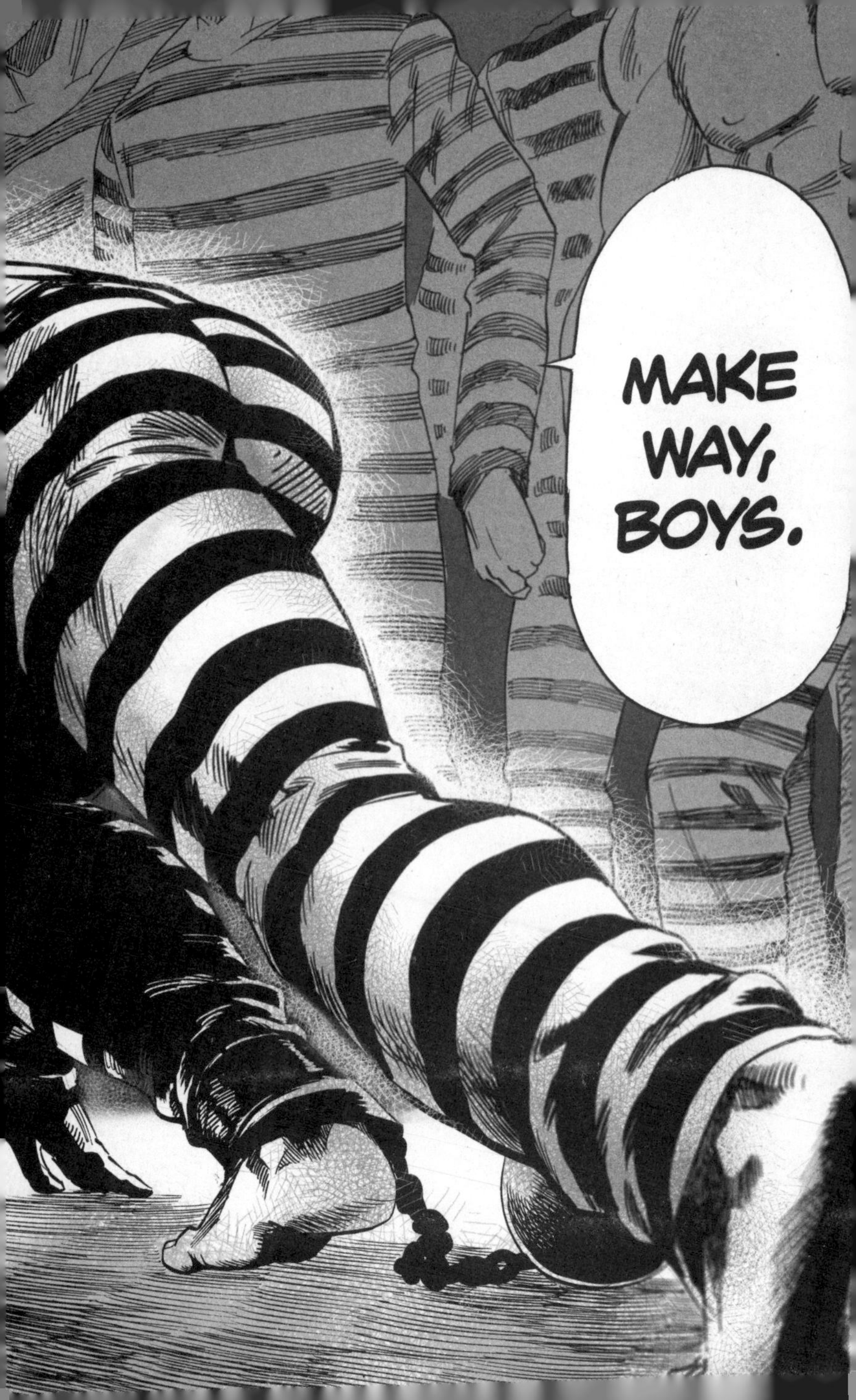
MAKE WAY, BOYS.

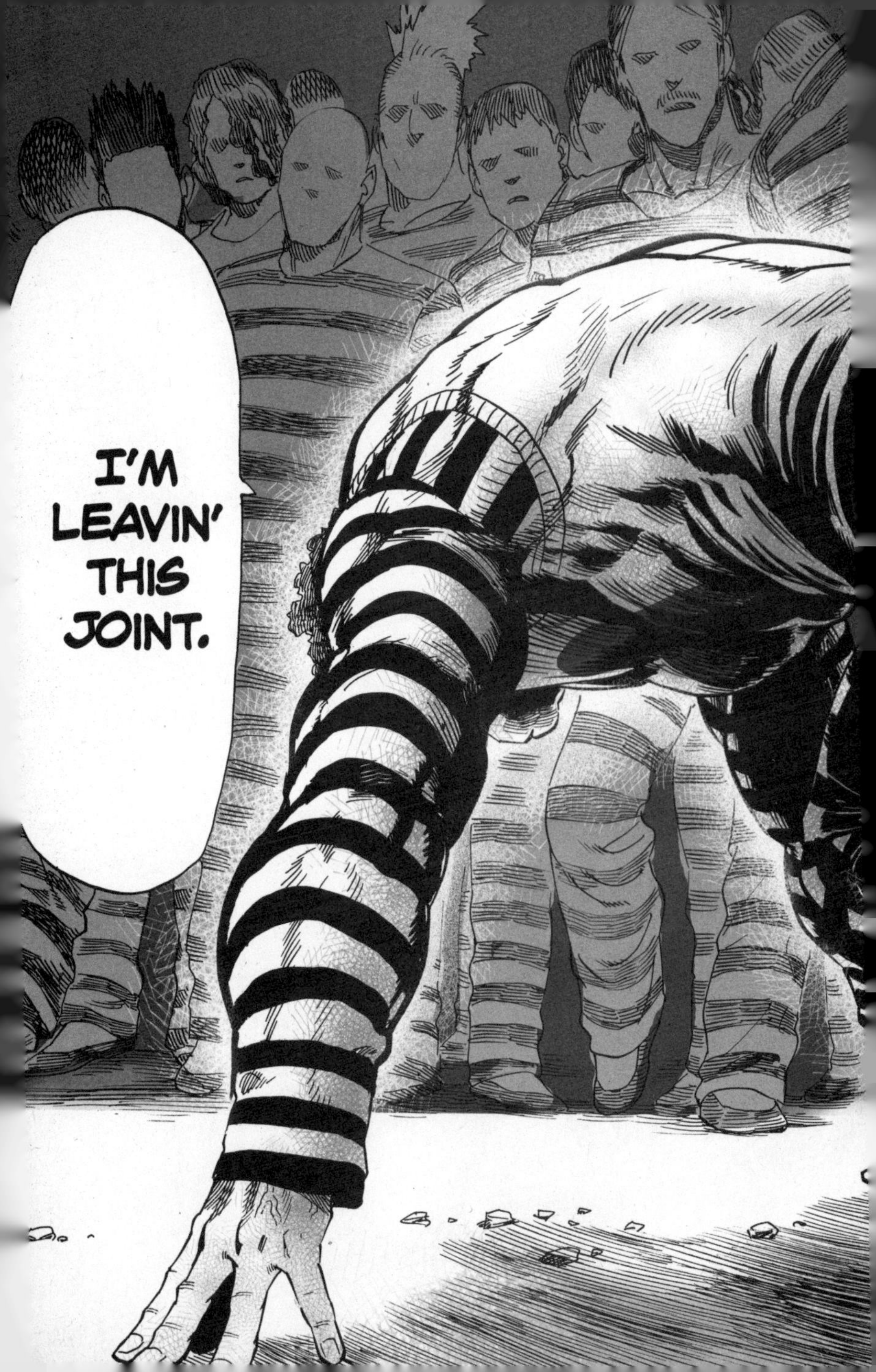
I'M LEAVIN' THIS JOINT.

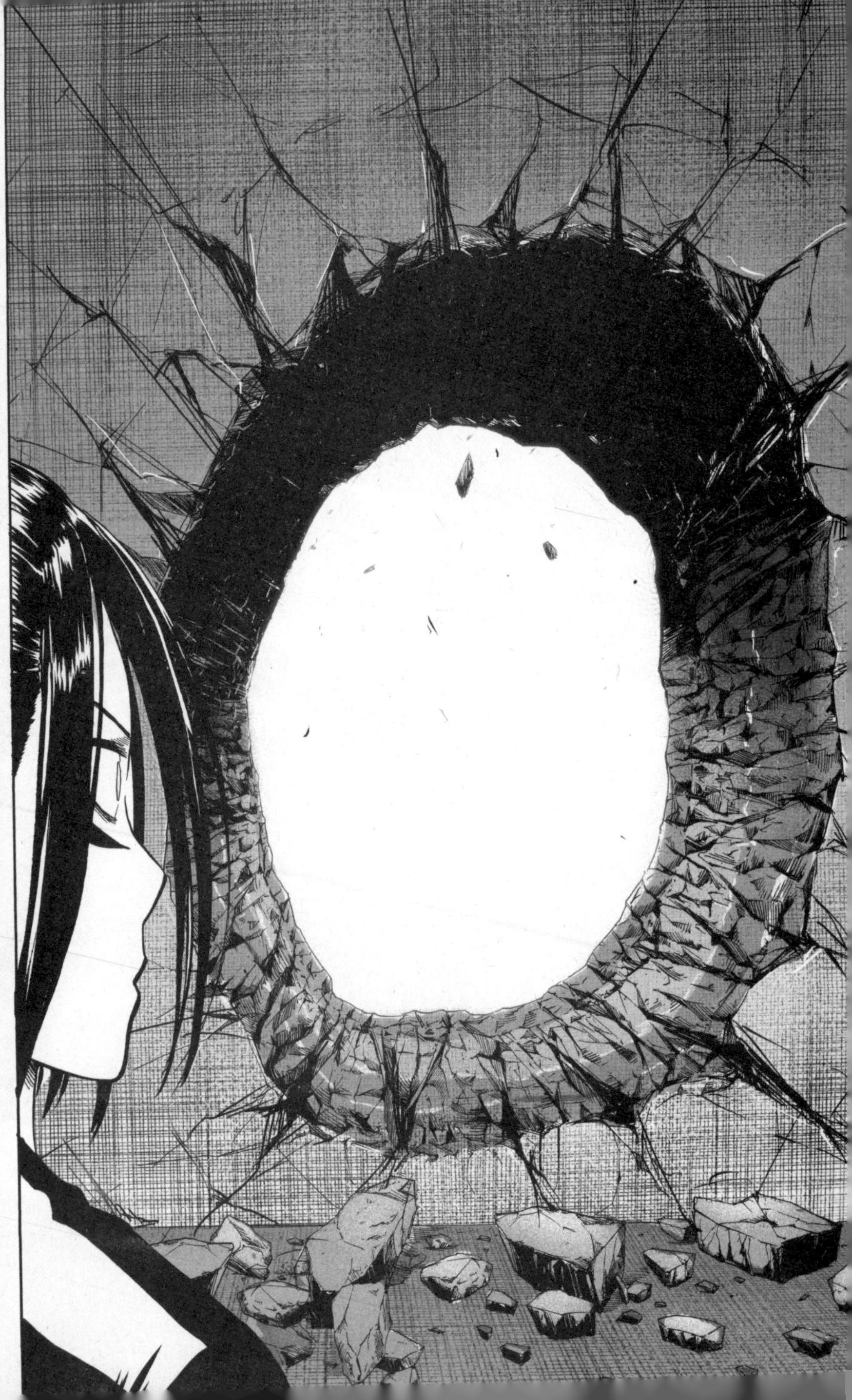

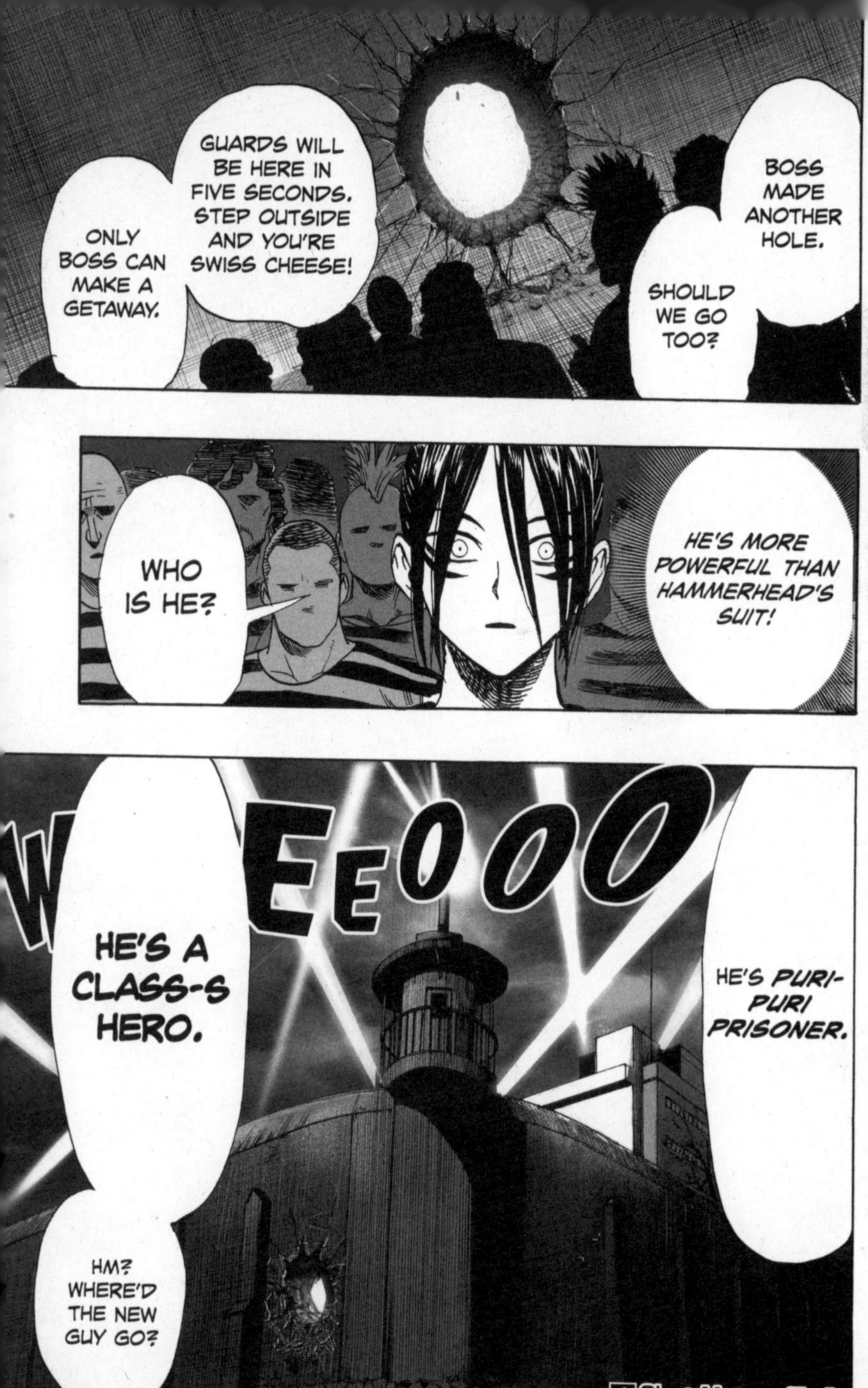
BOSS MADE ANOTHER HOLE.
SHOULD WE GO TOO?
GUARDS WILL BE HERE IN FIVE SECONDS. STEP OUTSIDE AND YOU'RE SWISS CHEESE!
ONLY BOSS CAN MAKE A GETAWAY.
HE'S MORE POWERFUL THAN HAMMERHEAD'S SUIT!
WHO IS HE?
HE'S PURI-PURI PRISONER.
W EEOOO
HE'S A CLASS-S HERO.
HM? WHERE'D THE NEW GUY GO?

4 Giant Meteor (End)

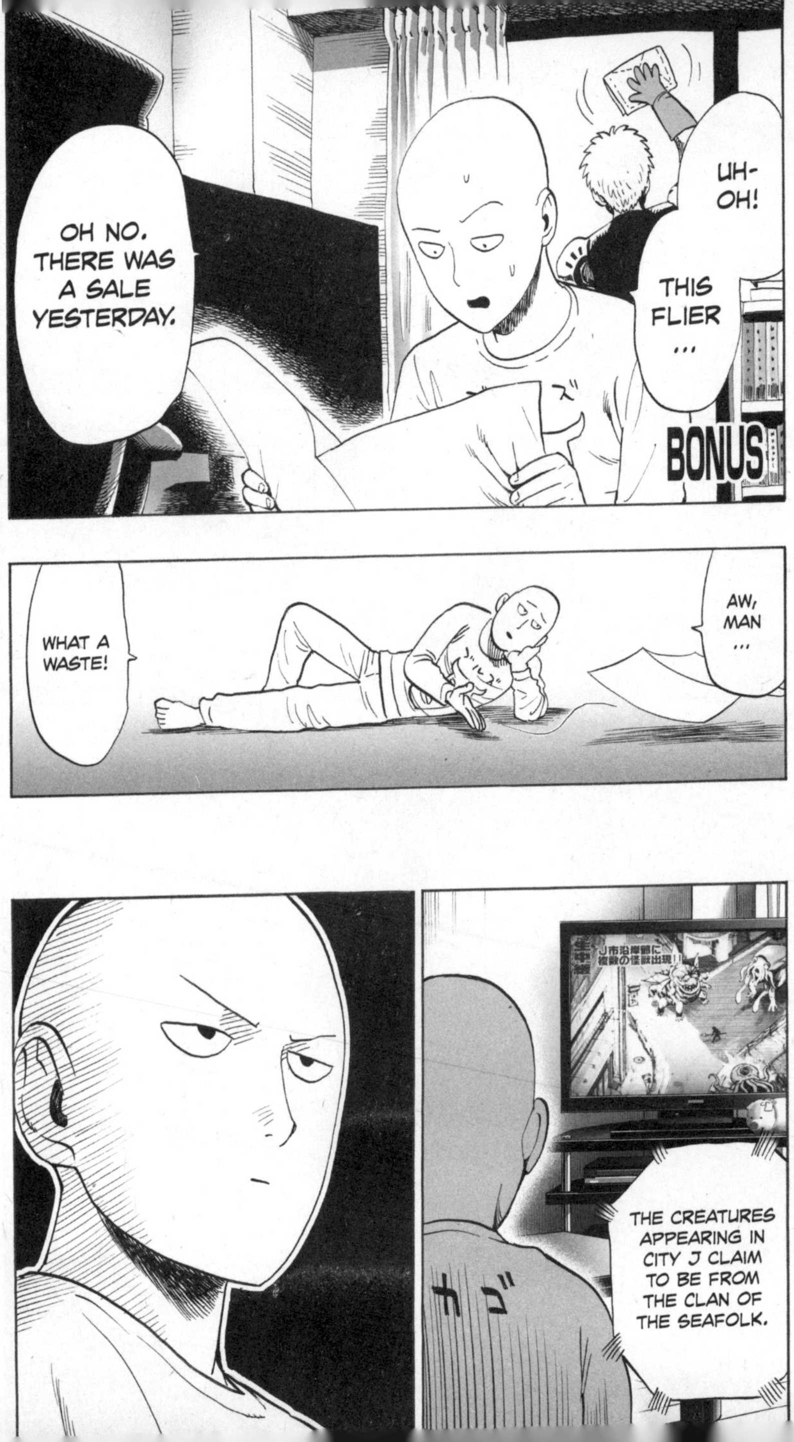
UH-OH!
THIS FLIER...
BONUS
OH NO. THERE WAS A SALE YESTERDAY.
AW, MAN...
WHAT A WASTE!
生中継
J市沿岸部に複数の怪獣出現！
THE CREATURES APPEARING IN CITY J CLAIM TO BE FROM THE CLAN OF THE SEAFOLK.

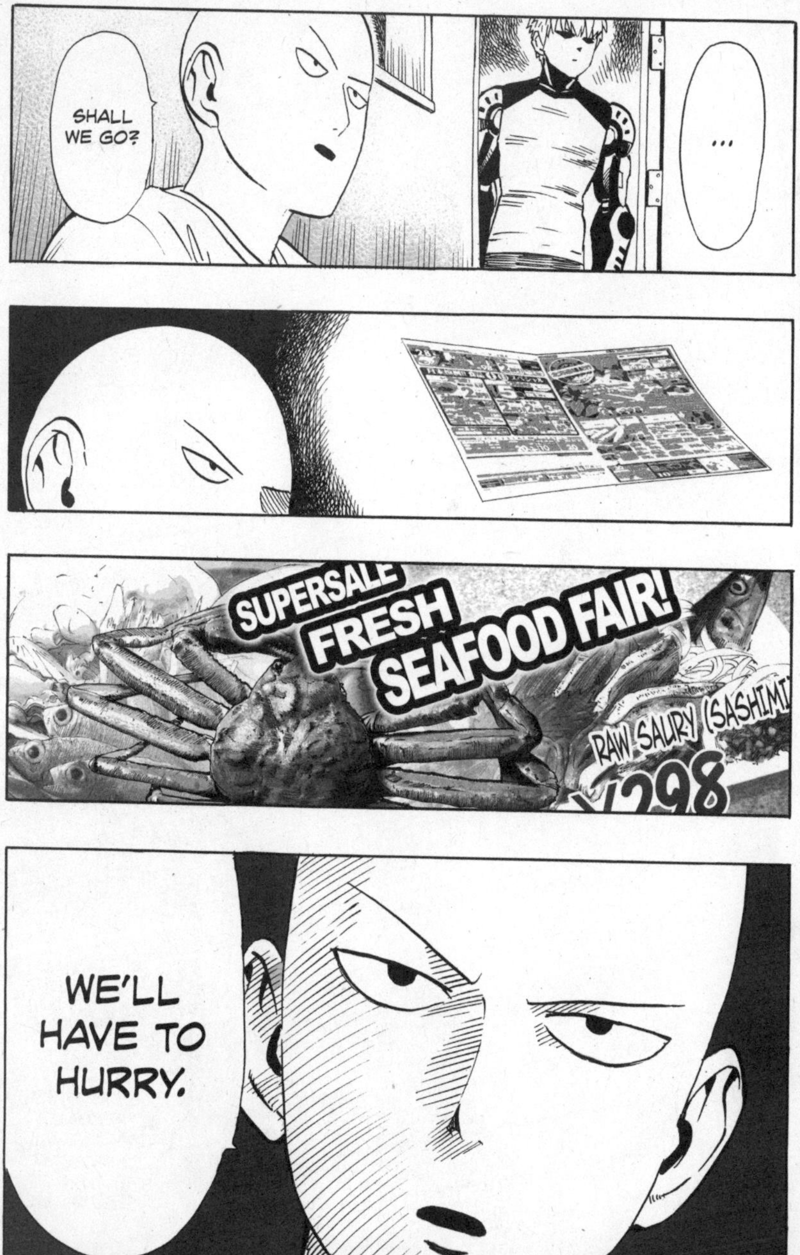
...
SHALL WE GO?
SUPERSALE
FRESH
SEAFOOD FAIR!
RAW SAURY (SASHIMI
¥298
WE'LL HAVE TO HURRY.
Bonus (End)

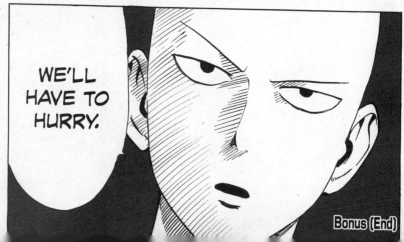

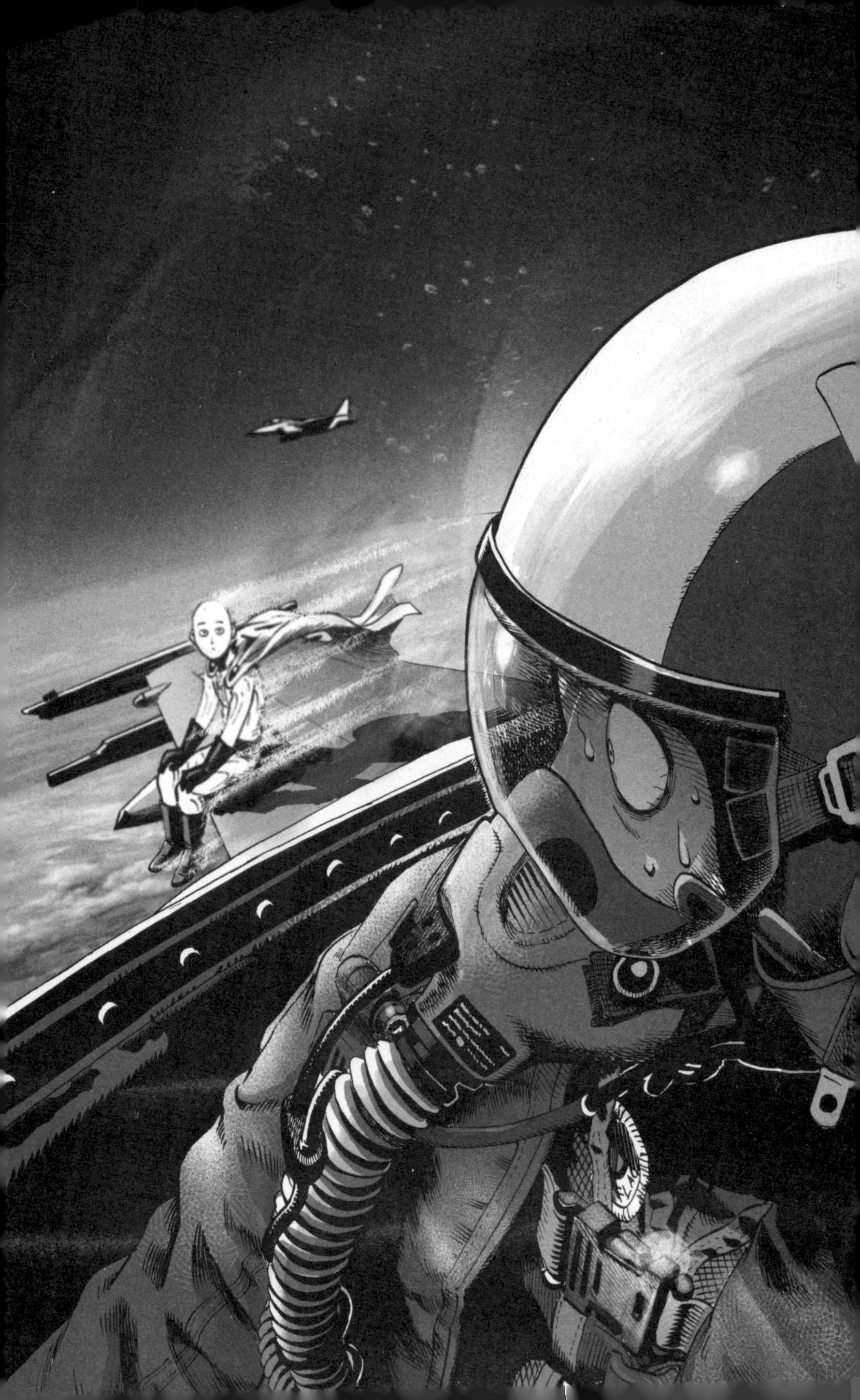

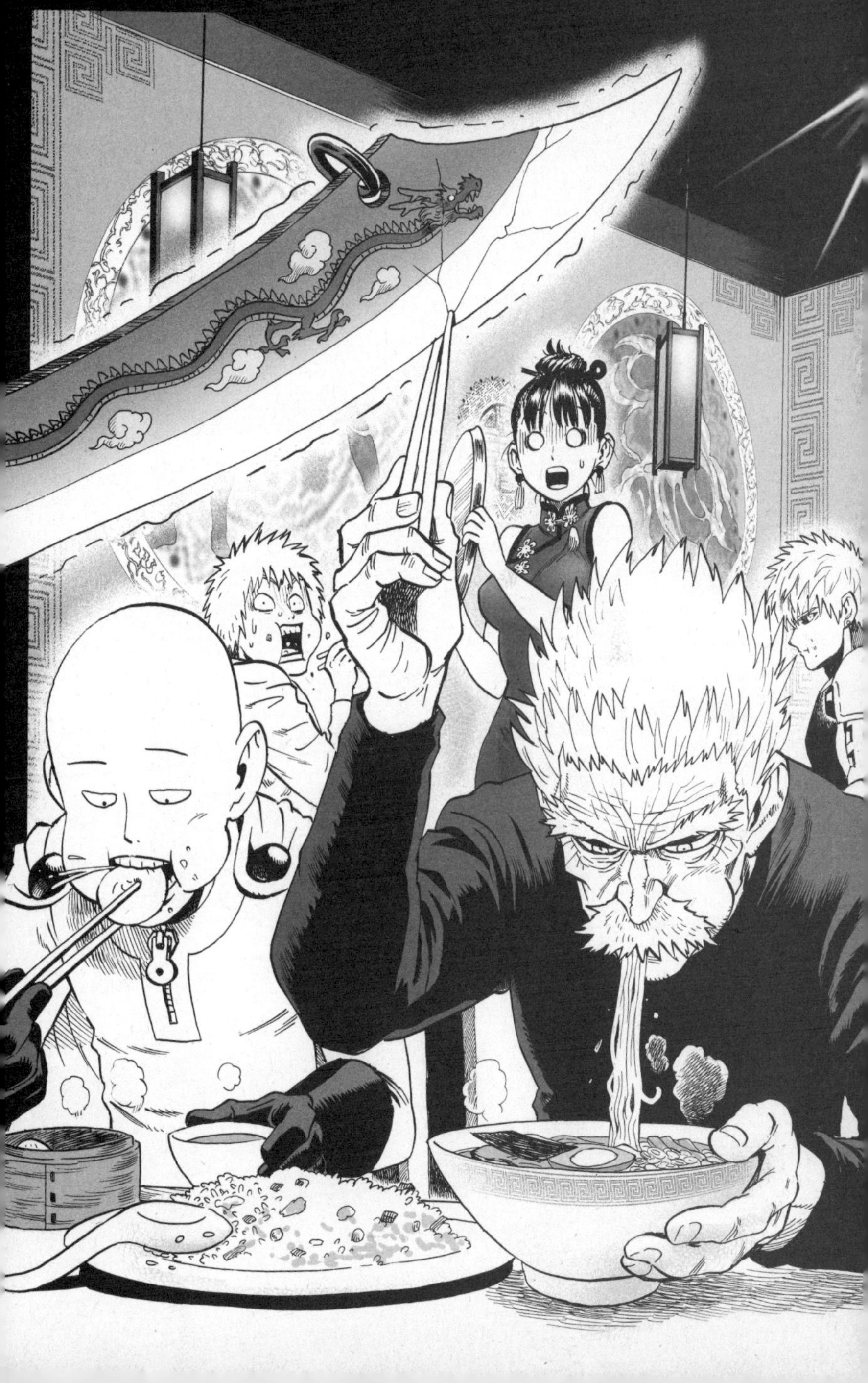

END NOTES

PAGE 8, PANEL 1:
The back of Saitama's shirt says Chicago and the front says Bulls.

PAGE 10, PANEL 1:
Saitama's bookshelf contains ONE's book *Mob Psycho 100*.

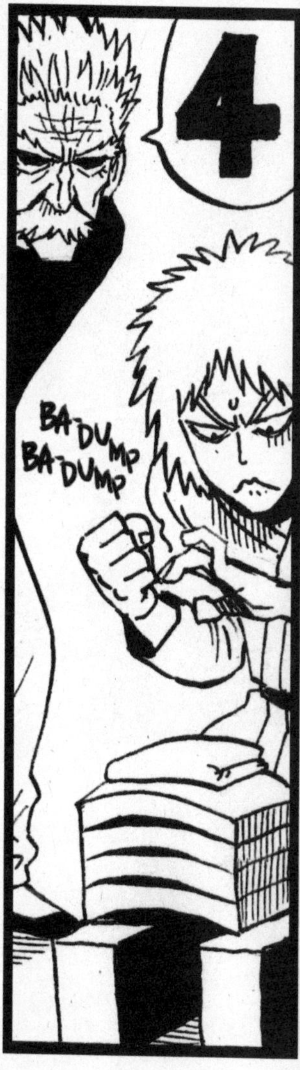
4
BA-DUMP
BA-DUMP

ONE-PUNCH MAN

VOLUME 4

SHONEN JUMP MANGA EDITION

STORY BY | ONE
ART BY | YUSUKE MURATA

TRANSLATION | JOHN WERRY
TOUCH-UP ART AND LETTERING | JAMES GAUBATZ
DESIGN | FAWN LAU
SHONEN JUMP SERIES EDITOR | JOHN BAE
GRAPHIC NOVEL EDITOR | JENNIFER LEBLANC

Printed in the U.S.A.

Published by VIZ Media, LLC
P.O. Box 77010
San Francisco, CA 94107

VIZ MEDIA
viz.com

SHONEN JUMP

10 9 8 7 6
First printing, January 2016
Sixth printing, July 2023

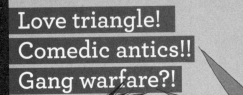

Hikaru no Go

Story by YUMI HOTTA
Art by TAKESHI OBATA

The breakthrough series by Takeshi Obata, the artist of *Death Note!*

Hikaru Shindo is like any sixth-grader in Japan: a pretty normal schoolboy with a penchant for antics. One day, he finds an old bloodstained Go board in his grandfather's attic. Trapped inside the Go board is Fujiwara-no-Sai, the ghost of an ancient Go master. In one fateful moment, Sai becomes a part of Hikaru's consciousness and together, through thick and thin, they make an unstoppable Go-playing team.

Will they be able to defeat Go players who have dedicated their lives to the game? And will Sai achieve the "Divine Move" so he'll finally be able to rest in peace? Find out in this *Shonen Jump* classic!

 SHONEN JUMP

 VIZ MEDIA

www.shonenjump.com
www.viz.com

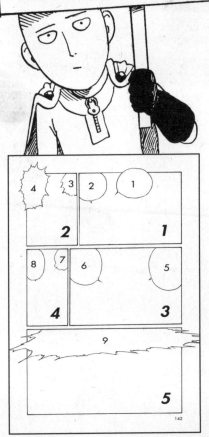

STOP!

YOU'RE READING THE WRONG WAY!

⭐ ONE-PUNCH MAN READS FROM RIGHT TO LEFT, STARTING IN THE UPPER-RIGHT CORNER. JAPANESE IS READ FROM RIGHT TO LEFT, MEANING THAT ACTION, SOUND EFFECTS, AND WORD-BALLOON ORDER ARE COMPLETELY REVERSED FROM ENGLISH ORDER.